Child Development

Child

MILLIE ALMY

TEACHERS COLLEGE
COLUMBIA UNIVERSITY

Development

Henry Holt and Company · New York

649
al 68

49578

20349–0115

Printed in the United States of America

Preface

PARENTS who wish to understand their children better, educators and other professional workers who wish to improve their effectiveness with children, and young people puzzled by their own life stories may look to the study of child development for information and insight. I hope that this book will serve as a useful introduction to the tremendous amount of literature which is available for them.

This book had its beginning in two major convictions. The first is that child development principles and the findings of research become meaningful only as their relevance to the lives of children become clear. Therefore, many pages of this book are devoted to actual descriptions of child behavior. In many instances these are drawn from my own studies of children, or have been contributed by students in my classes. I have also made use of a number of published case studies from various research centers.

My second conviction is that the significance of development is best grasped when the child's life experience can be viewed through succeeding age periods. I have centered the material in this book around the life stories of six young people, from birth to 18 years of age. Studies conducted by the Department of Maternal and Child Health, Harvard University, School of Public Health provided the material from which they were derived. These studies were longitudinal in character and permit the recognition of continuity as well as change in following the development of individual children.

Using the lives of young people as a point of departure, I have attempted to provide a framework within which the reader may build an understanding of child development principles. I have not tried to offer a survey of the vast amount of literature in which I have delved. I have tried rather to indicate something about the variety of research which is available and to stimulate the reader's interest in pursuing it. In deciding what to include and what to leave out, I have been guided mainly by my experience with students just beginning their study of child development. Undoubtedly in so doing, I have omitted important material which another writer might have selected, and have chosen some which he would have omitted.

My judgment in these and other matters has been both questioned and approved by those who have read the book in manuscript: Professor Freeman Butts, Professor Arthur T. Jersild, Professor Harold Shane, Dr. Harold C. Stuart, James E. Burnes, and Bracha Zeev. I am grateful to each of them for his own unique contribution in helping me to clarify my thinking and writing. The preferences and the biases the book reveals are, of course, solely my own.

This book was begun while I was teaching at the University of Cincinnati. It reflects some of the understanding I gained from the parents who brought their children to the nursery school there. I am grateful to them for their generosity in sharing their children, and their thoughts about their children with me. I also feel that my insights were both deepened and broadened through association in various ways with colleagues in the Department of Psychiatry and the Children's Hospital.

Most of the writing of this book has been done since I have become a member of the Psychological Foundations Department at Teachers College, Columbia University. The encouragement and support of my colleagues in Developmental Psychology, Professor Arthur T. Jersild and Professor Anne McKillop has meant much to me.

I wish that it were possible to give due credit for each instance in which I have used illustrations given me by students or by teachers with whom I have worked, but the list would be too exhaustive. Some of the incidents from childhood and adolescence were written anonymously and must remain so. I can, however, express my appreciation to Evelyn Dragiff, Norman Johnson, Elizabeth Stephenson, Doris Brigham, and Ubert Vincent for behavior descriptions which are quoted at some length. I am also grateful to Helen Burstein and Anne Truslowe for illustrations of children's art.

Several graduate assistants, Philip Jackson, James E. Burnes, Leah Anne Green, and Bracha Zeev, provided valuable help in locating and reviewing research related to various fields. Various members of the Teachers College library staff have made helpful suggestions and greatly facilitated our work.

At various stages the typing has been done by Phyllis Young, Ruth Engel, Viola Cyr, Priscilla Akin, and Elwood Layman. To Mr. Layman goes my warmest appreciation for good judgment, patience, and generosity in handling the numerous details entailed in the final preparation of the manuscript for the printer.

I cannot close this list of acknowledgments without mention of the understanding and interest which my parents gave to the production of this book. I can only hope that it is to some extent worthy of the high regard in which they held it.

M. A.

New York, N.Y.
January 25, 1955

Introduction

THIS IS A BOOK about human growth and learning from birth to maturity. Its subject matter is something each one of you has experienced personally. Once a squalling, helpless infant, you slowly gained independence, learned to walk and to talk, tested your growing powers in ways that both entranced and irritated your elders, gradually mastered more and more of the ways of the world, and then found yourself on the brink of adulthood, faced with exciting, delightful, and, at times, frightening new possibilities.

Now as an adult you are ready to study, with some degree of objectivity, the processes involved in your own growing and learning, and in all human development. You can observe the characteristic ways of behaving at 8 months and 8 years as well as at 18. You know that all human beings are alike in many respects, but you are also aware that there are wide differences. You probably would like to know how it comes about that people are alike and how it happens that they are different. Perhaps you are aware that many professions and many disciplines have something to contribute to your understanding. This book will attempt to bring together some of the information, the generalizations, and the principles from these fields which have a bearing on child development. Its primary focus, however, will not be to provide you with a résumé of the available research (there are a number of excellent books which do that) but to help you to apply your growing knowledge in an understanding way.

Perhaps you have not yet given much thought to the situations in which child development is likely to be useful. But surely if you are a student, you have already thought of marriage and having a family. You may have speculated about the children you are likely to have, and how you would like to raise them. Some of the experiences you have had, you would wish for them. Others you would avoid. Deep within you, you feel confident about your ability to be a " good " mother, or father. Or you are a little uneasy, uncertain that you can cope adequately with all that parenthood involves. In any event, you will feel more confident in facing this important job if you know something of what to expect from infants and children, what the world looks like to them, and what your own feelings about them are. You are less likely to feel, as young parents sometimes do, that the first baby should be a " practice " edition to give inexperienced parents a chance to learn from their mistakes!

It is not only in parenthood that one should find a study of child development helpful. In many professions it is essential to understand how human beings grow and learn. Educators cannot plan adequately for the school experience of children and youth without knowing a great deal about development. When does the child begin to learn most effectively in a group, under the tutelage of someone other than his parents? How does learning occur? Is the process the same for a 6-year-old as a 16-year-old? Are there stages of development when certain kinds of knowledge and understanding are acquired more readily than at other stages? What kinds of school experiences may be expected to further the healthy personality development of youngsters? These are a few of the questions the educator, from nursery school teacher to college professor, can ask as he turns to the findings in child development.

Members of the medical and nursing professions draw on child development understandings both in promoting health and treating disease. The pediatrician needs to know not only what immunizations are necessary and when, but also how the child may feel about them. He must become sensitive to the ways a child's behavior indicates that development is proceeding smoothly. The nurse knows that sick children (and sick adults!) may " regress " to an earlier stage of development, and she must be prepared to meet their needs on that level. At the same time she draws on her understanding of well children to provide challenge for convalescence and recuperation.

To a nutritionist, likewise, it is essential to know how children act and think and feel. She may know all the elements in an optimum diet, but the food she recommends will be useless unless it is eaten and enjoyed. She knows that food which gratifies a basic need may become a symbol of love and affection to the child. She is prepared for the conservatism of the young child and the enormous appetite of the adolescent.

Social workers, whether they deal mostly with children or with adults, with groups or with individuals, also draw constantly on an understanding of children. Will a particular foster home best serve infants or school-age children? What shall be done when a welfare client spends her rent budget on a dress for her 16-year-old daughter? Is an adolescent club group always in an uproar? These are some of the questions for which a knowledge of child development is required. In somewhat similar fashion an understanding of child development may aid and abet the lawyer or judge.

All concerned with the spiritual development of the individual, whether clergymen or religious educators or counselors, need insight into the ways of human beings as they grow toward adulthood.

Those whose professional lives are directed toward helping the emotionally disturbed and the mentally ill, such as clinical psychologists and psychiatrists, increasingly find that experience with a wide range of individuals of various ages is essential. They must be familiar with the more typical or usual patterns of development in order to appreciate the significance of deviation.

If your career is in business, in the arts, or in the physical sciences, you will likely not be able to make as direct an application of your child development understandings as you would in the professions just discussed. On the other hand, very practical uses for knowledge of child development sometimes turn up in newspaper and magazine production, radio and television. It is our opinion, however, that the personal use you may make of child development either as you look ahead to parenthood, or as you come to terms with your own childhood experience, is quite as important as is its vocational use.

The literature of child development is voluminous, but in relation to all that could be known about growth and learning, it provides only a beginning. There are still no final answers, and frequent contradictions do exist. The theories which are emerging and seem likely to stand the test of time can eventually only be validated in the lives of human beings.

The study of child development, therefore, as urgently as any science demands laboratory experience. The most appropriate setting for this, however, is not within academic walls. Rather, we observe children and youth in their natural habitats, at home, at their play, at school, wherever they may be. And we observe the child that lingers on in each of us as we ourselves grow toward maturity and old age. Strangely enough, this child within can be both a help and a hindrance to our understanding of growth and learning in other people. Only to the extent that we have learned to live comfortably with our own childhood do we become able to view another's experience without somehow distorting it.

Through "laboratory" experience we broaden our perspective on human growth and learning. Suppose, for example, that you have been brought up as an only child, or the youngest child in your family. You've had little experience with babies or young children. One day you find yourself entrusted with the care of a 2-year-old. He is extremely resistant to all of your suggestions. You are baffled by a "will" which seems as determined as your own. Perhaps your conclusion is "stubborn brat," but you are challenged to watch him with other people, and also to watch other 2-year-olds. You discover a strong element of "do it myself" appears in his reactions to everyone, but that pitched battles ensue only when the adults are adamant in their demands. Evidently there *are* ways of temporizing with 2-year-olds! You note that some of your two's persistence appears in the behavior of other 2-year-olds. You are about to make a fine generalization about two being an age of resistance when you come across a passive little "angel" who seems quite content to do whatever is expected of him and you are no longer so sure. Should you happen at this point to be transported to some foreign culture in which adult expectations for 2-year-olds are very different from those in America, you might become even more uncertain. Nevertheless, if you could observe widely enough, you would be in a fair position to state something about the behavior of which a 2-year-old is capable, that is, the growth and learning which are likely to have occurred up to that point.

Throughout this book we shall cite examples of behavior which seem to be typical of a particular age in a particular cultural group, and we shall try to help you look for such behavior. But we expect that you are interested not only in knowing that certain behavior occurs, but also why one kind and not another. Why, for example, is an occasional 2-year-old in our own middle-class culture so unassertive? To answer questions such as these we must study both the child, the circumstances surrounding him, and his life history.

Just as observation of many children of the same age gives us one kind of perspective on development, to see children growing through time gives us further perspective. We may find, for example, that a determined 2-year-old is pliable and cooperative when he reaches the age of 12 or 20. A quiet, shy 6-year-old may be reserved and reticent at 16, or he may be quite social and communicative. As the child grows up, there are many ways in which his personality remains the same, but there are also many ways in which he changes. The processes of growth and learning responsible for continuity and for change will likely be better understood as there is more research in which the same individuals are studied over a period of many years. Several research studies of this kind were initiated in the early 1930's. Some evidence is already available from them, but many of their findings have not yet been published.

This book places considerable emphasis on seeing children's behavior and development in the perspective of time. Chapter 1 begins with a description of six young people at the moment of their graduation from high school. You may wonder whether these boys and girls are real or fictional. They are real in the sense that they were evolved from case studies of six young people whose patterns of learning and growth closely resembled those of the six you will meet. But they are fictional in the sense that they have been created by the author expressly for the purposes of this book. You cannot expect that you may some day really meet any of these individuals, for as they are described they exist only in the mind of the writer. The incidents and situations devised are, however, limited to those for which there is some parallel in real life.

Chapter 1 raises a number of questions as to how the young people it describes came to be the kind of people they are. These are questions intended to stimulate your thinking about growth and learning. They are the kinds of questions which we might ask about any group of young persons. We may expect to find answers for them in our study of child development.

In Chapter 2 we begin to seek the answers by starting " At the Beginning." We consider important facts about the families into which our six young people were born. We discuss the various factors which contribute to the child's development even before he is born. We describe some of the characteristics of the six youngsters while they were still in the nursery for newborns.

Chapter 3, " From Then to Now — Child Development," is somewhat different from the other chapters in the book. In it we try to describe the kinds of processes which have likely been operative over the years so that the six newborn infants described in Chapter 2 became the six persons first met in Chapter 1. Unfortunately, no one theory exists which is adequate to cover all of these. Instead it is necessary to borrow insights from several disciplines and psychological points-of-view. This makes this chapter somewhat more abstract and probably more difficult than the others. You may wish to postpone a thorough study of it until you have finished the rest of the book. However, since it provides the structure on which the book is built, we recommend that you read it through at least once in its proper sequence.

Chapter 4, " Studying Children and Youth," offers suggestions for observing and working with children. It is intended to help you learn about child development from the children themselves.

In Chapter 5 and the chapters following it we consider infancy and the succeeding stages of development including adolescence. We continue to refer to the life histories of the young people given in Chapter 1, but we shall not get to know all that might be known about them. We have tried to include enough information to reveal major influences in the shaping of the personality of each young person, but there are many omissions. Some of these arise because the case studies which provided the patterns of learning and growth for our fictional young people emphasized certain areas of development less than others. In some instances, in attempting to highlight a particular influence, the author has overlooked others. The life history material should not be expected to explain precisely how each of the six young people came to be his particular kind of person. It should help you to develop insight into the many factors operative in personality development. We hope further that from it you may also acquire a deepened appreciation, understanding, and respect for human individuality.

Finally, a word about the "problems" found throughout the book. Some are "thought" questions which demand that you stop to think about the implications of the material you are reading. Some will draw on your growing acquaintance with the life histories. Others are intended to test your understanding of certain principles. Many of them do not have any one "right" answer but invite you to consider likely possibilities. Problems of this type may serve as a basis for class discussion as well as for individual study.

A second type of problem demands further reading. Many of these offer you opportunities to become familiar with original research and with child development as a specialized body of knowledge. Some of them are designed as cooperative enterprises for class use.

A third type of problem includes suggestions for observing and working with children. While no one student will be able to carry out all of these suggestions, the more time that can be given to actual contacts with children, the more meaningful the study of child development becomes.

All of these problems are set in bold-face type in order to set them apart from the rest of the text. As you turn now to Chapter 1, you will note that the material relating to the young people is also set in darker type than that used in the explanatory portions of the text. This type is used throughout the book whenever the life histories are cited.

Contents

High school graduation: a ceremony symbolizing the young person's progress toward adult status.

1

Adults in the Making

" TONIGHT YOU CROSS the threshold into the world of adult responsibility. . . ." The voice of the commencement speaker droned through the sticky heat of Franklin High School auditorium. The graduates, not yet accustomed to the dignity thrust upon them and stifling in their academic garb, wriggled apprehensively. Here and there a nod confirmed earlier predictions of forty-five minutes of boredom.

Jane Warner, annoyed that the seating arrangements had placed her best friend several rows behind her, noted briefly that she was in the direct line of vision of Andrew Drosky. Not that Andy would pay any attention to *her*. He was undoubtedly the best-looking boy in the Senior class, probably choosy about his girl friends. She thought that she ought to try to locate her family so she could tell her mother that she had seen them. Trust her mother to ask, nothing ever escaped her. Her eyes swept the crowd, searching her mother's new red hat, her father's bald head, her brother Jim's dark curls. Ah, there in the tenth row. Her father was frowning intently. Probably still annoyed with her plan to spend the night with Karen when he'd thought she ought to come home. " After all," he'd said, " We don't have a brand new graduate in our family every night of the week." Of course what he really objected to was Karen. It seemed strange that he had never liked her. Karen was so brilliant, so loyal, so far above the cheap kinds of girls she might be running around with.

Thinking of Karen, Jane's gaze shifted to her classmates. Take Pat Plummer. Now there was one her father liked, her mother too, for that

1

matter. Pat always made out to be a little on the shy side, especially when older people were around, or just girls. She didn't seem to say much around boys either, but the way she smiled up at them, and acted like she'd never heard or seen anything to equal them! Uncomfortably, Jane recalled how she'd tried to copy some of Pat's techniques, quite unsuccessfully. She really didn't know what it was about Pat. Maybe the way she danced, though you wouldn't think a fellow would care about a girl's being an exhibitionist. Pat declared she'd die of stage fright every time she danced, but Jane recalled that she'd been given a solo part in the Franklin Follies for three consecutive years. She suspected that Pat might be enjoying herself more than she let on.

Personally, Jane thought, she herself had *never* enjoyed any part of high school. Chemistry, maybe — and hockey. But not the chit-chat between classes and the awful scramble to get a date for the dances. Maybe when she got to college she'd find a man with interests more like hers. Someone who wouldn't call her a goon just because she liked poetry . . . " How do I love thee? Let me count the ways. . . ." Momentarily serene, Jane slipped into a pleasant fantasy.

Andrew Drosky, who had been somewhat similarly engaged in speculation about *his* family, his friends, and himself, suddenly found himself arrested by the marked change in expression on Jane's face. She looks almost human, he thought. Funny about girls — all so unpredictable. Just when you think everything is under control, because you like the same things, music for example, and books, and the same kinds of people and it looks like you're really good friends, they begin to pull the coy stuff . . . " But Andy, I thought we were going steady." One of these days he'd probably fall for that. And there would go his future. His future . . . What about that? Would he get to college or would the Army get him first? Maybe he'd enlist in the Marines, maybe the Air Force. But he would like to go to college, concentrate on social sciences, maybe psychiatry, find out more about people. Well, no matter what, from now on out no more wasting time. He'd wasted too much time, been too lazy, but not any longer. He knew he was smart, like the teachers always said; from now on he'd work and prove it. Might even be able to show his folks he amounted to something. He knew they weren't very pleased with him a lot of the time. His mother seldom looked at him with that " Here's my big beautiful son " like some mothers had. Like Dan Mallon's mom. Dan just couldn't do anything wrong.

In the row ahead of Andrew, Dan Mallon shifted his shoulders uneasily under the weight of his robe. He wished the speaker would get on a little faster. This was a big night for him, the first member of his family to graduate from high school, but he'd be glad when the ceremonies were over. Take it all and all, he'd been pretty darned lucky. His school record wasn't spectacular, just a good dependable average. He hadn't been a star athlete, but he'd made the grade with the rest of the guys, and he had a place with them. Got on all right with the girls, too. Nobody special yet, still playing the field, no use to get too involved now. Like as not he'd be in the Army soon. Lots of ways that kind of life appealed to him. Abruptly the speaker's voice cut across his revery . . . ". . . young men who have given their lives on the battlefields. . . ." Death — funny how he always felt so uneasy about that, the one thing he feared, he guessed. He wondered how the other fellows took it. Chet Brown, for instance. Bet he'd make a good soldier, always seemed to be spoiling for a fight. Funny his brother, Charlie, never seemed that way. Not that he couldn't take care of himself okay, but he just never seemed to have the chip on his shoulder that Chet had.

At that moment Charlie, too, was thinking of the differences between himself and his brother. He couldn't imagine being separated from him for any very long time, and yet it seemed they were no longer as completely companionable as they had once been. Chet's ideas about girls didn't jibe with his. Seemed like Chet had to " make " every girl he met, but when she succumbed, he was ready to move on to greener fields. Somehow, he, Charlie, didn't crave such variety. As a matter of fact, he wasn't at all sure that girls made very much difference to him, though he'd surely had his share. Thinking back it seemed as though some of the very best times of his life had been camping trips when he and Chet and their older brother Ted were pretty much on their own together.

As he mused on this, Charlie let his gaze wander over the faces of his classmates. He began clicking off mentally the girls he had dated, and the girls he had thought about dating. Pat Plummer — there was once he'd beat Chet. Jane Warner — he paused at her. Sometimes she was darned good looking, but when you tried to talk to her, she either clammed up or else made some smart crack that made you wish you'd minded your own business. Celeste Collins — funny about her, she wasn't really pretty but she was a good sport. He liked her.

Celeste, aware of Charlie's attention, smiled in his direction. How many of these fellows she had come to know in the past two years.

She smiled to herself as she thought of how scared she had been when she had first entered high school, how she couldn't talk to anyone, and used to wish the floor would open up to swallow her when she was called on in a class. She'd had just one friend in those days, now she had dozens. She wasn't quite sure what had made the difference. Maybe learning to swim so well and to dance, or maybe earning money after school and summers so she could have a permanent and buy nice clothes. Whatever it was, she felt pretty good about herself. If she'd made this much progress in four years, maybe when she got into a full-time job she'd do all right too, perhaps even find the doctor or lawyer she'd like to marry.

That so many of the young people in his audience were thus reviewing their pasts and their futures was no necessary reflection on the merits of the speaker. Indeed one of the proper functions of the commencement speech may be to offer the young person a few quiet moments when he may appropriately consider who he is, how he came to be, and what is his destination.

In cultures less complex and more primitive than ours, young people are initiated into adult status with ceremonies much more elaborate and ritualistic than any high school graduation. At the same time, the differentiation between the roles of youth and the roles of adults is much more clear cut than is the case with us. It is reported, for example, that some 40 percent of our young people never enter high school, and of those who do only about 50 percent graduate. Of these, some 13 percent go on to college.[1] Thus some adolescents achieve adult status (earning their own living, starting their families) without benefit of any initiation, some of them are initiated via high school graduation, others remain economically dependent for four years of college, and still others may not be fully independent until they have had as many as ten or more years of education and training beyond high school.

Becoming an adult in our culture is not a matter of passing through some ordeal or examination, or receiving some certificate or award. Rather it is a matter of learning to behave the way other adults do. Learning is complicated by the fact that there are so many

[1] Kuhlen, Raymond G. *The Psychology of Adolescent Development.* New York: Harper and Brothers, 1952. P. 461.

kinds of adults, so many different ways of behaving which pass as adult. Some people learn quickly and easily. Others learn slowly and painfully. Some individuals seem " mature " at 16, others are " immature " at 60. Small wonder that the establishment of a sense of his own identity becomes so all absorbing to the young adult-in-the-making.

In this process the older adults — parents, teachers, employers, neighborhood gang leaders, ministers, club workers, neighbors, and so on — all play their part. Probably none feel the weight of responsibility more than do the parents. So it was with the parents of the young people in Franklin High.

Mrs. Warner glanced around her with considerable satisfaction. The red hat had been a good buy. In it she felt as young and attractive as any mother around her. Focusing her attention on the graduates once more, she noted with relief that Jane's sullen expression had been replaced with a faint smile. What an enigma the girl was. Determined that her daughter should not suffer the heartbreak she herself had known as a young girl, Mrs. Warner thought about how hard she had tried to bring her up to enjoy a social life. And Jane had agonized every step of the way. She was bright, surely, but she had been interminably slow about developing any kind of grace. Only recently had she shown any concern with her appearance and mostly only to resist her mother's ideas. Certainly she had a mind of her own and was increasingly willing to express it. Remembering what she had recently read about adolescence being a time when young people had to untie the parental apron strings, Mrs. Warner wondered whether Jane's present open rebellion was indeed just " another phase," or whether it went much deeper. Sometimes she felt she must have misunderstood Jane all her life. And there didn't seem much she could do about it now. Maybe " hands off " would work, and yet Jane was still such a *baby*.

Three rows in front of her, Mrs. Drosky sat dreaming about *her* baby. What a precious little boy Andrew had been. She remembered how he looked in his white embroidered romper suit the first time she had taken him to nursery school, when he was only a little over 2. Those had been worrisome years, what with her husband out of work so much, but she had somehow always managed to keep the children clean and well fed. And she'd always been so proud of Andy then —

the way he started kindergarten when he was only 4 and the fuss the teachers had made over him. He'd always got along well with people, but in late years she didn't feel he'd lived up to his best potentialities. Sometimes she thought she'd failed him somehow. She knew she kept after him to do things too much.

Mr. Drosky, sensing her uneasiness, patted his wife's hand. He'd about given up on Andy. He just seemed to lack ambition. Maybe kids these days had too much. Not like when he was young and had to quit school, and live through the depression and then fight back by going to night school and gradually getting re-established. One thing, he'd stuck by his family. Not like Ted Brown who'd gone off to the Navy when it hadn't even been likely he'd be drafted. Stayed in, too, even after the war was over. Mrs. Brown didn't look over-concerned about her husband's absence on this important night either. Looked like she just about lived for the kids, and was pretty proud of them.

Mrs. Brown was pleased. They were good-looking youngsters, not the smartest, but they got on all right. People liked them. The manager of the " five and ten " where Charlie worked after school and Saturdays said he'd never known a boy he'd trust more, and the men at the gas station had told her Chet was a pretty reliable kid. Charlie, of course, was her special pride, as good as a woman when it came to helping her around the house. Beaming, she returned her attention to the speaker who was saying something about "the families of tomorrow."

Dan Mallon's mother knew in her heart she couldn't bear to think of Dan's leaving her to begin his own family. Already she was beginning to steel herself against his enlistment which she knew was coming soon. She could share him with the Navy, she supposed, but not yet with another woman. Ruefully she reminded herself that letting them go was part of being a good mother. She'd never believed in holding the reins too tight, and this was no time to begin. She supposed she'd been lucky. He'd been such a little hellion when he was 4 and 5 and then he'd begun to settle down until now you couldn't ask for a steadier, more responsible boy. Not unusual, just average, an average good kid.

Perhaps Mrs. Mallon's satisfaction in her son contained some elements not experienced by the mothers of daughters. Certainly little could mar that held by Mrs. Plummer. Just as she had felt when the nurses had laid her last-born in her arms that this, " the little one," was the most perfect, so on this night she regarded Pat as perfection itself.

Momentarily she forgot her uneasiness about the boy friend who reappeared so persistently, and who seemed so unlike anyone Mrs. Plummer had known before. Pat was still young. She adored her father, her mother, her home. She would not yet leave the nest.

In contrast, Mrs. Collins was thinking that soon Celeste would be settling down to going steady. She herself had been married young. The marriage had been a happy one. She would wish for Celeste someone with more ambition than her father had had, but his steady qualities and his thoroughgoing goodness were by no means to be despised. Celeste didn't seem to take much interest in work. She wouldn't want to help earn the living as she had done through the years. On the other hand, with her love of a good time, and her ability to pick becoming clothes, Celeste ought to do all right for herself. No need for anyone to worry over her.

No need, perhaps, and yet more than one of her teachers had. Miss Yates, her homeroom teacher in Sophomore year, recalled the pale, tense, frizzy-haired girl she had been and wondered whether she had fully gained control of her warring feelings or whether her apparent serenity was only a carefully held mask. She hoped the former, but she had seen too many youngsters go way up and then way down to be willing to rely completely on appearance.

Mrs. Jordan, one of the guidance counselors, mused along the same lines. The speaker of the evening, his conclusion now clearly in view, had seemed to imply that these youngsters setting forth into a not too friendly world would now reap what they had sown. Those who had worked hard would find the way made smoother for them, while those who had played too much would find their paths beset by the thorny demands of business and industry. His rhetoric is considerably better than his logic, and neither is outstanding, Mrs. Jordan thought as she folded her program. She'd known some of these youngsters' parents when *they* were in high school. She's oh'd and ah'd over some of these same 18-year-olds when their age was still reckoned in months. And she'd learned to be extremely careful about predictions where human behavior and development were concerned. The more I study people, the more I learn about the ways they grow and learn and change, the more impressed I am with the *variety* of possibilities in human personality, she thought philosophically as she turned her attention to the ceremony of diploma presentation.

Mrs. Jordan's viewpoint is one with which we shall be concerned throughout this book. We have described six young people all of whom have completed eighteen years of living.

These are the young people to whom we shall return again and again in the course of this book. You need not attempt to remember everything about them. We shall get to know them better as time goes by.

THE GIRLS

When the seating of the graduates was arranged all three of the girls found themselves among the shortest girls in the class. Jane and Celeste were almost exactly the same height, while Pat's extra inch was barely noticeable. Aside from this, there was little other resemblance among the three. The academic robes concealed their figures but without them one would have judged Jane the heaviest since her build was somewhat more chunky.

Jane Warner. As Andy had observed, the thing most people noticed first about Jane was her facial expression. It was often hard to tell whether something was annoying her, or whether she was merely " thinking hard." Her features were good. She had a round face, a small, well-shaped nose, brown eyes, and a pretty mouth. Her hair, which was a medium brown, showed a slight inclination to curl especially when she was warm. Relaxing after a strenuous and successful hockey game, or dreaming over a beautiful bit of poetry, she was a most attractive young person. But the corners of her mouth could turn down in a sulky expression and her comments were sometimes more sarcastic than she realized. Consequently, people who did not know her well were sometimes inclined to think that she was unfriendly. Jane's interests, apart from sports — and it was only in the middle of her teens that she had really cared much for them — were almost all intellectual. She had read a great deal, thought it was important to be informed about literature and current events and to do well in school.

Pat Plummer. In contrast, most everyone regarded Pat as a very friendly person. She was not nearly as sure of herself as she appeared to Jane. Jane knew her only casually, although their families had been acquaintances for some years. Pat operated on the principle that looking pleasant and being cheerful would see you through most situations, and, in general, it did. She had always loved clothes and spent a considerable amount of time selecting the sweater or the scarf which would accentuate her blonde hair and blue eyes. Lipstick and nail

polish must always match. She enjoyed dancing but had no other outstanding interests. The crowd of boys and girls to which she belonged
were movie fans, but they also spent many evenings at one another's
homes talking, listening or dancing to records, and eating. They, like
Pat, had few intellectual interests.

Celeste Collins. Despite the increased confidence she herself now
felt, most people would still call Celeste a shy person, especially in a
group. She was so often concerned with the impression she might be
making, that it was hard for her to be spontaneous, even though she
knew that one way to get along happily with other people was to be
interested in their interests. She had learned to select her clothes fairly
well. Her appearance was usually neat and trim, although never outstanding. Towheaded as a child, she had found the gradual darkening
of her hair something of a disappointment, but permanents had helped
her to manage it in attractive ways. She liked to dance and swim and
was moderately good at both. Celeste belonged to a group of young
people who were less closely knit than were Pat's crowd. Sometimes
there would be a dozen of them together; more often, only two or
three couples. Celeste usually went with one boy whom she liked, but
had no intention of regarding " seriously." She was " quick " at learning, but not very creative. She enjoyed the romantic stories in the
popular magazines but would not have cared at all for the poetry
that Jane liked.

THE BOYS

Andrew Drosky. Andy stood almost at the head of the Senior class
so far as height was concerned. With his broad shoulders and fine
physique he didn't really need crisp blond hair and deep blue eyes to
make him attractive. But he had those too. He also had what some of
his teachers termed " a way with people." He belonged to no one
crowd in the high school, perhaps because so many of the girls found
him interesting and were always arranging to have him invited to
parties. Had you asked Andy who his best friends were, he would have
hesitated. He had best friends, but they were outside the high school.
There was a recreational leader in a settlement house, and another
fellow who had just graduated from college. With them he shared interests in music, literature, and even philosophy.

Dan Mallon. When it came to height, Dan was about average. Lean
and muscular, with sandy hair and a cowlick he never quite succeeded
in subduing, he was far from handsome. He had no very distinguishing
features, just a nice " average " boy, as his mother said. He was in-

tensely interested in sports, especially basketball and football. Whenever the boys were gathered in a group you could be sure that as the
talk turned in the direction of the game just past, or the one to come,
Dan would take an active part. Aside from that he was usually rather
reserved and quiet. When the other fellows took girls out, Dan did
too, but he was not nearly so keen on dating as some of them.

Charles Brown. Charlie was only slightly taller than Dan, but a little
heavier. His light brown hair had some tendency to curl, and his eyes
were hazel. Girls who sometimes mistook him for his brother Chet when
the two were apart learned to notice that he had a " dimple " in one
cheek. This was a slight scar dating from a neighborhood fight when he
was 4. Like Dan, Charles was interested in sports, but he was not nearly
so intense about it. Games, like dating, dancing, the movies, were
pleasant ways of spending time so far as he was concerned. He also
enjoyed less social pursuits — being at home with the family, for example, and reading. He was not interested in intellectual matters to
the same extent as Jane, or Andy, but he did have a reflective, thoughtful turn of mind.

We have seen that in some ways these young people are very much
alike. All of them have now graduated from high school, all shared
similar educational and recreational interests, all of them have some
concerns about the future, all of them are in greater or lesser degree
sensitive to the opinions of their parents and peers. But in other
ways they are very different. Their attitudes toward themselves and
toward other people, their aspirations, the interests they seem likely
to pursue as they become increasingly independent are almost as
varied as their hair coloring, their facial contours, their height and
weight. What are the factors responsible for the similarities? Are
these six typical of 18-year-olds generally? Or American 18-year-
olds? Or only of Franklin High 18-year-olds? Raised in the same
community, having similar school experiences, going to the same
movies and skating rinks, subject to the same pressures of depression
and war, are their likenesses not to be expected? But what factors
account for the differences? To understand these we must go back
to the beginning, to a time even before they were born.

2

⌐⌐⌐

At the Beginning

A GENUINE READINESS to establish and guide the next generation is a mark of the mature healthy personality. It implies a considerable faith — faith in the future and in oneself. The prospective parent's feelings about bringing a child into the world depend in large part on his own experiences in growing up and his feelings about them. The person whose life has been such as to make him feel good about himself is likely to feel good about having children. The person who is bitter and unhappy is not likely to regard the possibility of parenthood so comfortably.

The young people being considered in this volume were born during the depression years of the thirties — a period when many parents hesitated to have children lest they be unable to feed, clothe, and educate them adequately. It is in this setting of part-time employment and joblessness, and later of public relief and work programs that we shall view the families into which these children came. However, as the sketches of the parents in Chapter 1 have indicated, all of them were hard-working, "respectable" people, capable of earning an adequate living, interested in providing comfortable homes and good education for their children. Now let us become better acquainted with them. As you read, you may wish to speculate on the kinds of babies likely to be born into such families.

11

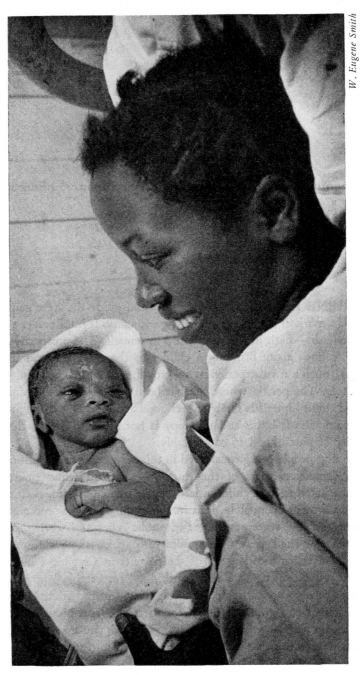

From the moment of birth social as well as biological factors shape the child's destiny.

The Families into Which Our Young People Were Born

Jane Warner's parents were in several respects the most privileged of the group. Her father, a tall, heavy-set man of 38 at the time she was born, was in excellent physical condition. He was a railroad engineer with continuous employment. His job enabled him to enjoy a considerable amount of free time at home. Being a good carpenter and handyman, he was able to do much to make the small apartment in which the family lived when Jane was a baby comfortable and attractive. A quiet, reserved person, he was content to limit his recreation to listening to the radio and occasional drives into the country.

Mrs. Warner, 28, a much more voluble person than her husband, had considerably wider social interests, but at least in the early years of her marriage she did not attempt to pursue them very much. She had graduated from a small college where she had majored in English. Ill-prepared for any kind of job, she had finally drifted into a librarianship. She had not been particularly happy as a librarian, for she felt that she should be doing something more important. When she was 26, she met Mr. Warner and married him shortly thereafter. She tackled home-making with full determination to make a success of it. There was no aspect of housekeeping which she did not try to do to perfection, even though it was very fatiguing.

The Warners were not particularly family " minded " and most of their relatives lived out-of-town. Consequently, Mrs. Warner had no relative in whom to confide or with whom she could share responsibility.

Pat Plummer's family presented a very different picture. She was the third child in a family which consisted not only of her older brother and sister but also grandparents and numerous aunts, uncles, and cousins. Her father, who was 40 when she was born, worked as an electrician. Since he had the only steady income, it went to support not only the immediate members of his family but some of the other relatives as well. The home was shared with these so that Pat's arrival only added to the congestion. Nevertheless, the house was well kept, and the various members of the household worked together in fine cooperative fashion. This in a sense was advantageous for Mrs. Plummer, 32, whose health was very poor during her period of pregnancy with Pat and for several years thereafter.

Like Jane Warner, Andrew Drosky was the first child. His parents, however, were considerably younger, his mother only 20 and his father 21.

Mr. Drosky, a slender man, inclined to underweight, had obtained employment as a clerk in an engineering office. His hope was to be able to acquire sufficient skills by going to night school to become a draftsman, but at the time of Andy's birth his progress was, he felt, very slow.

At the end of her second year in high school Mrs. Drosky had left school to become a clerk in a dime store. She had known and admired Mr. Drosky since they were children. Although generally able to control herself, she was rather a "worrier," and under sufficient provocation could become quite depressed. Her health at the time of Andrew's birth was fair.

Though she had as many concerns as Mrs. Drosky, Mrs. Mallon, a short, stout woman of 28, was better able to take them in her stride. In general, she was easygoing, although when provoked, she was quite capable of expressing herself in vivid, direct fashion. Except for occasional headaches she was in good health. She had completed two years of high school before clerking in a neighborhood store. She did not work following her marriage, even though Mr. Mallon's income was frequently marginal. Twenty-four at the time of Dan's birth, he had left school at 14 to work as a gas station attendant. Although he was rarely ill, a physical examination just prior to Dan's birth indicated that he was somewhat below par. Both of the Mallons enjoyed socializing and dancing, but following their marriage, they tended to center their recreation around their home. There was much visiting back and forth of the relatives on both sides of the family.

Like the Mallons, the Browns experienced many financial problems. As a cabinetmaker, Mr. Brown found work slack. In addition to supporting his immediate family, he shared responsibility for assistance to relatives. As a consequence there were times when even food was scarce. His wife, who had been a bookkeeper before her marriage, was of Spanish ancestry and had all of the volatility which people sometimes associate with the Latin temperament. She herself often commented that it was fortunate that she had had the experience of having one child, Theodore, five years before the twins arrived. Otherwise, even though she was a quite mature 30 at the time of their birth, she might not have been able to cope with them.

Mrs. Collins was the only mother in the group who worked rather consistently outside her home. She had left school at 15, taking a job in a garment factory. She worked at the factory well into the fourth month of pregnancy. A petite, talkative little woman of 24, she always seemed to regard her husband with some degree of awe. Her marriage meant a great deal to her. As she put it, before she was married she used to worry a great deal but after she was married there seemed no call to worry about anything. Mr. Collins had completed high school and had a secure factory job. Although it did not net him a great deal, it had been steady and he was sufficiently trusted by his superiors so that there seemed little likelihood of his losing it.

PROBLEM 1. On the basis of the above information, which families do you think might have the healthiest babies? The most intelligent? The happiest? On what factors do you base your hunches? What additional information do you think you would need to substantiate your hunches?

We cannot even begin to answer the questions we have just raised until we have some understanding of the interplay of heredity and environment, of the ways in which nature and nurture operate together in human development. We turn our attention first to the contribution of the child's biological inheritance, that is, the characteristics with which he is endowed at conception. We do this not because of any conviction that heredity factors are more influential in development (without the operation of both heredity and environment development could not take place) but rather because of the very practical consideration that the environmental factors are more easily modifiable. Parents, for example, may aspire to producing a husky boy baby destined for star player on the football team of papa's alma mater, but they cannot prevent nature from turning up with a dainty wisp of femininity. They can, however, adapt the nurture they provide. That parents and other adults significant to children can offer more adequate guidance when they are sensitive to the subtle as well as the more gross innate differences between individuals is one of the major theses of this book.

An analogy drawn by a young parent who was groping toward a better understanding of his two children may serve to illustrate the point. The father said, " As a draftsman I must draw plans for the use of a variety of kinds of metals. Unless I know the exact nature of each metal, how much stress and strain it will take, how it will respond to changes in temperature and atmosphere, I run the risk of making a plan which may be hopelessly inefficient or ruin the material. I wish I could know the strengths and weaknesses, the potentialities of my kids as well as I do those metals. If I did, I darned sure wouldn't make some of the mistakes I have in the past."

Children, of course, are much more complex than a sheet of metal. They are not merely shaped by their environment but they exert their own pressures on it, so that in a sense it must conform to them as well as they do it. This fact, however, only emphasizes further the importance of an understanding of individual differences in the understanding of human behavior and development.

HOW DOES HEREDITY CONTRIBUTE TO DEVELOPMENT?

Within the last fifty years scientists in the field of genetics have made tremendous progress in establishing the facts of heredity.

Scheinfeld, in *The New You and Heredity,* says:

Thus it can be said with assurance that the mechanism of heredity — among humans as among other living and growing things — now stands clearly revealed. While all of its intricacies are by no means clearly known, the basic principles are as unmistakenly clear as the workings of a watch. . . .

And yet, vitally important as all of this is, not much of it has seeped through to the general public, and even among many professional people the knowledge of modern genetics remains hazy.[1]

It is not within the scope of this book to convey as much information about heredity as the serious student of child development may wish to acquire. Rather we shall draw on the accounts of Scheinfeld and of Dunn and Dobzhansky for a few basic considerations which may be kept in mind in any attempt to understand human development. The reader will find it very worthwhile to turn directly to these sources for more complete information.

Biological Inheritance

Biological inheritance at conception. Conception occurs when a male sperm cell (one of the hundred million or so which may be present in a single drop of seminal fluid) reaches and penetrates a

---

[1] Scheinfeld, Amram. *The New You and Heredity.* Philadelphia: J. P. Lippincott Company, 1950. P. 2.

female ovum, or egg. Nature is considerably less prodigal with the ova than she is with the sperm cells. Normally only one such egg a month ripens in the mother's ovary. The ripe egg when released passes into the fallopian tube where it can be reached by one of the many million sperm cells.

Each sperm cell carries twenty-four tiny bodies called chromosomes, and it is these which are the hereditary contribution of the father. As the head of the sperm cell enters the egg and releases these chromosomes, the egg nucleus likewise lets go of its twenty-four chromosomes, the hereditary contribution of the mother. The new individual cell is thus provided with forty-eight chromosomes. As this cell divides and redivides, each new cell in the body (with the exception of the germ cells which carry only twenty-four chromosomes) duplicates the original forty-eight chromosomes.

The importance of the chromosomes lies in the fact that they carry the genes, living units, determining the life processes of the human being. They determine such obvious individual characteristics as eye, hair and skin color, facial features, size and shape of the body. They are equally influential in establishing the individuality of the organs, brain, nerves, heart, lungs, glands, and so on. Owing to both difficulties in observation and the complexities of function there is still a tremendous amount to be learned about the variety of differences which exist and their effect on the growth and development of the individual.

The genes, like the chromosomes, are paired, one of each pair coming from each parent. Each member of each pair is equipped for the same function (the determination of eye color, for example) but possesses greater or lesser ability to carry out that function. Thus the gene for brown eyes is said to be *dominant* over that for blue eyes. The blue-eye gene is said to be recessive, and blue eyes appear only when both members of the eye-color pair are blue-eye genes. Every child stands the chance of receiving from his parents for any characteristic two genes which are dominant; or one gene which is dominant and one which is recessive, in which the characteristic will be similar to what it would have been had it been produced by the two dominant genes; or he may receive two recessive genes, in which case the characteristic will be different. For such a characteristic as eye color, study of a man and woman and their relatives and ancestors can reveal, within limits, the kinds of genes they are carrying. Thus it is possible to make some prediction as to the appearance of their offspring. With organisms less complex and more easily subject to control than human beings, a knowledge of the laws of genetics has made it possible to breed selectively so that certain desired characteristics appear more and more frequently in each succeeding generation and the less wanted characteristics gradually disappear. Some of the difficulties inherent in applying these laws to human beings will become more apparent in the next section.

Unique inheritance for each person. The child's biological inheritance is unique for each individual. The only exception to this is the case of identical twins, which we shall discuss later. We do not know how many genes man has, but we may gain some idea of the possibility when we learn that the number estimated for the fruit fly, an organism which has been much used in the study of genetics, is as many as ten thousand. Dunn and Dobzhansky estimate that there must be several thousands of genes in the full set carried in a human sex cell. They state:

Since the baby gets one gene of each kind from each parent, it follows that it has two of each kind. If there are five thousand different genes in the egg and five thousand in the sperm cell, there will be five thousand pairs or ten thousand altogether in every cell composing the body of the individual. However, when sex cells, whether eggs or sperms, are formed in that individual there is an exact biological mechanism in the body which ensures that each egg or sperm will receive one gene of each pair. It is clear, therefore, that each parent transmits to its child always only one-half, never all, the genes which each parent has, but it will be, as we know, a different set of genes for every child.[2]

It should be noted that at birth each individual has in his body the already formed though not yet mature sex cells which will transmit his genes to his offspring. At present there is no known way of changing the composition of these cells to effect specified changes in the characteristics for which they are responsible. In other words,

    [2] Dunn, Leslie C., and Dobzhansky, Theodosius. *Heredity, Race and Society.* New York: Penguin Books, 1946. P. 44.

nothing which takes place in an ordinary lifetime is likely to change the nature of the germ cells which provide the individual's biological inheritance to his offspring. (The effects of atomic radiation have been under study, but results are as yet unknown.)

Dunn and Dobzhansky draw an analogy which may be helpful in understanding how heredity functions in a way guaranteed to insure uniqueness to each new individual:

> The set of genes present in a sex cell may be likened to a suit of cards, except that the hereditary " suit " has several thousand, instead of the thirteen " cards." Suppose that the maternal cards are red and the paternal black. The child has two suits, the red and the black one. Now when the child grows up and produces its own sex cells a full suit must be provided for each cell. But it does not matter whether only red, only black, or mixtures of red and black go into the outfitting of a cell. One cell may carry, for example, ace and queen of diamonds, king and jack of spades, while another cell may carry ace, king, jack of diamonds and queen of spades, a third may carry all diamonds, etc. We may carry this analogy still further. Suppose that the " hand " of one of the parents consists of diamonds and spades, and the " hand " of the other of hearts and clubs (the suits now represent the grandparental sets of genes). The rule of the game is that a parent must give to the child one card of each kind (i.e., one ace, one king, one queen, etc.) to make a complete suit. But the card is drawn at random from two of each kind the parent has. The " hand " which is dealt to the child is, therefore, contributed to equally by both parents and each parent contributes one half of the " hand " he himself has. What cards will the children have? The answer is that different children will receive different cards. By and large, the hand of a child will consist of cards of each of the four suits. But each card will be represented only in duplicate and therefore by two suits only. So there will be " hands " with the kings of diamonds and clubs, diamonds and hearts, spades and clubs, and spades and hearts. In other words, a grandchild inherits each kind of gene from only two, never all four of its grandparents.[3]

From this it should be quite apparent that once conception takes place the parent has no control over the genes which are " dealt " his child. He can, of course, avoid transferring to a future generation traits or tendencies carried by dominant genes by abstinence from sexual intercourse or by using contraceptive methods. It is considerably more difficult for him to prevent the transfer of characteris-

[3] *Ibid*. Pp. 46 and 47.

tics which are carried by recessive genes, since he is less likely to be aware of the fact that he carries them. If his family history reveals the presence of defects, abnormalities, or diseases, he may be able to learn about their genetic origin and transmission. Enough is known about some of these to warrant caution in the choice of mate and careful observation of any children born so that preventive and corrective measures may be taken as early as possible. By and large, however, the number of ailments to be blamed on heredity are relatively few in number when compared with those which are primarily caused by environmental factors.

Any parent who attempts to secure for his child any special attributes through inheritance is very likely to meet with some frustrations. The highly intelligent college professor who wishes to raise a son capable of carrying forward his pet researches has a somewhat better chance if he selects as his wife the brightest of the students in the subject he teaches than if he chooses the " pretty-but-dumb " waitress who serves his morning coffee, but the outcome is not guaranteed. His young hopeful may be bright but lean toward art and not toward science, or he may turn out to be a steady, plodding youngster with no special attribute beyond an ability for top-notch baseball pitching. Regardless of his abilities he may of course determine to be " his own man " and become anything but what his father wants him to be!

Nevertheless, the fact of each individual's uniqueness has many important implications for parents, and for all who share responsibility for guiding the young. The extent to which genetic factors are influential in the development of the individual is only beginning to be understood. Hall, in proposing a new area of study, psycho-genetics, states:

The individual is a purposive, striving, selective, adjusting, animated organism. He does not spring to life just because stimuli from the outside world fall upon him. Nor does he lapse back into passivity and desuetude at their termination. There are inner forces that regulate, control and precipitate his responses to the world. Psychologically these forces are called motives, intentions, values, interests, attitudes and sentiments. Physiologically they are hormones, neural impulses, and chemical states. Genetically they are forces residing within the chromosomes. These genetic forces must be extremely important in shaping the psychological destiny of the individual. . . . Accordingly an understanding of psychogenetics is a prerequisite for the development of a dynamic psychology.[4]

PROBLEM 2. Do you know any families in which there are children who seem to be " misfits "? In what ways do they differ from the other members of the family? To what extent do you think their differences may be due to genetic factors? To environmental factors?
PROBLEM 3. Two young parents are very much concerned over the fact that their first baby has been born with a clubfoot. They " confess " to the doctor that the baby was conceived before they were married. Could this fact have been responsible for the malformation? Why or why not?

Identical twins. Identical twins are to a large degree the exception to the rule of uniqueness of biological inheritance. There is one instance in which two (or more) individuals may have the same biological inheritance. That is when a single egg cell fertilized by a single sperm cell splits after it begins to grow. Most often the split results in two individuals, identical twins, but further division sometimes results in triplets, quadruplets, or even quintuplets. Not all multiple births are the result of a single sperm penetrating a single ovum. When more than one egg cell is fertilized, each child has a different biological inheritance, and the relationship is one of fraternity rather than identity. Identity is established when a close resemblance is found in such identifying marks as eye color, hair color and form, hair whorls, skin color, patterns of the palm, sole, and fingers and, in blood type, blood pressure, pulse, respiration, and brain-wave patterns.

Identical twins have furnished science with " natural " experimental material in which to study the interaction of nature and nurture. A method of " co-twin control " introduced by Gesell and Thompson has been used to determine the effects of training and of maturation in the acquisition of various kinds of skills. In this method one member of a pair is given special training during the period of experimentation while the other receives none. Since it can be assured that both grow at the same rate, any differences in

---

[4] Hall, Calvin S. " The Genetics of Behavior " in *Handbook of Experimental Psychology,* edited by S. S. Stevens. New York: John Wiley and Sons, 1951. P. 328.

performance at the end of the experimental period can be attributed to the training given.[5]

Information regarding identical twins reared apart has served to indicate the variety of ways environment plays a part in the development of temperament, interests, and abilities. Yet the similarities which are found even when twins have had rather markedly different experiences underline the importance of the biological inheritance as well.[6]

PROBLEM 4. One of the best-known studies of twins is that done by Myrtle McGraw, *Growth: A Study of Johnny and Jimmy*. The study focused on the effects of very early training in a variety of motor activities. Originally diagnosed as identical twins, Johnny and Jimmy were later found to be fraternals. In what ways would this finding alter the significance of the results? (For discussion of the study see *Readings in Child Psychology* edited by Dennis, pages 199–223.) [7]

Influence of inheritance on development. Many a parent, contemplating his first newborn, wondering what life may hold for him, has asked whether the baby will be what he " has to be " or whether he may be what his parent would like him to be. Had he put the question to scientists in the first decade or two of this century, a period when the science of genetics was just taking form, the answer would surely have been in favor of the baby's destiny being largely predetermined by the nature of his biological inheritance. In the twenties and thirties when experimentation had focused more on the learned aspects of man's behavior, the answer would more likely have suggested that the baby would be what his parents " made " him be. By the forties a reaction to this extremely environmental point of view was well under way. Gradually understanding is emerging that the development of the human personality is not *primarily* a matter of genetic endowment, nor *primarily* a matter of socialization and training, but rather an ever-changing yet continu-

[5] Gesell, Arnold, and Thompson, Helen. " Learning and Growth in Identical Infant Twins." *Genetic Psychology Monographs,* 6, No. 1, 1929. Pp. 5–120.

[6] See, for example, Newman, Horatio M., and others. *Twins, A Study of Heredity and Environment.* Chicago: University of Chicago Press, 1937; and Burks, Barbara Stoddard, and Roe, Anne. " Studies of Identical Twins Reared Apart." *Psychological Monograph General and Applied,* Vol. 63, No. 5, Whole No. 300, 1949.

[7] A complete list of the books referred to in the problems will be found in the Appendix, pages 472–477.

ous process involving both heredity and environment. From the latter point of view, genetic factors are regarded as setting potentialities for development, while the realization of those potentialities depends on environmental factors.

Some aspects of the child's biological inheritance are revealed at birth or soon thereafter, others become apparent as he grows, and still others may never be observed because the environment is not such as to disclose them. This is not because the child is genetically incapable of such a performance but rather because its possibility has never been brought to his attention. For example, a child may possess some artistic talent, but its existence may never come to light simply because he happens to live in a family and neighborhood in which his abilities as an athlete and fighter receive conspicuous acclaim.

PROBLEM 5. Make a list of genetically determined potentialities which you think might exist simultaneously in the same individual. On what environmental factors might their realization depend?

In the following consideration of the child's biological inheritance we shall begin with those factors which are most easily observable. Later we shall consider some of the aspects of the child's inheritance which are of equal if not greater importance but which cannot be so readily appraised.

Sex of the Child

The very comment with which most children are ushered into the world — "It's a boy," or "It's a girl" suggests the importance which is attached to the sex of the individual. And, despite our current emphasis on "equality," it is likely that sex as much as any one other factor, and perhaps even more, determines the nature of the individual's life experiences!

The sex of the child is determined at the moment of conception. There is at present no reliable way of telling it until the moment of birth. Interestingly, it is the father and not the mother who sets the sex of the child, but there is, of course, no way for him to know what it is to be. The father's responsibility lies in the fact that in the male cells the twenty-fourth pair of chromosomes is what is known as an XY combination, in contrast to the XX of the twenty-fourth pair in the female. When the male sperm cells are formed, the X's and Y's go separate ways, with the result that half of the male sperm cells have a twenty-fourth chromosome which is X and half of them have a twenty-fourth chromosome which is Y. But the female egg cells all have a twenty-fourth chromosome which is X. So, if the male sperm cell reaching a female cell at the time of conception happens to bear an X, the resulting combination in the new individual is XX, and a girl baby is on the way. If, on the other hand, the male cell which penetrates the egg is a Y-bearing cell, another boy is in process.

Although the twenty-fourth chromosomes tip the balance in the determination of sex, this does not mean that sex development is dependent on them. On the contrary, many of the other chromosomes carry " maleness " and " femaleness " genes, and each sex gets both kinds. Research is only beginning to open up the significant facts in this area, but findings that masculinity and femininity are apparently matters of degree rather than discrete traits have many implications for the understanding of human development.

PROBLEM 6. Of the parents described here and in Chapter 1 only two expressed a preference regarding the sex of the baby. Mr. Mallon " hoped for " a girl. Mrs. Brown was convinced that she was going to have a large baby girl. From the information given, how do you think they would react to the birth of boys? Can you discover any factors which might make for differences in the intensity of their reactions? What effect if any do you think their reactions might have on the babies?

Eyes, Hair, and Facial Characteristics

As has been implied, given sufficient information about a pair of prospective parents and their relatives, the geneticist can make a rough forecast as to what their children will look like. But such prediction must always consider the possibility of the exception. From the standpoint of the child's development, however, the important question is not his looks *per se,* but how they fit into the family standards for acceptable appearance. A flat nose, for example, may not be inappropriate on a rather broad face, but the fact that it lacks the aquiline characteristics which a proud mother associates with the aristocracy of *her* line can make its owner miserable. Oddly enough, very good features, if they set one off as different from the rest, may also distort the growing child's sense of self worth. In any event, what the newborn baby looks like, whether the parents gazing at him see him as a baby just right for their family, or vaguely resembling Uncle Herman whom they have always disliked, or their favorite Uncle Elmer, or as some kind of mistake nature ought never have made, may become an important factor in his development.

PROBLEM 7. As you review the families described here and in Chapter 1, to which do you think the appearance of the baby would have been most important? Why?

Body Type

That babies come in assorted sizes and shapes is common knowledge. Not too much, however, is known about the relationship between their early status in these respects and their eventual development. Although considerable research has been done on the relationships between the body build and temperament of adults, the results have been somewhat controversial.

The most extensive work in this field has been done by W. H. Sheldon and his colleagues. They distinguish three basic components of structural variation in the human physique: the endomorphic, soft, rounded, tending toward obesity and general muscular relaxation; the mesomorphic, athletic, muscular, heavy boned; the ectomorphic, flat-chested, linear, with stringy muscles. On the basis of measurement of different regions of the body, they have developed a classification of subtypes such that a complete " somatotyping " of an individual may place him in any one of seventy-six possible categories.[8]

Relatively little work with children under the age of 18 has yet been published. For the beginning student of child development the importance of this research is that it highlights one of the ways in which human beings differ from each other. Body type is likely to be an important factor in determining the amount and kind of food a youngster needs and is able to use to best advantage. Attempts

[8] Sheldon, William H., and others. *The Varieties of Human Physique*. New York: Harper and Brothers, 1940.

to push into a wiry ectomorph-type youngster the amount of food relished by an endomorph can lead to serious feeding difficulties. Since the individual tends from conception to grow toward a certain kind of structure, efforts to modify that structure except within certain rather narrow limits are apt to meet with failure. We can expect also that the child's body structure factor may be important in both the interest he shows in certain motor activities and the ease with which he tackles them.

Physical Growth Curves

In like fashion each individual seems to have his own unique pattern of growth. He makes progress toward the size and shape which will be characteristic of him as an adult at his own rate which is seldom constant but shows both spurts and plateaus. Some idea of the process can be seen by a study of the growth curves for height and weight for the children we have described earlier. (See Appendix, pp. 472–477.)

PROBLEM 8. Which children were the heaviest at birth? The tallest? At age 6? At age 10? At age 18? Can you locate the period at which each began to grow most rapidly, prior to puberty?

Measures of height and weight have long been used as an index of growth, but they give only a rough approximation of the child's progress toward physiological maturity. Since each child grows in his own way, there is little point in attempting to appraise his progress through reference to tables of average weight for height. In recent years various techniques have been devised which make better allowance for individual variation.

One of them is the use of percentiles. Table 1 shows heights and weights for children from birth to eighteen years. The number of the percentile indicates the position which a measurement would hold in a typical series of 100 (100 percent). Thus, the tenth percentile gives the value for the child who is tenth in a group of 100. Nine children will be smaller than he, and 90 will be larger. At the fiftieth percentile an equal number of children will be smaller or larger than the measurement.

Another technique which is quite commonly used was designed

by Wetzel, in which the child's height and weight are plotted on a grid or graph. The graph shows seven different channels, each of which represents the growth to be expected from children having a particular kind of physique. The assumption is that the child's progress will be continuous within the limits of a particular channel and that deviation suggests disturbance. However, because of the complexity of factors operative, interpretation is dependent on clinical examination.[9]

The important point for our consideration is the fact that the process of growth revealed in the growth curve shows such definitely individual characteristics. This individuality is even more apparent in growth curves based on measures of skeletal development. The cartilage and fibrous tissues which are preponderant in the skeletal structure of the child are gradually transformed into the harder and less pliable bones of the adult. This process which involves the deposit of calcium phosphates in the cartilage is known as ossification. The degree of ossification of certain of the long bones in the body, particularly those in the hand and wrist or the leg, provides a much better index of physical development than do measures of height and weight alone. Techniques for such measurement have been used in various longitudinal studies of children's growth.[10] A related technique which involves measurement of the muscles and overlying tissues of the leg area offers further support for the individual character of growth.[11]

Of course, the child does not merely increase in size, general stature, and complexity of skeletal structure. All of the body systems grow, and there is also development in ability to function. The relationships between the various aspects of growth, the degree to

[9] Watson, Ernest H., and Lowrey, George H. *Growth and Development of Children*. Chicago: The Year Book Publishers, 1951. Pp. 44–72 give an explanation of various methods of evaluating progress of normal growth.

[10] Greulich, William W. "The Rationale of Assessing the Developmental Status of Children from Roentgenograms of the Hand and Wrist." *Child Development*. 21 (1950), 33–44.

[11] Stuart, Harold C., and others. "The Growth of Bone, Muscle, and Overlying Tissues as Revealed by Studies of Roentgenograms of the Leg Area." *Monographs of Society for Research in Child Development*. Vol. 5, No. 3, 1940; and Stuart, Harold C., and Dwinell, Penelope H. "The Growth of Bone Muscle and Overlying Tissues in Children Six to Ten Years of Age as Revealed by Studies of Roentgenograms of the Leg Area." *Child Development*. 13 (1942), 195–214.

TABLE 1

Percentiles for Weight and Height of American Children*

PERCENTILES, BOYS			AGE MEASUREMENT	PERCENTILES, GIRLS		
10	50	90		10	50	90
			Birth			
6.3	7.5	9.1	Weight, lb.	6.2	7.4	8.6
18.9	19.9	21.0	Length, in.	18.8	19.8	20.4
			3 mo.			
11.1	12.6	14.5	Weight, lb.	10.7	12.4	14.0
22.8	23.8	24.7	Height, in.	22.4	23.4	24.3
			6 mo.			
14.8	16.7	19.2	Weight, lb.	14.1	16.0	18.6
25.2	26.1	27.3	Height, in.	24.6	25.7	26.7
			1 yr.			
19.6	22.2	25.4	Weight, lb.	18.4	21.5	24.8
28.5	29.6	30.7	Height, in.	27.8	29.2	30.2
			2 yr.			
24.7	27.7	31.9	Weight, lb.	23.5	27.1	31.7
33.1	34.4	35.9	Height, in.	32.3	34.1	35.8
			3 yr.			
28.7	32.2	36.8	Weight, lb.	27.6	31.8	37.4
36.3	37.9	39.6	Height, in.	35.6	37.7	39.8
			4 yr.			
32.1	36.4	41.4	Weight, lb.	31.2	36.2	43.5
39.1	40.7	42.7	Height, in.	38.4	40.6	43.1

* These figures are abbreviated and modified from data of H. C. Stuart, Department of Maternal and Child Health, Harvard School of Public Health, and H. V. Meredith, Iowa Child Research Station.

It can be seen that with increasing age, the measurements lie farther apart for each of the given percentiles.

Source: Watson, Ernest H. and Lowrey, George H. *Growth and Development of Children.* Chicago, The Year Book Publishers, 1951. Pp. 45–46.

PERCENTILES, BOYS			AGE MEASUREMENT	PERCENTILES, GIRLS		
			5 yr.			
35.5	40.5	46.7	Weight, lb.	34.8	40.5	49.2
40.8	42.8	45.2	Height, in.	40.5	42.9	45.4
			6 yr.			
40.9	48.3	56.4	Weight, lb.	39.6	46.5	54.2
43.8	46.3	48.6	Height, in.	43.5	45.6	48.1
			7 yr.			
45.8	54.1	64.4	Weight, lb.	44.5	52.2	61.2
46.0	48.9	51.4	Height, in.	46.0	48.1	50.7
			8 yr.			
51.2	60.1	73.0	Weight, lb.	48.6	58.1	69.9
48.5	51.2	54.0	Height, in.	48.1	50.4	53.0
			9 yr.			
56.3	66.0	81.0	Weight, lb.	52.6	63.8	79.1
50.5	53.3	56.1	Height, in.	50.0	52.3	55.3
			10 yr.			
61.1	71.9	89.9	Weight, lb.	57.1	70.3	89.7
52.3	55.2	58.1	Height, in.	51.8	54.6	57.5
			12 yr.			
72.0	84.4	109.6	Weight, lb.	69.5	87.6	111.5
56.1	58.9	62.2	Height, in.	56.1	59.6	63.2
			14 yr.			
87.2	107.6	136.9	Weight, lb.	91.0	108.4	133.3
59.9	64.0	67.9	Height, in.	60.2	62.8	65.7
			16 yr.			
111.0	129.7	157.3	Weight, lb.	100.9	117.0	141.1
64.1	67.8	70.7	Height, in.	61.5	63.9	66.5
			18 yr.			
120.0	139.0	169.0	Weight, lb.	103.5	119.9	144.5
65.5	68.7	71.8	Height, in.	61.5	64.0	66.7

which all of them may be impelled from within, and the effects of environmental stimulation of various kinds upon them are all matters on which there are some good tentative answers but as yet no final ones. Probably the consensus of opinion is that, to a much larger extent than we would have believed twenty or thirty years ago, the child is what he " has to be " and that his responses to our efforts at socialization and training are conditioned much more by his native uniqueness and his pattern of growth than we had originally thought. We shall have occasion to examine this idea and its implications many times in the rest of this book.

Body Chemistry

Changes in size and structure can be measured and plotted on a graph. Growth curves thus are made comprehensible to an individual with a minimum of technical knowledge. Understanding of the physiological processes of which growth is but one end product demands considerably more background. Nevertheless, if individuality is in part determined by one's physiology, the student of human growth and learning cannot afford to overlook such processes. Williams discusses some of the implications of physiological individuality:

It is common knowledge that we inherit from our forebears the size and shape of our noses, ears, eyes, hands and feet, even down to the minute markings on fingers and toes which are distinctive for each of us. It is not so commonly appreciated that the size, shape, and cellular composition of thyroids, adrenal glands, pituitaries, and sex glands vary greatly from individual to individual and that these characteristic anatomical features are likewise transmitted to us through inheritance.

Sensory reactions — those of taste, smell, sight, hearing, and the several skin senses — show a high degree of individuality, and many of the distinctive reactions which every individual exhibits are known to come down to him through his ancestors. . . .

But our individuality does not stop here. In the field of bio-chemical genetics it has become increasingly evident that there is often a one-to-one correspondence between the genes, the carriers of inheritance, and the enzymes, which catalyze the chemical reactions of metabolism. Beadle and coworkers have found that knocking out a single gene by X rays knocks out a single enzyme from the metabolic potentialities of the organism affected. From these observations it is inescapable that inasmuch as we differ from one another in inheritance so we must differ in the details of our metabolism. Dogs, which have a keen sense of smell, have made use of this fact throughout the ages to identify individuals. Each of us yields a distinctive blend of metabolic products.[12]

An example of the kind of evidence on physiological individuality which is now being gathered is found in studies such as that by Jost and Sontag in which a variety of physiological measurements, pulse pressure, salivation, respiration rate, and so on were found to be most alike for twins, next alike for siblings, and least alike for unrelated children. The authors believe that an " automatic constitution " may be at least partially an inherited characteristic, and should help to explain predisposition to many psychosomatic disorders.[13] Although the nature of the relationships are not yet clear, many students of human personality are inclined to believe that further study of physiological individuality may also throw further light on personality variation.

Intelligence and Special Talents

We cannot leave our consideration of the child's biological inheritance without some reference to the matter of intelligence and special talents, although there is probably no area which presents greater controversy or greater uncertainty. Practical observation has taught you that children meet new situations differently. One youngster pulling a cart seems baffled and does nothing when the wheel gets stuck on a stone, another calls immediately for adult help, while a third studies the situation, backs the wheel away from the stone, heads the cart in a new direction and goes on his merry way. You would probably say that the third youngster showed the most intelligence and the first the least. And, provided all the children were of the same age, your judgment is one with which experts would concur. Suppose, however, that the first child had been brought up in a deprived environment in which he had never encountered a cart, or any object with wheels. Would it be fair to

[12] Williams, Roger J. " Some Implications of Physiological Individuality " in *Feelings and Emotions,* edited by Martin L. Rymert. New York: McGraw-Hill Book Company, 1950. P. 269.
[13] Jost, Hudson, and Sontag, Lester W. " The Genetic Factor in Autonomic Nervous-System Function " in *Personality in Nature, Society and Culture,* edited by Kluckhohn, Murray, and Schneider. New York: Alfred A. Knopf, 1953. Pp. 73–79.

say that he was less intelligent until he had had some opportunity to "catch up" with the others in experience? The negative answer you have probably given points up one aspect of the role of experience in intelligent behavior. In colloquial terms we might say that a "brilliant mind" is of very little use if it is never stimulated to function. But in fairness we must raise another question. Can a "slow mind" be stimulated to catch up with or even run ahead of the bright one? Here we run directly against the old heredity-environment controversy that has so persistently plagued psychologists and educators. Our best tentative answer at present seems to be that while certain experiences can considerably improve the individual's *use* of whatever mental capacities he has, they are not likely to change the capacities themselves. There are apparently inherent differences in intellectual capacity.

We have, however, no really adequate method of measuring this capacity. The intelligence tests, by attempting to sample the individual's response to certain situations, give us an approximation of the differences in functioning of individuals. They do not, however, reveal in what ways the organism of the so-called "intelligent" person differs from that of the one who is "dull." Intelligence has been conceived of as a kind of unitary character, something which functions the same way in all aspects of behavior. Some research, however, has placed considerable emphasis on the variety of functions in intelligence. This raises the possibility that individuals of similar language ability (as measured by an intelligence test) might differ markedly from one another in the patterning of other mental functions. If this is the case, perhaps one's intellectual inheritance would come through the action of genes governing specific mental functions such as memory, perceptual speed, number facility, and so on. Such a theory makes provision for the individual who seems to have superior "practical" intelligence but does not do so well in verbal situations. Much more work needs to be done before we can be really certain of the nature of intelligence.

For our purposes, the important point is that certain aspects of the child's intellectual capacity will have been determined at the moment of conception. This in no way implies that his destiny is predetermined, but rather that the important educative forces in his life, his parents and his teachers particularly, must learn to reckon with the particular variety of capacities he has.

So far as special talents are concerned, the endowment of nature is sometimes clear and obvious (this is particularly true in the case of musical talent and mathematical aptitude), but more often discovery is dependent upon the child's exposure to individuals who are sensitive to his possibilities. And certainly, full realization of talent is impossible except through training and education.

We began this section with the question — How does heredity contribute to the child's development? We have seen that science does not yet have full and final answers to this question but we may be certain of the following:

Whatever contribution heredity makes is made at the time of conception. It is at that point that the ground plan for the individual is laid down. And it is, except for the case of identical twins, a plan which has never been used before and will never be used again. This can be said despite the fact that since the plan is for a human organism it will *resemble* the plans for all other members of the human species. In a sense, it is a plan which sets limits for what the human organism can become. But at the same time it is a plan which provides for contingencies almost limitless in number. It establishes the individual's sex, his facial and bodily characteristics, his ways of growing, his ways of responding to the world.

Yet we must not overestimate the role of biological inheritance. For without a nurturing environment, without learning, without socialization, the cell so miraculously endowed at conception would never become a mature human being. The parent who would like so much to know the nature of his child's " ground plan," who may wish for some clearer indication of what it is that the child " has to be," must remember that it is only with the help of his care and his guidance that the child can ever be what he " has to be."

THE PRENATAL PERIOD OF DEVELOPMENT

Heredity begins to play its part at the moment of conception. When does environment begin its action? We might almost say before conception, since the successful union of the sperm and the ovum seems to be to some extent dependent on the conditions within the body of the mother. Certainly from the moment of conception the environment is of crucial importance. Corner says:

> Man even in his earliest weeks faces uconsciously the unending problem of getting along in his world. Life is a paradoxical career in which the individual must both accept and contend with his environment, at once struggling for independence and adapting himself to cooperative action. Before birth this effort and adjustment are a matter of physiology alone; only later is the struggle complicated by problems of mentality and social custom and by those workings of the spirit through which a man must pilot his individual life to success or failure in his community, to achievement or martyrdom, to turmoil or inward peace. For the embryo in the uterus, pilgrim's progress begins with the process of attachment or placentation, by which the human child is to win his nine months of prefatory life. Thus early must he contend with his environment — which for the time being is the lining of his mother's uterus — and at the same time must adjust himself thereto.[14]

This process of placentation in which the ovum is implanted in the uterus wall is accomplished by the twelfth day following conception. It establishes the embryo's source of nutriment for the entire period of its uterine life. The placenta, the only means of communication between mother and child, provides an extremely specialized connection. Corner emphasizes that, " Not a single nerve fiber crosses the placental barrier; there is no channel for the transmission of feelings, or intentions, moods, memories, or ideas. The infant is in fact completely shut off from its own mother save for the exchange of simple chemical nutrients and wastes through a screen so fine that it will pass nothing but the smaller molecules of matter." This fact is one which we shall need to bear in mind throughout our consideration of prenatal development.

Once attached to the wall of the uterus the cell begins the rapid period of embryonic development. Differentiation or specialization of the cells which will eventually constitute the outer layers of the body, skin, hair, nails; the nervous system; the muscles; the circulatory, excretory, and glandular systems takes place.

Gesell, who sees all of development as a patterning process, and emphasizes that an understanding of mental function is dependent

[14] Corner, George W. *Ourselves Unborn*. New Haven: Yale University Press, 1945. P. 37.

upon an understanding of the early life history of the organisms, offers the following succinct description of prenatal development:

In the embryo, one lunar month after conception: brain, eyes, and hands are already taking form.

The heart soon begins its rhythmic beat.

The retina develops as an outgrowth of the brain.

The rudimentary hands likewise are coming into linkage with the nervous system.

In 2 months the embryo becomes a fetus.

This fetus is capable of small, almost imperceptible movements — flexor movements of trunk and shoulders.

In another month the neuromuscular organization penetrates to forearm and fingers.

The fetus at five months foreshadows the infant of the future: his body conformation becomes individual.

A vast network of nerves — countless sensory and motor neurons and connecting circuits have brought into being a total action system. This action system includes five hundred pairs of skeletal muscles which activate trunk, limbs, hands, face, mouth, and eyes.

.   .   .   .

By the seventh prenatal month a continuous neuron connection is established between the cortex and a more highly differentiated retina. The visual path is complete and capable of functioning. Brain, retina and oculomotor muscles have been linked. The eyes may move coordinately even in the fetus.[15]

Much discussion regarding developmental processes has stemmed from studies of fetal development in human beings and related studies of animals more accessible to observation. To what extent does an understanding of development in this period help us to understand later development? We shall consider briefly some of the generalizations which may be significant in this respect.

The Direction of Development

If you note carefully the changes which appear from one picture to the next in the illustration on page 36 of early development, you can detect that the head assumes tyically human characteristics before the neck, chest, or pelvis; that the upper arms are distinguished before the lower arms; the fingers still later; and that foot

[15] Gesell, Arnold. *Infant Development; The Embryology of Early Human Behavior.* New York: Harper and Brothers, 1952. Pp. 10–11.

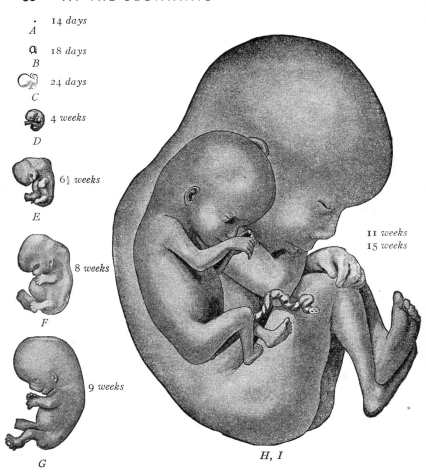

14 *days*
A

18 *days*
B

24 *days*
C

4 *weeks*
D

6½ *weeks*

E

8 *weeks*

F

9 *weeks*

G

11 *weeks*
15 *weeks*

H, I

Figure 1. A graded series of human embryos at natural size. (*Reproduced from Leslie B. Arey. Developmental Anatomy. Philadelphia: W. B. Saunders Company, 1946.*)

development is slower than hand development. It appears that the general direction of development then is from the head downward, and from the axis, or center of the body, outward. Such trends are not mutually exclusive, nor is it meant to imply that while development occurs rapidly in one area, nothing happens in another. Development goes on in all areas simultaneously, but the degree of differentiation or specialization in certain areas exceeds that in others.

PROBLEM 9. To what extent are the general directions of development characteristic of the prenatal period also apparent in the process of the learning to walk and to use one's hands?

Timing

All of our discussion thus far has implied the orderliness of development and the fact that various parts of the organism come into being at different times, but always in a certain succession. Either hereditary or environmental factors may operate in such a way as to alter the usual process of development, but the seriousness of their effect will depend largely on the time at which they function. The most damaging abnormalities are caused when such factors become operative during the time when the central nervous system is developing. Thus rubella, or German measles, if contracted by the mother early in pregnancy, may result in cataracts or deafness in the infant, but may have no effect at all if contracted in the later months of pregnancy.

PROBLEM 10. Timing appears to be an important factor in the development of the individual following birth. Can you think of any environmental influences which might affect a child adversely at one stage of development more than another? Consider, for example, learning to walk and learning to read.

Differentiation and Integration of Responses

So far we have been discussing how human *structure* develops. But the question of *behavior* is equally important. Under what circumstances does the individual begin to respond to stimulation? Research carried on with a variety of organisms but most notably with salamanders (Coghill), chickens (Kuo), and guinea pigs (Carmichael) together with some ingenious work with human fetuses (Hooker) has provided fairly definite answers. The once debated question as to whether the organism responds first as a whole, gradually differentiating out specific responses, or whether, conversely, specific responses are gradually integrated into the totality of behavior is revealed to be an inappropriate one. As early as the eighth week of human fetal life stimulation of the mouth has been found to result in flexion of the neck; from then on an increasing number of specific responses to stimulation have been observed. Almost simultaneously, however, these various reflexive behaviors recombine so that by the time of birth the child is capable of sucking, breathing, crying, grasping, and so on. Behavior, it appears, consists of responses which are increasingly differentiated one from another, and also increasingly integrated together.[16] We shall refer to this principle of organization again when we consider the nature of learning at later stages of development.

PROBLEM 11. Consider the baby's behavior during the period when he is learning to walk. What evidence do you find of differentiation? Of integration? Can you find evidence of differentiation and integration in the child's learning to read?

Is Any Prenatal Behavior Learned?

We have implied so much about the capacity of the fetus for response that the reader may be wondering to what extent these responses are modifiable. Does the fetus learn from his experience? This is an important question and the answer will have much bearing on our later discussion of environmental influences on prenatal development.

First, we must remind ourselves of the conditions of life for the fetus who is to be delivered as a full-term infant. He lies in a closed sac, surrounded by a pool of amniotic fluid, maintained at an even temperature. Whatever we know about how he responds to certain stimuli is based almost entirely on experimentation with animal fetuses or with human fetuses removed from the interuterine environment, or on those born prematurely. From such work we can be fairly certain that he develops a high degree of skin sensitivity well before birth; that the proprioceptive senses in muscles and joints are also well developed; the mechanism for smell is developed but because of the nature of the environment not likely to be in operation; the auditory structure appears to be blocked except for sounds of marked intensity; the visual mechanism is probably able to differentiate light and dark.

Is it possible to stimulate the fetus in such a way as to produce or

---

[16] Carmichael, Leonard. "Ontogenetic Development" in *Handbook of Experimental Psychology,* edited by S. S. Stevens. New York: John Wiley and Sons, 1951. Pp. 281–304.

alter responses? The evidence on this is controversial, although one experimenter (Spelt) working with women in their last two months of pregnancy was able to establish what appeared to be a conditioned response in the fetus. He applied to the abdomen of the mother an apparatus which vibrated at the same time as a loud noise was made. Then the movements of the fetus were recorded. After some fifteen to twenty such stimulations the loud noise was omitted and the fetus appeared to respond to the vibration alone.[17]

So far as learning is concerned, it should be noted that whatever modification may be obtained through conditioning of this sort is not "learning" of a very complex sort, and does not involve the central nervous system. The fetus has no experience that could be called conscious, and no means of remembering. Any processes, other than purely physiological ones, by which prenatal experience could affect later development and personality are at present unknown.

Environmental Influences on Prenatal Development

The preceding statement notwithstanding, a variety of factors can affect the fetus probably through influence on the body chemistry of the mother. Chief of these are nutritional deficiencies. It has been well established that mothers who have had an adequate diet during pregnancy are more likely to produce infants in good condition at birth. Abortions, premature births, still births, and neonatal deaths appear more frequently when mothers' diets are poor.[18]

Certain drugs are generally agreed to affect fetal development, others seem to have a transitory but not necessarily injurious effect. A variety of diseases, particularly those which are infectious, can if contracted at a crucial period in fetal development, seriously impair development. There is also some evidence that noninfectious functional disease such as hypertension may adversely affect the fetus.

[17] Spelt, David K. "The Conditioning of the Human Fetus in Utero." *Journal of Experimental Psychology.* 38 (1948), 338–346.

[18] For evidence on this point and citation of references see "Nutritional Requirements during Pregnancy and Lactation" by Burke, Bertha S., and Stuart, Harold C. in *A Handbook of Nutrition,* published for American Medical Association, The Blakiston Company, New York, 1951.

That diet, drugs, or disease may influence prenatal development is a generally accepted fact. That the mother's emotional attitudes may also have a bearing on the well-being of the fetus is considered more open to question. Perhaps the reluctance of some scientists to accept the possibility stems from an unwillingness to seem to be supporting certain old superstitions which are only now giving way to more rational understanding. There is no evidence whatsoever that a frightening experience, such as unexpectedly confronting a mouse, may produce a mouse-shaped birthmark, or that listening to beautiful music will insure the birth of a musical child. There is accumulating evidence, however, that an emotional disturbance which is so severe as to upset the mother's nutritional status may react adversely on the fetus. Psychosomatic medicine has shown very clearly that mind and body do not operate in two separate spheres, and there is no reason to believe that this is less true during pregnancy than during other periods of life. A study by Sontag, for example, indicates that children born to mothers suffering from marked emotional disturbances tended to have more than usual difficulties in the first weeks of life, including gastro-intestinal upsets and other illnesses.[19] The difficulty with such evidence is, of course, that association of factors — the mother's emotional disturbance in pregnancy and the child's illness — does not necessarily prove the first a cause of the second. The youngster's genetic potentialities may have been such as to make early adjustment difficult, or the mother's problems may have been reflected in inadequate care after birth. Whatever the precise causal relationships may be, it appears that, other things being equal, a tranquil, deeply satisfied woman is more likely to bear a serene baby than is one for whom life is perplexing and meaningless.

PROBLEM 12. Like any other six women, the mothers of our youngsters differed considerably from one another in emotional outlooks and attitudes. From the descriptions of them at the beginning of this chapter, which ones would you think more likely to find satisfactions in carrying their babies? Why? What factors do you think might tend to create tension?

---

[19] Sontag, L. W. "The Genetics of Differences in Psychosomatic Patterns in Childhood." *American Journal of Orthopsychiatry.* 20 (1950), 479–489.

PROBLEM 13. What kinds of attitudes toward pregnancy and the coming of the new baby do you find expressed among the expectant mothers and fathers of your acquaintance?

PROBLEM 14. For further evidence on current thinking about constitutional and prenatal factors in development, review and discuss the article by Ashley Montagu in *Readings in Child Development* edited by Martin and Stendler, pages 15–29.

At pregnancy every woman is confronted with the essential fact of her femininity. The more satisfied she is and the more accepting she is of herself, the more likely it is that she will find the period one of happiness and fulfillment, provided, of course, that she is in good physical condition. Various circumstances may, however, introduce considerable tension even though the prospective mother is basically serene. For example, of the families described here, two had incomes inadequate for subsistence, and two more lived under constant threat of unemployment so that worry about finances was often present. During the war years concerns for the safety of loved ones, the pressures of overcrowded housing, " doubling up " with relatives, and so on, sometimes complicated the adjustments of pregnancy.

According to some authorities, some of the measures which make pregnancy less menacing to the mother's physical well-being have in one way or another also contributed to tension and insecurity during pregnancy. Hospitalization procedures have drastically reduced the number of deaths at childbirth, but they have tended to depersonalize an important human experience. An overdependence on anaesthesia may lead women to think of the birth of their child as an " operation " to be undergone rather than a process demanding their full participation. Counteracting these tendencies has been an emphasis on " natural " childbirth. As set forth by one of its foremost proponents, Dr. Grantly Read,[20] an English obstetrician, this is " childbirth without fear." The mother from the beginning learns how the baby is growing in her body, and to relax and control her muscles so that she cannot only assist in the birth in the most effective fashion but can do so with full or nearly full consciousness. While there is good reason to question whether all women can

[20] Read, Grantly. *Childbirth Without Fear.* New York: Harper and Brothers, 1953.

participate as fully as Dr. Read's work suggests, the important implication is that the period of pregnancy can be considerably more relaxed and the delivery of the child facilitated by "humanizing" prenatal care. This involves giving the mother an opportunity to express her fears and to have her questions answered so that she understands the various changes going on within her body and develops a thorough understanding of the important part she has in the baby's welfare. Under these circumstances the best prenatal care involves not only attention to the mother's physical well-being but education and emotional support as well. This may be offered by the private physician, the nurse in a prenatal clinic, or by a total program which also includes discussion group sessions for prospective fathers as well as mothers.

In the United States until very recently hospital procedures have involved care of the newborn baby in a nursery separate from the mother's room. At the present time a few hospitals are experimenting with "rooming-in plans" as an adjunct to their prenatal and obstetrical care. The baby remains in or immediately accessible to his mother's room. Under these circumstances mothers learn to care for their babies almost from birth, and fathers can be permitted to hold them rather than merely viewing them through the window.

The intended effect of all these newer trends in the care of mothers and babies is to make the prenatal and neonatal period one of full anticipation and participation on the part of the parents so that to as full a degree as possible every baby may be a "wanted" baby. It is under these circumstances, it is believed, that youngsters are given the best start in the world.

BIRTH AND NEONATAL DEVELOPMENT

The young people whose growth we are following in this book were born some years before the first rooming-in plan was opened. So, like most hospital-born babies, they spent most of the first two weeks of their lives in a nursery for newborns, visiting their mothers only at feeding time. Let's take a look at some of them there:

Baby Warner sleeps quietly. Even when she's awake, she seems placid and content. The doctor's report says she is in excellent condition.

Pat Plummer is the smallest baby in the nursery. She did well the

first days, regained birth weight on the fourth day, but stopped gaining thereafter. At fourteen days, she is going home in " fair " condition. A slight spasticity is apparent in her movements.

That one who looks a little heavier than the others? That's Andy. Yes, he's doing fine now, has gained steadily since the sixth day. He weighs almost nine pounds.

And the one who looks a bit " beat up "? That's Dan Mallon. His delivery took a long time and was difficult. He's had a skin eruption which hasn't improved his looks any, but he's nursing well and the doctor says he'll go home in " good " condition.

Like Dan, Celeste Collins had a slow start, required resuscitation following birth. By two weeks, however, she has made some gains and is becoming a rather active baby.

Individual Differences in Newborns

Were we to observe these and other newborns over a period of hours their differences would be even more striking. Watching carefully, we might expect to note that some move about more than others. Some are more inclined toward relatively smooth movements while others are quite jerky. We might also discern that some seem more sensitive to stimulation than others. One startles when a door suddenly slams, others are undisturbed. Perhaps the baby's movements are only coincidental with the door slamming, but there is also the possibility that he hears the noise or feels the vibration, and we shall watch to see whether such behavior is repeated. We may keep an activity chart of each child's movements to see whether any typical pattern of activity is yet emerging. Although at this early period we do not expect to find a great deal of regularity, we may be able to detect some individuality.

Repertoire of Responses in the Newborn

Observation in the newborn nursery also affords us opportunity to study the repertoire of the newborn. In addition to the generalized movements described above, we may note that the babies cry, yawn, cough, sneeze, and hiccup.

PROBLEM 15. Perhaps your instructor can arrange an observation of newborn infants. See how many items of behavior you can observe in addition to those listed here.

If we chance to be present at feeding time, we can see some of the babies spontaneously turn toward the nipple while others seem to have to be directed to it. Most of them appear to be born with the sucking and swallowing reflexes in good working order, but a few seem to need considerable encouragement before they " catch on." Ribble, basing her conclusions on her clinical experience with babies, has reported that this difficulty is most persistent among infants who receive insufficient mothering.[21]

The behavior of the newborn includes a number of other reflexes (involuntary actions), some of which seem to be suggestive of later motor complex accomplishment and others which seem to bear little relation to later behavior. Among these is the Moro reflex observable when the infant responds to a blow struck on the surface on which he is lying with an arm movement resembling an embrace. Another is the Darwinian or grasp reflex. It is this phenomenon which a proud father has discovered when he boasts of his young infant's ability to suspend himself from his outstretched fingers. Still another is the Babinski reflex, the fanning out of the toes when the sole of the foot is stroked.

If we have observed behavior carefully and over a sufficient period of time, we can begin to draw certain conclusions regarding the nature of the newborn's activity. We note that most of it seems random and unco-ordinated. Yet as early as the first day of life the baby can turn his head slightly. Within the first month he is able to propel his body in one direction or the other although his squirming is not sufficient to turn him over. As we watch his transitions from sleeping to waking and see that his activity diminishes as soon as he is fed, we are keenly aware of the extent to which his behavior is governed by the state of his internal economy. Yet he is not unresponsive to the world outside himself. Hold a light in front of him, and his eyes fixate, however momentarily. Touch his cheek near his mouth and he will turn his head and begin sucking. Offer him a salt or bitter solution instead of his customary milk and he will reject it.

What is the significance of all this? Does the newborn baby

[21] Ribble, Margaret. *The Rights of Infants.* New York: Columbia University Press, 1943.

sense that he is in a world different from that he knew before birth? Does he find it less comfortable, more difficult? What goes on in his mind as he hungers, feeds, and quietens again? Do the stimulation of light, the touch of a finger on his cheek, the taste of milk have any " meaning " for him?

These are questions which have long tantalized man's speculative powers. All that is presently known, however, regarding the development of the baby's brain and nervous system indicates that for at least the first month of life there is little likelihood of his having any conscious awareness of his experiences. Indeed it is not until he begins to get about under his own powers of locomotion that he appears able to differentiate himself from the world around him. It is true that within the first month he exhibits adaptability and a rudimentary kind of learning. If, for example, he is fed on a regular feeding schedule, he will exhibit marked restlessness whenever the appointed feeding time arrives and food does not appear to be forthcoming. Such learning is not so complex as to imply consciousness on the part of the baby.

Despite the fact that the development of the cortex in the newborn brain structure is not sufficiently advanced for us to assume that the baby remembers his experience, we cannot discount the significance of birth and neonatal experiences in the life of the child. There is little, if any, scientific evidence to support the contention of certain psychoanalysts that birth is a necessarily traumatic experience for the baby. Nevertheless, it does mark a profound shift in his way of life. If he is to survive, he must give up an essentially parasitic existence and assume an active part in maintaining himself. He moves from a tranquil environment into one in which, comparatively speaking, he is bombarded with sensation.

One infant makes his way into the world slowly and as it were protestingly. Another seems almost eager to enter upon the trials and tribulations of the extra-uterine environment. This one wails almost continuously, his little body tense with apparent anguish. That one cries lustily whenever feeding time approaches, but subsides immediately when picked up. We cannot tell what meaning these experiences have for each baby. Often we cannot tell why one cries and another does not. We cannot predict that the apparently serene newborn will be the happiest adult. We cannot even predict with certainty that the one who seems so consistently distressed will always find life difficult. But our own warm and protective feelings may come welling up to tell us that the baby who seems comfortable and content is off to the best start. And eventually we may be able to verify our hunches with respectable scientific evidence.

Our study of the child after birth will be more meaningful if we know something of the variety of knowledge on which we can draw. In the following chapter we shall consider some of the research and theory which is available.

3

From Then to Now — Child
Development

THE STORY OF HOW the newborn infants described in the last chapter grew and learned; how these small bits of humanity, impelled only by organic needs for food, sleep, and activity became the six distinctly different individuals we saw in Chapter 1, each with characteristic ways of behaving, of feeling, of looking at himself and others, is the story of child development. In the lives of these young people we can find many illustrations of the processes of growth and learning. Yet the story as we tell it cannot be complete. This is partly because we do not know all that is to be known about the happenings in these lives — there may be many important occurrences for which we have no information. And partly it is because there are so many gaps in our knowledge about child development. In this chapter we shall consider the nature of the knowledge we have and the extent to which it can aid us in understanding children and young people.

CHANGING VIEWS ON CHILD DEVELOPMENT

Twenty years ago, before the children described here were born, there was much talk about " scientific methods " in rearing children.

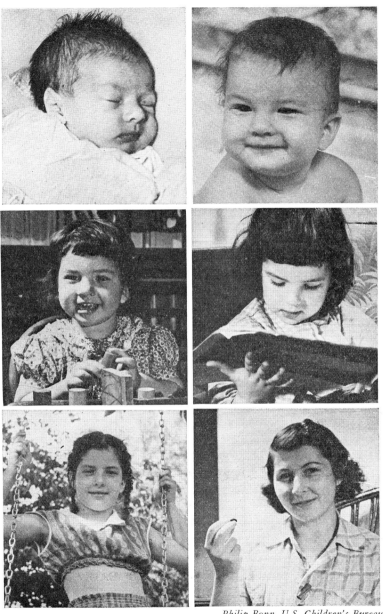

Philip Bonn, U.S. Children's Bureau

The continuity and the changes as the child grows from infancy toward adulthood: this is child development.

Today the emphasis has shifted. Parents are no longer admonished to offer their children "objectivity" and "efficiency." Rather it is hoped they can provide "love and security." Some who remember the days of rigid feeding schedules, early weaning, and rigorous toilet training, voice considerable skepticism as to the wisdom of child development "experts" who appear to have completely reversed themselves within a period of two decades. These shifts in thinking actually reflect increased knowledge and understanding about child development much of which has not derived from "scientific" child study. Rather it has come as professional workers have had opportunities to know children and their parents more intimately and have become more aware of the important role of emotions in all human relationships.

PROBLEM 1. Make an informal survey of child-rearing methods by interviewing individuals whose children have now reached the ages of 10, 20, and 30 years. Find out the methods they followed in feeding and training, whether they followed their own inclinations or pediatric advice. Or, if possible, review some of the popular women's magazines of each period to see what their parents' pages were recommending.

To understand the nature of the changes in sanctioned child care practices, we need to consider both the kinds of research which have been going on during these years, and the variety of influences which have affected the thinking of the child development experts.

Scientific Approaches to Child Development

The scientific study of human behavior, like the study of any other phenomena, proceeds on several fronts at the same time. There is the observation, collection, description, and classification of many kinds of data; theories are evolved which suggest ways of organizing the data and new data to be looked for; hypotheses are set up which can be tested and verified or rejected; a body of knowledge of accepted facts emerges. Implicit is the notion of predictability — under certain circumstances a specified behavior may be anticipated.

Until the second decade of the twentieth century, most of the studies of children were largely descriptive. The work of G. Stanley

Hall had focused considerable attention on the observation of children but the methods used were considered unscientific. In the early 1920's John B. Watson demonstrated that the behavior of infants and children could be studied in the psychology laboratory. Behavior could also be altered by changing some aspect of the carefully controlled laboratory environment. In what has become a classic example of his methods, Watson showed how a youngster with no fear of a white rat could be made afraid of it. A loud noise occurring at the moment of his interest in the animal made the child withdraw from it. After several repetitions of this experience his reaction to presentation of the rat was one of fear. Later experimentation indicated that the original interest and lack of fear of the animal could be reinstated by associating pleasant experiences with it.[1]

The times were ripe for the translation of Watsonian ideas into child-rearing recommendations. World War I had revealed shocking inadequacies in the mental and physical health of young adults. If consistent patterns of training in the early years could lead to the establishment of desirable habits, as the experimental findings with children and animals seemed to indicate, then certainly efforts to get parents to follow such patterns were worth while. At the same time, nutritional studies revealed the dietary components essential for good growth. Other research showed the extent to which infectious disease could be controlled by effective sanitation. Small wonder that the most effective mother was supposed to be the one who most closely resembled the " scientist," conditioning her child to eat by the clock a formula carefully calculated to maintain him in optimum health, in an environment as nearly sterile as it was possible to have outside a hospital nursery.

We have no way of knowing to what extent this strongly environmentalist point of view was actually accepted by parents. There is good reason to suspect that many who recognized that their role could not be equated with that of the scientist, accepted those recommendations which they found agreeable to themselves and their children, and rejected those which did not fit. Others, less certain

---

[1] Watson, John B., and Rayner, Rosalie. "Conditioned Emotional Reactions." *Journal of Experimental Psychology.* 3 (1920), 1–14.

of their own effectiveness both as parents and as human beings, were likely made uneasy and unsure by their realizations that what the scientists said should work, did not work for them. We may note in passing that the fact that so many parents *cared* about what the experts were thinking may reflect a characteristic value of the American culture. As a nation we seem to be committed to change and to improvement. Just as we accepted new methods of manufacture and more efficient ways of producing bigger and better crops, so we were willing to adopt whatever seemed likely to give us bigger, healthier, " better " babies and more " adjusted " youth.

In the long run the effect the work of Watson and his followers had on the child-rearing practices of the day is probably less important than the fact that it opened up the possibilities in scientific study of the behavior of infants and children. When the findings of the laboratory were found difficult of application in home and school, theories began to be questioned. Perhaps some of the factors which could not easily be controlled — the child's physical growth processes, the emotional responses of the adults in his total environment, the variety of learning experiences he had — were as important as the deliberate training he was given.

The Search for an Adequate Theory of Child Development

It has gradually become apparent that a scientific theory adequate to explain the many facets of child development must deal with much more than the observable behavior of the individual. According to Sears, it should focus on the actions of the child since these can be directly observed and indeed are the means by which human beings deal with each other.

But the actions cannot be limited to those of one person. Provision must be made for varying *interpersonal situations.* Thus we are concerned not merely with Johnny's behavior, but with the interacting responses of Johnny *and* his father, Johnny *and* his teacher, Johnny, his teacher, *and* his class. We are interested not only in action or performance at a particular time — such as Johnny's first awkward swipe at a baseball or his deft catch as a regular member of the team — but also in his acquisition or *learning* of the skill. Further, we cannot deal with this aspect of behavior without recognition of Johnny's potentialities for action. These have to do not only with Johnny's size, strength, and co-ordination but also with his motivation, the strength and direction of his drives, the importance which baseball has in his scheme of living. These potentialities for action, which taken all together constitute what may be described as *personality,* also change through time. Johnny grows, his strength increases, his co-ordinations improve, the interpersonal situations shift and baseball, about which he once cared little, becomes a major interest.[2]

At present no such comprehensive theory as that proposed by Sears exists. Instead some research focuses on actions, some on changing potentialities, some on learning, and so on. As Jersild has pointed out, child psychology has tended to be eclectic, drawing sometimes from the hereditarian and sometimes from the environmentalist point-of-view; adopting both the idea that there is something intrinsic and inherent in the process of development and much that can be accounted for in terms of the conditions infringing on the child, the variety of social and cultural influences to which he is exposed; drawing on research which appears atomistic and also on that which takes account of larger totality; recognizing both the conscious and the unconscious.[3]

If the growth, learning, and personality development of children growing up in the United States (not to mention those in other parts of the world) is to be understood, information from many fields of knowledge is necessary. Many professions and disciplines contribute — among them pediatrics, psychology, psychiatry, anthropology, sociology, education, and social work.

PROBLEM 2. What kinds of information would each of the above fields have to contribute to an understanding of the life histories of the six young people we have described in Chapters 1 and 2? Can you think of other fields from which knowledge might be drawn?

At one time each discipline tended to see children in its own light. Depending on the professional training of the expert, the

[2] Sears, Robert E. " A Theoretical Framework for Personality and Social Behavior." *The American Psychologist.* 6 (1951), 476–483.

[3] Jersild, Arthur T. " Child Psychology in the United States." *Teachers College Record.* 50 (1948), 114–127.

child was viewed as a biological organism, a social being, or a creature beset by psychological conflict. Yet, as early as 1930 recognition was growing that the *same* child was at once all of these and more. The White House Conference on Child Health and Protection called by President Hoover in 1930 brought together knowledge from various fields. This was published in a large and systematic series of publications.[4] The concept of the " whole " child began to correct the tendency to look at the youngster as a pupil, or a patient, or a client rather than as a total human being.[5] Recognition of the need to view the child as a totality and to see his development in the perspective time was implicit in much of the research initiated in the nineteen thirties. In a number of centers plans were made for longitudinal studies in which the development of a group of children would be followed for a period of years. In such studies the research workers often functioned as a team. The research team usually included psychologists and pediatricians and sometimes psychiatrists, social workers, and educators.

PROBLEM 3. Some of the important considerations necessary in a longitudinal study of children were outlined by Jean MacFarlane when the California Personality Study was begun. This article is included in *Child Behavior and Development* edited by Barker, Kounin, and Wright. Plan to have someone review it for your class. Discuss the changes which would likely be made if a plan for a similar study were being made today.

Following this discussion, if possible have someone review " Human Growth " by George W. Gray in *Scientific American*, 189 (Oc-

[4] The publications from the White House Conference on Child Health and Protection included the following:

  a. *The Handicapped and the Gifted*. New York: The Century Company, 1931.

  b. *Organization for the Care of Handicapped Children*, IV, B. New York: The Century Company, 1932.

  c. *Growth and Development of the Child, Part I: General Considerations*. New York: D. Appleton-Century Company, 1932.

  d. *Growth and Development of the Child, Part II: Anatomy and Physiology*. New York: D. Appleton-Century Company, 1933.

  e. *Social Hygiene in Schools*. New York: D. Appleton-Century Company, 1932.

  f. *Report of Committee on Physically and Mentally Handicapped: The Handicapped Child*. New York: D. Appleton-Century Company, 1933.

  g. *The Adolescent in the Family*. New York: D. Appleton-Century Company, 1934.

[5] Krogman, W. M. "Trend in the Study of Physical Growth in Children." *Child Development*. 11 (1940), 279–284.

tober 1953), 65–74. This article describes some of the findings emerging from another longitudinal study. How do the emphases in this study resemble and how do they differ from those in the MacFarlane plan?

Despite the attention given the " whole child " in much of the literature from the nineteen thirties on, the findings of interdisciplinary team approach to the study of children were not very well synthesized until after World War II. The Mid-Century White House Conference marked the first large-scale attempt to bring together knowledge from the various fields and to relate it to personality development in some systematic fashion. Speaking of the contributions of the various disciplines to the understanding of human behavior, Witmer and Kotinsky comment:

> In none of these areas has scientific investigation gone beyond a promising beginning. Nevertheless, the facts and ideas accumulated up to this time serve several useful purposes. They are sufficient for the formulation of meaningful questions, the base from which worthwhile research must start. They are sufficient to make us aware of the errors of the past and the present; . . . They are sufficient to make us recognize the dangers of hasty application and to give us promising suggestions for action.[6]

THE VARIETY OF CHILD DEVELOPMENT MATERIAL AVAILABLE

The research from which child development is drawn may be classified in a variety of ways. Since our concern is for the practical uses to which research may be put in understanding the behavior and development of children, we shall consider the available materials from the standpoint of whether they are primarily *descriptive, explanatory,* or *predictive.*

Descriptive materials are undoubtedly most numerous. Here we include studies which picture the child as he changes through time, or which show us the behavior of children of the same age under varying circumstances. Some studies are concerned with the " whole

---

[6] Witmer, Helen L., and Kotinsky, Ruth (eds.). *Personality in the Making, the Fact-Finding Report of the Midcentury White House Conference on Children and Youth.* New York: Harper and Brothers, 1952. P. 4.

child," while others focus on a particular phase of development, as physical, mental, emotional, or social.[7]

Explanatory materials are those which help us to explain behavior as it emerges. In this category we include both theoretical formulations of personality development and clinical material, the study of which offers clues as to why a particular individual behaves as he does. We are especially concerned here with the relationships between early characteristics and behavior and later development.[8] Such materials (provided we had sufficient information) would enable us to understand why the braggadocio that was characteristic of Dan Mallon when he was 5 seems to have disappeared by the time he finishes high school.

Predictive materials are those which help us to anticipate behavior and development likely to be characteristic of an individual at some future time. For example, information about the child's height before the age of 6 gives us an idea of the *probability* that he will reach a certain height at maturity. We cannot, however, be certain of the outcome. This element of chance is even greater in the prediction of behavior, because there are so many factors operating which cannot be controlled. Potentially, predictive materials hold great promise for more effective work with children. It would be helpful if the teacher were able to specify the conditions under which he knew that a particular child could learn a specific behavior. Difficulty, however, arises out of the fact that as the child acquires the expected behavior he may incidentally learn other behaviors or feelings of uncertain value.

Descriptive Child Development Material

Physical growth has probably been more adequately described than any other aspect of development. This does not mean, how-

---

[7] See Martin, William E., and Stendler, Celia B. *Child Development.* New York: Harcourt Brace and Company, 1953. Note pages xiv–xvii for a discussion of the types of studies included here and their contribution to the study of child development.

[8] In this connection Hartmann and Kris, in "The Genetic Approach in Psychoanalysis." *Psychoanalytic Study of the Child,* Vol. I. New York: International Universities Press, 1945. Pages 11–31 discuss what they call genetic propositions which "describe why in past situations of conflict, a specific solution was adopted; why the one was retained and the other dropped, and what causal relation exists between these solutions and later developments."

ever, that there is not still much to be discovered, particularly about the interrelationships among various phases of physical growth.

Normative studies. Many studies have been "normative" in character, that is, their conclusions have included indications of the average age at which the children in the group surveyed displayed a certain growth characteristic. Such studies provide a very useful framework for further research so long as their limitations are realized. If, for example, we wish to know whether a child's progress in physical growth compares favorably with that of other children we must select for our standard of comparison the average progress of a group similar to that of the group from which our child comes. Unless such factors as the techniques of measurement, race, sex, locale, and socio-economic status are equivalent, we have no reason to assume that the averages found in one group are equally applicable to another.[9]

Perhaps the most commonly known of the many normative studies are the ones conducted by Gesell and his co-workers. They observed the behavior of infants and children at regular intervals from birth on, and established norms in four major fields — motor, adaptive, language, and personal-social. They found, for example, that at the age of 15 months only 27 percent of the children they studied were able to build a tower of three or four cubes. When the same test was offered at 18 months, 77 percent of the children were able to pass it.[10] Thus, 18 months may be regarded as the age at which most children will be capable of this bit of adaptive behavior. Some children will of course accomplish this feat sooner, some later. One child may be advanced in motor behavior as measured by such activities as walking and climbing, and relatively slow in language or adaptive behavior. Gesell has indicated how norms may be used or misused:

Norms of behavior development, as measures of maturity, must be applied with even greater caution (than norms of height and weight). The lay person should not attempt to make a diagnosis on the basis of

9 Thompson, Helen. "Physical Growth" in *Manual of Child Psychology*, 2d ed., edited by Leonard Carmichael. New York: John Wiley and Sons, 1954. Pp. 292–334.

10 Gesell, Arnold, and others. *The First Five Years.* New York: Harper and Brothers, 1940. P. 322.

such norms. . . . Refined and responsible application of maturity norms requires clinical skill based on long clinical experience.

. . . For the psychological orientation of the reader we have drawn up a series of behavior profiles for advancing age levels. . . . When the profiles are read as a consecutive series they give a time-flow-map of the way in which a child matures. It is not intended that a single profile should be used to determine whether a given child is bright or dull, good or bad. Individual deviations are almost as normal as they are numerous. The norms enable us to detect the deviations.[11]

PROBLEM 4. The Gesell behavior profiles are based primarily on children studied in New Haven, Connecticut. Precise statements of socio-economic status are not reported but most of the children appear to have been from middle-class homes. Which of the following would you consider appropriate ways to use such profiles:

1. A teacher in a privately operated nursery school in Cambridge, Massachusetts, reads the behavior profiles for 3-year-olds before she begins to plan the daily schedule for her 3-year-old group.

2. A teacher in a nursery school in a Chicago slum area says that her children are " backward " when compared with the Gesell profiles.

3. An ex-teacher is disturbed because her own 4-year-old has not yet exhibited any of the boastfulness and bossiness described in the behavior profiles for 4-year-olds.

PROBLEM 5. Examine a copy of *Infant and Child in the Culture of Today* by Gesell and Ilg to see the kinds of material included in the motor, adaptive, language, and personal-social fields. In which of these fields would you expect to find the greatest differences between varying cultural groups? Perhaps you can check your thinking by also examining the study of Balinese children in *Growth and Culture* by Margaret Mead and Frances Cook MacGregor.

Studies of specific aspects of development. In addition to the studies which attempt to describe in rather comprehensive fashion the all-round development of children, many more are focused on one specific aspect, such as motor or social development. A great many of these have been based on observations made in nursery schools, frequently those operated in a university. Consequently, there is relatively more information about the behavior of 3-, 4-, and 5-year-olds from middle-class homes in relation to the equipment and materials usually found in nursery school and to their peers and their teachers, than there is about older or younger children, chil-

[11] Gesell, Arnold, and Ilg, Frances L. *Infant and Child in the Culture of Today.* New York: Harper and Brothers, 1943. P. 70.

dren from other socio-economic groups, or children in their family settings.

Many studies have explored the relationships between various aspects of development, but frequently because of the small and highly selected group studied, the relationships established could not be predicted to exist in another group. Where similar patterns appear in research carried on in different centers, it is of course possible to make broader generalizations than can be made where all of the data come from one group.

PROBLEM 6. An excellent example of research carried on in a nursery school is *Social Behavior and Personality* by Lois B. Murphy. Excerpts from this are available in *Child Behavior and Development* edited by Barker, Kounin, and Wright, pages 345–362. Review this study. What kinds of behavior were common to all three of the groups studied? Under what circumstances did the children in the study show sympathetic behavior? From what you know of children of similar age and circumstance today would you expect similar findings if such a study were to be repeated?

In recent years research increasingly has been concerned with children of all ages. The extent to which children in varying socio-economic situations resemble or differ from one another has also received more attention.

PROBLEM 7. The book *Father of the Man* by Davis and Havighurst is a popular account of a study of differences in child rearing in different socio-economic groups. Review this book, or the article by Davis and Havighurst which is reprinted in *Readings in Child Psychology* edited by Dennis, pages 512–530.

By now it should be apparent that many of the materials which are here classified as "descriptive," also have in them elements of explanation, that is, help us to understand why a particular youngster behaves as he does. Some also are to a degree predictive; that is, they suggest the circumstances under which certain kinds of behavior are likely to emerge. By and large, however, they do not offer too much help when it comes to the understanding of the individual child. We cannot get from them, for example, an explanation for the fact that Jane Warner as a newborn seems a comfortable, placid individual and by graduation time has become a discontented, rather unhappy person. Nor can we understand how Celeste Collins has shifted within her high school years from an unattractive, uncertain youngster into a young woman with reasonable self-assurance and confidence. For such understanding we turn to what we shall term "explanatory" materials, including not only research studies but also certain theoretical approaches not necessarily fully validated by scientific research.

Explanatory Materials

In the materials which we shall classify as "explanatory" emphasis shifts from the observable *actions* or behavior which is the center of concern in the descriptive materials to the *interpersonal situations* in which the child finds himself, and their influence on his developing *personality*. The child's feelings and the way people and things appear to him assume equal importance with what he does.

We shall select two lines of thought from those which have contributed their influence to these materials. One is psychoanalysis. The other is field theory, particularly as expounded by Kurt Lewin.

The influence of psychoanalysis. The influence of Freud on child development has been both indirect and direct. The finding that the difficulties adults have in their lives are so frequently rooted in childhood experience lent great impetus to the child study movement. Further, Freud's conception that personality development had a biological base and that its organization changed as the individual proceeded through various stages of growth made his theories extremely applicable to the study of children. Freud also ascribed to infancy and the early years sexual interests and strong feelings of love and hatred. Since many of these impulses are socially unacceptable, they are the source of considerable conflict, which besets the individual from a very early age. These ideas implying that the young child might be torn by impulses and emotions in many ways similar to those experienced by the adult met with considerable resistance. Researchers whose training was in the behaviorist tradition were unwilling to admit the possibility of such complex motivation on the part of the child. Nevertheless, there is little doubt that Freudian theories and the reports of analysts who worked with children considerably stimulated thinking about the inner life of the child. By 1950 Roger Barker could write:

> Theory in child psychology in 1950 is dominated by two trends. The first is the continuing controversy between proponents of psychoanalytic and nonpsychoanalytic viewpoints. Insofar as current research is guided by explicit psychological theory, psychoanalysis predominates. In fact, it can almost be said that the only comprehensive psychological theory of childhood that is influential at the present time is psychoanalysis. . . . The second trend in current child psychology theory is the application of learning theories to problems of personality development in children.[12, 13]

In discussing available psychoanalytic materials we should note that many of the ideas originally held by Freud have been modified in various ways both by those who have followed him rather closely and by those such as Jung, Rank, and Adler who have formed other schools of psychoanalytic thought. The nature of these modifications need not concern us here. Those who have come to be known as the neo-Freudians, particularly Fromm, Horney, and Sullivan, have been influential in translating some of the basic Freudian concepts into terms more acceptable to American scientific thought than were the original formulations.[14] One important thread which is most important for our purposes runs through all current psychoanalytic thinking. This is the assumption that it is the child's relationships with other people and his feelings about them which are important determinants in his developing personality.

The influence of field theory. The basic idea of the importance of interpersonal relationships is also found in the work of Lewin. His emphasis, which somewhat resembles that of Sullivan,[15] is always

---

[12] Barker, R. G. "Child Psychology." *Annual Review of Psychology,* Stanford, Calif.: Annual Reviews Inc., 1951. Pp. 1–23.

[13] For an interesting statement of the rationale for resistance to some of the Freudian concepts, see Anderson, John E. "Personality Organization in Children" in *Readings in Child Psychology,* edited by Wayne Dennis, New York: Prentice-Hall, 1951. Pp. 476–490.

[14] The positions of the various psychoanalytic schools in regard to the development of the personality has been succinctly described in Blum, Gerald S. *Psychoanalytic Theories of Personality.* New York: McGraw-Hill Book Company, 1953.

[15] Some of the parallels in the thought of Sullivan and Lewin are discussed by Murphy and Cattell in an article on "Sullivan and Field Theory" in *The Contributions of Harry Stack Sullivan,* edited by Patrick Mullahy. New York: Hermitage House, 1952. Pp. 161–179.

on the immediate life situation rather than on the life history. According to Lewin, the child and his environment (both physical and social) have to be viewed as variables which are mutually dependent upon each other. For example, " How a child sees a given physical setting (for instance, whether the frozen pond looks dangerous to him or not) depends upon the developmental state and the character of that child and upon his ideology. The worlds in which the newborn, the one-year-old child, and the ten-year-old child live are different even in identical physical or social surroundings. This holds also for the same child when it is hungry or satiated, full of energy or fatigued." And also, " The state of the person after encouragement is different from that after discouragement, that in an area of sympathy or security from that in an area of tension. . . ." [16]

PROBLEM 8. Select some area with which you are very familiar, such as a park, a near-by beach, or the toy department of a large store. Assume the roles of children of varying ages and backgrounds, and describe the area as it would most likely appear to them.
PROBLEM 9. Review the material describing the young people and their parents in Chapter 1. Find as many illustrations as you can of the principle of the reciprocal interaction of the child and his environment which has been set forth here.

It must be clear that Lewin's approach like Freud's provides only a conceptual framework for thinking about human behavior. Many of the factors entering into the psychological field of the child, for example, are—at least in our present state of knowledge—difficult or impossible to measure. These would include " such *specific* items as particular goals, stimuli, needs, social relations, as well as much more *general* characteristics of the field as the *atmosphere* (for instance, the friendly, tense or hostile *atmosphere*) or the amount of freedom." [17]

Projective materials. In such a conception, " personality may be viewed as (the) dynamic process of establishing and maintaining

[16] Lewin, Kurt, " Behavior and Development as a Function of the Total Situation." *Field Theory in Social Science.* New York: Harper and Brothers, 1951. P. 239. (For an extremely lucid presentation of Lewin's point of view applied to development, see " The Field Theory Approach to Adolescence " in *The Adolescent, A Book of Readings,* edited by Jerome M. Seidman. New York: Dryden Press, 1953.)
[17] Lewin, *op. cit.* P. 241.

and defending the individual's private world." [18] Direct access to the individual's private world to his ways of viewing himself and the world outside is impossible. However, the nature of the private world may be inferred by the use of *projective techniques*. These are "methods of studying the personality by confronting the subject with a situation to which he will respond according to what that situation meant to him and how he feels when so responding." [19] The child's play with dolls and housekeeping toys, his creations in clay, paint, and finger paint, as well as his responses to certain specially constructed personality tests can all be studied with a view to understanding his "private world." For example, the child who arranges the dolls in rigorous order, or who attributes to them only mean and hostile qualities, probably has an inner life rather different from the youngster who arranges the dolls according to occupations appropriate to them, and allows them to express a variety of emotions. In recent years these methods have been used in many research studies.

Predictive Materials

The more we study children, particularly when we rely on explanatory materials, the easier it is to see why prediction in child development is so difficult. There are too many interrelated factors operating to change the direction in which an individual seems to be going. Nevertheless, prediction is an important aim in any science, and attempts to predict future growth and learning have provided a great variety of information about children.

Predicting intellectual accomplishment. As we indicated in Chapter 2, much work has been done with the prediction of children's physical growth. Considerable attention has also been focused on the development of intellectual ability. The efforts in 1904 of Alfred Binet, a French psychologist, to devise tests which would indicate the degree to which children were teachable led eventually to the construction of standardized intelligence scales which are, with certain revisions, still in use today. In these tests the child's responses to standard questions put him by a qualified examiner are used to

[18] Frank, Lawrence K. *Projective Methods.* Springfield, Ill.: Charles C. Thomas, 1948. P. 8.
[19] *Ibid.* P. 46.

determine his *mental age*. The questions have been presumed to relate to matters which would be sufficiently within the everyday experience of all youngsters as to rule out environmental influences. For example, at 3 years the child is expected to answer appropriately, among others, the question, " What must you do when you are hungry? " At 8 years he is asked to identify " what is foolish " about such a statement as " Walter now has to write with his left hand because two years ago he lost both his arms in an accident." The problems proposed increase in difficulty with increasing age and include tests of vocabulary, memory, comprehension, reasoning, and conceptual abilities. The *mental age* when divided by the child's *chronological age* gives an *intelligence quotient* or I. Q.[20]

In the nineteen-twenties it was generally assumed that an intelligence quotient derived from an individual test provided a fairly reliable index to later accomplishment. However, in the nineteen-thirties repeated tests on the same children and tests of children from a variety of environmental situations began to throw doubt on some of these assumptions. Considerable controversy has since been waged over the constancy of the I. Q. Although difference of opinion still remains, there is general agreement that measurements of intelligence, particularly those made before the child reaches puberty, are subject to many influences which may reduce their predictive value.

The testing movement has not been limited to testing of intelligence but has covered practically every aspect of human endeavor. Among its important consequences have been not only the increasing number of psychological tests available and refinements in both their construction and use, but even more important from the standpoint of child development, many longitudinal studies and investigations in the fundamental nature of individual differences.[21] A present trend is toward studies of the interrelatedness of various phases of growth. Prediction of one aspect of the child's living becomes a matter of studying not only measures of that particular phase but a number of related measures. Olson, for example, has

[20] Terman, Lewis M., and Merrill, Maud A. *Measuring Intelligence, A Guide to the Administration of the New Revised Stanford-Binet Tests of Intelligence.* Boston: Houghton-Mifflin, 1937.

[21] Anastasi, Anne, and Foley, John P., Jr. *Differential Psychology.* New York: Macmillan Company, 1949. Pp. 24, 25.

found that the child's educational achievement (many of his studies have focused on progress in learning to read) can be anticipated from a longitudinal study of measures of the child's growth as a whole.[22]

Difficulties in the prediction of learning. Since so many factors, including intelligence, rate of growth, and previous experience, are influential in the child's learning, it is no simple matter to predict what he may learn in a particular situation. Indeed, much remains to be known about the nature of the learning process in human beings. This is true despite the thousands of studies related to learning which are to be found in psychological literature. The majority of these have dealt with the learning of animals and college students rather than with the learning of infants and children.

A basic difficulty in the prediction of learning is that we still do not know enough about the nature of the learner, nor about how learning affects him. It is, for example, uncertain whether the increased ability to solve problems and to retain information which is associated with increasing age is primarily a matter of the increasing maturity of the organism, or of the fact that the older individual has a greater reservoir of previous learnings on which to draw.

Learners differ from one another in many ways in addition to rate of growth. In Chapter 2 we noted the nature of some of these differences. The effects of these on learning have not received much attention, but it is reasonable to assume that the child who has, let us say, keen visual acuity may confront early learning situations rather differently from the child with " average " visual and auditory responses and a markedly sensitive skin. To what extent these early and probably inherent differences in individuality may affect later learning is problematical.

How learning affects the learner is also a matter open to considerable speculation. We have earlier raised the question as to when learning begins. We hold a bottle in front of the newborn baby. He continues to cry. We nudge the nipple against his lips, and he begins to suck. Perhaps two months later when he cries and we hold the bottle in front of him he quiets immediately. Is this not rudimentary learning? What has happened to the baby that he responds differently? What changes have taken place within the organism? [23] Another important question relates to imitation. The baby's repertoire of vocal noises is sufficient for the acquisition of any language. What are the processes responsible for his learning to imitate the sounds of the language spoken by his parents? These are questions to which answers are still being sought.

Even if we cannot know the nature of the neurophysiological changes which take place as the infant grows and learns, we cannot ignore the cumulative effect that such experiences have on him as a learner. Assuming for the moment three infants of equal capacity — one of whom is regularly fed, bathed, and changed but deprived of toys and play, another who is fed, bathed, and changed and played with for a few minutes during and following each bath, while the third is continuously played with during all his waking moments — it is likely that each would have a very different repertoire of established responses to bring to a new learning situation. The first infant, as we can verify from studies of institutional children, would perhaps not be as " ready " for learning as the last two. Just what the differences in learning readiness of the latter two might be, we do not know but it is safe to hypothesize that they would not be exactly equivalent. Depending upon the feeling tones which had accompanied the play experiences they had had, they might view learning from a different perspective. The fact that the same learning situation can mean different things to different individuals primarily because of their differing backgrounds of experience with learning becomes even more obvious as we consider older individuals.

As we contemplate the complexities of human growth and learning, we may perhaps be as much impressed by the extent to which science has been able to make predictions about it as by the tremendous gaps there are. It is clear, however, that for some time to come we are likely to have to draw for our understanding of child development more heavily on explanatory materials than from

[23] D. O. Hebb in *The Organization of Behavior*. New York: John Wiley and Sons, 1949, sets forth a neurophysiological theory of learning which postulates two types of learning, one the primitive sort described above, and the other, the more efficient learning possible to the older child and adult.

thoroughly validated research. From a practical standpoint this need not handicap us too much. We shall, it is true, not be able to predict with any degree of certainty how a particular individual will react in a particular set of circumstances, and certainly we shall not be able to say, " Given this baby with this kind of physique and response tendencies, if we provide these and these experiences he will turn out to be such and such an adult." [24] We are left rather with the necessity for proceeding on our hunches and for using our intuitions as well as our intellects. Our understanding, then, may depend as much on our own integrity and our own capacity for caring about what happens to other human beings as it will on the extent to which we are able to master the facts of child development.

A PRACTICAL APPROACH TO UNDERSTANDING CHILD DEVELOPMENT

Following are three anecdotes taken from the lives of the young people with whom we are concerned in this book.

Jane Warner, at 2½ years of age, was observed playing by herself. She had several dolls, a large doll bed and a doll carriage, and a number of doll blankets. She commented, " I cover baby up. This doll baby on the left side. This doll baby on the right side." Then she evidently had some difficulty arranging the blankets to her satisfaction, for she muttered, " I can't tuck babies in." She turned instead to the carriage, and taking some of the available doll blankets, said, " This is gween, this is bwue." She reached for one from the bed and said, " I want dis too." As she covered the doll in the carriage she said, " Let's have baby rest."

[24] To say that much remains to be known about learning is not to discount the importance of current research. Especially relevant are efforts to apply learning theory to personality development. See, for example: Mowrer, O. Hobart. *Learning Theory and Personality Dynamics.* New York: The Ronald Press, 1950; and Dollard, John, and Miller, Neal E. *Personality and Psychotherapy.* New York: McGraw-Hill Book Company, 1950.

For a discussion of some of the problems involved in such application of theory see Nowlis, Vincent. " The Search for Significant Relationships in a Study of Parent-Child Relationships." *American Journal of Orthopsychiatry.* 22 (1952), 286–299. Research carried on by Robert Sears such as that reported in the " Symposium in Genetic Psychology," " Effects of Frustration and Anxiety on Fantasy Aggression," *American Journal of Orthopsychiatry.* 21 (1951), 498–505, exemplifies the use of learning theory in the study of aggression.

Dan Mallon, at 7, lived in a neighborhood in which there were few youngsters of his own age. He tagged around after some 14- and 15-year-olds who sometimes took time to coach him in boxing. In school he often threatened to punch some of the other boys, but never made good on his promises.

Celeste Collins, who at 13 was a shy, passive, round-shouldered girl with stringy, dull hair and stubby, bitten fingernails, seemed to place some confidence in her Sunday school teacher. One day she talked to her about her experiences in eighth grade. Although she was doing acceptable work, she said that she didn't like school or the teachers. " They are too crabby. The men teachers aren't too bad, but the women teachers are awful. They don't explain things or they use too long words."

These anecdotes become meaningful only as they are related to the total ongoing development of the children. But it is difficult to think of all the facets of development at the same time. Suppose we look first at the *biological* aspects of development which are revealed in them.

Biological Factors in Development

In the first incident we note a 2½-year-old engaged in an *activity*. From continued observations of this kind, we could begin to generalize something about her customary patterns, the vigorousness of her movements, their tempo and rhythm. To some extent these will have been modified by the nature of the social experiences she has had, but her particular physique is a basic determinant.

She does not manage the blankets perfectly but with sufficient success to make us sure that doll-bed making is no novelty to her and that she has already made considerable progress in fine muscle co-ordination. We can, if we wish, compare her height and weight now with similar measures six months ago and with the measures of other children of the same age so as to determine whether she is growing relatively " fast " or " slow." We must remember, however, that at this age growth is slow and gain in weight small as compared with earlier and later ages. Therefore, very slow progress for a time at this age is not significant.

Like her motor activity, Jane's language tells us something about her *ability to learn*. The words she uses are the product of her experience, but the fact that at the age of 2½ she has this much of a repertoire, and that she is already dealing with the concept of left and right, suggests not merely that she has been taught but also that she is quite " teachable."

The anecdote about Dan Mallon is not particularly revealing about the biological aspects of development. There is some indication of zest for vigorous activity, but we are left in the dark as to its quality. We have no basis for comparing his development with other 8-year-olds, or for appraising his ability to learn.

The description of Celeste Collins suggests a physique not functioning at its best. If an apparent lassitude were characteristic with her, it might reflect a predisposition to placidity, or poor nutrition, or it might have its origin in feelings of inadequacy about herself or her body. The fact that she is doing " acceptable work " tells us a little, but not very much, about her learning.

As we focus on the biological factors which may have been operative in the development of these youngsters, we cannot avoid consideration of the *social* factors. Let us examine those more closely.

Social Factors in Development

Jane Warner's play reveals immediately some of the customs of the world in which she has been brought up. Babies, in the American culture she knows, are *tucked* into bed. They are not carried in a sling around the mother's waist, nor strapped to a cradle board. And her comment about having baby rest may imply they are not let to fall asleep when they choose but must rather " rest " when the mommies think it best for them. Even the fact that she finds it appropriate to play with dolls is further evidence of cultural influence. Had she been brought up in Samoa, for example, she might have regarded the dolls as something to look at rather than a toy. The concepts of left, right, blue, and green which she seems to be acquiring (the anecdote does not reveal whether they are yet stable) are also culturally determined.

Her play further reveals that she is developing an awareness of social roles — those behaviors customarily associated with certain positions in society — as she imitates the mother caring for her babies.

The older the child is the more apparent the influence of social factors becomes. Thus, in the incident regarding Dan Mallon, we can detect the operation of influences beyond the immediate family group. In this instance three are evident, the neighborhood, the school as represented by the teachers and the adults, and the peer groups as represented by the youngsters in Dan's own grade. We can see here how various groups tend to structure or "institutionalize" behavior. The hitting and fighting which occurs so spontaneously among 7-year-olds becomes "boxing" among the 14- and 15-year-olds. The incident also raises some interesting questions regarding the learning of social roles. Dan evidently knew how to behave acceptably as a 7-year-old with 14- and 15-year-olds, but he appears to have been somewhat less adequate as a 7-year-old among 7-year-olds.

Celeste Collins has come into contact with at least two social institutions outside the family — the school and the Sunday school. In both she has had certain kinds of learning experiences. Whether in either instance she has learned all that it was intended she should learn is not clear. What is evident is that she has learned much which was not taught deliberately including a distaste for school and a stereotype about woman teachers. We may well inquire as to whether the school was really so bad or whether Celeste was at this point in her development somewhat inclined to see most adults as not very helpful. Such a query pushes us to consider another aspect of development, one that we shall call *psychodynamic*.

Psychodynamic Factors in Development

Here our concern is not with the directly observable behaviors but with the psychological processes involved in those behaviors. We wish to understand both the continuity in personality (Jane Warner is as recognizable as Jane Warner at 18 as she was at $2\frac{1}{2}$) and the changes that occur (Celeste Collins at 18 is still a quiet, somewhat retiring person but not so markedly shy and passive as at 13). To do this we must consider how the individual organizes his experience, what goes on in his "private world." Direct access to this is of course impossible. Much must be inferred. Many times we can verify our hunches in the later behavior of the individuals with whom we are concerned, but since this is not always possible and since at certain points our understanding of the nature of the psychological processes may be inadequate, we cannot hope to achieve complete insight.

Robert W. White, whose *Lives in Progress, A Study of the Natural Growth of Personality* is concerned with the psychodynamic study of normal people, has this to say about it:

> To some extent the psychodynamic study of man bridges the gap between biological and social ways of thinking. On the one hand it is concerned with drives, learning and the general process of adaptation. On the other hand it deals with the social environment, particularly that portion of it, the family circle, within which the child accomplishes his earliest learnings and first adaptations. Owing its original impetus to Freud's work with neurotic patients, it is still based largely on knowledge obtained in the course of treating maladjusted people. If this circumstance has somewhat limited the scope of the findings, it has at least served to keep the focus of interest on the individual and his development. Psychodynamic study never overlooks the personal meaning of experience. Its basic material is the pattern of urges, anxieties, defenses, and values that appears in the individual life.[25]

Personality development. The term " personality " may be used in a variety of ways. In this book we shall use it rather broadly to refer to our concept of all that the human being is, including his potentialities for action. To understand the individual from this point of view, we may think of him as gradually developing a system of inner controls whereby he is able to perceive reality, think, and act in ways which both satisfy his own needs and impulses and are acceptable to the society in which he lives. In Freudian terminology this system corresponds roughly to the individual's *ego*. We shall use this term throughout the remaining chapters to refer to these processes of control, management, and execution.

Before we concern ourselves with the functioning of this control system, it may be well to consider the needs and impulses for which it is responsible. The basic origin of these is undoubtedly biological. Something of their nature can be discerned by thinking of what the human animal might be like if he were stripped of socializing

---

[25] White, Robert W. *Lives in Progress, A Study of the Natural Growth of the Personality.* New York: The Dryden Press, 1952. P. 295.

influences and lacked the power of thought. The primitive strivings necessary for the growth, maintenance, and reproduction of human life thus revealed may not seem to bear too much resemblance to the motivations of the adult. Such lack is likely testimony that the ego has succeeded in governing them by " moderating their intensities and determining the modes and times of their fulfillment." [26] The extent to which such moderation is easy or difficult will depend in part on the strength of individual drives and impulses. In line with the point of view of individual differences presented in Chapter 2, we should expect them to vary considerably from one person to another. To use an analogy from Murray and Kluckhohn, " Some ' egos ' are sitting in the saddle of a docile Shetland pony, others are astride a wild bronco of the plains." [27]

The likening of the ego to a rider originated with Freud. It has also been likened to a steering mechanism or organization [28] and, when functioning adequately, to a democratic organization in which all the various forces in the personality may express their demands and have them listened to. Reconciliations are then made between conflicting interests, and demands are mediated by compromise, trading, concession.[29] Such comparisons may help you to understand the scope of the functions of the ego. However, we hope that you will not lose sight of the fact that what we are dealing with is merely a way of conceptualizing certain processes in personality development.

Ego processes. In order better to understand the processes with which we are presently concerned, let us turn our thinking to the descriptions of our six young people as they appeared in Chapter 1. We find in them six different personalities, none yet fully " mature " but each revealing, in his own way, a functioning ego. Each knows or *perceives* the world around him, has not merely a sense of how things look, sound, smell, feel, taste, but also an awareness of their

[26] Murray, Henry A., and Kluckhohn, Clyde. " A Conception of Personality," in *Personality in Nature, Society and Culture,* 2d ed. New York: Alfred A. Knopf, 1953. P. 24.

[27] *Ibid.* P. 26.

[28] Spitz, René. " Psychiatric Therapy in Infancy," *American Journal of Orthopsychiatry.* 20 (1950), 623–633.

[29] Alexander, Franz, quoted in Symonds, Percival M. *The Ego and the Self.* New York: Appleton-Century-Crofts, 1951. P. 13.

relatedness, and of the predictability of events. Each perceives the same objective situation in his own unique way in the light of his particular background of experience. Consider, for example, how differently Jane and Pat might look at a problem in chemistry, a basketball, a ballroom for dancing, and each other. Are not both Jane and Andy somewhat more critical of their peers than the other youngsters?

But it is not only the world outside that is perceived. Each also has a perception of *self*, an awareness of body, of actions, of feelings, of a past and a possible future. As the individual grows in maturity, these become unified into a more or less consistent self, a concept which may be quite realistic or quite distorted depending on whether the individual's experiences have been such as to make him feel comfortable in his own skin, or uneasy and unsure.

Each young person *thinks*. In Chapter 1 we find them fantasying, wandering somewhat aimlessly through their private worlds, but each is also capable of putting his mind to a problem, disregarding interruptions, working out a logical solution. True, some would be able to work their ways through more complex and more abstract problems than would others, but all six are quite capable of rational thought.

Further, each of them *acts*. We do not see them in action, but we know that they have made and will continue to make decisions, that they schedule and plan their activities, that they solve conflicts and choose the course they will take. Beset by impulses at odds with each other they repress, or inhibit, or channel some and express others. Action, it may be noted, does not always occur without pain. Sometimes they know its source, for it comes from a disapproving outside world. In other instances it comes from their own guilt and anxiety, and they are less sure of the origin of the discomfort. A major task of the healthy ego is to put impulses and drives to the service of activities which are at one and the same time satisfying to the individual and to society.

Perceiving, thinking, acting, these are obvious expressions of human personality, functions of the individual's inner control system.[30]

[30] This statement of ego processes is drawn in part from Symonds, *op. cit.* Pp. 7–17.

The role of learning. But you may ask, does not learning play an important part in all these functions? Doesn't the adult have a more adequate control system than the child, and may not all of its manifestations simply reflect the fact that he has had more opportunity to learn? This is an astute question and deserves a better answer than we are presently able to give. There is no doubt but what learning processes *are* fundamental to all of these functions. Unfortunately, as we have suggested earlier, there is as yet no completely adequate and integrated theory as to how the variety of learnings involved do take place. We believe that the student who is interested in acquiring a practical understanding and appreciation of human development will find it more helpful to deal with the processes of personality development as we are describing them here than to apply any one of the current theories of learning to them. We shall, however, as the book progresses endeavor to describe the kinds of learning which do go on at each stage of development.

The role of conscience. Some of you may also be concerned with direction. Is there nothing by which the individual is to " shape " his personality, no guide lines as to what is " good," " desirable," or " right "? It is at this point that the ideas of *conscience* and *ideals* become useful. The individual does need some standard against which to judge his behavior. In infancy this is pretty much lacking, but as he grows, his parents begin to demonstrate in one way and another what they regard as proper. Their standards are his standards. Gradually, however, his social world widens, he develops positive relationships with individuals other than his parents, and they, too, serve as models for him. The conscience which he derived from his parents and which was appropiate for a child is no longer adequate to him as an adult, and it must be revised. This does not mean that each generation throws out old standards and establishes new ones as those who are fond of carping at young people sometimes seem to imply. It does mean, however, that each individual, if he is to be an adequate adult, must come to terms with the standards and values he holds and with their significance for his behavior.

As we consider the musings of our six young people, it seems evident that none of them has yet attained a sure sense of direction, and it is likely that to a greater or less degree all of them are still struggling with a somewhat childish conscience. All of them, however, have some picture of the ideal selves they would like to be. How realistic these may be we shall leave for consideration after we have come to know them better. At 18, or thereabouts, they must in a sense face the adequacy of the personality they have already developed. Adolescence is sometimes regarded as the last chance society has to shape its young people, but it may equally well be regarded as the individual's opportunity to begin to put his own life in order. Tremendous changes may take place, and an adolescent with little to build upon may sometimes erect a sturdy structure even at this late juncture. More often, however, the adequacy with which he meets the demands of early adulthood depends on what has gone before. Failure to meet past crises leads to equal failure in maturity.

It is readily apparent that the demands of the impulses and drives as well as the expectations of society change as the individual grows older. Likewise, the perceptions, the thoughts, the actions of the young child differ from those of the adult. This book is concerned with the nature of these changes through time. It assumes that as the child develops, as he learns to mediate between the demands coming from within and those from without, he adds new strengths, new components to his personality. The nature of these components and the approximate periods in which they are evolved has been set forth in a scheme of the "Growth and Crises of the Healthy Personality" by Erikson,[31] and we shall use his structure in organizing the remainder of this book.

Crises in personality development. The basic assumption which Erikson makes is that very much as biological organisms have a basic *ground plan* from which the various parts arise all in their proper time until all have become a functioning whole, so there are certain inner laws operative in personality development. (At this point you may find it useful to review the section on prenatal development, particularly noting the statements about "Timing" in Chapter 2, page 37.) These inner laws, Erikson believes:

[31] Erikson, Erik Homburger. "Growth and Crises of the Healthy Personality" in *Personality in Nature, Society and Culture,* edited by Kluckhohn and Murray, *op. cit.* Pp. 185–225. Also, Erikson, Erik Homburger. *Childhood and Society.* New York: W. W. Norton and Company, 1950. Pp. 219–234.

. . . create a *succession of potentialities for significant interaction* with those who tend him. While such interaction varies from culture to culture, it must remain within the *proper rate and the proper sequence* which govern the *growth of a personality* as well as that of an organism. . . . Personality can be said to develop according to steps predetermined in the human organism's readiness to be driven toward, to be aware of, and to interact with, a widening social radius, beginning with the dim image of a mother and ending with mankind, or at any rate that segment of mankind which " counts " in the particular individual's life.[32]

The diagram in Figure 2 illustrates Erikson's conceptualization of the healthy, mature personality or ego. The growth stages, from infancy to mature adulthood, may be read downward at the left of the diagram. The designations which are given are derived from psychoanalytic concepts. The first four stages may be thought of as corresponding roughly to the first year of life, the years from 1 to 3, from 3 to 6, from 6 to 12, and the last four as occurring after the age of 12. Variations in the age of reaching puberty as well as the differentiating effects of life experience make it difficult to label these stages as to years.

Each of the boxes in the diagonal represents what may be regarded as the central problem of that period. As Witmer and Kotinsky have interpreted Erikson, every problem:

. . . has to be solved, temporarily at least, if the child is to proceed with vigor and confidence to the next stage. These problems, these conflicts of feeling and desire are never solved in entirety. Each shift in experience and environment presents them in a new form. It is held however that each type of conflict appears in its purest, most unequivocal form at a particular stage in a child's development, and that if the problem is well solved at that time the basis for progress to the next stage is laid and a degree of " sturdiness " in personality secured for the future.[33]

At any stage in development we may think of the unlabeled boxes below the diagonal in Figure 2 as representing the strength in personality which the individual has achieved through the working through of that particular conflict at a previous stage, whereas

[32] Erikson (in Kluckhohn and Murray), *op. cit.* P. 187.
[33] Witmer and Kotinsky, *op. cit.* P. 6.

	TRUST VS. MISTRUST	AUTONOMY VS. SHAME, DOUBT	INITIATIVE VS. GUILT	INDUSTRY VS. INFERIORITY	IDENTITY VS. ROLE DIFFUSION	INTIMACY VS. ISOLATION	GENERATIVITY VS. STAGNATION	INTEGRITY VS. DISGUST, DESPAIR
ORAL SENSORY	TRUST VS. MISTRUST							
MUSCULAR-ANAL		AUTONOMY VS. SHAME, DOUBT						
LOCOMOTOR-GENITAL			INITIATIVE VS. GUILT					
LATENCY				INDUSTRY VS. INFERIORITY				
PUBERTY AND ADOLESCENCE					IDENTITY VS. ROLE DIFFUSION			
YOUNG ADULTHOOD						INTIMACY VS. ISOLATION		
ADULTHOOD							GENERATIVITY VS. STAGNATION	
MATURITY								INTEGRITY VS. DISGUST, DESPAIR

Figure 2. Erikson's eight stages of man. (From Erik H. Erikson. Childhood and Society. New York: W. W. Norton & Company, P. 234.)

76

the boxes above the diagonal represent potentialities for the development of such strengths.

The mature healthy personality, according to this conception, would be one combining feelings or senses of *trust,* a warm, serene confidence in people; of *autonomy,* of self-worth; of *initiative,* enterprise and imagination; of *industry,* duty and accomplishment; of *identity,* the full realization of one's self as continuous and individual; of *intimacy,* the sharing of emotional closeness with other human beings; of *generativity,* creativity, productivity, and the genuine wish for parenthood; of *integrity,* conviction and commitment to the meaning of life itself.

We shall leave a more precise definition of these components of the healthy personality to emerge as we deal with each stage of development.

Thus far we have described personality development as a process during which the individual develops a system of relating himself and his needs and drives to the physical and social world in which he lives. We have indicated some of the components of the mature healthy personality and the periods at which they become the point of focal attention in the personality. We have implied that these components arise out of the resolution, more or less temporary, of certain conflicts, but we have not discussed the nature of the factors determining their successful resolution.

It would be pleasant to be able to present these entirely in positive terms, to suggest that if as the child grows his parents are able to provide adequately for his needs and impulses; if they reward his behavior appropriately, he will automatically and at no pain to either himself or them resolve his conflicts adequately. Such a presentation would, however, be quite unrealistic. Development, even when it is healthy and " normal," always involves some pain. As Jersild says, " Every hurdle a hazard, every gain at a price." [34] The 5-year-old who becomes a " *big* boy " and goes off to school enjoys the new-found maturity, but he loses the gratifications of being mother's *little* boy. And he runs the risk of anxiety as to whether, now that he is *big,* she really does still love him.

The role of anxiety. It is doubtful whether personality develop-

[34] Jersild, Arthur T. *Child Psychology.* New York: Prentice-Hall, 1947. P. 52.

ment can be understood without dealing with the lurking *anxiety* with which, it seems, all human beings must eventually come to terms. This anxiety has been variously defined and is used in different ways by different schools of psychological thought. The basic element in it as it is subjectively experienced appears to be a state of tension and dread difficult to relate to any real danger. Although it resembles fear, it differs in that its source is unknown and consequently there seems to be no means of combating it. Some writers distinguish between what they regard as "normal" anxiety, the avoidance of which seems to be an essential motivation in socialized beings, and "neurotic" anxiety which so cripples the individual that he is unable to cope effectively with the demands of society and still retain sufficient sense of his own integrity. Some see anxiety as having its origin in the birth process, others in the infant's dread of separation from the mother. Our concern here is not to pinpoint its origin but rather to suggest that very early in development it becomes a possibility for the child. Erikson says:

> In childhood, of course, fear and anxiety are so close to one another that they are indistinguishable, and this for the reason that the child, because of his immature equipment, has no way of differentiating between inner and outer, real and imagined dangers; he has yet to learn this, and while he learns, he needs the adult's reassuring instruction.[35]

Each stage of development as we shall see brings with it new dangers. The way the child learns to cope with the particular dangers associated with the period, and thus to avoid the attendant anxiety, helps to determine the effectiveness of the developing ego. The child who experiences anxiety repeatedly and pervasively will never be able to become the effectively functioning personality that Erikson has described. On the other hand, the child who never confronts anxiety (if this be possible in the world in which we live!) will equally surely never become a mature personality.[36]

Anxiety is a difficult concept with which to work for a number of

[35] Erikson, *Childhood and Society, op. cit.* P. 364.

[36] Harry Stack Sullivan sees the self-system (which corresponds roughly with the idea of ego, personality, or control-system as we have been using the term) as, " An organization of experience for avoiding increasing degrees of anxiety which are connected with the educative process." *The Interpersonal Theory of Psychiatry*. New York: W. W. Norton and Company, 1953. P. 166.

reasons. It is not only that the term has different meanings. We live, so it seems, in an " age of anxiety." Consequently we have all experienced it. To a greater or less degree it has distorted us and our perceptions. We are not comfortable in its presence, and we would rather not have to deal with it. We try to give it other labels. The 3-year-old who is unable to " light," going from toy to toy at a frantic pace has " excess energy "; the blank-faced first grader who never raises his voice above a whisper is " shy," the brightly painted 12-year-old girl who tags after boys already out of high school is " boy-crazy." We prefer to classify their actions rather than to deal with their discomforts.

On the other hand, the very fact that we have been anxious can, under some circumstances, help us to be more sympathetic, more understanding, more compassionate. The unspoken yearning of the 8-year-old camper for the familiarities of home strikes a responsive chord in us. We, too, have been lonely. We are sensitive to the confusion of a young fellow at his first dance. We do not laugh for we, too, have known the agony of inexperience.

A further difficulty arises from the fact that whatever our response to the presence of anxiety in other people may be we sometimes find it impossible to know why we are affected as we are. Some experiences have perhaps been too painful, and we have repressed them. We cannot, except under the protection of therapy, expect to bring these to the forefront of our consciousness. We can sometimes, however, learn to be aware that we have such touchy spots and recognize our inability to cope with them rationally.

Another limitation in using anxiety as a pivotal concept in understanding personality development comes from the fact that anxiety seems so negative and so destructive whereas growth itself seems positive and constructive. In a sense, however, this problem is one of perspective. It is a matter of seeing the conquest (and recomquest) of anxiety always as a means to the end of fuller sensitivity, richer self-awareness, increased productivity, and greater compassion, rather than focusing on the abolition of anxiety as an end in itself. The psychology of development must, it seems, deal with pain as well as pleasure, very much as any adequate philosophy of life must also deal with death as well as life.

Summary

In the chapters which follow we shall endeavor to use as a framework for our understanding of each stage of development the ideas developed in this chapter. We shall need to consider these questions:

1. What are the important biological factors to be considered in this period of development?
2. What are the important social factors which influence this period of development?
3. What are the psychodynamic factors to be considered in this period of development?

    How do children perceive their world and themselves?

    What are their ways of thinking?

    What are their ways of acting?

    With what anxieties must they cope? What defenses are they developing? What strengths are they adding to their personalties?

In addition, if the study of child development is to become really meaningful, you will need to spend a considerable amount of time studying live children and youth. The following chapter offers suggestions as to some techniques and methods for getting to know youngsters of varying ages.

4

Studying Children and Youth

NO MATTER HOW WELL you know the child development materials, the theories, and the research which we have discussed in the last chapter you will not really understand child development until you begin to apply your knowledge to the study of children and young people. In the chapters which follow this one you will have some opportunities for such application as you follow the life history material relating to the youngsters we presented in Chapter 1. But the experience of studying human beings who are met only in print is in many respects quite different from studying real live human beings. Written characterizations of individuals do not change. The Jane, Pat, and Celeste, the Andy, Dan, and Charles we have described cannot respond to the warmth of your interest and friendliness. They cannot avoid your glance, or meet it with a grimace. You may find some of their qualities intriguing, or annoying, or baffling, but the way you feel about them will make no difference to their " behavior." In contrast, the children with whom you come in direct contact will react to you. They will in a sense be different because you " study " them. Thus it is important that you find as many opportunities as you can to know children. In this chapter we shall discuss how you may find situations in which to study children and some of the techniques which will help you

One learns about children through living with them.

to gain from such study. Some of these will need to be adapted to the particular circumstances in which you find " your " children.

LOCATING A " LABORATORY "

Look around you! Have you younger brothers and sisters? Nieces, nephews, or cousins? Do you peek inside the baby carriage that your next-door neighbor rolls out to the front porch every morning? Do you travel by bus and train? How can you avoid knowing children? You live in a college dormitory? Then you may have to exercise some ingenuity to find children, but the assignment is not an impossible one.

Perhaps your college has its own nursery school. Over the years, thousands of students have first learned about child development through observation and participation in a laboratory nursery school since it offers continued contact with the same children. Such a facility can add tremendously to the depth of your understanding, but it doesn't give you much breadth. You need to know babies, and toddlers, and school-age children as well as 3-, 4-, and 5-year-olds; children growing up in large families and living in crowded conditions as well as children living in small families with houses of their own; children of bus drivers and day laborers and the children of college professors, lawyers, and doctors; children at the end of a long day when they are tired, cranky, and resisting getting ready for bed, as well as when they are filled with fresh enthusiasm for the wonders of a new day; children with the handicaps of physical or mental disability as well as those on whom fortune has smiled more graciously.

In some colleges provision will be made for you to have such broad experiences. You will have opportunities to visit a variety of child-caring agencies as well as schools of different kinds, and perhaps even to spend some time in families with children. However, some of the most interesting situations cannot possibly be prearranged. For example, one student reported that she had not really understood how a child might be " in " a family, but not feel a member of it, until during a dinner date she observed the social interactions among a father, mother, and two youngsters at a neighboring table. We do not mean to suggest that the student's social life should now become dedicated to child study, but we do wish to stress that the study of children need not be limited to the laboratory nursery school or the field trip.

Informal Observations of Children and Youth

The first step in studying children is to go where they are — five-and-ten cent stores; the toy, children's clothing, and shoe departments of large stores; supermarkets; the barber shop specializing in children's hair cuts; parks and playgrounds; zoos; museums; the neighborhood movie theater on a Saturday afternoon; skating rinks. These are all places rich in opportunities for casual and sometimes fairly detailed observation of children and young people.

What you learn depends on you. How much you learn under these circumstances depends not only on your abilities to " see," but also on your own interest and friendliness. In some situations, about all you need to do is to look and listen. In others, you may want to get additional information. Try to relate yourself appropriately to the situation. You won't be able to learn much about small babies, for example, without asking questions. Most mothers respond rather quickly to a warm, appreciative glance in the baby's direction and some comment on his smile, his beauty, or his sturdiness. If you are willing to listen, they'll often spontaneously tell you his age, his weight, how he takes his feedings, and whether he sleeps through the night. An occasional mother may be suspicious of your motives. (Men students seem to have a little more difficulty with this type of observation than do women.) You can, if you wish, justify your interest by the fact that you are taking a course and have been given an assignment, but it is perhaps more fun to see how much you can learn without revealing your student status and without asking direct questions. Need we remind you that your role is not to make judgments about the babies. " He *looks* like a girl! " " Isn't she awfully tiny for six months? " " What are you doing about those big ears? " are not comments likely to further rapport.

Getting acquainted. Young children will probably continue their play without taking too much interest in you. They may want to know what you are doing and will be satisfied that you are " enjoying the sunshine," or " writing," or " doing school work." Or they may want to talk further with you. Students are often concerned as to how to make conversation with young children. It is usually better to let them give you the lead than to begin with the inept questions grown-ups so often use — " What is your name? " and " How old are you? " One may ask you to look at the sand cake he has just made or to watch him " skin the cat " on the climbing apparatus. But you must be prepared for surprises, such as the little girl who edges up to you and confides that today she is wearing her best pink pants with ruffles! This has been an important event for her, and she is ready for you to share her pleasure over it. In contrast is the child whose approach seems an affront — " Where did you get those ugly shoes? " or " Hi, you old stinkpot." These are the ones who will really test your child development aplomb! What is your reaction? Do you want to retaliate? Or are you curious as to what may be back of the child's comment? " Ugly " may mean " different " and " fascinating " to the child. Or his question may be an inept way of saying, " Let's get acquainted." The same goes for " stinkpot," which may indicate a genuine distrust not of *you,* really, but of adults in general, or it may be the youngster's idea of a " bombshell " sure to get your full response.

Older children aren't so likely to shock you, nor are they so likely to let you in on their " inner worlds." They've learned how to protect themselves from adults, to carry on unaided their own games and secret clubs and gangs. On the other hand, they aren't likely to object to your presence unless you indicate that you are inquisitive or that you want to take over what they are doing.

Much the same responses will come from adolescents. However, as young college people you may be in the position of being more accepted and " looked up to " than would be the case if you were older. Because of this, it is often possible for college students to make unusually fine " studies " of high school youth in their recreational activities and even in " bull sessions."

The advantages in the kinds of informal study of children and youth we have just described lie in the variety of experience and the freedom that it gives you. Except for your ethical responsibility not to respond in a way likely to be damaging to children, you do not have to be self-conscious about what you do and say. If your approach to the mother of an infant in a baby carriage is so awkward that she begins to wonder about kidnapping, not much harm has been done. You can review the experience and try again. If the frankness of 4-year-olds discomfits you, you can retreat momentarily without losing face with anyone, except perhaps yourself. Of course, if you are to learn from such experiences, you do have to come to terms with your own feelings about them.

Don't be an expert. The main hazard in informal observation probably comes when you try to get information from other adults, and fall into the trap of letting them regard you as an " expert." " Do you think it's normal for Janie to cry so much? " " What should I do about Tommy's temper tantrums? " " Ought Mildred go to nursery school? " are questions you can't answer. Gradually you will learn how to weigh the evidence necessary to provide answers to such questions, and you will also understand that the only one who can really answer is the parent himself. You may find it helpful to try to think through what answers a particular parent would be likely to find " right " for a particular child, and why. In the beginning of your study, however, you will be likely to be glad to fall back on your student status to avoid getting into too deep water.

Study of Children and Youth in More Formal Situations

In addition to the kinds of observation described above, a great deal can be learned from the study of youngsters in agencies and institutions providing an ongoing program of activities. These include nursery schools; the children's wards and children's playrooms in hospitals; day care centers; institutions for neglected, delinquent, and handicapped children; settlement houses and community centers; boy scout and girl scout troups and similar clubs; public, private, and parochial schools; Sunday schools.

It is of the utmost importance to bear in mind that every one of these agencies has its own purposes and functions to fulfill. Its primary concern is not to provide students with an opportunity to study children. The only exception to this is probably the laboratory school, which has been established to serve a dual function. This means that students must expect to direct their study in a way which does not run counter to the program of the center in which they are observing or participating. It also implies an obligation to learn about the nature of the agency as well as the children it serves.

Frequently arrangements are made for students to go in groups to such agencies. The director, or person in charge, talks with them about the agency, what it does, how it is financed, where its children come from, and so on. Then students are shown the physical facilities and have some opportunities to observe the children. Such "field trips" are very useful in developing a picture of the variety of social forces affecting children and a sense of the kinds of responsibilities the community assumes for its children. Sometimes, however, they are frustrating to students who wail on their return to the college: "We didn't see the children" or, "The children paid no attention to us" or, "I asked about that one little boy, but they wouldn't tell me anything." Such comments indicate certain misunderstandings. Any program can "take" only a limited number of disruptions by visitors. In general, the younger the children and the more emotionally upset, the more difficult invasions by groups of adults are. The failure of young children to run to the visitors often may only mean that the program is satisfying and relationships with staff members sufficiently warm so that other adults are not sought out. And an unwillingness to discuss a child may reveal nothing more than an ethical responsibility to protect him and his family from the curious. It is possible to have too precious an attitude toward youngsters. Certain schools and centers have found that their youngsters have much to gain from the experience of sharing their activities with visitors. But in the long run it is the agency which must decide how permissive toward visitors they can be. After all, it is their staff which must go on living with the children!

Visiting a variety of institutions contributes considerably to a broad view of child development, but for the deepening of understanding actual participation in the ongoing program of some agency is very much recommended. Such participation is often arranged and supervised by the college as part of the "laboratory" course in child development. Or students may volunteer their services to an agency and may have no supervision other than that of the agency. In such instances it is helpful for both the student and the agency to have a clear understanding of the nature of the responsibilities the student assumes, to whom he goes for help, whether he is committing himself for one semester or more, whom he notifies if it is impossible for him to attend and so on.

LEARNING WHAT TO LOOK FOR

We have discussed at some length how to locate children to study. The next problem is what to study. If your experiences are to be focused on "participation" rather than on "observation," you may find yourself so busy "doing" that you have no time to worry over what you "ought" to be studying. We are inclined to think this is all to the good. Our own bias is in favor of starting the study of children with "participation," using "observation" as a tool to help individuals to participate more effectively. Practically, this cannot always be managed, and you may find that your first assignment is to just observe. The material which follows tends to assume that you are *not* a mere "side-lines" observer, a kind of recording machine, but that you are also active with the children.

Doing What Comes Naturally

After you have located a group of youngsters with whom you are going to spend some time how do you begin studying them? Why not try whatever seems most natural for you? Here are a few ways which have been "right" for some students, as they themselves described them:

In the nursery school, sitting quietly in a chair at the side of the room, making jotted notes about the names and appearance of all the children so as to be able to identify them.

Sitting quietly on the side lines, picking out the most "interesting" child, watching him as he moves from one activity to another.

Asking the teacher if she might help with the dressing. Noting names on the children's cubbies helped her to learn the names of the children.

Noticing where the books were kept and making himself available when a youngster asked for a story.

Settling down on the floor beside two boys who were building a tremendous "garage." He himself had always liked construction and was probably as much intrigued with the possibilities in the blocks as with the boys.

In an after-school play program for 7-, 8-, and 9-year-olds: Just watching until he saw an opportunity to hold the propeller of a model airplane steady for a boy who was having difficulty attaching it.

On the playground, initiating the construction of a snow fortress in place of a free-for-all snowball fight.

In an adolescent girls club: Expressing enthusiasm (genuine) for the singer over whom the girls were currently swooning.

Working on a simple braided bracelet, listening, and watching, but saying little.

On the base of these beginnings, each of these students was able to build the confidence, the comfortable-within-himself feeling which was the first step to being able to understand the feelings and responses of the youngsters, and his own reactions to them.

What you feel does make a difference. In the past the study of children was thought to be mainly a matter of learning to observe them " scientifically," that is, objectively and without allowing one's emotions enter into the process. Now the difficulty of ruling the emotions out is better understood. Rather than attempting to eliminate the effects of emotions of the observer on the observation, we ask the observer to include his feelings so that we can better appraise how they may have affected his perceptions of whatever he has observed. The fifth nursery school incident above illustrates the difference nicely. The student in recounting his experience said that he felt " drawn " to the building. His account of the accomplishments of the boys was quite glowing. Had we asked him to eliminate his feelings from the observation, we might have noted some distortion in it — no one else saw the structure as tall as he did! — but we would have been unable to locate its source.

As we shall see when we discuss the recording of children's behavior, we maintain an interest in describing as objectively as possible what the children did or said, but we also provide an opportunity for the observer to record his reactions as well as those of the child. It is particularly important for people who work with youngsters to learn to know how their responses may affect the children, as well as how the children's responses affect them as adults.

Doing What Is Expected

Having urged you to begin the study of children in the way which seems most natural for you, we must now caution you that in certain situations you cannot be permitted as much freedom to find your own way as suggested above. Where a great many students are studying children in the same situation, or where the program is complex, or the children particularly sensitive to changes in routine, it becomes necessary to prescribe the limits within which students are to operate. You may be asked to do nothing except observe, and to carry on that observation from a particular vantage point!

In any event, there are some expectations which will likely be set for your behavior, in whatever setting you are. Following are some suggestions for meeting such expectations.

Take it easy. Understanding of youngsters doesn't come in a day or a week. Don't expect to get all the answers at once. First you have to learn what questions to ask!

Assume all the responsibilities of a good guest, but expect none of the privileges, at least at first. Show your appreciation of the courtesy being offered you by the agency by conforming to its rules and regulations. Don't *assume* that participation two or three hours a week makes you eligible to use the phone, stay for lunch, or borrow crafts materials. (In some centers it does, but others can't afford such generosity, and none like to feel that you take it for granted!)

Keep your focus on the children. Some agencies have the kind of relaxed easygoing kind of program which almost seems to operate itself. But the adults responsible for it know what is going on, and they will expect you to know also. It will be especially helpful to you if someone has time to talk with you occasionally to help you to understand it better. On the other hand, you can learn considerable just by being a good observer.

Learning to Obtain More Information

The first time children are observed is usually exciting. You find a good way to get into the group, or a comfortable way to watch. You learn the names of the children. Then, frequently, one of two things happens. You see so much that you can't decide what is important. Or you see no more than you did at first, and you wonder what use observing can possibly be to you. If you are participating, you are a little less likely to get caught in either of these dilemmas because you have discovered that some of the things you want to do with children don't work out very well. You want to know why, but you are not very sure how to go about finding out.

Gaining perspective. Some students feel that the best way to observe is to concentrate on one child. There are some advantages in this, particularly when you begin to notice not only what he does and says and how he relates to other children and to adults, but also which situations he seems to find satisfying, which disturbing, and how he recovers from an upsetting episode. The difficulty with such absorption in one child is that frequently there is no frame of reference from which to view his behavior. In a nursery school, for example, a 3-year-old may be all sunshine and smiles one moment, but dissolved in tears the next. You feel a little uneasy as to the significance of this, but you are not sure but what it may be expected at this age. Perspective in the beginning stages of child development study often comes from comparing the behavior of children in similar situations. The 3-year-old you are interested in cries when someone grabs a toy from him. What do the other children do when a toy is grabbed? Which ones respond similarly? Which ones respond differently? In what other ways are they like him or different from him?

Another way to get a perspective on a single child is to try to broaden your observation to include not him alone, but the interpersonal situations in which he is involved. Here you begin to look not only at his responses to others, but also at theirs to him. This may give you some hunches as to how others beside yourself feel about him.

Testing out hunches. As you begin to become familiar with the repertoire of behavior which is possible in your group, you may be ready to test out certain hunches about these interpersonal relationships. What happens when John and Mary play together? Why are they as a " pair " so different from John and Susan? What is it that Mike does that acts like a charge of dynamite in any group he stays with over ten minutes? Why does a committee with Linda as a member always seem to produce so much? Is it what Ben *says* that settles the ruffled feelings of the girls after the boys have teased them, or is it something else?

Still another way to expand your observation is to select a second child on whom to concentrate, perhaps deliberately choosing one to whom you have not felt so much attracted.

Or, you may find it helpful to organize your observations for a time around one aspect of development, listening to language, or trying to find how many ways anger may be expressed, or how children react to various kinds of frustration, or how they express affection.

As you build experience, you will also want to begin to relate your observations to the ages of the children you observe, so that you become increasingly sensitive to the difference in potentiality between, say, a 4-year-old and an 8-year-old.

With young children you may learn most from them just by watching and listening, but with older children and youth it is also possible to obtain information more directly, conducting informal interviews to learn what their hobbies are, how they spend their out-of-school hours, what they would like to be when they grow up, how they feel about their school experiences, and so on. Such interviewing should usually be planned in advance and the nature of the information you are seeking discussed with those who are in charge of the youngsters. However, even casual encounters with older children can yield material of this kind if you are willing to follow the conversational leads the youngsters give you, and are not too intent on finding out only what *you* think is important.

KEEPING RECORDS

Looking for all the kinds of information suggested above, *and* finding it, will be of little help in understanding development unless you keep a record of it. Children's responses do change through time, and the degree of change cannot be fully appreciated unless there is some basis for comparison. Therefore, it seems important to learn to be a record keeper.

It is possible to carry record keeping to an extreme. In the early days of nursery schools, for example, teachers were sometimes so busy writing down their observations that they hardly had time to respond to the children. One little girl who attended such a nursery school, frequently played " teacher " at home, an activity which consisted entirely of walking about with a pencil and pad in her hands! Records are, after all, only a means to an end. Unless they are so regarded, they may detract from rather than enhance the understanding of children.

There are three kinds of record with which the beginning student of child development should be acquainted. These are the *diary* or *running record,* the *anecdotal record,* and the *log.*

In the *diary record* the observer attempts to include all of the child's behavior as it occurs continuously through a given period of time. The diary record has been the basic tool in much child development research, particularly at the nursery school level.

The *anecdotal record* describes an incident of child behavior, but does not attempt to include all of the details.

Both are techniques for obtaining evidence as to how development is proceeding. They may be used to study individual children or groups and the interrelationships among children and adults.

The *log* is kept over a period of weeks or months. It includes anecdotal records, but may be focused on the reactions of the observer or on a group rather than an individual.

Most students find that they need considerable practice before they become skillful in using these techniques. For practical purposes the anecdote is used more frequently than the diary record. However, since learning to make a good diary record also involves learning to observe more carefully, the individual who becomes skilled in the use of the diary record is usually able to pick out the important details necessary in the anecdote. The following suggestions which are focused on the diary record are consequently relevant also to the anecdote and the log.

The Diary or Running Record

The objective of the diary record is to describe in language *all* of the behavior of the individual. It is an attempt to make in words a talking, moving picture so vivid and clear that the reader will know what happened almost as though he had been present. This means that the observer must be alert not only to the *gross* behavior, such as the movements of the body and the words spoken, but also to the *finer details* of behavior. On a gross behavior level one might record: " John walks into the room, says ' Hello ' and sits down." With more attention to the finer details the record might read:

"John saunters into the room, his gaze shifting over the other youngsters. As he goes down the aisle toward his own place, he lets his fingers trail along the surface of each desk he passes. When he reaches his seat, he looks directly at the teacher, grins and says ' Hello! ' rather loudly, then drops into his chair."

Although more descriptive than the record of gross behavior, the above tells us little of the *quality* of the behavior. We do not know whether John was tense and anxious, or whether he was relaxed and at ease. The following supplies some of this needed information:

" John saunters into the room, his gaze shifting *eagerly* over the other youngsters. As he goes down the aisle toward his own place, his fingers trail *gently* and casually along the surface of each desk he passes. When he reaches his seat, he looks at the teacher, grins *openly* and says ' Hello! ' *in his usual rather loud* voice. Then he drops comfortably into his chair."

If in the above *apprehensively* is substituted for *eagerly, tap nervously on* for *trail gently and casually along, defiantly* for *openly, in an unusually* for *in his usual,* and *sits down tensely* for *drops comfortably,* Our picture of John's behavior changes completely.[1] We see that he is tense rather than relaxed.

Reading the signals of behavior correctly. The accuracy of a diary record obviously depends on the ability of the observer to read the signals of behavior correctly. He should learn the variety of subtle ways in which tension may be manifested, such as the tightening of various muscles, particularly around the mouth and eyes, shifts in posture, speech inhibition, and the equally varied ways in which human beings indicate that they are comfortable and at ease. Getting to know a particular youngster well is in part a matter of learning his characteristic modes of emotional expression, his signals for difficulty and well-being.

Observers differ markedly in the extent to which they are able to perceive behavior accurately. As Jersild puts it, " What one perceives ' objectively ' may be, to a large degree, a projection of one's own subjective state and thus tell more about oneself than about

---

[1] This material is adapted from material originally prepared by L. J. Stone. See Hartley, R. L., and others. *Understanding Children's Play.* New York: Columbia University Press, 1952. Appendix, pp. 339–350.

the people whom one observes."[2] Thus, in the behavior incident described above, one observer, himself inclined to react in a hostile manner toward teachers and authorities in general, might be prone to see defiance in all of John's gestures, while another more favorably disposed toward the school situation might see the identical behavior as a manifestation of John's at-home-ness. How then can we be sure that the *quality* words we find in a diary record are really relevant to the actual feelings of the individual described? How can we validate our observations? Sometimes it is difficult, if not impossible, to verify what we think we have seen. There is, however, an additional aspect of the diary record which provides certain safeguards. This is the inclusion, either at the end of the record, or parenthetically, of the observer's own *feelings, impressions,* and *interpretations.* For example, in addition to describing John's behavior in the incident above, one observer might note, " I find this boy very likable and attractive. Today I think he wanted to be the center of attraction, but somehow I felt that was all right. It is difficult for me to be very objective about him." Another observer might say, " This boy often irritates me. I feel that I am only beginning to see that his apparent cockiness is but a cover-up for his lack of sureness." In both instances John arouses feelings which tend to alter the perceptions of the observer. Both observers, however, in adding their own feelings to their impressions and interpretations, are supplying a necessary perspective for validating their observations. They can review their records and note that depending on how they felt, they saw John's behavior in different ways. Perhaps they will need to explore their own feelings further in order to arrive at an understanding of what they saw. John's behavior, for example, may irritate the observer because it represents to him a lack of confidence with which he, too, has struggled. Only as he comes to terms with this is he likely to be free to understand how John really feels.

Checking validity. The validity of an observation may be checked not only by comparison with another observer, and out of one's own life experience, but also by further observation. If John's opinion of himself is somewhat shaky, there will be other times when he puts

    [2] Jersild, Arthur T. " Understanding Others Through Facing Ourselves." *Childhood Education.* 30 (May 1954), 411–414.

on some kind of bravado. If his apparent confidence is genuine, it will tend to reveal itself further in new situations. When the observer becomes an active participant, he can test out his hunches regarding a youngster's feelings somewhat more directly. He may comment in a reflective way about a child's apparent feelings, " I guess that seemed pretty unfair," or, " Maybe you're not sure what the other kids will think." Or he may, especially with a young child, act more directly. Thus, noticing that a 4-year-old becomes hyperactive and jittery when there are many children playing together in the playhouse at one time, he may hypothesize that the child is anxious lest he hurt or be hurt by someone. He offers him an interesting opportunity to play where there is less confusion and notes that he relaxes almost at once. Or he introduces some rules which reduce the risks of a melee and observes that this child more than any other accepts, abides by, and quotes them the while his movements becomes less frenzied and his voice drops from its high pitch. In these situations he may not have been able to identify fully the source of the child's anxiety, but he has surely verified the fact of its existence.

In an actual diary record the bit of John's behavior with which we have so far been concerned would represent a very small fraction of the total, covering fifteen minutes or a half hour. It is difficult for one observer to continue such intensive and detailed recording for a much longer period without some rest. The lapse of time should be noted as the record progresses so as to give the reader a sense of the child's pace.

Every record also needs a setting. For example, a record including the bit of John's behavior which we have just described, might begin:

> The fifth grade is just settling down following lunch hour. Miss Brown is seated at her desk on one side of the room. I have a chair in the back. All the children except John are present. The room is very quiet.

Included in the description of the setting are the people present, the activities going on, and anything which may have happened to indicate that the situation is either " normal " or different from usual. The observer's subjective reaction to the situation may also be included. For example, as you start a record on one child, you may want to note that you have picked him out because he seems to you so handsome.[3]

The following form, which may be varied to meet special requirements, has proven useful for diary records:

Name of child _____ Name of recorder _____
Date _____
Setting:

Time	Child's Behavior	Observer Reactions

Anecdotal Records

Anecdotal records, in contrast to diary records, do not attempt to include *all* of a youngster's behavior through a given period of time. They are, rather, descriptive of incidents which the observer believes reveal significant aspects of the child's personality. Frequently written following an incident, rather than during it, they may be regarded as a kind of shorthand for accomplishing an end similar to that of the diary. Like the diary, they are of value only to the extent that they describe behavior accurately and distinguish adequately between what the child did and said and what the observer

[3] The importance of permitting the observer to see his subject subjectively before he attempts an objective record has been stressed by Katherine Wolf, who finds it an essential step in establishing human rapport. See her " Observation of Individual Tendencies in the First Year of Life " in *Problems of Infancy and Childhood,* edited by Milton Senn. New York: Josiah Mary, Jr. Foundation, 1953. P. 102.

felt and thought. In writing anecdotes, students need to guard against generalizations and evaluations which are little more than impressions. For example, " Richard is a hyperactive, energetic child, always getting in somebody's way " tells much less about Richard than does the following anecdote:

Richard and Robin were building with the blocks. In reaching across Richard to pick up a triangle, Robin knocked down a pile of Richard's blocks. Richard turned on Robert and would have hit him with a block, had I not taken it away from him. He left the blocks and went over to the easels where Sally and Lou were painting, grabbed a brush from the green paint and made a mark on Sally's picture. She slapped him.[4]

The Student's Log of Child Development Observations

The log is another type of record useful to the student of child development. In it he includes what seems to him to be significant anecdotes concerning the children and his own personal feelings, reactions, and thinking. It is a report of his progress toward understanding and insight into human behavior — his own as well as that of the youngsters. It is especially useful when the student is an active participant and begins to see the variety of ways in which children respond to him and he to them. To keep a good log is not always an easy task, for its effectiveness depends to a large degree on the student's willingness to be honest about himself, and this is sometimes painful. Where such a log is reviewed by an instructor in child development, the student's personal reactions are regarded as confidential between him and his instructor. Although the log may not be required, many students have found it useful to keep it as a source of information to be drawn on for a variety of other child development assignments.

Photographs, Movies, and Recordings

The student of child development who has easy access to cameras and recording equipment may be interested in the possibilities for using them to supplement other types of records. If his technical

[4] Chapter II (pages 21–41), " Learning to Describe Behavior " in *Helping Teachers Understand Children* prepared for the Commission on Teacher Education, American Council of Education, Washington, D.C., 1945, contains a number of excellent anecdotes which are specific and descriptive as well as illustrations of some which are poor because they are judgmental, interpretative, or generalized.

skills are good, he may be able to introduce his tools so casually as not to destroy the spontaneity of child behavior. Most youngsters will want to find out how a camera or a recorder works, and may want to make themselves the center of its attention. Gradually, however, they can become accustomed to it and go about their affairs without being unduly distracted. Using a simple box camera, one can record vividly the infant and toddler's characteristic ways of sitting, crawling, pulling himself up, grasping, reaching, his pleasure or dismay when confronted with a new toy or a new playmate, and so on. A snapshot can preserve the complexity of a kindergartner's block building and catch the satisfaction a group may feel when their cooking products have turned out exceptionally well. The recorder may capture the flavor of the young child's language, while older children will sometimes talk more freely to the machine than they will to an audience. Students will undoubtedly think of other ways in which audiovisual techniques may be effectively used to study children, recognizing of course that there are many situations in which they would be most inappropriate.

Other People's Records

Many schools and other agencies have in their files considerable information about the children they serve. This may include reports about home backgrounds, physical examinations, psychological tests of various sorts, records of school progress, and perhaps notes regarding the child or his parents, written by teachers, psychologists, or social workers. Such material may be sketchy and deal largely with the obvious, or it may be very detailed and go deeply into the motivations of the individual involved. In the latter case, confidentiality is essential. Because of this, many agencies are not free to share their records with students. Whether or not this is a handicap to the beginning student of child development is debatable. Certainly knowing the objective facts about a youngster's background, such as where he lives, where his father works, how many brothers and sisters he has, and so on, can save students much useless conjecture. Information that the child seems to be more favored by his mother than by his father or that he appears jealous of the baby is helpful at the point when the student is beginning to question the meaning of some of the child's behavior. At an earlier stage, however, he may feel more compelled to look at the child described in the record than at the child presently before him. Records are useful when they can be used to supplement the student's own observation and hunches. In and of themselves, they have relatively little value for the beginning student of child development.

All of the information available about a child, including his developmental history as revealed in interviews with the parents, physical and psychological examinations, and a variety of observations of current behavior may be brought together in what is known as a *case study*. The material regarding the six young people whose development we shall follow throughout this book is illustrative of that which might be included in such a study. To prepare a case study which does full justice to a child demands a good background of theoretical knowledge and great skill and sensitivity in evaluating evidence. For this reason, the author does not regard it as a basic technique for the beginning student in child development.

THE ETHICS OF STUDYING CHILDREN AND YOUTH

Whether you study children in a community center, your neighbor's backyard, or at the college nursery school, you have certain responsibilities for confidence which are completely different from those expected of you in any other laboratory situation. A story of a minor blow-up in the chemistry laboratory very likely reflects only on your own ineptness. But the tale of a temper tantrum in the nursery school may be misinterpreted to mean that either a child or his upbringing is inadequate. The burden of responsibility for their children's personality development which modern parents carry is heavy enough without adding to it the apparent censure of students. Even though your comments about a particular youngster may not be intended as judgmental, they may be so interpreted. Consequently it is better to avoid identifying the children when you wish to comment to friends on an interesting incident that happened at the nursery school or on the playground. Make it a rule to discuss the meaning of the behavior of a particular child only with your instructors or with other students in child development who are bound by the same ethical standards as you are.

5

~~~~~~

During Their First Year

THE SIX YOUNG PEOPLE whom we first met in Chapter 1 and described as newborn infants in Chapter 2 were 2 weeks old when their mothers took them home from the hospital. (Before World War II hospitalization for maternity extended over a longer period than is customary now.) This chapter will focus on Infancy, the first 12 to 15 months of life. During this stage of development human beings can do little for themselves. They must depend on others for nurture and survival. And yet, if all goes well, their helplessness gradually decreases, they pull themselves to standing positions and, as the second year of life rolls around, begin an independent locomotion which takes them out of infancy into the wider world of toddlerhood. Growth, accompanied by increasing complexity in behavior, occurs more rapidly in infancy than in any ensuing period of life.

We closed Chapter 2 with a statement as to the probable importance of infant comfort and contentment. In this chapter we shall consider the factors which seem to contribute to babies' serenity and security and examine their role in personality development. We shall bear in mind the extent to which the experiences each infant has depend on the adaptability and responsiveness of the adults who care for him, especially his mother. Whether he is fed when he is hungry,

The adults in his world contribute to the baby's developing sense of trust.

changed when he is uncomfortably wet, warmed when he is chilly, soothed when he is sleepy, or stimulated when he is bored, depends on his mother's ability to " read " correctly his activities and his cries.

Only through so doing can she adequately meet his needs. Perhaps the most pervasive and certainly the most obvious need in infancy is the need for food. Within the first year the baby customarily triples his birth weight. Small wonder that his small stomach demands frequent fillings, nor that the mother's breast, or its bottle substitute, should loom large in his list of satisfactions. Indeed, many authorities see the infancy period as dominated by these " oral drives." However, as we shall see, satisfactory infant development is dependent on a number of factors in addition to the important one of ready gratification of hunger.

We can imagine some of the excitements of the arrival of our six new babies in their respective homes. All but Pat and Charlie were first babies and so each must have created a very special stir: relatives and neighbors visiting to comment on their resemblances, and prophecy as to their futures; mothers wondering whether they would eat and sleep as well as they did in the hospital; fathers feeling considerable pride in their offspring and at the same time perhaps a little uneasiness in their new roles.

To the extent that the mothers felt comfortable and sure of themselves, and that the fathers were able to contribute their love and assurance to the newly established mother-child pair, we might anticipate that the care of the babies would go smoothly. Under such circumstances we should expect the mothers to find it relatively easy to sensitize themselves to the infants and provide adequately for their needs. But we must not fail to recognize that infant care involves two individuals. The baby, too, assumes an active part in the relationship. In examining the biological aspects of development during infancy, we shall inquire into some of the ways in which the individuality of the baby may manifest itself, as well as into the growth which is to be expected during this period.

BIOLOGICAL ASPECTS OF DEVELOPMENT IN INFANCY

Just as development in the prenatal period follows an orderly process, so postnatal development takes certain customary patterns.

Head raising precedes sitting, sitting comes before standing, standing before walking, and so on. Our knowledge of the sequences of development in infancy is drawn from both intensive studies of small groups of infants, such as those by Buhler [1] and Shirley,[2] and from normative studies, such as those by Bayley [3] and Gesell.[4] Normative studies, as we have indicated previously, establish the age at which a majority of the children studied are able to perform a given function. Relatively few children will fit precisely the average pattern of growth which such studies reveal. Rather, as Gesell has noted, " The growth career of each infant assumes a distinctive pattern. The range of individual differentiation is wide and diverse. Only in extremely similar monozygotic twins do we find a high degree of developmental correspondence between two individuals." [5]

Trends in Infant Development

Although the rate of growth in the first year of life is rapid in comparison to later years, it is decreasing in relation to the prenatal period. Weight at birth for normal full-term infants may vary from 5 to $11\frac{1}{2}$ pounds. By 6 months, the range may be from $11\frac{1}{2}$ to 26 pounds; at 1 year, twenty-five infants in one hundred weigh more than 24 pounds, twenty-five others less than 20 pounds. Body length at birth may measure from $17\frac{1}{2}$ to $22\frac{1}{2}$ inches. About an inch a month is gained from birth to 6 months. At 1 year, the tallest 25 percent measure above $30\frac{1}{2}$ inches and the shortest 25 percent below 29 inches.[6] By 9 months, both boys and girls will have reached half of the sitting height that they will have attained by 17.[7]

Different parts of the body grow at different rates. After eight

---

[1] Buhler, Charlotte. *The First Year of Life.* New York: John Day Company, 1930.

[2] Shirley, Mary. *The First Two Years.* Vols. I, II, III. Minneapolis: University of Minnesota Press, 1933.

[3] Bayley, Nancy. *The Development of Motor Abilities During The First Three Years.* Washington, D.C.: Society for Research in Child Development, National Research Council, Monograph No. 1, 1935.

[4] Gesell, Arnold, and others. *The First Five Years of Life. A Guide to the Study of the Preschool Child.* New York: Harper and Brothers, 1940.

[5] Gesell, Arnold. " The Ontogenesis of Infant Behavior " in *Manual of Child Psychology,* 2d ed., edited by Leonard Carmichael. New York: John Wiley and Sons, 1954. P. 364.

[6] Rand, Winifred, Sweeney, Mary, and Vincent, E. Lee. *Growth and Development of the Young Child.* Philadelphia: W. B. Saunders Company, 1946. P. 117.

[7] *Ibid.* P. 120.

weeks of growth the head and chest regions slow down, and the lower limbs begin to grow somewhat more rapidly. The baby just beginning to walk is still markedly " top heavy." [8]

As we have suggested in Chapter 2, progress toward maturity is better reflected in the growth of the skeletal system than in measure of weight and height. Figure 3 shows graphically skeletal growth

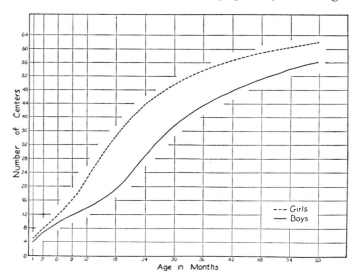

Figure 3. Mean number of ossification centers from birth to 60 months. (*From Sontag, Snell, and Anderson.* American Journal of Diseases of Children. *58[1939], 955. Based on Fels Institute Material.*)

in infancy, in terms of the mean number of ossification centers — areas in which the cartilage and membrane are being replaced by bone.

Studies of roentgenograms (x-rays) of the leg area of children at successive ages show that from birth to 6 months, the most rapid growth rate is in the amount of skin and subcutaneous tissue, but from 6 months on, bone and muscle grow more rapidly. Girls at all ages tend to have a higher percentage of skin and subcutaneous

[8] Thompson, Helen. " Physical Growth " in *Manual of Child Psychology, op. cit.* P. 307.

tissue and a lower percentage of bone and muscle than do boys.[9]

The eruption of the teeth occurs in an expected sequence with most infants, although individuals may differ somewhat in the exact order of tooth eruptions. The timing of the occurrence of successive teeth differs more widely, however, between individuals. Some acquire their first teeth, usually the lower, front, central teeth (incisors) at or before 6 months, while others will not do so until 12 months or later. Infants whose first teeth appear early tend to have all subsequent teeth, both primary and secondary, appear early also. This indicates that an attribute of individuality is that of having teeth erupt early, at an average age, or late.

Motor development. As the baby grows, his behavior becomes more organized and more complex. During the first year of life, at least, the stimulation for the emergence of new skills and abilities seems to come more from within than from without. Thus, the fact that one child may walk when he is 12 months old and another not until 16 months, is attributed to genetic differences rather than to environmental factors. For example, Hopi children, bound to cradle board throughout infancy, have been found to begin walking at about the same time as do children who are not so restrained.[10] However, as we shall see later, severe deprivation, either physical or emotional, may result in retardation.

On the basis of Gesell's findings, these are briefly the developments which we expect to occur in the period of infancy with which we are here concerned:

From being unable to lift his head, or fix his vision in the first week of life, during the *first quarter* (4–16 weeks) of the first year the infant gains control of his twelve oculomotor muscles.

In the *second quarter* (16–28 weeks) he comes into command of the muscles which support his head and move his arms. He reaches out for things.

[9] Stuart, Harold C., and others. " The Growth of Bone, Muscle and Overlying Tissues as Revealed by Studies of Roentgenograms of The Leg Area." *Monographs of the Society for Research in Child Development,* Vol. 5, No. 3, 1940. Pp. 44–45.

[10] Dennis, Wayne, and Dennis, M. G. " The Effect of Cradling Practices Upon the Onset of Walking in Hopi Children." *Journal of Genetic Psychology.* 56 (1940), 77–87.

In the *third quarter* (28–40 weeks) he gains command of his trunk and hands. He sits, he grasps, tranfers and manipulates objects.

In the *fourth quarter* (40–52 weeks) he extends command to his legs and feet; to his forefinger and thumb. He pokes and plucks. He stands upright.[11]

Later in this chapter we shall examine the extent to which the infant's personality development, his ways of perceiving his world and the people in it, his thinking, and his feelings are conditioned by his abilities to bring things into his field of vision, to move out, and to explore.

PROBLEM 1. If possible, observe the repertoire of behavior of an infant whose age you do not know. Can you correctly estimate his age from what he does? Try to observe babies in each of the four quarters of the first year of life. Note their progress toward sitting and walking, the kinds of eye-hand co-ordinations they reveal. What insights do you get as to how the world must appear to them?

PROBLEM 2. If you have an opportunity for recurrent observations of the same baby, keep notes on the progress he makes in eye-hand co-ordination (looking, reaching, grasping, manipulating, poking). Is there evidence that his responses to people parallel this progress?

Some idea of the variations in progress toward walking which may characterize " normal " healthy infants is revealed in the following series of excerpts from the pediatrician's notes regarding some of the infants on whom our interest has been focused.

Three months examination

Celeste — Cannot raise head.

Pat   — Sits, head well up, back convex.

Dan   — Cannot elevate head.

Six months examination

Andrew — Not quite sitting.

Celeste — Sits very straight, but with prominent abdomen (has been propped in high chair for last month).

Charles — Sits with rounded back.

Pat   — Sits.

Dan   — Sits steadily.

[11] Gesell, *op. cit.* P. 339.

Nine months examination
Andrew — Sits, stands, does not crawl.
Celeste — Sits steadily.
Pat   — Not yet standing.
Dan   — Sits steadily, stands steadily, crawls.

Twelve months examination
Andrew — Not quite standing alone, walks with support.
Celeste — Stands unsteadily, walks.
Charles — Walks with support.
Pat   — Stands unsteadily, crawls.
Dan   — Walks without support, unsteadily with a wide base.

Were more complete records available, we should undoubtedly find that these babies differed not only in the ages at which they were able to walk steadily, and in the modes of acquiring the ability, but also in a variety of other ways, probably genetic in origin. Until recently most of the research in infancy as in other stages of development was so focused on the discovery of the " typical " that individual differences tended to be given second consideration, if not overlooked. At present, certain non-normative studies of infant behavior, while not yet definitive, promise to offer some important new insights as to the nature of some basic underlying differences in personality development.

Individuality in Infants

These non-normative studies start from the premise that just as infants differ in size, body type, and rate of growth, so they differ in tempo, rhythm, and sensitivity to various kinds of stimulation. The extent to which these differences are primarily hereditary or conditioned by experiences in utero and during the birth process, or by the emotional states of the infant or his parents, has not been established. But these studies do serve to indicate the nature of infant individuality and suggest some of the reasons why some babies seem to take life so easily, while others find it so burdensome.

Differences in activity. An early study of this kind by Fries and Lewi[12] is concerned with the kind of activity a newborn infant

12 Fries, Margaret, and Lewi, B. "Interrelated Factors in Development." *American Journal of Orthopsychiatry.* 8 (1938), 726–752.

shows in response to certain stimuli. On the basis of observations of motor activity, sleep, and feeding behavior of infants together with their responses in physical and neurological examination, Fries has distinguished three activity types within the normal range. She finds that some infants tend to be quiet, some but moderately active, and some definitely active.

PROBLEM 3. If possible, observe several young infants in similar situations. Compare or contrast their activity. Do their mothers regard them as more or less active than other babies they have known? How do they respond to unexpected sounds, to bright colors, to new tastes, to being held closely? Do their mothers regard them as more or less " sensitive " than other babies they have known?

Much remains to be learned regarding the ways in which the child's activity type may be influential in his personality development. However, it is readily apparent that the very active infant will have somewhat different needs from the placid baby. A mother who is herself inclined to placidity may be overwhelmed by an infant who in a sense is always " on the go." On the other hand, a normally placid baby may seem lethargic to a volatile, high-strung mother. Child-rearing techniques which the parent finds successful with one child may thus be ill-adapted to another.[13]

Differences in sensitivity. Not only do babies appear to differ in characteristic activity, but also in sensitivity to varying kinds of stimuli. One infant becomes apprehensive and upset when he hears a drum for the first time, another responds with apparent interest and pleasure. One restless baby quiets when his blankets are wrapped tightly about him, while another bursts into frantic crying. A mother who finds she must exercise great vigilance to protect her baby from diaper rash notes that her neighbor's baby is never troubled with any skin irritation. All infants tend to be somewhat conservative about tastes which differ markedly from that of milk, but even here individual differences are apparent. One baby accepts without much fuss anything offered him in the guise of food, while the next will

---

[13] The possible effects of activity type in parent-child relationships, ego development and the defense mechanisms are considered at some length in Fries, Margaret, and Woolf, Paul. " Some Hypotheses on the Role of the Congenital Activity Type in Personality Development," in *The Psychoanalytic Study of the Child,* Vol. VIII. New York: International Universities Press, 1953. P. 48.

consume one brand of canned carrots with evident relish, and vigorously reject another brand.

Escalona,[14] who has devoted considerable study to such individual differences in infants, has found that not only is it likely that different babies have very different experiences under identical kinds of stimulation, but also that their ways of reacting to the stress or tension of continuous stimulation, are equally varied. Part of her research, which has been filmed, shows the responses of infants 4½ to 6 months of age to perceptual overstimulation (repeated presentation of such objects as cup, spoon, ball). Some babies react to mounting tension by shifts in posture and movement, others by facial grimaces. Respiration and circulation are affected in some. In others social responsiveness, or the length of the attention span, or the quality of use of the object presented may deteriorate.

Differences in needs for food and rest. Infant individuality, as we might expect, also manifests itself in those important processes which occupy a major part of the infant's time in his first year — eating, sleeping, and eliminating. Had this text been written in the years when our six youngsters were babies, these processes would likely have been singled out for special treatment as " habits " to be acquired through correct training. Research then under way, however, was beginning to point toward what might be called the inherent wisdom of the baby for knowing when he was hungry and how much and what kind of food would satisfy his hunger. Some pediatricians and psychologists wondered whether the baby might not also know something about what sleep habits best fitted him and when he could really comprehend what was expected from him in the way of eliminative control. But a considerable number still subscribed to the idea that if parents could only learn to use the correct techniques, their babies would soon be lapping up all the elements in a prescribed optimum diet, sleeping quietly through the night, and using a " toidy " chair at least as early as 6 months.

Current thinking on these matters does not neglect the importance of the parents' methods for socializing the baby, but sees the

[14] *Eight Infants: Tension Manifestations in Response to Perceptual Overstimulation.* New York: New York University Film Library. Also: Leitch, Mary, and Escalona, Sibylle. " The Reaction of Infants to Stress " in *The Psychoanalytic Study of the Child,* Vol. III/IV, *op. cit.,* 1949. Pp. 121–140.

success of any technique as depending in part on its appropriateness to a particular infant and his stage of development.

In the next section we shall consider eating, sleeping, and elimination from the standpoint of the infant's basic equipment for these functions.

Eating, Sleeping, and Elimination

One of the major differences between prenatal and postnatal existence is that as an independent human being the infant must ingest and digest his own food, where previously those processes were carried on by the mother. Although immature, his digestive system is in working order at birth. He feels the pangs of hunger, but it will be some time before he will associate those feelings with the satisfaction of eating. (At about 4 months many babies will quiet at the sight of the bottle.) His mouth structure appears well adapted to taking in food by sucking, but his swallowing apparatus functions only involuntarily. Not until he is several months old, is he able to swallow food unless it is placed in the back of his mouth.

Learning to eat. The supposedly simple and satisfying processes of sucking and swallowing may present real complexities to some babies, even those who are healthy and adequately cared for. Escalona describes their difficulties vividly.

There are those . . . as late as four weeks and beyond, who take the nipple and begin to suck, but respiration is still dominated by the crying pattern and either one of two things happen. If the milk flows freely, they choke and have to be taken off the breast until they recover. If milk does not flow except as it is pumped out through the sucking motion, the baby gets nothing and cries and wriggles about at the breast.

. . . A large proportion of babies are not fully capable of the integrated motions that go into sucking. They nurse by fits and starts, now clamping down so tight that nothing comes, now failing to swallow so that the mouth fills to overflowing, opens, the nipple is lost, and the milk runs down their necks; failing to coordinate swallowing and breathing, the fluid goes down the trachea and they choke, cough, sneeze and gasp.[15]

[15] Escalona, Sibylle. "Emotional Development in the First Year of Life," in *Problems of Infancy and Childhood,* edited by Milton Senn. New York: Josiah Macy, Jr. Foundation, 1953. Pp. 13, 14.

Not only do babies differ in their ways of getting food, but also in their ways of passing it along the digestive tract. According to findings revealed by Rand, Sweeney, and Vincent, the range of time for passage through the gastro-intestinal tract is from four to twenty-eight hours. The average for breast-fed babies is fifteen hours and slightly longer for the bottle-fed.[16]

Most newborn babies learn to take milk and water without difficulty quite quickly and when this is accomplished they usually tolerate orange juice and some form of Vitamin D, in addition to the basic diet of milk. Soon thereafter, soft cereals and pureed vegetables and fruits are usually acceptable, customarily being introduced gradually some time between 3 and 6 months of age. Foods which require mastication, that is " chewier " foods in chopped form, are not well handled until some months later.

Considering that infants of the same size, age, and activity type may differ in sucking and swallowing abilities, in the complexity of food they can tolerate, in the length of time digestion takes, and probably in many other different ways, we should expect that their food requirements would also vary. That this in fact is the case, has been substantiated by the work of Davis who found that even fairly young infants can, when given an adequate variety of natural foods to choose from, select a diet that is adequate and optimum for their nutritional needs.[17]

The nutritional outcome of the study was of course dependent on the fact that the foods offered the children were such as to supply all the requirements needed for growth. In no way does the study minimize the importance of adequate dietary provisions.

PROBLEM 4. A report of Clara Davis' experiments is included in *Readings in Child Development* **by Martin and Stendler, pages 69–74. Plan for a member of your class to review this article. Discuss its implications for the feeding of infants. How would you interpret the findings to parents?**

The following selected notes from the pediatrician's records on two of our babies are indicative of some of the variations in eating pat-

[16] Rand, Winifred, and others. *Growth and Development of the Young Child.* New York: W. B. Saunders Company, 1946. Pp. 166–169.

[17] Davis, Clara. " Self-Selection of Diet by Newly Weaned Infants." *American Journal Diseases of Children.* 36 (1928), 65–79.

terns which may arise. It should be noted that both mothers had been urged to feed their babies on a regular schedule, and that early weaning (certainly in the first year) was customarily recommended at that time.

Jane

22 days	— Breast fed every 4 hours. Takes 25 minutes. Seems satisfied, sleeps through.
5 weeks	— Mother thinks baby is uncomfortable as she squirms after each nursing for 15 minutes.
7 weeks	— 2 a.m. feeding omitted.
3 months	— Mother wants to wean baby.
4 months	— Bottle feeding supplement begun. Baby only satisfied with 6 a.m. feeding.
6 months	— Does not always take full amount of formula.
7 months	— Getting 24 ounces of milk, but has little appetite for it. Taking cereal, vegetable, potato and fruit pulp, egg yolk.
8 months	— On three meals a day.
9 months	— Satisfactory.
1 year	— Appetite good.

Andy

5 weeks	— Breast feedings, every 4 hours, 10 minutes at each breast. Spits up a great deal.
7 weeks	— Doing well with breast plus complementary feeding.
8 weeks	— Fussy. Cries almost constantly in day time.
3 months	— Now taking breast satisfactorily, but does not seem satisfied.
3½ months	— Baby fights breasts and sometimes vomits after trying to nurse. Never seems satisfied even after complementary feeding. Spits cod-liver oil if more than 1 teaspoon given. Also spits orange juice. Weaned from breast.
5 months	— Eats hungrily.
6 months	— Eating everything well and is happy. Start vegetables.
9 months	— Eating well.

PROBLEM 5. From the material on these children and their parents in the preceding sections, can you recall anything which might suggest reasons for the slight difficulties presented here? Can you think of important factors which have not been mentioned?

Sleeping. Shortly after the period in which our babies had been learning to adjust themselves to prescribed four hour schedules, research by Gesell and Ilg [18] suggested the feasibility of feeding babies on " demand " schedules. The findings indicated that infants fed as often as their restlessness or crying suggested they were hungry and who were allowed to take as much or as little as they chose, developed as well as or better than babies fed on a rigid schedule.

We shall postpone for later consideration the question of the baby's feelings about being made the arbiter of his own feedings, and its possible effect on his personality. We are rather concerned here with the establishment of his capabilities and his unique qualities.

Sleeping patterns are closely related to eating patterns, particularly in the first months of life. The infant wakes to eat, eats, and then sleeps again. Gradually, however, the length of time he can go comfortably between feedings begins to increase, he sleeps through the night and starts to have longer waking periods in the day. Not too much is known about the mechanism of sleep, but it appears to be a function which undergoes developmental changes. Gesell and Ilg [19] distinguish three phases to the sleep cycle: going to sleep, staying asleep, and awakening. Not until 16 weeks or so does the infant's " waking mechanism," dependent upon development of some of the higher nerve centers of the brain, begin to operate smoothly. Just as he learns to waken by choice, so he must learn to release into sleep. Gesell and Ilg suggest that sleeping difficulties may be accentuated by the stimulation of modern culture. However, they especially stress the fact that the infant's nervous system is not complex enough for complete voluntary control until well after 15 months.

The individual variations in sleep patterns are wide. Some babies, as their parents say despairingly, seem to insist on turning night into day. Some require considerably less sleep than others. They are not necessarily less healthy or less happy, but have rather developed a pattern unique to them. Some babies, on the other hand, reveal in

[18] Gesell, Arnold, and Ilg, Frances. *The Feeding Behavior of Infants.* Philadelphia: J. B. Lippincott Company, 1937.

[19] Gesell, Arnold, and Ilg, Frances. *Infant and Child in the Culture of Today.* New York: Harper and Brothers, 1943. Pp. 301–310.

their wakefulness a sensitivity to tension and a kind of anxiety, the source of which is sometimes difficult to locate.

Elimination. Voluntary eliminative control, like the control of sleeping and waking, also appears to be dependent on the development of fairly complex mental processes. Some babies tend to have such regular bowel movements that an alert parent can " catch " them at the appropriate moments. This gives the illusion that the baby is " trained," but it is not until the reflex mechanism of defecation comes under cerebral control that a habit is really formed. Voluntary control of urination usually comes somewhat later than bowel control. Although the variation from child to child is wide, it appears likely that both of these functions are likely to remain on an involuntary basis throughout the first year of life.

PROBLEM 6. A study by Myrtle McGraw, " Neural Maturation as Exemplified by the Achievement of Bladder Control," describes the phases in the attainment of bladder control. This study is reported in *Readings in Child Psychology,* edited by Dennis (pp. 180–190). Review this study and discuss how its results might be interpreted to parents.

PROBLEM 7. Following is an excerpt from the records on Jane Warner

> 6 months — Bowels regular, one movement a day. Mother starting to train to nursery chair.
>
> 7 months — Is trained to use toilet chair. Mother used suppository for four mornings before placing on chair and leaving alone. For a week or more she has had a bowel movement (without the use of a suppository) following the morning feeding.

Evaluate this statement in the light of your present understanding of the acquisition of voluntary control. Do you think this early regularization of Jane's habits would have beneficial, detrimental, or neutral effects on personality development? Why?

PROBLEM 8. Plan with your classmates to pool as much information as you can get about the eating, sleeping, and eliminative habits of infants of your acquaintance. If possible, interview mothers and observe babies to obtain answers to such questions as what kinds of feeding schedules are maintained for babies of 3, 6, 9, 12, and 15 months; what foods are relished and which disliked; what are babies' customary sleeping and waking times at these ages; what sleep difficulties are encountered; what regularities in eliminative functions have been noted; what attempts at training, if any, have been made.

Significance of Biological Aspects of Development in Infancy

At no other period in life, it seems, is the individual's ability to cope with his world, to feel, to think, to act, so much determined by his physical and motor development. At no other period is the increase in complexity more rapid or more obvious, and yet, as we have seen, Nature sets some rather definite limits to what the infant can do. Sometimes, however, it is difficult to be sure of how these limits operate, for even the very young human organism shows a remarkable adaptability. The 6 months' infant can grab a spoon (or chopsticks!), but his motor co-ordinations are still so inept that, unless there's an adult about to see that the food thereon gets into his mouth, he may well starve in the midst of plenty. But it makes little difference to him whether the food that does come is spooned from a can, or prechewed in his mother's mouth. If he's an Otomi Indian he'll probably accept a *tortilla* more readily than a cracker. (How well nourished he may be will, of course, depend on his total diet.) He may be fed every time he cries, or only three or four times a day, and still survive. He may be breast-fed to 2, 3, or even 5 years of age, or he may be cup-fed from a few days after birth.

We have good reasons to believe that certain kinds of experience (feeding on a rigid schedule and early weaning for example) may make demands on the infant's biological economy which are detrimental to his optimum development, but much more evidence is needed. We do not know the extent to which some babies may be more resilient than others. We know very little about how it feels to be a baby and extraordinarily little about how he learns and adapts to adult expectations for him.

SOCIAL FACTORS IN INFANCY

To a certain extent the biology of the infant determines the expectations that are set for him. Whiting and Child say:

Child training the world over is in certain important respects identical. It is identical in that it is found always to be concerned with certain universal problems of behavior. . . . In all societies the helpless infant, getting his food by nursing at his mother's breast and having digested it, freely evacuating the waste products, exploring his genitals, biting and kicking at will, must be changed into a responsible adult obeying the rules of society. . . . Child training everywhere seems to be in considerable part concerned with problems which arise from universal characteristics of the human infant and from universal characteristics of adult culture which are incompatible with the continuation of infantile behavior.[20]

Child-rearing Practices

Despite the similarities in infant needs, ways of meeting them vary widely. Each adult who cares for a child has himself been brought up in a group of people sharing a common way of life which to some extent prescribes what his child-rearing techniques and attitudes shall be. Thus, in one primitive society (the Chenchu tribe of India) custom dictates the nursing of children until the age of 5 or 6, while in another (the Marquesans) weaning before the age of 1 year is the accepted pattern.[21] In relatively simple societies few individuals are likely to attempt to change the customary way of doing things, for they will have had no other models from which to learn. In complex societies, such as ours, the choices are considerably wider. Today's young mother, if she follows the example set by *her* mother, will likely put her baby on a definite three- or four-hour bottle-feeding schedule. Yet her pediatrician may incline toward a flexible schedule, and recommend breast feeding, while her best friend has been bringing up her babies completely "self-demand." However, this apparent freedom of choice does not extend so far as we might at first think. No sane American mother is likely to consider disposing of her first baby because it turns out to be a girl, or binding her feet to keep them from growing, nor will she be willing to turn her baby over to a nurse for strengthening, even though all of these practices have at one time or another been completely acceptable in certain civilized societies. It is almost as unlikely that she will contemplate carrying her baby about in a sling (though a few mothers of conviction have done so), completely dispensing with crib, carriage, and high chair. Each of these possi-

[20] Whiting, John W. M., and Child, Irvin L. *Child Training and Personality: A Cross-Cultural Study.* New Haven: Yale University Press, 1953. Pp. 63–64.
[21] *Ibid.* Pp. 69–71.

bilities in some way or other goes against the traditions, the ways of thinking, the standards, and the values of the "typical" American woman.

Child-rearing practices are part of the total pattern of custom of the group of which the parent is a member, and in which he himself has been socialized. Anthropological studies have indicated that the individuals in any culture tend to share many personality characteristics. Those common elements form what may be regarded as a basic personality type for the culture. The culture's child-rearing practices tend to reflect the attitudes of this typical personality structure.[22] At the same time they seem to communicate such attitudes to the child so that he early begins to learn those the adult has already learned.[23]

PROBLEM 9. Some of the issues relating to the possible effects of child-rearing practices have been reviewed in a critical article by Orlansky. An abridgment of this may be found in *Readings in Child Development* edited by Martin and Stendler (pp. 321–334). Plan for several members of your class to review and discuss this article.

We cannot expect any one-to-one relationship between a particular child-rearing practice and adult personality development. The child's initial learning in relation to a particular procedure may be modified by his later experience. However, we can be sure that the early training the child receives does effect his personality, both as an infant and as he grows up. We shall find it profitable to consider some of the more usual variations in child care. In this chapter we shall concern ourselves particularly with the infancy period. According to a scheme of analysis employed by Whiting and Child in their study of *Child Training and Personality* there are five systems of behavior which occur and are subject to socialization in all societies. A system of behavior is defined as a " set of habits or customs motivated by a common drive and leading to common satis-

[22] Kardiner, Abram, and others. *The Psychological Frontiers of Society*. New York: Columbia University Press, 1945. Pp. 1–46. See also: Linton, Ralph. *The Cultural Background of Personality*. New York: D. Appleton-Century Company, 1945. Especially pp. 125–153.

[23] Mead, Margaret, " National Character," in *Anthropology Today*, edited by Kroeber. Chicago: University of Chicago Press, 1953. Pp. 644, 645.

factions." The first three of these systems — *oral, anal,* and *sexual* — are presumed to be motivated by the primary or innate drives of hunger, elimination, and sex. The fourth and fifth systems — *dependence* and *aggression* — are motivated by drives which are probably acquired rather than innate. The dependence system arises out of the fact that some degree of care and nurture is experienced by and comes to be desired by every human being. The aggression system also appears to develop out of experience. The individual learns, as it were, to want to assert himself, his needs, and his demands.

Whiting and Child suggest that

No child can grow up completely without frustration, and aggression is very likely to occur as a response to frustration. Moreover, parents and others, with whom a child interacts, are very likely in any society to comply with a child's aggressive demands at least part of the time. Therefore, we expect aggression to " pay off " to some extent in all societies and hence become learned as a drive.[24]

Child-rearing practices in relation to each of these systems of behavior may be studied from the standpoint of the extent to which they permit the child initial indulgence, the age at which they begin to expect socialization, and the severity with which they impose it.[25] We may ask, are the child's primitive impulses in this area allowed free rein? Is the expression of these impulses encouraged, tolerated, or ignored? How old is he when he is expected to begin to check or reorganize them? Are new patterns to be learned gradually or all at once? Are the old behaviors punished and how severely? Are the new behaviors rewarded and in what fashion?

In this chapter we shall devote most of our consideration to socialization of the oral and dependence systems, giving briefer attention to the others. We shall describe some of the patterns which may be found in families in the United States.

Expectations for the feeding of babies. Traditionally, few Americans have regarded themselves as epicures. They enjoy a " good " meal, and on occasion they may linger over its courses, but unlike some other nationalities (the French, for example) they do not center their activities around the pleasures of the palate. Food (and

---

[24] Whiting and Child, *op. cit.* Pp. 45, 46.   [25] *Ibid.* Pp. 67, 68.

drink) is an important accompaniment to conviviality, but not an end in itself. It is primarily valued for its health and energy-giving qualities. The food pages in the most popular women's magazines are directed much more to the improvement of family nutrition than to the creation of exotic dishes or new taste sensations. While these pages, of course, do not condition the character of American food habits, they do reflect an important American value, namely a practical interest in matters scientific. Along with this goes a willingness to accept and try anything which seems likely to make for greater efficiency. To some extent American attitudes toward food also reveal a lingering trace of early puritanism, which tended to regard as sinful all the pleasures of the flesh.

From these points of view feeding the baby becomes primarily a matter of seeing that he stows away whatever foods are currently recommended as insuring him optimum growth and development. The idea that the process should also afford the baby sensory and visceral satisfaction seems relatively new. It is also one which is likely to create some uneasiness among individuals who hold traditional attitudes toward food. Every mother, depending on the attitudes of her particular cultural group, contemplates feeding her baby with certain preconceived notions about food and its significance in life. These to some extent influence both the feeding techniques she chooses and the way she uses them.

Some evidence of how expectations for feeding behavior in the United States compare with those in other societies can be drawn from the Whiting and Child [26] study to which we have previously referred. The nursing and weaning procedures reported in a group of middle-class families were compared with those in fifty-two primitive societies. All the societies but one gave their babies more initial indulgence than the American group. Babies in the American group were also weaned earlier than in all of the other groups but one. The severity of the weaning process was also greater for American babies, than for the majority of other societies. Our concern here is with the fact that early socialization procedures differ from one society to another. The effect of such differences on personality development will of course depend on what happens to the infant

[26] Whiting and Child, *op. cit.* Pp. 69–73.

later and in other areas of his living. Unfortunately comparisons with societies as complex as our own are not available.

The United States is, of course, much too large a country with too many culture groups for us to assume that the attitudes toward food we have so far described are the only ones prevalent. Over the years a number of studies have explored the diversity of customs in various groups in the United States. Some have focused on groups newly arrived in this country. Some have dealt with slum dwellers, others with farming people, miners, mountaineers. Recently much research has explored the hypothesis that the customs adhered to by the individuals and their families tend to resemble each other most when they have similar socio-economic status. According to this thinking, the American social structure is being increasingly stratified into differing social classes. The lines between classes are far from fixed, and the criteria for establishing an individual's class membership are not the same in all studies. Although they may be further subdivided, at least two major classes are usually found. The most influential is the middle class, in which the majority of the families enjoy relative economic security, have some recognition in the wider community, and belong to organizations which receive public notice. The lower class, in contrast, tends to be harassed by economic insecurity, to live in neighborhoods lacking in recognition in the large community, and to belong to relatively few groups other than churches and labor unions.[27]

We can anticipate that the baby born into a home where it is not always certain where the next meal may be coming from, where brothers and sisters are clamoring for whatever food is to be had, and where there is no attendant ritual of place settings and courses, may have very different feeding experiences from the baby born into a middle-class home. How the important differences can best be measured is less clear.

An early study by Davis and Havighurst [28] found that lower-class

[27] Kluckhohn, Clyde, and Kluckhohn, Florence. "American Culture: Generalized Orientation and Class Patterns," in Conference on Science, Philosophy and Religion, Conflict of Power in Modern Culture, edited by Bryson, Lyman, and others. New York: Harper and Brothers, 1947. Pp. 106–129.

[28] Davis, Allison, and Havighurst, Robert J. "Social Class and Color Differences in Child-Bearing." American Sociological Review. 11 (1946), 698–710.

mothers tended to be more indulgent in offering children opportunities for oral satisfaction than are middle-class mothers. More lower-class children were breast-fed only, were fed at will rather than on schedule, and were permitted to suck longer than twelve months. On the other hand, middle-class children were more often held while they were being fed.

In contrast to these findings, a more recent study reports few differences between the classes in infant-feeding practices. Both groups modified feeding times to fit the infant's hunger, neither weaned abruptly, both made the transition from sucking to drinking gradually, and neither pressed the child greatly to give up sucking.[29]

PROBLEM 10. Plan for several members of your class to review the articles suggested above. Discuss the possible reasons for the discrepancy in findings. What is the significance, for the student of child development, of studies which present contradictory evidences?

In child-rearing areas other than feeding, more consistent differences have been found, as we shall see. So far as feeding is concerned, however, it appears that establishing a mother's socio-economic status is not going to tell us too much about her expectations for her baby. Before we shall be able to judge that she is permitting him genuine indulgence of his oral impulses, we shall need to see how the mother handles the baby's first attempts at grasping the nipple; whether she helps him to a mutually comfortable position for nursing, fusses over or ignores his ineptness; whether she regards his lusty sucking as delightful or disgusting, his turning away while breast or bottle is still full as evidence of satiation or a personal affront. We shall need to know not only *when* she weans him from breast or bottle, but how. Does she anticipate his readiness for cup and spoon so that they replace the breast or bottle gradually, or does she make the transition abruptly? Does she perhaps postpone the transition, enjoying, as it were, his extended babyhood? Whatever she does, is it with a sense of inner conviction and rightness, or is she merely playing her mother role according to the rules-of-

[29] Maccoby, Eleanor F., Gibbs, Patricia K., and others. "Methods of Child-Bearing in Two Social Classes," in *Readings in Child Development*, edited by Martin and Stendler. New York: Harcourt, Brace and Company, 1954. Pp. 380–396.

the-game established by her neighborhood, or her crowd, or her mother-in-law?

It is our conviction, the basis of which we shall delineate further when we discuss psychodynamic factors in infancy, that the important element in socialization may not be the particular technique the adult uses, but rather his intent. The apparently identical technique may have quite different results when used by a mother whose relationship with her child is characterized by warmth and love or by one whose feelings are predominantly hostile.

Expectations for eliminative control in infancy. As we have indicated, voluntary eliminative control is not usually attained until the second year of life. Nevertheless, in the United States toilet training is often begun before the baby's first birthday. Such early training, particularly when relationships between parent and child are already difficult, may have an adverse effect on personality development. However, since it is not until the second year of life that the baby's eliminative processes apparently become meaningful to him, we shall give most consideration of this aspect of socialization in the next chapter, devoted to the toddler. In the Whiting and Child study [30] American middle-class children were rated as being trained earlier than all but one of the primitive groups.

Expectations regarding sexuality in infancy. The first year of life may be regarded as a period of self discovery. The baby "finds" his fingers, his toes, *and* his genitals. Early in this year, the boy baby may have experienced erection of the penis. That he attaches any special significance to these experiences, is quite unlikely. However, if the adult who cares for him has strong feelings about such activity, the situation may be considerably altered. Except among lower-class groups there appears to be a trend today toward overt acceptance of baby manifestations of genital interests as normal and natural. Mothers who feel uneasy about them are advised to distract the baby's attention with a toy. Whether this device may not still convey the mother's negative feelings to the child is an open question. The problem is, however, considerably less acute during the infancy period when the infant is less capable of attaching a specific meaning to the mother's attitude than he will be later on. In the third or

[30] Whiting and Child, *op. cit.* P. 7.

fourth year of life his emotional investment in matters relating to his genitals is apt to be marked. Consequently, we shall consider socialization of sexual behavior at length in the chapter on the power-testing period.

Expectations regarding dependence. To what extent is the infant nurtured and protected, to what extent is he left to his own devices? In the United States the range of practice is wide. Most commonly the baby's own mother is the one who cares for him — feeding, changing, bathing, playing with him, and putting him to bed. With one mother this may occupy the major part of her time. Each phase of the routine becomes an elaborate ritual of affection and tenderness. Another spends the same time, goes through the same motions, but with little of the spontaneous warmth of the first. Still a third accomplishes the same results, but in half as many hours. One investigates every whimper and move, another usually waits for what she terms the " three-bell alarm." Many mothers have other children and other duties. An unknown number of women with small babies work outside their own homes, leaving them with relatives or neighbors or in foster homes. In rural areas and migrant work camps even small babies may be taken into the fields to be cared for by a small brother or sister or just left to wait while mother helps with hay or picks beans. Professional health and welfare workers for a variety of reasons do not favor the employment of mothers of children under two years. (See pages 188–189.) Nevertheless, in 1951, 16 percent of all women in the United States who had children under the age of 6 were employed.[31] The likelihood that many of these children are less than 2 is very great.

In contrast, there are the women at the other end of the economic scale, whose separation from their babies is a matter of custom — those who employ a full-time baby nurse. This is perhaps less common here than in privileged groups abroad, but numbers of youngsters are so brought up.

Some mothers engage baby " sitters " frequently to look after the infant while they shop or play bridge. Some regard the " sitter " as a necessity of life, others as a luxury. Some insist on having the

---

[31] Women's Bureau, U. S. Department of Labor. *Handbook of Facts on Women Workers.* Bulletin No. 242. Washington, D.C., 1952. P. 21.

same person each time, others settle for the first available teen-ager, or take whatever middle-aged woman an employment agency sends. In contrast, some parents rarely, if ever, employ a sitter, nor do they greatly alter their leisure pursuits even when the infant is very small. Rather the baby goes perhaps in a basket, perhaps in arms, wherever they go. This pattern, characteristic in rural areas, was observed on college campuses following World War II and persists in many suburban sections where most of the families are young.

Just as babies may have nurturing experiences differing widely both in amount and quality, so they may be encouraged toward, pushed into, or hampered from exercising the independence of which they may be capable. Americans probably tend to value manifestations of independence rather highly. For example, in comparison with the other cultures in the Whiting and Child study,[32] the American middle-class group was found to start independence training earlier than some other groups. Further we may note the pride which so frequently attaches to the fact that a particular baby at an early age sits *by himself,* or *wants to feed himself.* Some observers have seen a tendency to urge the baby on, to put, as it were, the responsibility for feeding on him, in the phrase so frequently used by mothers to the infant, even in the lying-in period — " Come on." [33]

The major struggles toward independence, the point at which the baby's growing abilities make a considerable degree of separate activity possible, are, however, not arrived at until walking is attained. They seem to dominate the period of toddlerhood, become somewhat less acute during the ensuing years of childhood, and are reinstated in new form in adolescence.

Expectations regarding aggression in infancy. Whether one defines aggression in terms of reaction to the frustration involved in failure to obtain a needed satisfaction, or more broadly in terms of assertion and demand, it is evident that some of the behavior of the infant takes on qualities of aggression. Whiting and Child [34] in their study of cultural differences in the treatment of aggression, focused on five aspects: temper tantrums, physical aggression, verbal aggres-

---

[32] Whiting and Child, *op. cit.* P. 97.
[33] Henry, Jules, and Bogg, Joan. " Child-Bearing, Culture and the Natural World," *Psychiatry.* 15 (1952), 1261–71.
[34] Whiting and Child, *op. cit.* Pp. 98, 99.

sion, property damage, and disobedience. They found that the attitude of a society toward aggression appeared to be continuous, not varying much with the age of the child.

It appears likely, however, that there are differences in the meaning which adults attach to aggressive behavior at different stages of development. Thus, a temper tantrum in a 9 months' infant may be regarded with more equanimity than one occurring in a 3-year-old. Studies of children's anger outbursts indicate that they both increase in number and change in character throughout the preschool years.[35] This points to increasing assertiveness on the part of the child and corresponding restriction on the part of the adult. Adult concern for the control of aggression, at least in middle-class American homes, is probably not nearly so great in infancy as in the toddlerhood and power-testing periods. Little evidence is available on this.

Following are some notes made regarding our six babies during their infancy.

Jane
    3 months — Mother notices baby sucks thumb after some feedings, removes it.
    7 months — Mrs. W. gives excellent care to child. Subscribes to Parents Magazine, reads it from cover to cover.
              Baby is sucking thumb a good bit.

Pat
    15 months — Mother comments on enthusiasm of all the relatives for baby. Both those who live with them and those who live in the neighborhood adore her. She has never lacked for company or someone to play with her when she is awake.

Andy
    9 months — Mrs. D. comments that Andy eats and sleeps well. Has a room by himself. Not yet toilet trained.

Dan
    12 months — Mrs. M. is pleased that D. is getting along so well now. The first few months he cried a lot, but now he seems happy and is very active.

[35] Goodenough, F. L. *Anger in Young Children*. Minneapolis: University of Minnesota Press, 1931.

Charlie

12 months — Mrs. B. talks a good bit about the differences between Charlie and Chet. Charlie is not so husky, but he is more active.

Celeste

12 months — This year has been a difficult one for the Collins family. Mr. C.'s hours of work have been cut. Mrs. C. would like to find employment, but so far has not been successful.

PROBLEM 11. Each of the above comments gives some clue as to the nature of the social environment each of these babies has. Discuss the implications of each statement in relation to the child-rearing techniques likely to be employed by the parents. What additional information would you like to have?

Significance of social factors in infancy. From the moment of birth, the infant is cared for and responds to other human beings who have acquired certain accustomed ways of feeling, thinking, and acting. As they handle him, feed, bathe, and protect him, talk to or about him, indulge or deprive him, they are teaching him in the most elementary way to be a human being like themselves. It will be several years before he will have learned their customs relating to food and to elimination, longer before he takes on all their patterns of sex expression and finally becomes not merely an independent person, but one capable of both asserting and maintaining himself, and nurturing a new generation. Nevertheless, the important process of socialization has begun.

Having considered the pressures of growth, of impulse and drive which characterize the infant as a biological organism, and the kinds of social expectations which are set for him, we shall now turn, as it were, to view him from within.

PSYCHODYNAMIC FACTORS IN DEVELOPMENT

How can we hope to know the baby's inner experience? He has no words to tell us of the sensations coming to him from within or without. We can try to feel as we think he may, but when we do so, it is with a nervous system so very much more complex than his that it is doubtful whether we can even approximate his state of mind. Further, we bring to the attempt so many meanings from our own years of living that we are prone to create images that represent our own wishes and desires more than the impressions of the newborn.

These are very real hazards, so great that until recently most infant psychology consisted of attempts at accurate and detailed descriptions of behavior and the conditions under which it arose without much attempt to infer its significance for the infant. Several influences have combined to shift this emphasis. Of special importance is psychoanalysis. Within the psychoanalytic field there has been increasing interest not only in amplifying and developing theory, but also in verifying it through wider observation than is possible in the clinical setting. A good bit of research into the nature of infantile experience (and its effects on later development) has also been carried on by nonanalytically oriented psychologists in order to test analytic theories. Progress in pediatrics and public health (which has advanced to the point where most of the dread diseases of infancy are now well under control) has also freed some of the researches in those areas to study infancy from a new point of view.

We lack neither justification for an attempt to explore the inner world of the infant, nor material on which we can draw. Unfortunately the latter is not of a nature that we can know that the inferences we make are necessarily correct. It can, however, make us more alert to the possible meanings of the infant's behavior, and perhaps make us more understanding of it.

Earlier we set forth the idea that as the individual grows, he develops a control system — a means of organizing and scheduling his behavior. He attaches meanings to the sensations coming to him from within and from without. He thinks, calling to memory events that have occurred previously, and anticipating coming experience. He acts, chooses to do one thing and not another. In short, he has a conscious awareness of his own functioning. The question of how and when this occurs is fundamental to our understanding of the inner world of the infant. In the following section we shall consider what the process may be, keeping in mind that because experimentation is still limited to a large extent, we can only surmise.

The Beginnings of Awareness

Now, with due concern not to read into the situation more than an immature organism can experience, we shall try to think what it feels like to be a baby of, say, 4 weeks or less. Much of the time his existence can only be characterized as vegetative. But it is punctuated by sensation, vague, undefined and probably largely undifferentiated.

Light and darkness; harshness and softness; cold and warmth; sleep and waking; the contours of mother's face as seen from below, vis-à-vis or even from above; being grasped and released; being moved and moving; the sight of moving people, curtains, blankets, toys; all these recede and approach and comprise the totality of experience in whatever constellation they occur at each split second in time.[36]

We must think of the baby at this point as a creature without time, for at this stage of his development each hunger pang, each swallow of milk are likely experiences without relation to each other. There is as yet no *outside-me* or *inside-me,* indeed no *me* at all. Yet in some as yet undefined way the sensations he has may be affecting the neurophysiological structure which underlies his perceptual capacities.[37] If this is indeed the case, then we can imagine that the child who has, say, an unusually sensitive skin surface and is also roughly handled as he is bathed, clothed, and held may, even in these very early weeks, be developing neural connections of a sort which will influence his later perception and learning in areas having some connection with skin sensitivity. This is of course still largely a matter of conjecture, and undoubtedly difficult to establish.

Changes in behavior. Under what circumstances are these vague, unrelated sensations differentiated into " from within," " from without," " before," and " after "? Although we do not know the exact nature of the process, shifts in the baby's behavior may suggest some of the changes which occur. For example, Buhler [38] found that by the third month babies responded to grown ups with a smile.

---

[36] Escalona, *op. cit.* P. 25.
[37] This possibility seems to be implied in theories developed in Hebb, D. O. *The Organization of Behavior.* New York: John Wiley and Sons, 1949.
[38] Buhler, *op. cit.* P. 56.

Spitz,[39] in an attempt to determine whether the baby could differentiate between the face of a human being and something resembling it in configuration and movement, presented infants with masks depicting various expressions. He noted that the point at which the infant appeared to discriminate in this fashion came sometime between the third and the sixth month.

Another observable change in behavior occurs in the baby's response to his own hands and to objects put into them. As his vision reaches sufficient maturity so that he sees small objects, and as his motor co-ordinations become more sure, during the period from 16 to 28 weeks, his behavior begins to look more directed and purposeful. Whether or not he yet associates changes in the outer world (the disappearance and reappearance of his rattle, for example) with his own manipulations of it, is not certain. But it seems likely that out of many similar instances some sense of *me* and *not-me* may begin to arise.

Important as the maturation of sensory and motor equipment is to the baby's ability to discriminate between an outer and an inner world, the relevance of another factor should not be overlooked. This is the influence of the human nurture the baby receives. We have earlier indicated how this may vary in kind and quality, but we have not discussed its significance in the mental life of the infant.

Discrimination between the *me* and *not-me* may be facilitated or hampered, depending on the extent to which the care the baby receives is consistent and, in a sense, predictable. According to Escalona,

> Other things being equal, those babies whose experience has a definite rhythm and sameness to it especially with respect to vital situations such as feeding and bathing may somewhat earlier and somewhat more easily acquire a sense of themselves as entities to whom things happen and who can make things happen.[40]

Still within the area of speculation, we may consider the possibility that the mother's play with the baby (the endless variations of "peek-a-boo," for example) serve in a sense to stimulate and

[39] Spitz, René. "The Smiling Response." *Genetic Psychology Monographs,* 34 Vol. 6, 1946. Pp. 57–125.
[40] Escalona, *op. cit.* P. 26.

strengthen the baby's dawning awareness of a continuity of *me* and discontinuity of *non-me*.

Anna Freud describes the infant's progress toward such differentiation in somewhat different terms.

The inner world of the infant in the first days and weeks of life consists essentially of the two contrasting feelings of the pleasure-pain series, . . . pain arises under the impact of body need (or irritation from outside), pleasure when the need is satisfied (or the irritants removed).[41]

Gradually the infant learns the objects which bring pleasure. When he is hungry, a " mental picture " of the mother, the milk, the breast, or the bottle will arise. Having so often experienced that the actual appearance of these has put an end to his hunger, the infant expects " his own mental image " to produce a similar result. Such an hallucination, however, brings no relief. Not until the real object has appeared, does satisfaction occur. It is thus that the infant " learns to distinguish between an inner image and the perception of a person in the outside world."

This differentiation is not made once and for all. Anna Freud cautions:

While the observer sees the infant as a separate entity, he has to realize that the infant himself has as yet no correct conception of where he himself ends and the environment begins.

She goes on to speculate on the development of the infant " self."

When constructing inwardly a first picture of his own self, the infant . . . takes as being part of himself whatever feels nice, satisfying, pleasurable, and rejects as not belonging to himself whatever is painful and disagreeable. According to this infantile form of discrimination, the mother, being " nice," is regarded by the infant as an important part of himself. . . . Only through the painful experience of losing his mother periodically does the child learn very gradually in the course of the first year that the big pleasure-self he has constructed in his mind is not all his own. . . . The observer can watch the infant for increasing signs that he is learning to recognize the true extent and limits of his own body. Actually, the first inside picture which the human individual has of himself is an image of his body. While adults think in terms of a " self," infants think, or rather feel, in terms of body.[42]

[41] Freud, Anna. " Some Remarks on Infant Observation," *The Psychoanalytic Study of the Child*, Vol. VIII, *op. cit.* P. 12.

[42] *Ibid.* P. 13.

PROBLEM 12. As you observe infants of different ages, note whether or not they seem to have awareness of the limits of their own bodies. What evidence of " pleasure " derived from the body do you observe?

Many psychologists would prefer to use terms referring more directly to the state of the organism such as *equilibrium* or *tension* rather than *pleasure* or *pain* which are more likely of subjective interpretation. They find it difficult to conceive of the baby's *images* as " mental processes far removed from words and conscious relational thinking, and determined by the logic of emotion." [43] Nevertheless, there is general agreement that the baby's dawning awareness, his beginning abilities to distinguish *me* from *not-me,* to attach meanings to sensations, and to develop rudimentary memories are dependent on the sensory and motor experiences he has. Increasingly, the importance of the emotional quality of these experiences is recognized. It has, for example, been observed that babies, deprived of warm human contact, tend to develop repetitive sensory and motor patterns of a bizarre kind.

We turn now to a more detailed consideration of the nature of the baby's perceptions, thoughts, and actions during the months after some sense of " me-ness " has probably begun to develop. We shall assume in this consideration that he is one of those fortunate babies who has been born into a loving family and that his tempo and rhythm are sufficiently similar to theirs so that life proceeds relatively smoothly.

Changing Perceptions in Infancy

As the baby grows, his world becomes less and less one of diffuse sensation and increasingly one of many differentiated perceptions. This does not happen all at once, and there are probably intermittent times when he is sleepy or hungry or fatigued or anxious, when the world loses its specific qualities and he knows only vague feelings.

Can we surmise the meanings he may be acquiring at, say, 7 or 8 months as he sits in his chair and surveys the world of things around him? Perhaps he is soon to have his bath, and his mother

---

[43] Isaacs, Susan. " The Nature and Function of Phantasy " in *Developments in Psychoanalysis,* edited by Joan Riviere. London: The Hogarth Press, 1952. P. 89.

has given him an empty powder can to play with. He grasps it in his fist, puts it in his mouth, takes it out, transfers it to the other hand, mouths it, bangs it on the chair arm, drops it, whimpers, bangs his fists instead. Mother can substitute a bath toy and the same repertoire will likely be repeated. Anything which comes within his field of vision is something to be reached for; if it is bright, all the more enticing — if red so much the better — but what is reached for is not always grasped. He is not yet a good judge of distance and does not yet see things in perspective so that a bright flower held in front of him may look about the same as the one in the pattern of his mother's apron. Whatever comes into his hand is twisted and turned, held now this way, now that, and eventually tasted and banged. How else can any object be exploited if he is to learn its size and weight, its form, its texture, its temperature, or its sound? Some objects have already acquired an emotional investment for him. Thus he may respond with much cooing and babbling to the sight of the bath toys with which his mother lets him splash, but with grimaces and protests to the approach of a washcloth which has been known to get soap in his eyes.

By the time he has lived another four or five months and reached his first birthday, the world of objects will have taken on many new meanings. If we look in on him before his bath, we're less likely to find him sitting in a chair than to find him crawling underneath it. There's a tiny but intriguing bit of fuzz there that he must capture. This bit of behavior suggests a major change in the nature of his perception. He is capable of considerably finer discrimination. He now sees objects in perspective, and everything has taken on greater complexity. He is more aware of details. The powder box is not merely round, hard, and good to bang, but it has intriguing holes into which he tries to poke his index finger. He seems, too, to have a dawning sense of relatedness. If he drops the powder box (and he likely will), he is no longer so vague and unconcerned, but may go after it — probably on all fours. If you sit down beside him and roll the can to him, he may even roll it back to you. If the box has a cover which comes off, he may twist and turn the two parts together as though he senses their belongingness.

One sees, too, some sense of "before" and "after" in repetition which is no longer completely aimless. Memory is growing apace. One day, Mommie accidently drops the beloved red bath toy behind the laundry hamper. Baby is fussy, wonderfully elated when it is found. Next day, Mommie says, "Where's duckie?" and he crawls to look for it behind the hamper.

Space, time, and reality meanings are shifting. But just as the world of things takes on new meaning, so is the world of people invested with increasing significance.

When the baby was 5 months or so, faces became more than mere configurations, and he began to notice strangers. Whereas previously, as a serene happy baby, he had more or less accepted all comers, he now became sensitive to differences, and according to Spock [44] might "take alarm at anything unfamiliar such as a visitor's hat or even his *father's* face." Upsetting to family equilibrium as such behavior may be (of course not all babies will manifest their growing abilities in precisely this fashion), it marks the beginning of a new sensitivity to people which is essential for the child's social learning. It seems likely that out of it develops the baby's readiness to imitate. Gesell and Ilg say, in discussing the forty weeks' infant,

. . . greater perceptiveness makes him more sensitive . . . he is becoming responsive to demonstrations and to teaching. He has a new capacity for imitation. Accordingly, he "learns" new nursery tricks like pat-a-cake and bye-bye.[45]

This capacity, we think, has a strong emotional component. The baby's satisfaction in the use of his body is enhanced by his pleasure in the relationship with the adult. Until he has had the repeated experience of having his own body needs met, he cannot to any marked extent develop the capacity for modifying his behavior to fit the patterns set by someone else.

Changing Social Relationships

In any event, by the time he is a year old, the fortunate infant, with whom we are immediately concerned, is likely to have devel-

----

[44] Spock, Benjamin. *Common-Sense Book of Baby and Child Care.* New York: Duell, Sloan and Pearce, 1946. P. 149.

[45] Gesell and Ilg, *op. cit.* P. 117.

oped a considerable degree of sociability, at least with the members of his family and people he is accustomed to seeing every day. With strangers he may warm up slowly. This fact in itself suggests that in a sense a core of resiliency is beginning to develop within his personality. He can, in his own baby way, fend off the adult whose demeanor indicates that he regards infants as puppets to be manipulated rather than human personalities.

Relationships to adults. There is, unfortunately, not much evidence about the effects on the infant of relationships with adults other than his mother. There is ample testimony that tremendous risks to physical, mental, and emotional development arise whenever any infant is deprived of his mother. But we still do not know very much about what happens when care of the baby is shared by several adults, nor about the extent to which other adults may influence the baby's development when the mother is the one who takes most of the care of the infant. For example, the role of the father, at least during the infancy period, has generally been thought to affect the baby only indirectly. Bowlby says,

Not only do they provide for their wives to enable them to devote themselves unrestrictedly to the care of the infant and toddler, but, by providing love and companionship, they support her emotionally and help her maintain that harmonious contented mood in the aura of which the infant thrives.[46]

There is considerable need for studies which will explore the infant's reaction to all of the adults with whom he has close and extended relationships, including fathers, maids, grandparents, lodgers, and so on.

Reporting on the International Seminar on Mental Health and Infant Development held in England in 1952, Margaret Mead comments:

There was one interesting and unexpected development from the three weeks concentration on young infants — and that was a quiet, stubborn, recurrent insistence upon the role of the father, that men as well as women could give care and emotional strength to children.[47]

[46] Bowlby, John. *Maternal Care and Mental Health.* Geneva, World Health Organization, 1952. P. 13.

[47] Mead, Margaret. "Sharing Mental Health Insights Around the Globe." *Understanding the Child.* 21 (October, 1952), 102.

Relationships to children. Similarly, we need more information about the infant's reactions to the child members of his family. Particularly in lower-class groups, one often sees girls of 9 and 10 caring for small baby brothers and sisters. Do they represent to the infant an extension of the parental protection? One would expect that the older youngster would be able to give warm, protective care only to the extent that she herself had had the same. But there is also the possibility of a small infant offering certain satisfactions to a child who had herself suffered some deprivation. It is a fact that in our culture brothers and sisters can and usually do experience much jealousy, rivalry, and competition. But our studies of the matter have perhaps tended to look too much at the hostile aspects of the relationships, thus losing sight of the positive potentials in it. In most families the experience of the infant is likely to be mixed. He may be subjected to certain personal indignities, as was the case of a 1-year-old who was liberally salted and peppered by his 2-year-old brother. But he is also played with in ways which may very well add to his pleasure and enjoyment and perhaps also facilitate development. For example, a 6-year-old boy was the first member of the family to excite a " dancing " response from his 5-months-old sister. The baby's laughter and the way in which she caught his rhythm in the motion of her hands appeared to excite considerable joy not only in him, but also in the watching parents. In another instance, a 3-year-old frequently quieted her 1-year-old sister.

The question of how the infant feels about a smaller infant in the family is equally complex. It is sometimes assumed that because he " is not old enough to understand," he may not experience any jealousy (if that word correctly describes the experience of a 1-year-old). What seems more likely is that what " new baby " means to him will depend pretty much on family circumstances. If *his* infancy has been pretty serene, if he has had his share of satisfactions and has developed an ability to socialize a little, *and* if his mother has sufficient resources (emotional and domestic), his equilibrium may not even be disturbed. Sometimes, however, the mother finds it impossible to give the detailed attention the small baby needs and the equally important but different attention the year-old needs, and then the older baby may feel deprived and unhappy.

The infant growing up with a twin has experiences quite different from the singleton. To what extent these affect his perceptions in the first year of life is not too well known. There have been numerous studies of twins, but relatively few focused on personality development in its very beginning. This again seems to be an instance which depends on the mother's ability to cope with multiple demands and give each infant full satisfaction. In addition, each baby constantly sees himself in the other (particularly in the case of identicals) and appears to tend to imitate him. The need for social response is in a sense taken care of in a closed circle. Under these circumstances, one would expect that differentiation might take place relatively more slowly and some sense of *me-ness* be more difficult to achieve.

The fact that a considerable degree of socialization, but not necessarily a sense of personal identity, can develop within the twin relationship raises some interesting questions about the ways in which infants in general tend to relate to one another. Genuine socialization — a give and take and mutual appreciation — is generally believed not to develop until sometime in toddlerhood or beyond and then to be dependent on prior good relationships with adults. However, Freud and Dann [48] observed intense group relationships within a group of six orphans who had experienced severe deprivation since they were less than a year old, but who had evidently found solace in each other. Although their behavior was in no sense " normal " or typical for their age, they were able to acquire a new language and gave other evidence that they had survived their experience comparatively well.

The study lends support to the idea that under certain circumstances the infant's relationships with his peers may be a source of considerable satisfaction and support to him.

The Beginning of Language

We have been discussing the baby's world of people and things and the meanings he is acquiring without reference to *verbal* communication. For some time the infant, and perhaps the toddler as well, deals more in impressions and images of experiences than they

[48] Freud, Anna, and Dann, Sophie. " An Experiment in Group Upbringing," *The Psychoanalytic Study of the Child*, Vol. VI, *op. cit.*, 1951. Pp. 127–168.

do in actual words. Yet language development begins in infancy, and many adult words probably call up such associations long before the child is able to talk. Mastery of spoken language usually develops rapidly between the ages of 1 and 5, but the elements from which speech develops are the sounds of early infancy. Cooing and babbling which are observed about the third month of life continue until about the end of the first year when the first words are heard. It has been suggested that the child's first comfort sounds are really expressive and later become playful babbling.[49] The early babblings are eventually transformed into intelligible speech, probably through a roundabout process of imitation in which the child, hearing the adult word, is stimulated to utter a babbling sound and eventually responds to a particular sound with a corresponding sound.[50]

PROBLEM 13. Of the six babies in whom we have been interested, Pat is the one having the largest speaking vocabulary. At the age of one year, her repertoire consisted of eight words. Other areas of her behavior were not correspondingly outstanding. What factors do you think might have influenced this aspect of her development?

Undoubtedly basic to the whole process of language development is the infant's progress in development in other areas, particularly physical and motor, and the kinds of experiences he has with communication, both verbal and nonverbal. Infancy is the period in which not only the mechanics underlying speech develop, but equally important meanings begin to be attached to those objects and occurrences for which words will eventually be learned.

At all stages of development the way one views the world is basic to thought and action. In infancy this is especially true. The baby's immaturity limits his thinking just as it limits his capacity for independent action. As long as he remains incapable of getting about, so that the world must, in a sense, come to him, and as long as his needs for food, sleep, elimination, and activity are pervasive, we may expect his thinking processes to be tied to his own organic activity and movements. These, it appears, may even for a time dominate

[49] McCarthy, Dorothy. "Language Development in Children," in *Manual of Child Psychology,* edited by Leonard Carmichael. New York: John Wiley and Sons, 1954. P. 507.
[50] *Ibid.* P. 519.

his picture of outer reality. This kind of thinking is sometimes referred to as *autistic,* and as we shall see, continues to function to a greater or lesser degree throughout life. According to Piaget:

> Autistic thought is sub-conscious, which means that the aims it pursues and the problems it tries to solve are not present in consciousness; it is not adapted to reality, but creates for itself a dream world of imagination; it tends, not to establish truths, but so to satisfy desires and it remains strictly individual and incommunicable as such by means of language.[51]

There is little reason to suppose, however, that this is the only kind of infant thinking. To the extent that he is developing a sense of *me-ness,* a differentiation between inner and outer reality, we see in his behavior the glimmerings of directed thought and incipient language.

Similarly, the activities of the infant are more suggestive of potentiality for independent action than they are of realization. His grabbing of the spoon from his mother's hand long before it can be used effectively to carry food to the mouth; his food likes and dislikes; his zest for taking apart and putting together (or attempting to) the pans and their lids; his insistence on standing up even before he has learned how to sit down; his joy at responding to " Where's baby? " all of these are signals that assure us that the infant of a year, or fifteen months, just on the brink of toddlerhood, is no mere creature of his own impulses and drives, but a human being with already visible potentialities for purposeful action.

The Role of Anxiety in Infancy

Thus far we have concentrated our attention toward the infant for whom life goes smoothly. He has had the advantages of being nurtured by a " good " mother, whom he loves and to whose expectations he adapts without undue difficulty. His experiences have been such as to establish a fundamental sense of trust and confidence in the world of people and to a more limited extent in the world of things. This is not to say that he has never been frustrated, never suffered uneasiness or pain. But assurance and satisfaction

[51] Piaget, Jean. *The Language and Thought of the Child.* New York: The Humanities Press, 1952. P. 43.

have somehow counterbalanced the unpleasant in such a way that his expectations are generally positive.

Not all babies move toward toddlerhood and the hazards (and joys!) of independent locomotion with such an orientation. There are some who appear distrustful, uncertain, and, some observers would say, unready to venture away from whatever meager comforts they find within their own small bodies. Disease and hereditary defect are often important determining factors in such seeming reluctance or difficulty. Sometimes, however, disturbances in interpersonal relations seem to be operative. Anxiety contributes to the basic distrust.

We shall make no attempt to analyze the nature of the infant's experience when he is anxious, but shall rather indicate the circumstances under which it is believed anxiety arises and the kind of behavior which ensues. Anxiety occurs most frequently and manifests itself most dramatically when the baby is deprived of a close relationship with a mothering person. Its effect has been illustrated in a description of an "experiment" instituted by the Emperor Frederick II, who

. . . wanted to find out what kind of speech children would have when they grew up, if they spoke to no one beforehand. So he bade fostermothers and nurses to suckle the children, to bathe and wash them, but in no way to prattle with them or to speak to them, for he wanted to learn whether they would speak the Hebrew language, which was the oldest, or Greek, or Latin, or Arabic, or perhaps the language of their parents, of whom they had been born. But he labored in vain, because the children all died. For they could not live without the petting and the joyful faces and loving words of their foster-mothers.[52]

The symptoms of deprivation may be described as:

listlessness, emaciation and pallor, relative immobility, quietness, unresponsiveness to stimuli like a smile or a coo, indifferent appetite, failure to gain weight properly despite the ingestion of diets which . . . are entirely adequate, frequent stools, poor sleep, an appearance of unhappiness, proneness to febrile episodes, absence of sucking habits.[53]

[52] Salimbeme. "The Emperor Frederick II" translated by M. M. McLaughlin in the *Portable Medieval Reader,* edited by J. B. Ross and M. M. McLaughlin. New York: The Viking Press, 1949. P. 366.

[53] Bakwin, Harry. "Emotional Deprivation in Infants," *Journal of Pediatrics.* 35 (1949), 512.

Direct observation of children in institutions, hospitals, and foster homes, studies of the early years of individuals who later develop mental illness, and follow-up studies of children who have suffered deprivation in their early years offer confirming evidence as to the devastating effects which prolonged deprivation of mother love can have on personality development.[54]

Further research is needed to establish the circumstances under which some children do survive a considerable amount of deprivation and the specific ways in which personality development may be affected. The reluctance of many individuals to accept a finding, which in a sense is little more than an affirmation that the human organism develops human potentialities more effectively when nurtured by a human being than by an incubator, is to some observers a curious reflection on present-day humanity.

On the basis of present knowledge, deprivation appears to be most devastating when it occurs during the second six months of life, that is at the time when the baby is developing a slight sense of *me-ness,* an incipient ego. The effects on later personality appear to include an absence of inhibitions, superficiality in relationships with others, poor performance in intelligence tests, and an inability to form concepts. Youngsters so deprived do not learn songs, rhymes, and stories easily, are slow in achieving time and space generalizations, and even in adolescence do not remember or recall the past very well.[55]

These findings have important implications for the care of infants who for whatever reason may have to be separated from their mothers. Time was when only as a baby in the infant ward of a hospital began to show symptoms of listlessness, loss of weight, and so on did the prescription — " t.l.c." appear on his chart indicating that a nurse was to pick him up, and give him individual *tender, loving care.* Now, however, there is sufficient recognition of the fact that baby needs mothering so that some hospitals encourage mothers of infants to remain with the babies whenever possible. Similarly,

[54] Bowlby, *op. cit.* P. 15. This book offers a comprehensive *survey* of the available research.

[55] Goldfarb, William. " Psychological Privation in Infancy and Subsequent Adjustment." *American Journal of Orthopsychiatry.* 15 (1945), 247–255. See also pp. 30–45 in Bowlby, *op. cit.*

when the mother is separated from the baby because of such reasons as death, illness, or desertion, foster home care rather than institutional care is considered preferable.

It is not necessary for the baby to be separated from the mother for him to experience anxiety in his relationships with her. Some mothers are ill-equipped emotionally to give an infant all the loving care he needs. Not fully grown-up themselves, they are disturbed by what seem to them to be his incessant demands. Others seem to lavish love and attention, but find it difficult to accept the baby's right to become a person, rather than a kind of plaything. The baby, lacking a control system of his own to take care of his impulses, drives, and needs, uses his parent's, in a sense, until his own develops. If the parent's is inadequate, the baby is likely to be apprehensive and uncertain. However, despite the fact that he may have grave difficulties because his mother is emotionally disturbed or mentally ill, it appears that the baby who has had some kind of relationship with a mothering figure is likely to be better off in later years than the child who has known complete deprivation. He has, as it were, something more on which to build, and appears to be better equipped to establish positive relationships with some other human being, even though doing so may be exceedingly difficult for him.

There is some reason to believe that occasionally infants experience a good deal of anxiety, not because their mothers are inadequate, but because they happen to come along when the mother finds living unduly complex and is tense and upset. During World War II, for example, many mothers found themselves left alone to care for a small baby. Living conditions were crowded, tempers short. Therefore, a mother, worried over the safety of her husband, concerned lest the baby wake someone in the next room, was hard put to give him serene assurance when he was hungry or colicky or wakeful. Just as there were jittery mothers, so there were many jittery babies. Yet many of these settled down into reasonably steady first graders and school children after their fathers came home and family life returned to a more even keel. Often during the years before 6, they were a little more wary of new experiences, somewhat more inclined to balk at changes in routines, a bit more " sensitive " than children whose infancies had been less hectic, but many apparently have survived without too great warping.

In our wish to emphasize that anxiety experiences in infancy can have serious effects on the baby's developing personality, we should not overlook the fact of the tremendous constructive powers which seem to be implicit in human development. Some babies build wonderfully well on what appears to be a mere fragment of the love and affection that ought to be their due. Babies may differ in their abilities to resist anxiety. Thus one baby becomes upset and fussy when his mother worries over the adequacy of a meal she is preparing for guests. Another's placidity is unruffled when the mother experiences intense anxiety over the illness of a loved member of her family. There are many aspects of anxiety and its relation to infant development which are not yet fully understood. We are, however, reasonably sure that an infant cannot feel intense and prolonged anxiety without its having some effect on later personality development.

Contributions of the Period of Infancy to Later Personality Development

Erikson defines the central conflict of this period as that between trust and mistrust. We are now in a position to understand the nature of the conflict. It is represented by the baby's experiences when he is hungry. By the time he has developed an awareness that food *will* come, that he can even wait a bit and still be sure of its coming, he has begun to resolve the conflict. But basic trust is no mere matter of food. He *trusts* the people in his world. He learns, also, to trust his own body, his ability to grasp that for which he reaches. As objects begin to take on familiarity, he begins to trust the world of things, and he develops a degree of control over them.

By and large all of the babies with whom we have been concerned appear to have established a good sense of basic trust in infancy.

Jane in infancy illustrates particularly well the principle that what matters in the child's development is not the specific child-rearing techniques used, but the nature of the relationship between the mother and the child. Jane was trained early and fairly strictly. She was apparently a placid baby whose " natural " inclination might have been to take the breast or bottle a little longer and to make transitions a little more slowly. Nevertheless, the period went well for her: there were no illnesses, and she appeared bright and happy.

Pat's infancy period was characterized more by ups and downs. She had a difficult start, being tiny at birth. She was a third child and was cared for as much by the relatives as by her mother. Yet she, too, at 12 months was a happy active infant.

Andy, too, appears to have established a sense of basic trust without much difficulty. His mother seems to have been somewhat more permissive about training than was the custom of the day, since he was not yet trained at 9 months. Or perhaps he was more resistant.

Like Pat, Dan had initial difficulties, his being with feeding. In some respects his mother was rather tense, and he tended to be rather active. To all appearances, however, the period went well.

Charles' mother appears to have been able to meet the needs of two babies quite adequately. Her experience undoubtedly contributed to this. The economic conditions in the family were marginal at the time. Nevertheless, Charles, too, seems to have a good start.

There were factors in Celeste's infancy which could have been quite disturbing to her basic sense of trust, including pressures on early training and a very precarious financial situation. Even so, Celeste makes good progress, and there is reason to believe that she has developed infancy resources fairly well.

It is in infancy that a reservoir of security is formed, from which love, affection, and compassion may be drawn all the rest of life. This is not to say that the individual will not add to and transform it, nor that the love of a baby for its mother is the same as the love of man for woman, or of parent for child. But it does suggest that a capacity for warm, spontaneous human relationships can only be acquired from experiencing them. If this basic principle were better understood, we should likely be more understanding of children (and adults) who are mistrustful, more willing to express our human concern for them, less likely to be retaliative and punishing. Unfortunately, modern living has tended to make many of us brusque and brittle, inclined to be wary of our own warm feelings, fearful of " softness," so that we often fail to draw on our own potentialities.

It is also in infancy that a basic orientation toward learning is established. Trust in a loved adult frees the child to perceive the regularities, the relationships in the world outside himself. The mistrustful child, it appears, does not so readily apprehend these. The nature and condition of the child's learning may alter as he grows older, but first learnings appear to be fundamental and at least to a degree determine the later attitudes.

The relevance of basic trust to later living and learning implies that adequate loving care in infancy may be a potent factor in the ultimate realization of full human potentiality. Are there, then, any measures which assure infants of this basic personality component?

DESIRABLE GUIDANCE IN INFANCY

We know of no formulas, no prescriptions for the " best " way to bring up babies. In so far as is humanly possible, every infant is surely entitled to have at least one adult who cares for and about him. But this does not *guarantee* a confident infant. What seems most likely to insure trust is a relationship with an adult who not only loves him, but is able to sense fully his unique characteristics and hence his unique needs. Such an individual feels with the infant, but at the same time retains a sufficient sense of the baby's need to grow, to become a person in his own right, so that he helps him, when the time is ripe, to learn to wait and thus to trust.

Where once it was thought that certain techniques might assure the baby a basic sense of security, that breast feeding and late weaning were essential, now it is recognized that what is " right " for one mother and her baby may be " wrong " for the next mother and her baby. Consequently, mothers are now encouraged to trust their own feelings and the baby's reactions and do what seems best for them. This is a boon to those mothers who are self-confident and self-acceptant. But it is less assuring to those who have never learned to trust themselves and may even be used to the disadvantage of the baby by a mother who is very hostile and emotionally sick. It is likely, however, that the great majority of mothers have considerably more potentiality for giving adequately and sensitively to their children than is currently realized.

We can think of nothing which is more likely to be " good " for infants than for their parents to have the strong conviction that they too are cared about, that their problems and difficulties matter to someone else. Parents today, it seems, pay a high price for civilization and its benefits. With new knowledge of nutrition and disease prevention, better understanding of the dynamics of personality development, more is expected from them than ever before. Yet these expectations are imposed at a time when in many respects living is becoming increasingly impersonal. In many areas of life, conformity is the order of the day, and free and spontaneous expression of feelings, of doubts and misgivings is frowned upon. We can but wonder what might happen to infants if every set of parents could feel assured of their importance as human beings and could know that someone cared when they were anxious or upset. We are not thinking of professional services at this point (although these are vitally necessary), but of relatives, friends, and neighbors who, it seems, in less complex times were much more relied upon than is the case today. In this connection the author has observed that mothers who brought up infants in World War II in strange communities were often beset by loneliness and the strong conviction of their own inadequacies in child rearing. Their retrospective comment was, " If only there'd been someone to talk to or someone just to take the baby for a few hours."

In our emphasis on the contribution which good warm human relationships can make to parenthood and thus to the adequacy of infant care, we do not mean to imply that there are no ways that are better than others nor that specific information about how babies grow and develop is unimportant. There are many things of which we are fairly certain and which parents have a right to know. Included among these are the nature of an adequate diet and good physical hygiene, the general order in which baby capabilities develop (sphincter control in relation to sitting and walking, for example), the way babies perceive their world, how each one differs from other babies, and how they tend to express their satisfactions and their anxieties. Some parents will acquire this knowledge from their own living in families. An increasing number perhaps will learn it in high school and college. But it will also continue to be a function of pediatricians, nurses, social workers, teachers, all who have professional contact with parents, to convey such information along with equally important understanding and sympathy. It is to be hoped that under such circumstances parents will become not only more alert to the ways in which their own feelings contribute to the infant's welfare, but more willing to face those feelings and to seek, if need be, psychological or psychiatric help for themselves.

So it will still be the parent who carries the major burden, but also the major joys and satisfactions in child rearing.

Here we are in agreement with Jersild:

> In their dealings with their children parents have a new opportunity and a new incentive for advancing their growth through continuing the process of self-discovery and self-fulfillment which began when they themselves were infants. This is, or might be, the greatest reward that comes from having children. And a paradoxical feature of it is that a parent in whom the channels for self-discovery have been open for some time will be most eager to keep them open and have the humility and courage to do so. The more a parent is able to perceive and accept in his awareness of what goes on in his relationships with his child, the more he recognizes how much there is yet to learn.[56]

[56] Jersild, Arthur T. *Child Psychology*. New York: Prentice-Hall, 1954. Pp. 85, 86.

The toddler explores his world.

6

‮⎍⎍‬

Beginning to Be Independent Persons

BABIES STILL, but on their feet, into everything, becoming people with minds of their own — these are the toddlers. From the first unsteady steps at 15 months or so to the sure and nimble gait of almost 3 is a period of venture and exploration. But the field of investigation is circumscribed by the necessity of keeping mother, or some loved adult, as a point of safe return. It is a period of growth toward independence: from being fed to feeding oneself; from being one to whom food is brought to being one who comes to meals; from eliminating involuntarily to eliminating at one's own volition; from being confined in a crib or playpen to roaming the house or apartment; from handling and mouthing objects to manipulating them with increasing skill; from being dressed by someone to helping to dress oneself; from babbling to talking. Like growth at other stages of development, it brings new satisfactions, but it also involves giving up old ones.

The toddler, like human beings of whatever age, is at times ambivalent. He feels two ways. He would like to be big, but it is comfortable to be small. So he moves forward slowly, or he moves three steps back. But he moves, for the growth urge is strong, and not easily quelled. If expectations set for him are reasonable so that he can comprehend what he is to do; if he is comforted when he falls, but is set again upon his feet; if his progress is approved and his mistakes understood, he will grow not only in his abilities to do, and in *me-ness,* but also in worthy selfhood.

As the toddler grows, so do his parents. As he gives up, so do they. They willingly relinquish the infant whose complete dependence gratifies their need to protect for the 1- and 2-year-old who often breaks, spills, and messes, and sometimes spits, kicks, and bites, but who is frequently completely charming even in his ineptness.

We define toddlerhood, which is the subject of this chapter, primarily in terms of the baby's achievement of a sense of his own abilities and limitations in dealing with the world of people and things. This central concern, which Erikson calls *autonomy,* extends throughout the period of the child's developing skill in walking and learning to talk. Chronologically, we shall think of it beginning at the onset of walking and extending through the second and third years of life, when the baby is a 1-year-old and a 2-year-old. Obviously there are no hard and fast lines dividing one stage of development from another. Not all texts recognize " toddlerhood " as a separate stage. Many deal with " infancy," including the second year, and the " preschool period," including the sixth year. The baby, as we indicated in Chapter 5, may reveal some degree of independence even before his first birthday, and he does not fully establish a sense of selfhood until well beyond his third birthday.

The World of Toddlerhood

Something of the flavor of life as it is experienced by a young toddler is apparent in the following excerpt from the descriptive portion of a diary record:

October 25

Dick has dark eyes and hair, small features, and a slight small-boned figure. His face wears a constant alertness, has a kind of studying questioning quality. His arms are always bent as he stands or walks. He moves in a bumpy run with legs spread, balancing from side to side with his head bobbing up and down.

The observation takes place on a community garden lawn in the rear of the house where Dick lives. He has spent much time there from his earliest carriage days on and has been used to seeing people of all ages and sizes there as well as many cats and dogs. Today his mother is with him and two women friends, Laura and Jane. Observer is a stranger to him.

Dick starts backing up as the observer draws near to sit down on the ground about fifteen feet away from his mother. He backs up until his mother says "Look out!" and then he sits suddenly. He leans forward, on both arms, and as he pushes, his behind goes up first, then he's straight up and waddling toward the hedge. He hides, peeks out, says "Hi!" Mother says, "Here's a leaf," holding it out toward him. He runs to her, reaching with right arm more than with left. She says, "Blow." She blows.

He takes the leaf, blows on it, holds it by the stem, turns his whole body, and drops it.

Mommy says, "Where is it?" She picks up another and blows. He takes it. She says, "Give it to Laura." He stands confused, eyes puzzled, reaches it to Mommy who puts it in her mouth, holds it by the stem in her teeth. He quickly pulls it, puts it in his teeth, and says, "Bo!" He tastes it, makes chewing motions and a wry face. Mommy says, "Put it in your hair, like this," and she puts it in her hair. . . .

He sees a kitten coming toward him. He moves his fingers, says, "Kiki," reaches, points, turns his head to look at Mommy. He smiles, sees a leaf, picks it up, and puts it by the stem into his mouth. His mother says, "Please," and he takes the leaf in his hand and runs to her.

Mother says, "All gone." He sits suddenly, or falls facing her. He brushes off his overalls, with full sweeping strokes of arms, more right than left and moving his whole upper trunk, pushes himself up — pushing on hands, rocking back, and then up. He falls into Mommy's lap; she cradles him in arms, then rubs off his face. He pulls away, she lets him go easily, he sits beside her and says, "Coming, airplane," and points straight up with right arm.

Mother says, "I don't see any."

As he pushes up, picks up magazine cover in right hand and drops it again as he turns to run with both arms out, all in one related motion. He stops and turns toward Mommy. She says, "Shall I blow? You blow." He runs to Mommy, stoops with knees bent, behind out, looking at Mommy, and says "Maper," as he looks at magazine cover. Mommy says, "Yes, paper."

He listens, hears airplane, and says, "Coming, airplane. Oo-oo-oo-oo," and gets up to run with arms up, then runs back, arms waving. Stops in front of Mommy, picks up cigarette, puts it in mouth and chews it. Mommy pulls him down on his back in her lap, pulls what she can from his mouth with her fingers, then stands him up. He is still spitting, so she carries him into the house for a drink. (Interval about 2 minutes.) She brings him out, leading him by the left hand; his right hand waves a cookie. . . .

He mouths his cookie, staring. He sees a cat, says " Kiki," runs toward her, sees children on gate swing, stops to look fascinated, and stands mouthing cookie, not biting, putting the whole piece into his mouth and out again. Then he bites and chews the cookie up. He runs by to mother and behind her and reaches for her hair. (It's long and black, done up in a bun.) She says, " Don't you pull my hair," and as he still reaches chuckling, she snatches him up in her arms and cuddles him laughingly.

He is up and away again, running to the swing. He edges up too close and moves back bending in the middle as it comes toward him. As he moves too close again, his mother calls to one of the children, but just then he hears an airplane, turns, moves away, says, " Airplane," points up with right arm, and runs to mother as if all in one motion, says " Oo-oo-oo-oo " as he runs. He stops at the edge of the walk near her, stands, reaches with arms and bends at hips as if falling, squats at the edge of the walk, pushes up, trips, falls flat forward, pushes up on feet in an instant squat, and then standing again, runs toward kitty, pointing. As the kitty goes, he sees the gate open and goes to push it, it reopens and he backs up; when he pushes it again, it reopens and after backing up, he moves around it to walk inside.

PROBLEM 1. Describe the progress you think Dick has made toward mastering the skills of walking. Describe his progress in eye-hand co-ordination. How does he appear to perceive the leaves, the kitten, the magazine, the airplane, the cookie, his mother's hair, the gate? To what extent do you think these perceptions depend on his motor development? What does the record suggest about his relationships with his mother? To what extent do you think his perceptions may be dependent on his relationships with her? Is there any evidence of developing selfhood?

In toddlerhood the child's view of his world is still considerably dependent on his growing abilities to use his body effectively. We shall turn now to consider his progress in physical growth and sensorimotor development.

BIOLOGICAL ASPECTS OF DEVELOPMENT IN THE SECOND AND THIRD YEARS

The baby grows so fast and seems to continue to change so rapidly in the toddlerhood period that it is easy to overlook the fact that the rate of growth is actually beginning to slow down. Parents often forget this and become very anxious when the toddler appears to eat less than he did. The reason for his leveling off is that he does not need so much to " grow on."

Physical Growth

Reference to Table 1 in Chapter 2 will show that if a boy-baby's weight were to fall right at the 50th percentile for the first three years of his life, he would have gained 27.7 pounds over his birth weight, but 14.7 pounds of this, or better than half, would have been gained in infancy. As far as height is concerned, almost as much is gained in the first year as in the next two together. Growth is, however, more rapid in the second year of life than in the succeeding years. An apparent tendency for babies receiving optimum diets to grow at rates better than average continues through this period.

Skeletal development. Even though the rate of growth slows down, important developments are taking place. The centers of ossification which, as we have indicated previously, are a good index to maturity, continue to be laid down. Bone growth, according to roentgenological studies of the leg, continues to exceed muscle growth until the age of 3 years. The rate of growth of skin and subcutaneous tissue rapidly declines.[1]

" Teething." The beginning of toddlerhood (12 to 15 months) is a midway point for the eruption of the deciduous or " baby " teeth. On the average, by this time the child has already acquired two lower and four upper incisors. The first molars may put in appearance between the tenth and sixteenth months, and the cuspids and second molars are likely to have completed eruption by 30 months. Although the sequence of eruption is generally regular, there are wide differences in the ages at which these teeth appear.[2]

As Spock indicates, since the baby is teething almost all of his first two-and-a-half years, it's easy to see why so many ailments were

---

[1] Stuart, Harold C., and others. "The Growth of Bone, Muscle and Overlying Tissues as Revealed by Studies of Roentgenograms of the Leg Area." *Monographs of the Society for Research in Child Development,* 5, No. 3, 1940. P. 45.

[2] Stuart, Harold C., and Stevenson, Stuart S. "Physical Growth and Development," *Mitchell-Nelson Textbook of Pediatrics*. Philadelphia: W. B. Saunders Company, 1950. P. 30.

once blamed on teething. However, he does think it is possible that teething may lower resistance so that infection may get an easier start.[3]

Posture. Toddlerhood brings with it changes in proportion and also in body mechanics. When the child begins to stand and walk, he tends to toe out and keep his feet apart. This gives him a certain amount of stability, but he continues to topple easily throughout this period. The weight of his body also falls on the inner part of his foot, and until about three years the pronation increases. If he is healthy, well nourished, has adequate opportunity for activity and no structural defects, his tendency to toe out and to pronate will correct itself later on.

In the same way, the tendency to a protruding abdomen, which is normal in the toddler, gradually lessens. As he grows, he becomes more erect. He does not lean forward so much. The fall that would bruise his forehead at 2, cuts his lip at 3.

Sensorimotor Development

Just as the child does not achieve an erect posture until the age of 3, it is not until about that time that he becomes able to use his hands more flexibly and without involving his whole body in the process. He no longer needs to keep his vision fixed on the object he wishes to grasp, nor does he have to extend his fingers in anticipation before he takes hold of it. " Such behavior displays the advancing maturation of the cortical areas of the brain and their influence on the visual mechanism." [4]

A rather detailed knowledge of the toddler's equipment for motor activity is essential to understanding him. Without it, we are likely to be merely amused, or baffled, or bored by his ineptness. If, on the other hand, we can feel what it is like to be only recently accustomed to an upright position; to have to pay attention to one's walking and running because those processes are not yet automatic; to live in an intriguing world of objects which call for manipulation, but may demand a precision of co-ordination that one is

---

[3] Spock, Benjamin. *The Common Sense Book of Baby and Child Care.* New York: Duell, Sloan, and Pearce, 1946. Pp. 158–159.

[4] Watson, Ernest H., and Lowrey, George H. *Growth and Development of Children.* Chicago: The Year Book Publishers, 1951. P. 131.

still lacking — then we shall be able to regard the toddler as a person of accomplishment and skill.

Learning to walk. One clear indication of the recency of the toddler's acquaintance with the upright position is the precarious way he maintains it. Not until 20 months or so is he able to hold his balance with one foot off the ground. Not until well toward his third birthday can he maintain his equilibrium when another child playfully shoves him. Much of the puppylike, all-fours play of 2-year-olds seems to be generated by the fact that they are so readily pushed over and find it easier to continue their frolics without bothering to right themselves. On the other hand, when the toddler wants to assume a sitting posture in place of a standing one, that, too, presents difficulties, at least until 18 months or so. Gradually he learns to count on reaching the seat he aims for, but it is a long time before his facial expression indicates complete confidence in the outcome.

The toddler may " walk " at 15 months, but it is not until he is 3 or so that the process has become really automatic. In the meantime he " practices " to make it so. Even while his balance is precarious so that he is still inclined to stagger, he walks backward and sideward as well as forward. At 18 months he pushes a chair in front of him, or pulls a wheel toy. By 2 his steps are still short, and much less free-flowing than those of the 3-year-old, but he is sure enough of himself to elaborate simple walking and trotting a bit. His arms tend to go with his legs, but he is beginning to be able to carry things as he goes. He can perform the (to him) precarious stunt of walking on a board elevated three or four inches from the ground. He can manage a kiddy car, but a tricycle on which one must balance *and* push with alternating feet is something else again.

Toddlerhood is likewise a period for practice in reaching and grasping. By the time he is walking comfortably, the toddler is relatively adept in his reaching. His hands do not miss the mark as they did in infancy. But reaching is still a whole body matter that takes the trunk and the arm along with the hand until well after 3 years. To provide necessary balance, he often extends both hands even though only one is to be used for grasping. There is no question of his ability to " get " the object he reaches for, even as early as

15 months, but precision in its manipulation comes more slowly. Take the matter of holding a spoon. It is clutched in an overhand fist grip well up to the second birthday. Frequently the child unwittingly picks it up with the hollow side down. To turn it over to get it *under* the food is a complex adjustment. Or he may pick it up correctly, but somehow in the process of directing it mouthward, his wrist turns and the mouthful must wait for a new start. Watching him pick up tiny objects, like peas, one is aware of his potentialities for precision. With larger objects, however, his fingers tend to work all together.

Related to progress in grasping is progress in releasing, which appears to develop somewhat more slowly. It is in a sense easier at this stage of life to get something than to let it go. The nature of the toddler's problem in release can be seen when he is watched as he tries to imitate the block play of his older brother. He places one block in an upright position; it wavers but stands. He puts a second one atop the first, but this time his hesitation (which he cannot control) shakes both blocks. His " building " crashes.

Handedness. Handedness is usually established sometime during this period. Whether or not it is innate or environmentally determined is not certain. However, there are a sufficient number of children who show very early a preference so strong as to suggest that any attempts to change involve disruption of an extremely complex and well-established motor pattern. Other children continue an ambidextrous approach until as late as 18 months or so and do not appear upset by encouragement of the use of the right hand.

PROBLEM 2. If it is possible for you to have a play period with a toddler, you can learn a good deal about his motor development (as well as about his social responses and yours!) through a simple game of ball. After you seem to feel comfortable with each other, roll the ball toward him. How does he respond? What does he do if you ask him to throw it to you? Notice his general body stance. How does he grasp the ball? How does he release it? Does the size of the ball make a difference in the way he handles it? Compare your observation with those of your classmates on other toddlers. In what ways do their children respond similarly to the one you observed? In what ways do they respond differently? How do you account for such similarities and differences?

PROBLEM 3. If possible, arrange to keep a running record of the activities of a toddler at meal time, or when he is playing by himself. In what specific ways are his accomplishments limited by his motor ineptness? Are there any instances in which he is more skillful than you would have anticipated? Try to observe the adult's handling of him also.

Eating, Elimination, and Sleeping

The skills necessary to independent eating likewise reflect increasing maturity of the neuromuscular systems. Another factor in eating is that the child's range of choice of foods is considerably widened by the fact that he has equipment for chewing. How he uses this may depend in part on how he is introduced to new foods. Both psychological and physiological principles support a policy of gradually accustoming him to foods which are coarser and need careful chewing. Unless he has become used to chewing in infancy, the toddler may be reluctant to accept foods which are coarse. Digestive systems also vary. Some appear to be more sensitive to roughage than others. Small portions of new foods and slow transitions to new textures enable the adult to determine the toddler's ability to handle a more grown-up diet without ill effects.

Appetite in the second and third years is inclined to fluctuate. The toddler continues to be the best judge of how much food he needs and, provided his ability to discriminate is not spoiled by the introduction of sweet and rich foods, appears also to be able to " select " the appropriate ones.

Increasing maturity is also apparent in developing abilities for sphincter control. From 12 to 16 months the ability to retain may develop rapidly, but the ability to release is not acquired until several months later. With the ability to release somewhere from 18 to 21 months, considerable progress toward voluntary control is made. However, as Gesell points out, the toddler seems to learn backward in this area. The first evidence of progress may come when he points out that he has wet after the act has occurred. Later he is able to " tell " during the act, and not until sometime later (24–27 months) is he able to announce his intentions before the act.[5]

[5] Gesell, Arnold, and others. *The First Five Years of Life.* New York: Harper and Brothers, 1940. P. 247. Also Watson and Lowrey, *op. cit.* P. 102.

Sleep patterns shift during this period as the infant develops greater awareness of his world. His ability to drift out of it through sleep seems to become more complex. His total sleeping time decreases. He may take only one nap instead of two and is sometimes most resistant to sleep when he is most fatigued. Gesell sees the ineptness in releasing and voluntarily holding on, which characterizes muscular activity, reflected in these changing sleep patterns.[6]

Nature and Nurture

We discuss the biological aspects of development because we believe that the nature of the human organism sets certain limits to what the individual at any given stage is able to do. Thus we do not expect the toddler to be able to play a game of tennis, read a book, or even tie his shoe. However, we must not overlook the fact that as a biological organism he does not exist in a vacuum. In one environment, emphasis may be put on a particular potentiality whereas another environment may stress a different one. The older the child gets, the more likely it is that his experience may have helped him to develop a particular skill, where another skill may lie dormant. This raises a question as to the extent to which the skills of the toddler are as restricted by an inherent growth pattern as our description has seemed to imply. May it not be that if the 18-month child were given much practice in tieing a shoelace, he would develop adeptness even at this early age? In the nineteenthirties a number of studies concerned themselves with various aspects of this problem of the contribution of nature or maturation and nurture or training to the individual's learning. A study by McGraw in which a pair of twins were taught a variety of motor skills including roller skating and tricycling before they were 2 years old excited much interest. Most of the previous work had indicated that the motor behavior of infants was not subject to improvement with practice. This study did not settle the problem, but it threw new light on some of the issues involved. It appears that the circumstances under which the motor performance of infants and toddlers may be modified by opportunities for practice vary

[6] Gesell, Arnold, and Ilg, Frances. *Infant and Child in the Culture of Today.* New York: Harper and Brothers, 1943. P. 305.

considerably. Among the important factors are the stage at which practice is begun, the extent to which the new performance remains appropriate to the child's body proportions and structure as he grows older, and the emotional connotations the performance has for the child.

The general implication in this and other studies has been that there are certain " critical periods when any given activity is most susceptible to modification through repetition of performance." [7] This corresponds to the principle of *timing* which we discussed earlier (see page 37).

PROBLEM 4. McGraw restudied the twins when they were 6 years old. Her report of the later consequences of training is reprinted in *Readings in Child Psychology*, edited by Dennis, pp. 199–233. The same collection includes a reprint of a study by Josephine Hilgard, " Learning and Maturation in Preschool Children," pp. 167–179.

Review these articles and plan to use the findings in a discussion on appropriate play activities for this age.

Another study which suggests that the young child's motor behavior patterns may be considerably modified by his experience is the Mead and Macgregor analysis of the activities of Balinese children. According to this study, Balinese infants tend to progress from sitting to squatting to standing in contrast to the American sequence of creeping, standing, and walking with squatting coming after standing. The Balinese grasping patterns also differ in that they emphasize extension and outward rotation, rather than the inward rotation and good opposition of the thumb and forefinger which characterizes American children.[8] There is little evidence as to whether similar studies conducted in other societies or by other observers might reveal different modifications in the sequence of motor behavior.

Significance of Biological Aspects of Development in Toddlers

Clearly, the toddler's behavior is conditioned by the expectations of his social environment as well as limited by his own inherent

[7] McGraw, Myrtle. " Maturation of Behavior " in *Manual of Child Psychology,* edited by Leonard Carmichael. New York: John Wiley and Sons, 2d ed., 1954. Pp. 332–369.

[8] Mead, Margaret, and Macgregor, Frances. *Growth and Culture.* New York: G. Putnam's Sons, 1951. Pp. 181, 182.

growth patterns. Never again, however, will his learnings be as much dependent on the state of his maturity as a biological organism as in these two years, and of course, the year which preceded them.

We shall consider now the social expectations which may be held for the child of 1 and 2 years of age, how they may vary from one cultural group to another, and what they may teach him overtly and subtly about himself and his world and the people in it.

SOCIAL FACTORS IN TODDLERHOOD

Just as in infancy, the total development of the toddler is affected by his social environment, by the adequacy of the food available, and by the amount of exposure to disease he must undergo. Some environments offer tremendous hazards to adequate development and present much greater risks for survival than others.

Toddlerhood is a period of rapid and intense socialization. Bit by bit the child is acquiring the behavior patterns typical of the group to which his family belongs. At 15 months he grips a spoon in his fist and carries it unsteadily to his mouth. By 3 years his characteristic way of holding it may reflect the way his mother has encouraged him to hold it. Food may be something dipped from a big kettle and offered on a plate, or it may be a slice of bread grabbed out of a wrapper and spread with jelly, or a ritual of washed hands, tied bib, dinner first, then dessert, and again, washed hands.

At 15 months the approach to objects is manipulative and exploratory. But by 3 years many of the things in the child's world are invested with new values, depending on the kinds of socialization he is undergoing. Water, for example, may be for splashing, dribbling, enjoying, or it may be " messy," " chilly," " full of germs." A jar of cold cream may offer delightful sensations of slippery smoothness and fragrance, or it may be simply " not-to-be-touched "; a living-room couch something to be jounced upon or something to be avoided; a long flight of steps a challenge to one's growing motor skills, or a threatening danger; a book or magazine an object to carry, or pages to tear, or a source for mutual enjoyment with an older child or adult. People, too, change their functions. From prime sources of satisfactions or vague parts of the background of experience they emerge as an all-seeing cop who may come to lug one off to "jail," a doctor with an ever-ready "needle," a genial grocer with an open cooky box, a "maid" with whom one can or cannot behave as one does with Mommy, and so on. The little girl next door is to be copied ("Sally Lou stays clean when she plays in the sandbox"); the boy down the block is to be avoided (he has "bad habits"); a husky 2-year-old is to be fought (Hit him back, don't let him get away with it!); another is to be protected (Don't hit him, *tell* him!).

In all of these and many other ways the members of the toddler's family are structuring his world for him. They are teaching him to seek these experiences and avoid those, to feel that certain objects and specific ways of using them are good while others are bad, and likewise that certain people and certain kinds of relationships are more desirable than others. Some of this teaching is done deliberately and consciously, but there is much which the toddler's elders convey to him of which they themselves are but dimly, if at all, aware. Nor is the toddler himself alert to the significance of all that he learns to imitate and to anticipate. He is still very much in a period of trial and error in which he may respond now one way, now another, to a particular situation. However, as he experiences approval in some situations, disapproval in others, he gradually learns to pattern his behavior in the fashion of the other members of his group. We shall discuss this progress more specifically when we consider his personality development in greater detail. For the present we are primarily concerned with the variety of patterns he may be expected to acquire during his second and third year.

These expectations, just as were those held for infants, are determined by the experiences the parents themselves have had and the customs commonly held in the group in which they live and the values they hold. The question of what to expect and how much to impose patterns of adult living on the child who seems in so many ways still a baby is a difficult one, particularly in the American culture. Our traditions change. We are committed to improvement, to acceptance of new ideas, new ways of doing things. Consequently, we are not sure that the expectations our parents held for us as toddlers are necessarily the ones we want to hold for our children. At the same time as a democratic culture we respect individuality, and resist authoritarian imposition. Some observers have pointed out that in contrast to certain other cultures in which the child takes a preponderantly spectatorship role vis-à-vis his parents, who are models showing him how to act, in America the child exhibits achievement and self-sufficiency vis-à-vis his parents who take a spectatorship role.[9] Where these values hold, it appears that parents are more likely to be uncertain in their expectations, more likely to permit the child to do now one thing, now another, so that he is less clear about what he can do and what he can't and perhaps also less clear about himself as a worthy or worthless individual.

With these possibilities in mind we shall examine some common expectations for socialization in the second and third years of life.

Expectations for Eating and Related Behavior

As we have indicated, the toddler has already developed several sources of satisfaction in addition to the one of being nursed either at the breast or by bottle. Nevertheless, oral activity, whether it be eating or sucking, chewing, or tasting and mouthing of toys and objects continues to loom large in his repertoire of behavior. Parents' attitudes toward such manifestations vary.

Weaning. In the American culture babies are frequently weaned from the bottle before 15 months of age. However, some may cling to it, particularly at bedtime, well into the second or even third year. In line with what we know of individual differences, we should expect to find a good bit of variation in the age of giving up nursing, depending on the child's particular needs for this kind of activity, but the parent's feelings about the matter are probably equally if not more important.

PROBLEM 5. **When our six babies were infants, late weaning was definitely frowned upon. Nevertheless, two of them continued with bottles in the second year. At 18 months Pat was getting two bottles and Charles four daily.**

From what you know about these babies and their families, can you think of any reasons why these two might be more likely to be weaned late rather than early?

[9] Ruesch, Jurgen, and Bateson, Gregory. *Communication — The Social Matrix of Psychiatry.* New York: W. W. Norton & Company, 1951. P. 221.

One reason parents sometimes offer for continuing the bottle into the second year is their concern over the fact that the child doesn't seem to be getting as much food as he did earlier. Babies in the second and third year are often capricious in their appetites, and as we have indicated, are growing relatively more slowly so that the quantities needed in proportion to their body size are not so great. Seeing that the child is adequately fed is such a tangible way of demonstrating love and affection that some parents may well feel rebuffed when the child no longer needs what he once did.

Thumbsucking. Other parents feel that extended nursing is a good preventive of the thumbsucking which may appear as early as eight to twelve weeks, but which seems to become most annoying to parents when it continues beyond the first birthday. Recent studies, including one of babies who were cup-fed from birth, tend to indicate that thumbsucking cannot be attributed to any single cause.[10] Children who are deprived of love and affection frequently seem to find comfort in this fashion, but cherished youngsters who are loved may also be thumbsuckers. Sometimes this pattern seems to be tied with sleep habits and appears only when the child is fatigued. Other children rarely suck their thumbs during the daytime but will when feeling embarrassed or shy. Not uncommonly sucking activity becomes focused on a particular object, as a fuzzy blanket, which becomes the child's comfort wherever he goes. Parental resistance to these grubby fetishes seems to serve only to enhance their value to the child, although the time is likely to come when he will be grateful for their help in giving it up.

Learning to eat independently. The transition from being fed to eating independently often provides another test of the parent's ability to accept babyishness and encourage toward maturity at one and the same time. Baby's first manifestations of interest in the spoon are probably important indications of his dawning sense of social expectations for him. But progress from those first grabbings of the spoon to the stage where he dispatches neatly and independently all of his dinner may be marked by countless spinach sham-

---

[10] Sears, Robert R., and Wise, George W. "Relation of Cup-feeding in Infancy to Thumbsucking and the Oral Drive." *American Journal of Orthopsychiatry.* 20 (1950), 123–138.

poos, beet baths, and milk showers. Some mothers, it appears, do not mind such messiness and some seem even to aid and abet it. Others deny the baby any opportunity to help himself until they feel reasonably sure that he can be about as neat as they are. Still others use techniques which permit the child to participate in the eating process through holding the spoon, a piece of toast and so on, but prevent him from getting fists and face into the bowl or cup. Although no one of these methods is likely of itself to have disruptive effects on personality development, each provides basic learning which may be influential in later attitudes toward food.

In general, it seems easier for the child if he is expected to relinquish his baby satisfactions gradually and only as he is able to find pleasure in more grown-up behaviors. However, here as in other areas, the important element appears to be the parent's feeling about the matter rather than the particular technique used.

PROBLEM 6. If possible, observe several different mothers' ways of helping their babies learn to eat by themselves. Or pool your observations of one mother from Problem 3 with those of your classmates. How much is the baby allowed to participate in the feeding process? How is his ineptness handled? Does his mother tend to ignore it, or does she restrict his movements, or redirect them, or attempt to distract his attention? What is your feeling about the appropriateness of the techniques used for the particular baby you are observing? What do you feel about the relationship between the mother and the baby? If you were handling this same baby, what would your techniques be? Why?

A comparison between mealtime in the Warner household when Jane was 2 and in the Plummer household when Patty was also 2 suggests some of the ways in which expectations for eating may vary.

Jane usually eats by herself, either sitting in her high chair or at her own small table. Until she was 21 months old, she ate very well, but then became very fussy, particularly about milk. Only with great effort was Mrs. Warner able to get even a pint " into her." Recently her mother has found that it is better not to pay too much attention to her idiosyncrasies. She now allows her twenty minutes for a meal. If at the end of that time Jane has not finished, her mother starts to take the food away. She will then complete the meal without further interruption.

Patty eats her breakfast with her Daddy, usually sharing a cruller with him. Her lunch is frequently eaten with one of the relatives. She sits at a small table by herself, but is continually getting up to see what is going on. If she repeats this too often, she is put in a room by herself until she can be " good." She eats " everything," including a great deal of candy, coke, and other sweets between meals. From a nutritional standpoint her diet is low in a number of important elements.

PROBLEM 7. In what ways is mealtime in these two homes consistent with other aspects of the family living? What is each of the girls learning?

Expectations for training in elimination. As we saw in our discussion of infancy, some parents attempt to train the child to function at a particular place and time well before he is a year old. But it seems likely that training in which the child is an actual participant is not accomplished until the second year of life.

Techniques for training. Depending on the extent and permissiveness of attempts to " regulate " the baby while he is still an infant, training practices may be ranked as initially restrictive or initially indulgent. In the Whiting and Child study which we cited earlier, the American middle-class parents were rated as more restrictive in this respect than all but two of the primitive societies.[11] With but a single exception, they also began training earlier than the other societies. The crucial aspect of toilet training seems to be, however, its severity and the kinds of techniques used to foster control. If no attempts at training are made until the child is able to talk and has developed strong motivations for pleasing his parents and conforming to the ways of his group, he sometimes seems to train himself.

Whiting and Child [12] rated the severity of training of American middle-class children as equivalent to the most severe in any of the primitive societies they studied. They were using for the comparison findings from the Davis and Havighurst study [13] in which the middle-class group had been found to be more severe than the

[11] Whiting, John W. M., and Child, Irvin, L. *Child Training and Personality.* New Haven, Yale University Press, 1953. Pp. 73–77.

[12] Whiting and Child, *op. cit.* P. 77.

[13] Davis, Allison, and Havighurst, Robert. " Social Class and Color Differences in Child Rearing." *American Sociological Review.* 11 (1946), 698–710.

lower-class group. More recent studies [14] have found the lower-class groups to be more strict and their training procedures more likely to be accompanied by punishment and scolding for accidents and by " shaming."

For a comparison of the expectations of two different families regarding eliminative habits we can turn again to Jane Warner and Pat Plummer.

Jane at the age of 2 is well enough trained so that she rarely has an accident in the daytime. She has occasionally been spanked for this. She is occasionally wet at night. She is usually picked up at 9:30 p.m. and again at 1:00 or 2:00 a.m., but goes back to sleep immediately. When she asks for the toilet, her mother helps her pull down her panties and get seated, then leaves her until she calls " All through." Her mother then tells her to wash her hands which she does.

At 2 years and 8 months, Patty has established bowel control, but wets her pants once or twice a week. She has been slapped, spanked, and put in a dark room for this. Her mother reminds her to go two or three times each morning and afternoon, saying " We go to bathroom " and seeing that she is unbuttoned before she leaves her. After urination, she pulls up her own clothes. In the case of a bowel movement, she calls her mother who wipes her. She is not allowed to use toilet paper herself. Nor is she allowed to pull the chain. Her mother washes her hands for her.

PROBLEM 8. To what extent are the expectations implied here typical of those which have been set for these children in other situations? What other factors, than the kind of training given, may make Patty somewhat slower in learning control?

Parental attitudes. As in our consideration of expectations for feeding in infancy, we are faced with the fact that we cannot estimate the effects of training on a particular child solely from a knowledge of the techniques used. For example, current child-rearing literature, which may be quite influential among middle-class mothers, tends to emphasize a permissive, easygoing approach to training. Spock says, " If you want to be completely natural, you can leave bowel training almost entirely up to your baby " . . . and, " A

---

[14] Maccoby, Eleanor, and others. "Methods of Child-Rearing in Two Social Classes," *Readings in Child Development,* edited by Martin and Stendler. New York: Harcourt, Brace and Company, 1954. Pp. 380–396.

child will usually become dry in the daytime somewhere between 1½ and 2½ years even if you don't do anything about it." [15] He wisely indicates in addition some things which a mother who wants to do something can do. Suppose, however, that several mothers decide to accept the idea of "doing what comes naturally." One finds the idea right and appropriate for her and her child. She has no negative feelings about her child's baby satisfactions or about diapers or laundry, and she has implicit faith that her child will at the appropriate state of readiness begin to function in a more mature fashion. Another, although she may not be able to admit it even to herself, finds the whole procedure irksome, and regards each month that the baby "stalls" as that much more evidence of his unreasonable demands upon her. Still another derives, again without awareness on her part, somewhat more satisfaction from her baby's need for complete care than she does from his need to grow up. In subtle ways which we do not yet fully understand each of these mothers "teaches" her child something different about the control of his eliminative functions.

Some authorities have regarded socialization in this area as a pivot on which the other learnings in toddlerhood are dependent. We shall consider this point of view when we discuss personality development in a later section. However, we cannot lose sight of the fact that socialization expectations for other systems of behavior, especially independence and aggression, may either reinforce or temper expectations for eliminative control.

Expectations for Independence

When the child develops abilities for walking and running, for holding on and letting go, and begins to be able to use the language of his elders, he no longer needs the same all encompassing protection necessary to him as an infant. He can to some extent be "on his own." This may mean different things in different societies. According to Mead's observations among the Munduugumors of New Guinea, for example, "As soon as a child can walk, it is set down most of the time and permitted to fend for itself. But it is not allowed to wander far because of the fear of drowning. . . . The

---

[15] Spock, *op. cit.* Pp. 196–201.

mothers have to remain more tense and attentive, and are forever screaming at wandering children or snatching them back violently at the riverbank." [16] In contrast, the Manus baby, as soon as he

. . . can toddle uncertainly, is put down into the water at low tide. . . . As he grows older, he is allowed to wade about at low tide. His elders keep a sharp lookout that he does not stray into deep water until he is old enough to swim. . . . *But the supervision is unobtrusive.* . . . His whole play world is so arranged that he is permitted to make small mistakes from which he may learn better judgment and greater circumspection, but he is never allowed to learn to make mistakes which are serious enough to permanently frighten him or inhibit his activity.[17]

The question is not only when the baby is put on his own and whether abruptly or gradually, but also how much is expected from him. All of these aspects of training for independence can be considered as we look at expectations for independence within the American culture.

Factors related to expectations for independence. Many early studies of social class differences in independence training indicated considerable middle-class emphasis on independence, particularly in terms of the child's learning at an early age to feed himself, dress himself, and so on. It appears, however, that other factors may be at least as important as his family's socio-economic status in determining the independence expectations for a particular toddler. One of these is the responsibilities of his mother. If her hours are filled with a round of household drudgery, labor-saving devices are few and space limited, she may be inclined to give less close supervision to him than the middle-class mother who has been brought up to regard her child rearing as an important part of her responsibility.

The number of children in a family, and the toddler's position in relation to them, may determine the age at which he is expected to relinquish his baby position and perhaps even begin to share, in his own fashion, responsibility for a younger brother or sister. On the other hand, if there are children older than he, toddlerhood may mean merely that he turns from being dependent on his mother to

[16] Mead, Margaret. " Sex and Temperament in Three Primitive Societies," *From the South Seas.* New York: William Morrow & Company, 1939. P. 197.
[17] Mead, Margaret, " Growing Up in New Guinea," *From the South Seas, op. cit.* P. 27.

being dependent on them. The last baby, whatever the class position of his family may be, remains a baby for some time, either because the older children regard him as such or because his parents are themselves reluctant to have him grow up.

Housing conditions may either promote or hinder the early development of independence. The middle-class mother who lives on the tenth floor of a large city apartment house dares not let her toddler go down to the street alone. She, or some adult, must be in constant attendance. In the suburbs, the same child might play contentedly in a back yard with only occasional supervision. In slum areas in cities one often sees 2-year-olds in the street, but inspection usually reveals that they are accompanied by an older brother or sister who may or may not be permitting them independent action.

Unquestionably, the areas in which a child is encouraged to function independently will vary greatly. Thus, the lower-class toddler may be physically less protected than the middle-class youngster, but he may have relatively less expected from him. He may be supposed to go to toilet by himself, but he may not have to learn the accompanying ritual of wiping himself, flushing the toilet, and then washing and drying his hands which is expected of middle-class children. He may feed himself, but without having to acquire certain specified ways of holding his utensils or learning to say please, thank you, and excuse me. He may dress himself, but once a day will probably suffice where the middle-class child may have to shift from overalls to pajamas for a nap, and possibly into another suit for an afternoon visit or even supper with the family. He may be expected to pick up his toys, but he does not have to sort through the quantities which the middle-class child may possess. Nor is he expected to demonstrate cleverness with them that middle-class parents hope their child will show. And it is not a matter of too much moment if his vocabulary develops rather slowly, whereas middle-class parents may be considerably disturbed if their child is not talking early and well.

Possibly more important than actual social status in such matters as these is the family's attitude toward their position. Upper-lower-class parents with a sense of the possibility of improving themselves, getting a better job, or moving to another and better neighborhood, may be more inclined to set high standards for the toddler's independent behavior. Families content with their lot, accepting what has sometimes been called a "common man" status, may encourage independence, but not push for outstanding performance.

It is clear that to encourage the child to independent action is also to offer him additional opportunities for self-assertion. Where much pressure is put on the toddler for achievement, particularly where more is expected than he is comfortably able to accomplish, we should expect that rebellion and accompanying aggression might occur.

Expectations for Aggression in Toddlerhood

To the extent that negativism and temper tantrums are expressions of aggression, toddlerhood is a period when aggression runs high. There are many times when the 1-to-3-year-old is thwarted, sometimes because socialization imposes certain demands on him, again because he is inept in getting what he wants or explaining his needs to someone. Not yet able to focus his anger very well, he either goes into a kind of blind rage, beating himself against the floor perhaps, or he simply balks. Sometimes he expresses his anger by hitting, kicking, or biting the "offending" adult. Less often he has a vocabulary equal to the occasion and can express his rage verbally as well as bodily. His ineptness may sometimes result in property damage, and he is often disobedient, often without any awareness of the nature of his error.

How the adult perceives these incidents and what he does about them may depend on the nature of the experiences he himself has had with aggression, and how aggression is regarded in his particular culture group. The parent who is himself troubled by hateful feelings may regard the baby's expressions of rage with apprehension and a desire to quell in the child all its manifestations. Or he may unwittingly encourage them. Particularly in groups where there is much open aggression, the baby's strong feelings may be admired and even praised. The toddler's tantrum may excite little more than such a comment as, "Takes after his pa. Won't let anyone put anything over on him." On the other hand, in groups with strong authoritarian patterns, aggression may be tolerated only so long as it is not expressed directly toward the parent. Then it must be restricted at all costs.

Middle-class expectations for aggression. American middle-class culture, although tending to promote competitiveness in many aspects of social living, looks with disfavor on the direct physical expression of aggression. According to some authorities, the control imposed on aggression in this group is relatively severe. Others, particularly among the better educated, see something of an ambivalent tendency. Thus the parent, recognizing that the toddler's temper is in part occasioned by his lack of experience, is inclined to be tolerant of it. Nevertheless, it makes him uneasy so that he tries to temporize, " ignoring " the child's behavior, offering him various inducements to be " reasonable," and often feeling upset that he hasn't himself enough patience and tact to prevent all such outbursts.

The American home, particularly in the middle class, is so filled with objects intriguing to the eyes and fingers of a small child, and the American sense of property rights so strong, that destruction of property early becomes an important issue in his socialization. The ways of coping with the problem are varied. Some parents operate on a policy of substitution — " That's Mommy's vase. Baby can have *his* ball." Some emphasize the forbidden with " No-no's " and perhaps slaps. Others accentuate the positive, trying to see that the baby is always provided with things he *can* do. They remove all breakable objects from the living room or expect him to remain in his playroom. Prohibition is thus implied, but never specified. Some take a kind of *laissez-faire* attitude in which anything goes as long as the child is viewed as " only a baby." Although one of these methods may tend to be used more characteristically than another in a particular family, all of them may be tried. There is no one pattern for teaching the American middle-class child property rights, nor is there any one way of handling his transgressions in this area. In this, as in other aspects of his socialization, expectations will vary depending on the social and economic position of his family, where he lives, and most importantly on the particular parents he has. Such variations are apparent when we look at the variety of social factors which were operative in the lives of our six youngsters. Some of those which may have been particularly significant during toddlerhood are included in the following comments:

Jane Warner. Jane's father and mother were never beset by the financial worries which threatened most of the other families. They lived in a quiet, well-kept, orderly home, in a neighborhood where there were almost no children.

During this period Mrs. Warner was injured in an automobile accident. She was not very well for some time thereafter and worried greatly about herself and also about the safety of the members of her family. Mr. Warner took increasing responsibility for Jane, of whom he was exceedingly fond. His work schedule permitted him considerably more time with her than was possible for those fathers who always worked in the daytime.

Pat Plummer. Patty's father's work was " steady," but throughout the period of her toddlerhood he was on part time so that the income was never very adequate. In addition to this, her mother was in extremely poor health, spending some time in the hospital. Fortunately the relatives who were so close at hand were able to help take care of Pat.

Andrew Drosky. Although the Droskys did not live in as good a neighborhood as the Warners, their apartment was pleasant and well kept. Andy had a room completely to himself. His father was steadily employed, and there were no outstanding economic problems during his toddlerhood.

Dan Mallon. The big social event in these years for Danny was of course the birth of his sister when he was 2½. Living for his family was already somewhat complicated since the income was marginal. Fortunately, Mrs. Mallon was a " good manager " so that they probably made out better than did other families with the same amount of money. Their apartment was small, and Danny was already sleeping in his parents' bedroom. However, when the baby came, her crib was put in the living room.

Charles Brown. These years were extremely difficult ones for the Browns. Mr. Brown never knew whether he would have a day's work or not, and though the family did not find it necessary to have public assistance at this time, it is obvious that it was avoided only by much scrimping and " making do."

Celeste Collins. Mr. Collins was another father who had irregular employment. His plant was closed down for a period of over six months when Celeste was a little more than a year old and again when she was almost 3. Her mother did find work, and Celeste was cared for by her father and grandmother. The Collins' apartment was small and very crowded.

PROBLEM 9. Discuss the ways the social factors cited above might have influenced these children's personality development.

Significance of Social Factors in Toddlerhood

In toddlerhood, as in infancy, the society in which the child lives impinges on him more importantly through his parents than directly. It is still his parents and the immediate members of his family who convey to him the customs, the standards, and the values of his culture. He is barely beginning to venture beyond his house and backyard except under their protection. Yet he has a growing ability to interest himself in and hence to learn from those outside his own family circle. Whether he is exposed to many people or few, travels much or little, has an abundance of toys or none, lives in a world limited to real experience or enhanced by books, radio, and television, eats food adequate to maintain life or to promote optimum growth, is cuddled or exposed to a variety of hazards — all these are, at least in part, determined by social factors. All of these influence the way he learns and what he learns. All have a part in shaping his " inner world."

PSYCHODYNAMIC FACTORS IN TODDLERHOOD

Between his first and his third birthday the child begins to talk. Through this new-found ability he reveals to us something of the nature of his perceptions, the way he thinks, and the confusions he may experience. But there is much which he cannot communicate, for he has yet to learn the names for many of the objects and actions in his world and the designations for his feelings and emotions as well. If we are to understand him, we must still feel with him as well as listen to him. We can still only surmise the meaning of much of his behavior. However, his activity is increasingly so much more organized that clues are more readily identified than was the case in infancy.

On the other hand, the period of toddlerhood is difficult to generalize about. Shall we focus on the toddler of 18 months or shall we consider the 2-year-old or the almost 3? We shall consider much longer age spans as we study children from birth through adolescence, but never shall we find one in which development is more varied or more rapid. We cannot assume that the outlook of the child just leaving the period much resembles that of the child just entering it.

This rapidity of development poses another problem. By the time the child is nearly 3, there has been so much growth and so many shifts in his ways of looking at his world that it is easy to expect from him a degree of differentiation and organization which he has not yet achieved. In order that we shall not overestimate his abilities, we shall examine the nature of his progress toward developing his own controls and toward becoming an independent person before we consider the changing nature of his perceptions, his thinking, and his activity.

Ego Development in Toddlerhood

The infant has a beginning awareness of the world outside himself and an incipient sense of *me-ness*. But it is apparently not until the second year of his life that he becomes clearly aware of his separateness from the various sources of his satisfactions. Not until the third year is he able to exercise much deliberate control of his behavior and begin to consider the wishes and desires of people other than himself. It is at this point that he appears to have an increased awareness of self. He begins to function in a more social and less infantile fashion.

It is assumed that two factors contribute to this gradual change in the child's outlook. One is a new kind of body awareness; the other a new view on his relationships to his parents.

Growing abilities. Growth brings with it increasing abilities to regulate body processes and to explore and manipulate the outer world. Until the achievement of voluntary sphincter control paralleling the development of abilities to grasp and release, the infant's "image" or "mental picture" of his own body would appear to be a diffuse succession of sensations, some unpleasant and some pleasant, with

the shift from the one to the other somehow associated with the intervention of another person. Grasping and releasing add a new di-
mension to the picture. The baby can hold on or he can let go, as
he discovers in learning to control eliminative functions as well as in
motor co-ordination. Further, as he moves about, sees himself in comparison to the adults in his world, and finds he can control some
of the objects with which he comes in contact, he is no longer so
prone to see himself as the center of the universe.

As was the case when we discussed the "inner world" of the
infant, some see this description as one which reads too much adult
meaning into the child's experience. Nevertheless, there is agreement
that independent locomotion and improved co-ordination are important factors at this stage.

Relationship with parents. As the child gains power to use his
body, he also becomes aware of his limitations. Whereas previously
the intervention of the parents on his behalf may have seemed to
be subject to his control, it now becomes evident that he is dependent on their cooperation. Not only does he have to learn to wait
for satisfaction of his needs, but they are beginning to expect him
to function, not as he pleases but according to their wishes. As it
becomes obvious that he is not omnipotent, but subject to regulation
and restrictions, he learns that the surest way to satisfaction and the
most effective avoidance of the unpleasant comes through acceptance of the adults' standards as his own.[18]

There is much to be learned. And what is approved in one situation may be disapproved in another situation which to the toddler
seems identical. Thus, exploring the coffee table in his own house,
the toddler comes upon a metal ash tray. It is empty. No one comments as he examines it, bangs it on the floor, makes it for the
moment a toy. But the same ash tray with cigarette butts in it
becomes a forbidden object. Further, a china ash tray probably looks
about the same as a metal one to the toddler. Certainly it is equally
intriguing. But whether it is empty or full, he finds that an attempt
to reach for it brings a reprimand.

Parents cannot avoid exposing children to confusions and conflicts

---

[18] Ausubel, David. "Negativism as a Phase of Ego Development." *American
Journal of Orthopsychiatry.* 20 (1950), 796–805.

such as this. They are inevitable as an immature mind, just beginning to be able to see relationships, confronts a complex outer world. Further, it is likely only through these processes of learning to limit his behavior that the child develops the mental organization he must have if he is to cope with the world effectively.

The toddler's interpersonal relationships help to determine the kind of self he feels himself to be and the effectiveness with which his own system of control develops. If the adults who care for him are more loving and kindly than hostile and demanding, the child is likely to picture himself as more good than bad. If he is guided more through reward for his correct behavior than through punishment for his errors, he will not only acquire the kinds of controls the adults wish him to have, but he will continue to hold the adults in affection and continue to wish to please them.[19]

A child can be socialized largely through fear. Severe punishment consistently given will effectively and rather quickly condition him against certain behaviors. But the same punishing experiences may engender fear and hatred toward the parents and seriously hamper the adequate development of his own inner control system. Just as he senses his parents' disapproval of the behavior from which he feels he would get satisfaction, so he comes to feel that he himself is disapproved and unworthy. He is no longer free to explore and to expand but tends rather to constrain and restrict his activities. Fortunately, this is not the course of socialization for most children. More usually the child is punished for some of his behaviors and rewarded for others so that he learns pleasantly that there are many things which he can do and many areas of his living which he can control, even though there are also many things which he cannot do. Even so, the limitations placed on him by his parents (and by society) often seem more than he can bear. He is enraged that the world goes not as he wishes. Provided the adults who are important to him continue to provide basic understanding and affection, he can survive these episodes without destruction of his feeling of self-worth.

[19] Mowrer, O. H., and Kluckhohn, Clyde. "Dynamic Theory of Personality," *Personality and the Behavior Disorders,* edited by J. McV. Hunt. New York: Ronald Press Company, 1944. Pp. 86–93.

Excerpts from two records of the behavior of toddlers may clarify the progress of ego development in toddlerhood. They show some of the ways in which the child is developing increased ability to control and direct his impulses.

In the first excerpt, a student of child development who is also a father, is observing the behavior of his young son, aged 16 months. The record is made while the father is still in bed on a Sunday morning. (The comments are the author's.)

Behavior	*Comments*
The baby's mother had sent him to look for his daddy. He first ran to the cellar door touching the knob, smiling and excited, saying "Daddy! Daddy!" (I had been working in the cellar the day before.)	The toddler is no longer merely absorbing affection and care as is the infant. His interests are directed toward the world of people and things outside. The ability to remember, even in a limited way, gives continuity to experience.
Mother said, "Daddy is not in the cellar," and the baby ran to the kitchen calling "Daddy." On his way, he saw my portable typewriter and touched it.	People are associated with objects and places. There is a beginning sense of relationship.
Then he spied the vacuum cleaner in the hall. (This is one of his favorite playthings. He likes to push it around and unwind the cord.) He touched it, climbed on it, said "Mine." He played with the cord a few minutes and then went to the back room, calling "Daddy."	But the world is very challenging and one can always be distracted. Perhaps, what does "mine" mean? This is a wonderful object. Does it seem a virtual extension of a dimly perceived self? One is distracted, but one *can* keep a goal in view.
When he did not find me there, his facial expression seemed to show disappointment. He next ran into the bedroom where he finally found me. His face was beaming. Running up, he said, "Hi Daddy!" and I answered "Hi Baby!"	Here we see the toddler looking to the adult as a source of pleasure. (Even if the father is not "objective" about the facial expressions, his description tells us a good bit about the nature of his relationship to his son.)

Behavior	*Comments*

He ran to the hall and pushed the vacuum cleaner into the bedroom. He played with this a few seconds, all the while saying "Mine."

Next he found a balloon that he had left the night before. He had a wonderful time squeezing, biting and pushing it about. He laughed aloud. Brought the balloon to me, saying "Baboon, baboon!" I thanked him and took it from him.

Basic sensory experiences — smoothness, color, tautness, buoyance, but not yet differentiated.

What's in a name? This kind of "sharing" is not to be confused with genuine altruism. His father's pleasure but adds to his.

He looked around the room and spied the lamp on the night table. Stood in front of it, saying, "Pretty, pretty," but not touching. (He had been told many times before not to touch.) His expression seemed to show longing to touch, but he hesitated.

Here is the basic dilemma. Impulses not very different from those which took him to the vacuum and the balloon push toward the lamp, but the remembered prohibition operates from somewhere within. Whether it would have been effective in Daddy's absence, we do not know.

He danced around the room to the other side of the bed. Found an ash tray, and, before I could stop him, he picked up a discarded cigarette and put it in his mouth.

Is it the size, shape, and texture of a cigarette which offers such enchanting manipulative possibilities? Or is the important element imitation of the loved adult? The toddler has to learn when such imitation is permitted and when it is forbidden.

I quickly reached over and tickled him, which distracted him long enough for me to remove the cigarette from his hand.

Wise use of the toddler's distractibility prevents many a battle. But there are certain situations of real danger when he will have to be removed, regardless of his immediate feelings. Further, as he grows and his awareness of self becomes more differentiated, he may insist

Comments

on testing his ability to get his own way. Failure to do so may excite his rage, but the essential fact that he cannot control all of his world must be worked through.

The second excerpt is taken from a student's notes on a boy not quite 3 after he had been in nursery school a few weeks. The comments are the author's. The behavior is typical of 2-year-olds. When compared with the record above, it shows considerably greater maturity, but a basic similarity in mental outlook. Some of the distractibility seen here might not have appeared had a record been made in the security of the child's own home, or even had it been made later in the morning when the child had had more opportunity to settle into the school situation. It is characteristic of the toddler that his organization and control tend to deteriorate in situations with which he is unfamiliar. However, we are inclined, on the basis of his behavior in other school situations later in the year and his generally happy outlook, to regard the following as representing no more disturbance or anxiety than is felt by most " old " 2-year-olds or " young " 3-year-olds in their first group experiences.

Behavior of T	*Comments*
9:12. Into playroom, sees cart, pulls it a few feet. Sees truck, grabs it. J tries to take it away. Both say, " Mine."	The sense of self as represented in the comment " Mine " seems a little clearer here than in the preceding record. Note, however, that at least with J it is wanting an object which makes it " mine," rather than actual possession of it.
Teacher steps in, suggesting J could use truck on shelf. T takes truck, then moves to color cone. He dumps pieces off, throws one, rolls others back and forth. Sees L with puzzle. Leaves cone, goes to L, embraces her, trying at the same time to grab the puzzle. She walks away. He goes back to cone, rolls one piece over floor.	The 2-year-old tends to see only what is immediately in his vision. Each object, in a sense, calls for his attention.

What is the attraction here? The puzzle or another human being? In either event, T's communication skills are not adequate to the situation. |

Behavior of T	*Comments*
9:15. Goes to where student is helping children build with large blocks. Says, " I wanna get in." (There isn't any room.) He turns away, then comes back, pushes against child already in the building, saying " I go in the house." The child who is in the way resists. T hits him.	Here there is apparent recognition of his own ineptness. He looks to the adult for help, but it is not forthcoming. Now his behavior is purposeful. He is not to be distracted. He reveals a typical 2-year-old concept of space — where one can fit, two should fit also! Again frustration and in response this time aggression. Adults have their problems, too! The student evidently felt his controls were not adequate to such a complex social situation.
9:17. Student takes him by the hand, leads him to another section of the room, says, " This can be your house," indicating a corner back by shelves. He stands there, watching the children building, turns to toy telephone and dials. " Mommie? Mommie, I'm at school." He repeats this.	Was her hunch correct?
	The adults at school deny the help he asks, he turns back to a more sure source of solace and direction. Did the call to Mommie offer reassurance for renewed effort? If so, it symbolizes the 2-year-old's relationship to his mother and the use he makes of her in directing his own behavior.
9:20. Back to big blocks. Says, " I build now." No one protests, so he moves a block. " I want this here."	The other children are as distractible as he. The issue of acceptable social behavior does not have to be resolved this time.

The other children drift away from the block corner.

The general trend of development in the period of toddlerhood is toward increasing differentiation and organization. The child, as both his behavior and his language reveal, is increasingly aware of himself as a separate entity. He is increasingly able to manipulate and arrange if not control the physical world about him. However, he continues to seek his satisfactions in an infantile, self-centered way until he has resolved conflicts with other people in a way acceptable to him and is willing to renounce his babyish ways sufficiently often for more social ones. Until this has happened (and it occurs only gradually), he is very dependent on adults, particularly his parents. In a sense their control systems function for him at those points where his is weak or not yet sufficiently well established. This immaturity manifests itself not only in his relationships with other children and adults, but also in his ways of perceiving the world around him.

Changing perceptions in toddlerhood. The world of things must at times seem completely baffling to the toddler. So often his motor skills are adequate to part but not all of the manipulation necessary to mastery of some object. Or he can see some of the relationships, but not others. Take the simple matter of dressing himself. Clothing these days seems relatively simple, but many hazards confront a 2-year-old in getting into pants and shirt, shoes and socks. The first problem would appear to be, " Which is the front of the pants? " But this often does not occur to the 2-year-old until he has them on and finds he can't walk very comfortably. If they are long trousers, he's really in for difficulty. If they are put on the floor or on the edge of a chair for him and he starts from the front, he does fine until he reaches the point of pulling them under his rear. Somehow the idea that he must stand to solve this problem is for some time quite incomprehensible. If the shirt buttons down the front and is held for him, he's sure to turn his body about so it will go on backwards. Socks are not quite such a problem since fortunately they can go on either foot. Of course, he may put a shoe on first, and he can't distinguish left from right. Then there is the matter of the laces referred to earlier. (The author recalls one independent miss of 18 months who was adamant about lacing her own shoes. For weeks each day following her nap she worked away on them, pushing the laces in and out, here and there, always ending with a pattern which could *not* be tied, always furious when the adult had to redo them, and always insistent that " *Me* do." A beautiful illustration of infantile ego.)

There are innumerable problems of space and distance. As already suggested, a box or any kind of open space seems to beckon to

2-year-olds. One child comes, then two, the space is full, but another and another are clamoring to get in. Or the three-piece puzzle lacks one piece, about two inches in diameter. Thoughtfully the toddler poses above the empty space a three-inch piece that belongs with another puzzle. Carefully he pokes one edge against another, then tries to make it fit by pushing it. Again, the box of cubes the toddler wants most is just out of reach on the shelf. He seems to see that a box would bring him nearer. So he moves one near the shelf. It isn't quite high enough, so he gets a second box. He puts it just on the ragged edge of nothing, for he perceives the gross relationships, but not the more precise ones.

A great deal of the toddler's time is spent using objects in ways which may seem to the adult merely repetitious and even futile. The endless arranging and rearranging of floor blocks in what seems to be no special pattern; the careful spooning of pebbles into pail so that they may be poured out and respooned; the scribbling on a sheet of paper, the call for " more," and the same scribble repeated; the soaping of the hands over and over and the insistence " They not clean! " all of these are the elements from which learning and eventual problem solving and concept formation are made. Unfortunately the point at which the child makes a generalization or works out a solution to a problem often goes unobserved, or is lost in the excitement which a simple experiment on the child's part may create in an adult more interested in orderly living than in intellectual development. For instance, the wisdom of a $2\frac{1}{2}$-year-old's observation that, " Water doesn't stay in this [sieve]," is likely to fall on deaf ears if his parent is confronted with a bathroom floor six inches deep in water!

Many problems cannot be solved because the child is not yet able to see all the elements in it. An example is the situation in which an object is lost. The child sees only the path by which the object departed from him and tries to recover it only over that same path. Woodcock in *Life and Ways of the Two-Year-Old* [20] describes such an incident in which the solution is arrived at by demonstration and later reused.

[20] Woodcock, Louise. *Life and Ways of the Two-Year-Old*. New York: E. P. Dutton & Company, 1941. P. 161.

Somers was dropping pebbles through a knothole in a board lying across two blocks. He was heard squealing with displeasure and was found to be trying to recover one of his pebbles by clawing down with his fingers through the knothole, which was not more than an inch across at its widest part.

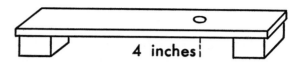

4 inches

The pebble being about four inches below the board and the hole being too small for more than his fingers, he could have no success. He was asked, " How are you going to get it out? "

Somer's solution came promptly, " Mi(ss) Wood'ock? "

He was not given help at once, but he was obviously at a deadlock with the problem. After a while, he was shown that he could lift the board and find his pebble. (It could have been reached from in front without lifting the board, but it was not known which pebble he wanted.)

When the board was replaced, he again dropped a pebble through the hole, started to claw for it, then said, " Move duh board " and did so.

Perception of adults. We have already indicated some of the ways in which the parent serves as a pivot for the activities of the toddler. This central focus appears to be reflected in the way he views the other adults who enter his world. The general trend of his interests is friendly, though he is often suspicious of the individual who appears in a new and, to him, undelineated role. Thus, he may have a host of adult friends to whose greetings he responds cordially so long as they stay in their accustomed places. When the doctor, whom he knows so well in his office, is suddenly encountered in the street, he may react as to a stranger. Adults with whom he has continued contacts are often rather quickly put into the role of parent surrogate, although there are considerable differences among children in the ease with which they make such shifts.

Much of our knowledge of the toddler's ways of viewing adults has come from observations made in nursery schools which included 2-year-old groups. Nursery school experience is now felt to be beneficial only to certain 2-year-olds where it is possible to be extremely flexible about the length of their day and the frequency

of their attendance. Teachers who understand their special needs
are essential. In order to be comfortable without their mothers in
the school situation, most 2-year-olds must first establish a close
relationship with another adult. This relationship develops slowly
as the teacher demonstrates that she, like Mommie, can be relied
upon to " fix " a recalcitrant toy, to help one out of a baffling pre-
dicament with another child, and to assist in the complex business
of dressing, undressing, and toileting. Eventually, if Mommie with-
draws from the picture, the 2-year-old must sense that this adult will
also offer him solace when he is grieved or lonely. When the 2-year-
old needs such comfort, he demands the full focus of the adult's
attention. Somewhat the same trends seem to operate in the toddler's relationships to baby sitters and others who may offer him
temporary care. Occasional toddlers are not merely suspicious of
new adults, but sometimes regard them with outright fear or hostility. Sometimes the source of their feelings is difficult or impossible to locate. The appearance of the new person may be associated with an upsetting experience, as in the case of the child who has
just had an unhappy experience with his doctor and refuses for
a time to have any association with unfamiliar men. Or the child
may feel that the newcomer is going to be substituted for the parent. He is enraged at the possibility of loss. Again, the child may feel
threatened by an adult who makes too rapid an approach, or by one
who is overpowering in his desire to smother the child with " affection," or by one who in more open ways reveals hostility.

Perception of self and other children. The toddler's perceptions of
children of his own age are apt to change considerably during this
period, depending, it seems, on how his own awareness of self
progresses. A study by Ames [21] of children in a nursery school setting indicates typical progress in this respect. At 18 months most of
the toddler's remarks are directed to himself and his own activities.
At 2 these remarks continue, but he adds comments about his relationships with his teacher and statements or entreaties directed toward obtaining or protecting objects. By 2½ most of his conversation is directed to his teacher, but remarks to the children are next

[21] Ames, Louise. " The Sense of Self of Nursery School Children as Manifested
by Their Verbal Behavior." *Journal of Genetic Psychology.* 81 (1952), 192–232.

most frequent. By 3 he devotes most of his conversation to the other children and has even begun to use the pronoun, " We."

As for the toddler's perceptions of children who are older or younger than he, much the same factors are operative as when he was an infant. He can view the older youngsters as menaces to his security (which they may well be if they tend persistently to maul and tease him) or he may see them as delightfully interesting sources of satisfaction if they are kindly and considerate. Child development literature has tended to emphasize the fact that the toddler (as well as the older child) finds his most satisfying companionship with his own kind — children who are at about the same stage of development and have similar interests and abilities. That one toddler can share with another a delightful, warm, and affectionate though occasionally stormy relationship cannot be doubted by anyone who has worked with children of this age. But the potentialities for satisfying experiences between children of different ages have been rather overlooked.

It is likely that the toddler's perception of children younger than himself does not differ materially from the way he sees children of his own age, often as much as objects as human beings. Undoubtedly, however, these perceptions are modified when he has experienced the coming of a new baby in his own family and certainly a baby in his family assumes quite different meanings from those attached to a baby in someone else's family. The relationships which are influential in these instances are, it appears, fairly similar to those affecting the infant. The toddler's own progress toward selfhood and his feelings about his own worth will, of course, be of considerable moment in determining how deeply disturbing the experience may be.

Only one of the six children with whom we have been especially concerned experienced the coming of a new baby during the period of toddlerhood. Dan was 2½ when his sister was born. He had been told of her coming somewhat in advance of the birth and gave no outward evidence of being upset. However, his surprised comments on the fact that she had eyes and his bewilderment at the fact that though she cried she could not talk, are indicative of the confusions typical of the period.

Language and thinking. The thought processes of the toddler are about as difficult for the adult to understand as are those of the infant. If we assume that a description of the inner world is possible, it appears that the toddler is no longer so likely as was the infant to confuse his inner " pictures " of the world outside himself with reality. Isaacs [22] says, " It is ' realized ' that the objects are outside the mind, but their images are ' in the mind.' " These images are " intensely vivid, concrete and often confused with perceptions. Moreover, they remain for long intimately associated with somatic responses; they are very closely linked with emotions and tend to immediate action." [23]

The fact that the toddler is beginning to use language is not too much help to us. The words he says clearly tell us what he has learned, but not much about the process of acquisition. An increase in average vocabulary from 3 words at 12 months to 272 at 2 years and 896 at 3 years, as found in one study, indicates how much learning may be going on in this period.[24] But individual variations, both in the number of words the child knows at a particular time and also the way he learns them, is very great. There have been a great many studies of children's vocabulary which, as McCarthy [25] points out, are as noteworthy for the differences in the way the sequences are described as for the similarities that are found. Much more intensive study of the relationships between the vocabulary development of children and their personality development is needed before the process of language development and its significance to the child is fully understood.[26] In the meantime we are not completely sure why the language development of girls is so generally advanced beyond that of boys, nor why twins are generally more retarded than singletons. Explanations may be found in the child's relationships to

[22] Isaacs, Susan. " The Nature and Function of Phantasy." *Developments in Psychoanalysis.* London: The Hogarth Press, 1952. P. 105.

[23] *Ibid.* P. 104.

[24] Smith, M. K. "Measurement of the Size of General English Vocabulary Through the Elementary Grades and High School." *Genetic Psychology Monographs.* No. 24, 1941. Pp. 311–345.

[25] McCarthy, Dorothea. " Language Development in Children," in *Manual of Child Psychology, op. cit.* P. 504.

[26] See McCarthy, *op. cit.,* especially pages 602–613 for an excellent discussion on these points.

his parents, particularly in the ways in which he identifies with and imitates mother or father.

All of the six youngsters we have been studying had some nursery school experience. The following comments taken from notes made by their teachers when they were between the ages of 2½ and 2 years 8 months show a characteristic individuality in their speech, and also a range of differences in maturity, which are about what one would expect to find in any group of this age.

Jane Warner. Jane is a deliberate, alert little girl who notices everything and talks a good bit.

Playing with the color cone, she removed the rings from the stick, saying, " Oh, it fell down! " Then she stacked the rings on top of one another, calling the result, " A big, big barn." Later she held the stick in her hand and started to put the rings on it. When she got to the top, she shook her head and commented, " Not room."

She has a nice streak of independence. She found some jackstones and said, " What dis? " I told her, " Jackstones." She said, " What dese jackstones for? " I demonstrated and immediately she said, " I do it."

At juice time she was eager to help herself saying, " Me pour it."

At rest time, when I told her to lie down, she said firmly, " I sit up."

Pat Plummer. Patty continues to seem wispy and nervous. Any new occurrence in the group seems to disturb her and add to her babyishness. Her speech is very poor in both quantity and quality. Her consonants are confused and she seldom talks in complete sentences. Examples of her conversation: " Me . . . a . . . ha . . . dis." " More . . . a . . . dis . . . home."

Andrew Drosky. Andy has had a difficult time at nursery school. He is unused to being with children, and his ego seems badly deflated by the discovery that he must share attention. He keeps making demands for attention. When he cried after his mother had left, he said, with an air of pathos, " My cough is choking me."

When he is not being noticed, he says, " I am funny, aren't I? " " Am I a monkey? " " What do I look like doing this? "

He has a drawling, exaggerated way of speaking. Repeats everything he hears said. His voice is very loud, seems to reflect his tension.

He became interested in Anne, tried to throw his arms about her and hug her despite her protests. Finally she pulled his hair. He said, " She doesn't like it when you touch her, I guess."

Dan Mallon. Dan has not been at nursery school much in the last couple of months. He was cared for by an aunt while his mother was having the new baby.

An interesting example of his use of language and degree of determinism came when he visited Miss Sullivan's (the nursery school director) office. She had shown him a small covered box of cubes which he liked very much. After he had played with them for a while, she wanted to see what he would do with a new puzzle; therefore, she had him put the cubes in the box and cover it. Then she offered the puzzle. He looked at it and then said, " You had better take this. You had better put that over there, and I had better have the blocks."

Celeste Collins. Celeste is slow moving, clumsy, seems timid, slow, and awkward, particularly on the playground. She spends a good bit of time working with *little* things, cubes, pegs, and so on. She has recovered from her initial unhappiness, but still seems tense and constrained. She plays by herself and appears happier then than when in direct contact with other children. But she was heard singing softly,

" We wash in school. In school we wash. Then we go home.

I'm going to dirty my hands
I'm going to dirty my face
I'm going to dirty my dress
I'm going to dirty my hair
I'm going to dirty my piggie toes."

PROBLEM 10. In what ways do these descriptions resemble what you might have anticipated from your knowledge of these children? If they differ from your expectations, how do you account for the differences? What do they reveal about each child's self-awareness?

The Role of Anxiety in Toddlerhood

Our description of ego development in toddlerhood has implied the points at which the toddler is most susceptible to anxiety. Overwhelming uncertainty and uneasiness may overtake him when he finds himself in a too unfamiliar situation. He seems to become more alert to the feelings of the adults about him. Sometimes his apparently frantic and often inept efforts to please adults also suggest that he is feeling anxious.

As long as the child is in the process of constructing his own inner controls, he is dependent on adult help to strengthen and support them. This makes him particularly vulnerable to the loss of the adults on whom he has most relied. Separation of the toddler from his mother, it is believed, has potentialities for almost as devastating effects as it has for the infant. Studies now in progress in London may eventually throw considerably more light on the nature of the child's inner experience when he is deprived for a period of the figure to whom he has been closely attached and for whose affectionate approval he has been willing to renounce many of his baby ways. It has already been noted that among a child's common responses to his mother after separation are an intense clinging to her which may last for weeks, months, or years, or a rejection of her as an object of affection, either temporary or permanent (the latter is rare).[27] The determining factors which operate so that one child is but briefly disturbed and another upset for years have not been ascertained.

A major reason for the shift away from providing group experience for 2-year-olds in nursery schools and day-care centers in this country has been the growing recognition that many of them suffer so much separation anxiety that they are unable to derive much benefit from their opportunities to socialize with their peers. Where group experience has appeared to be " good " for 2-year-olds, it has been in those instances where the child has an evidently well-developed sense of selfhood along with sufficient inner controls so that he is already able to communicate in language, to relate himself to adults other than his parents, and to enjoy spontaneous play. Even in these instances anxiety is often evident.

PROBLEM 11. In the preceding sections of this chapter re-read all of the descriptions of children in nursery school. Pick out the behaviors which you think may be indications of anxiety. What clues might the teachers use to decide whether or not the situation was unduly upsetting to the children? How might they help the children to deal constructively with their anxieties?

As in infancy, anxiety may be engendered through the child's relationships with his parents. When his parents are too anxious, too hostile, or too immature to consider how his inner controls are devel-

[27] Bowlby, John, and others. " A Two-Year-Old Goes to Hospital," *The Psychoanalytic Study of the Child,* Vol. VII. New York: International Universities Press, 1952. Pp. 82–94.

oping, they may unwittingly impose on him outer controls which are too rigid or too demanding or insufficient to help him grow. When the child's experiences with his parents are persistently of this nature, a vicious circle of anger and anxiety are set up which may seriously hamper his development of a sense of worthy selfhood.

Again, we must emphasize the fact that the growth impulse is strong and that the toddler whose parents are unfortunately inadequate is sometimes helped to realize his potentialities for selfhood through the kindly offices of some other adult, or perhaps even of an older child who somehow conveys to him the particular strengths he needs. We know a good deal about the destructive effects of anxiety, but not so much about the factors which may help some children to resist it. Nor do we know what price to the developing personality such resistance may cost.

Contributions of the Period of Toddlerhood to Later Personality Development

Erikson [28] defines the central conflict of the period of toddlerhood as that of autonomy versus shame and doubt. What is necessary for its successful resolution is a continuing faith in existence (the trust of infancy) that is not jeopardized by uncertainty about the rightness of the impulses which have come with a more powerful muscular equipment. Growth brings new abilities to do for oneself, to explore the world around one, and to be in a sense, independent. The child needs to feel as secure about himself as a walking, " doing " person as he did when he was a babe in arms. Healthy personality development is furthered as the child learns to govern himself according to the abilities he has thus far developed and to feel comfortable about them. The child whose mutual relationships with his parents are such as to help him achieve this has a sense of personal dignity. He has been given enough freedom of choice so that he can rely on himself. The impossible has not been expected of him so that he has not come to compare himself unfavorably with those more capable than he and thus to doubt him-

---

[28] Erikson, Erik. *Childhood and Society.* New York: W. W. Norton & Company, 1950. P. 223.

self. Nor has he been so filled with rage at his ineptness as to make him ashamed of his smallness.

Autonomy, like trust, is an attainment not just for this period but provides the base for a self-reliance and adequacy throughout life.

Let us now turn to the youngsters we have been studying to see the extent to which their behavior suggests that they have developed attitudes of autonomy and self-worthiness.

PROBLEM 12. Before you read the following material, you may find it interesting to review preceding sections which describe various aspects of these children's living. Consider the factors most likely to contribute to feelings of worthy selfhood. Are there any factors which contribute to self-doubt?

Jane Warner. Of Jane's competence there can be no question. She talks well, is able to see relationships in the world around her, makes friends with her teachers and, to a lesser extent, as one would expect, with children. There is good evidence of her developing sense of selfhood. Her personality makes itself felt. She expresses her own wishes and desires in a " fussy " attitude toward eating, in some resistance toward toilet training, and in occasional temper tantrums. In general, she is regarded as a " good " child who conforms fairly well to what are rather carefully held standards for her behavior. That these controls are not developed without some tension is suggested by the fact that she develops a habit of playing with her lip which just avoids being finger sucking.

It is, of course, impossible to know what Jane's real feelings are, but as we watch her carrying through routines, exclaiming over picture books, directing her dolls in close imitation of the way her mother directs her, only occasionally expressing her own feelings, we may wonder whether she has perhaps too much taken into herself the ideas and attitudes of her mother. Does she have sufficient sense of her own worthiness, apart from conformity to the patterns which have been set for her?

Pat Plummer. Patty, unlike Jane, is not pushed toward conformity; indeed, there even seems to be considerable indulgence. On the other hand, perhaps because her mother is frequently ill and she is cared for by relatives, she does not seem to develop a very strong push toward independence. It should be noted that she herself had a fair number of illnesses during this period, which, though not serious, may have discouraged either her mother or her relatives from expecting her to do very much for herself. By the time she is 3, it appears that she has not yet really established a strong sense of autonomy, either because she does not have as strong drives toward independence as do some youngsters or because she has been sufficiently protected so that she has been able to find no outstanding advantages in developing greater independence.

Andrew Drosky. Andy, almost more than any of the other children, appears to be still dependent on adult approval. He functions pretty well when this is forthcoming, which suggests that he has yet to complete his emancipation from his mother. Until this is accomplished, his sense of selfhood is limited, for his control system is adequate only when she is present, or when he can make someone else assume a role of admirer similar to the one she has held.

Dan Mallon. In Dan we see some of the behavior so often associated with 2-year-oldness. "He has a mind of his own," and there appear to be rather a number of battles of will with his mother. We are not always sure who wins out, and perhaps Dan isn't either. Dan has as much or more freedom to exercise his own growing abilities as any of the six.

Charles Brown. As is so often the case with twins, it is difficult to tell just how much progress Charles makes toward a sense of separate selfhood. His actions tend to be seen always in relation to Chet's, and vice versa. Both of them are active, but there is no evidence of any strong push toward independence during this period.

Celeste Collins. Celeste's sense of selfhood seems to be somewhat mixed. As early as 2 she reveals one aspect of her picture of herself when she says to another child, "You watch C'este. C'este knows how to walk." On the other hand, she lacks sufficient confidence to relate herself to other children very well. Perhaps we can say that she sees herself as competent in some areas, but has doubts about herself in others.

PROBLEM 13. In the light of the above statements and the other material in this chapter, what strengths, either in himself or in his environment, do you think each will probably rely on most as he moves into the next period of development?

No one of these children appears to have resolved the conflict between worthy selfhood and doubt or shame with complete success. The variations which we see here are about the same as those which we should expect to find in any group of healthy toddlers. The dif-

ferences in the vigorousness with which these children seek independence may be attributed partly to biological factors, partly to
the kinds and amounts of encouragement or discouragement toward independence their environment has provided them. Out of
these unique experiences each child has developed some sense of
selfhood. How each child sees himself, how much he is disturbed by
doubt about his worth or feels ashamed of his behavior will perhaps become more evident as we study him in the ensuing years.

Desirable Guidance in Toddlerhood

It is doubtful whether any other stage of development demands
more patience and understanding on the part of parents than does
toddlerhood. The baby wants increasingly to explore and to do
things for himself. He is unsocialized and must be trained in some
of the ways of the world. In what areas can he have choice and
freedom and in which ones must parents make the decisions regardless of how he may feel about them? This is a difficult question and one for which a precise answer is impossible.

Much depends on the particular child and his parents. Some
parents are extremely sensitive to the shifts in the child's abilities to
deal with his world. They are able to adjust their demands to his
growing skills. Other parents find it difficult to sense the child's
readiness to take over certain controls for himself. Some children
reveal rather clearly such readiness, while others are more complex
and what is likely to be best for them is not so easy to ascertain.

Parents provide the best guidance they can with whatever inner
resources they have at their disposal. Just as in infancy, they are
most effective when they themselves feel basically confident and have
convictions regarding their own self-worth. When they are unhappy, anxious, or hostile, it is difficult, if not impossible, for them
to sense the child's needs. Rather than seeing his ineptness, his accidents, and his efforts to impose his baby-will on theirs as marks of
his immaturity, they tend to take them to mean what they might
in an adult. They may assume that he is capable of decisions far
beyond his abilities and withdraw their control, or they may decide
that his obstinacy must be quelled and attempt to impose more and
more control on him.

When parents are deeply troubled, advice regarding guidance is not of much avail. Their own needs are likely to be so great that they distort whatever suggestions are given in order to suit their own unconscious purposes.

However, most parents and many others, who are in one way or another responsible for the guidance of toddlers, may find certain principles helpful.

Consistency helps. An understanding of the toddler's inexperience and his need to learn through experience of a consistent sort is essential. This principle applies equally to the " Do's " and to the " Don't's " which he is expected to acquire. Take, for example, the matter of " getting into things." To put a baby who is just learning how the world feels and tastes, what objects are " heavy " and which are " light," which smooth and which rough, into a living room filled with fragile keepsakes not to be touched, is to expose him to endless and unnecessary frustration. On the other hand, to assume that nothing should be forbidden him, is to take an unrealistic view of the nature of modern living. There are some objects which are dangerous, which can be kept out of reach — cleaning fluids, matches and so on — but there are others, such as electric cords and plugs, which the toddler must be trained to avoid. Whatever these may be, it is important that his attempts to get at them are always forestalled. If he is sometimes scolded when he starts to play with a cord dangling from the toaster, another time spanked, and the next time ignored, he has no way of knowing what is expected from him. When his approach to the toaster always meets with disapproval and he is distracted from it to some other object of interest to him but lacking in danger, he is not so likely to become confused.

In the early months of toddlerhood, especially, deeds are much more effective than words. The baby needs considerable experience before he comprehends fully " No! No! " " Hot! " or " Sharp! " Such simple phrases as these, however, are more intelligible to him than more complex explanations. Indeed, even through the third year, directions given in the form of positive statements accompanied by action usually produce good results whereas talking alone is often useless. For example, " Let's find Panda " may detract the toddler from his path toward the television set controls, but, " Now don't go near the television set, you'll spoil the picture," is almost guaranteed to impel him to twist the dials. (One ingenious father has rigged up a board with plastic knobs which satisfies nicely the manipulative interests of his 18-month-old son in this situation.)

Conviction helps. No doubt, an important reason for the greater effectiveness of the adult who acts instead of merely talking is that he is a person of conviction. He is not afraid to exercise the control which he knows the child needs. As the child grows and develops better understanding, the adult can rely more on language and give him greater choice. But the choices must be appropriate to his stage of development. Thus a 2-year-old may choose between red socks or green socks, but he cannot be expected to make a decision as to whether or not he will wear a jacket on a cold day. Adults sometimes unwittingly get into trouble because of a tendency to offer the child a choice he cannot really make. For example, " Do you want to come in and have lunch now? " is almost sure to be answered with, " No," whereas the simple statement, " Time for lunch," would have been accepted.

Understanding the toddler's view helps. Another difficulty in guiding the toddler arises when the adult's pace is too fast for the child. The youngster, immersed in his play and lacking the time sense which the adult has learned, cannot make transitions readily. Thus, if he is peremptorily called for lunch, he will balk, but if given the signal that it is time for lunch and a few (but not too many) minutes to finish what he is about, he will come quite readily. Frequently, the " No " of the toddler does not really mean " No," but rather, " Not just yet," and it is his way of expressing his independence.

A general emphasis on the positive, indicating to the child what is to be done next in a simple way which does not offer him a chance to refuse, does not mean that all unpleasantnesses are to be avoided. There are bound to be some situations in which the child will insist on something other than what the adult knows is best. In his frustration, he may even go into a temper tantrum. This, of course, is no time for the adult to change his mind and " give in," for to do so only gives the child an unrealistic idea of his own power. Most children, when they sense that the adult's decision is really not to be modified and that he is not unduly concerned by their outbursts, recuperate fairly quickly. However, some will keep themselves in a state of frenzy for an hour or more unless the adult intervenes with some face-saving gesture. When temper tantrums occur very frequently and persistently, the adult will want to consider whether too much may be expected from the toddler, whether he may be unduly fatigued, or perhaps anxious.

How to handle the situation in which the child is to receive something which will make him uncomfortable, but which is nevertheless necessary, is difficult at all ages, but particularly so with the toddler who cannot yet comprehend explanations. For example, adults may say regarding the treatment for a minor cut, " This won't hurt," even though they know it well may. Far better to say, " This will hurt a little," and make the necessary application followed by whatever comfort the child is most likely to relish, than to attempt to inveigle him with some falsehood. Even when he does not clearly understand the words, he seems to sense and be made uneasy by the adult's deception.

The same principle holds in preparing the toddler for any new situation. Because his concept of time and use of language is limited, not much can be done by telling him what is to happen in advance, but one can accustom him to the new and unexpected gradually. Thus, an opportunity to get acquainted with a new baby sitter on an occasion when mother is *not* going to leave him, makes it easier when mother does have an evening out. If the toddler is to venture into unfamiliar territory, it is comforting to take some well-known and well-beloved toy along. Many toddlers, when they must be separated from their mothers, find solace in having her leave with them a familiar garment of hers, as a scarf or a sweater.

Desirable guidance for toddlers appears to depend very much on the adult's ability to see the world from the toddler's point of view. When he can do this, he will sense the child's need to keep the familiar close to him, to find the adults predictable and reliable, to proceed at his own pace, to experience transitions gradually, and to be not too much talked at. When the adult finds the toddler persistently too baffling, too annoying, or too stubborn, it is time for him to turn the focus of attention away from the child to ask, " What happens here? " " Is the difficulty in the child or in me, or in the relationships between us? " The toddler, like the child of any other age, may bring the adult face to face with the child he once was. Difficulties in understanding him and in guiding him may stem in part from the fact that he has never quite understood or come to terms with his own childish rages and fears. He has never completely experienced autonomy and hence finds it hard to help another to begin to be an independent person.

Testing out some basic skills.

7

~~~~~~

Testing Their Powers:

Biological and Social Aspects of Development from 3 to 6 Years

THE PERIOD FROM 3 to 6 years, on which this chapter is focused, is a period in which children try out, embellish, and develop the basic skills they have acquired earlier. Should a 3-year-old by some mischance awaken one morning to a house in which there were no adults, he could, if he were not unduly frightened, pull on enough clothing for protection. He would be unable to tie his shoes, but he could slip into them and probably manage pants and a shirt and a jacket. If he were hungry, he would know where to look for food and perhaps could work out some arrangement to climb to the shelf where bread or cereal might be kept. He could undo a cellophane wrapper or a cardboard carton. He might be able to open the refrigerator and, if he succeeded, could pour himself a glass of milk, not necessarily without spilling. Or, he could go to a next-door neighbor and explain his plight in rudimentary fashion — "Mommy gone" or "I want my breakfast."

Obviously, the 3-year-old cannot maintain himself very long without adult assistance, but he has already established the elementary patterns of motor and social behavior, which will gradually be elaborated into independent functioning. The years from 3 to 6 are ones in which the child develops increasing ability to control his own behavior. By the time he is 6, he is not so impulsive as at 3. His perceptions are no longer so dominated by his emotions. He lives more in a world of reality and less in a world of fantasy. He can understand a number of relationships in the physical world. His sense of time, though limited, is sufficient so that he can look ahead to tomorrow and even next week. He is not so distractible and can direct his thoughts more effectively. He knows his actions have consequences for other people and is more alert to their responses and feelings. His conscience has begun to function more effectively.

Such competence does not develop suddenly or all at once, and many children at 7 or older are still in the process of arriving at it. In general, however, it is during the period from 3 to 6 that the child tests out his growing powers in both imagination and reality and learns what his potentialities may be. No aspect of living goes untouched by his vivid, ebullient imagination.

Poised at the top of the climbing apparatus, he is the pilot of an airliner or perhaps a Superman about to take flight. Pedaling his tricycle " no hands," he becomes the circus stuntman he has seen on television. He puts paint to paper, and before him are the castles and the dungeons of his mind, the aspirations and the fears which he cannot yet verbalize. He builds a mighty skyscraper with his blocks, destroys it with a well-directed kick, then seizes on the opportunity to summon the fire engines and to man the hoses. This ability to transform the humdrum objects of reality into manifestations of his own impulses and desires carries with it some threat, for the actual realization of some of these would indeed be terrifying. But this same ability also enables him to visualize a variety of relationships in the world around him, to set up hypotheses regarding them, and eventually to apply the method of science to testing them. In like fashion he tests his powers in the world of people. His language shocks. Will it also harm? The adults he knows engage in such fascinating occupations. How far can he go in being like them? Like Daddy, can he drive a car, make a scene at breakfast? People get in his way. Small brother takes some of the care and attention that once belonged to him. Can he perhaps wish him away?

Over and over again, the child in these years tests out limits. How far can I go? What is real and what is only imagined? What are the consequences of this bit of action? How is the world organized? What can be depended upon? What is predictable? These, of course, are not the child's words, but as the adult watches, these seem to be the questions he is asking. To the extent that his experience enables him to test his powers as fully as possible, but always within the limits of safety to himself and to those around him, he emerges with a considerable awareness of reality and confidence in his own abilities to deal with it. He has a sense of initiative which will serve him well as he grows toward adulthood.

BIOLOGICAL ASPECTS OF DEVELOPMENT

The powers which the 3-to-6-year-old tests are many and varied, but the extent to which each flourishes will depend in part on his physical vigor and the general progress of his development. The experience of the child who is advanced in muscular co-ordination and skill will differ markedly from that of the child who is still awkward and inept. The child who is weak and sickly will not see himself in the same way as will the one who is strong and energetic.

Physical Growth

This is the period when individual differences in rate of growth and activity drive, rhythm, and tempo begin to show themselves more markedly than in previous periods, although not as much as in ensuing years. The older a child grows the less likely is it that we can predict his behavior from knowledge of his age. Some slight indication of this can be seen as we examine the growth records of the six youngsters in whom we have been interested.

As the charts in the Appendix (pages 472–477) show, all six children at 3 years of age lacked only a pound or two of being the same weight. With the exception of Andy, who was tall from birth, they were equally close together in height. By the age of 6 the differences in weight, excluding Jane who was 10 pounds heavier than any of the rest, had increased to 4 pounds. The differences in height, again with the exception of Andy, remained about the same.

PROBLEM 1. Study the growth curves that are shown in the Appendix. During this period, which children tend to retain their position in relation to the norms for height and weight? Which ones shift position? What factors might account for such shifts? Suppose that our group of children had included one whose height and weight tended to fall at the ninetieth percentile, and another whose height and weight tended to fall at the tenth percentile, what would the differences between the two be at 3 years? At 6 years?

As we have indicated previously, height and weight alone do not indicate very much about the progress the child is making. However, the fact of falling at either extreme of one's group, may considerably affect personality development. For example, a child whose body type is such that he is very tall in relation to his peers, may have expectations set for him which are considerably beyond his actual maturity. A child who is quite tiny may be " babied " more than is actually necessary for his stage of development.

Skeletal development. Some idea of the child's progress toward maturity can be ascertained from measures of his skeletal development. Between 3 and 5 years ossification centers will have been formed for most of the bones of the fingers and thumb and the wrist bones will be in process of formation. Girls, on the average, tend to be more advanced in skeletal development than boys.[1] They have, however, a smaller percentage of total weight in bone and muscle than do boys.[2]

Records on all of our children are not available for this period but there is an indication that Jane and Celeste tend to be somewhat advanced in skeletal age, while Andy is slightly behind.

PROBLEM 2. Explain why a child's position so far as skeletal age is concerned does not necessarily correspond with his position in height and weight.

During this period the length of the legs increases relatively more than the rest of the body. The pelvic girdle widens somewhat and the characteristic toddle of the young child is replaced by a more flexible gait.[3] The child's posture is, of course, dependent not only

---

[1] Rand, Winifred, and others. *Growth and Development of the Young Child.* Philadelphia: W. B. Saunders Company, 1946. P. 126.

[2] Stuart, H. C., and others. " The Growth of Bone, Muscle and Overlying Tissues as Revealed by Roentenograms of the Leg Area." *Monographs of the Society for Research in Child Development.* Vol. 5, No. 3, 1946. P. 44.

[3] Rand and others, *op. cit.* P. 131.

on skeletal structures, but also on muscle development. Muscles tend to develop rather rapidly from the fifth year on, with the large muscles, particularly those in the legs and back, somewhat in advance of the finer muscles in the hands. Posture and the child's ability to use his body effectively are dependent on the child's general health and well-being, both physical and emotional.

Posture and body mechanics. Contrasts in posture and in characteristic ways of using the body can be seen in the following comments taken from records of our children's physical examinations and nursery school activities during these years.

Jane Warner. Jane was a child of short build, with particularly short legs. Her posture was generally poor. Leg and back muscles were good, but abdominal muscles weak. Most of her play throughout this period was of a sedentary kind. She showed very little interest in activity.

Pat Plummer. Until she was 4 years old, Patty also tended to be a rather slow, heavy, inactive child. Her fine muscle co-ordinations were initially clumsy, but tended to improve somewhat more rapidly than the large ones, perhaps because she did not care to exert herself with any kind of large equipment. From 4 on, however, she took more interest in active play and began to manage her body somewhat better than before. Her posture, however, remained poor.

Andrew Drosky. Andy was a well-built little boy, capable of excellent use of his body, but, at least in nursery school, inclined to somewhat aimless activity which did not reveal his full capabilities. Some improvement in the amount of large muscle activity and in the skill with which he used his hands was noted from the age of 4 years on.

Dan Mallon. Danny, always an active youngster, was generally skillful in large muscle co-ordinations. Even at 6 smaller co-ordinations tended to be somewhat awkward. At 4½ he lacked subcutaneous tissue, his posture was becoming poor, and other signs suggested chronic fatigue and malnutrition.

Charles Brown. Charlie was another active boy. In contrast to Danny, however, he was skillful in both large and small co-ordinations. His posture was excellent.

Celeste Collins. A well-built youngster, Celeste, nevertheless, made a poor showing in large co-ordinations. At 3½ years of age she was still wheeled about outdoors more often than she was encouraged to walk. At 4 she was anemic and chronically fatigued. Her posture continued to reflect her lack of vigor.

PROBLEM 3. Discuss the ways in which each child's characteristic motor patterns might either reflect or influence his picture of himself. What influence will they have on the character of his "power-testing"?

PROBLEM 4. If possible, observe the posture and characteristic ways of using the body of several 3-to-6-year-olds. Consider the effect on each of nutritional status, body type, opportunities for activity, and emotional stress.

Teeth and the development of the jaw. Early in this period, development of the deciduous teeth is completed. Calcification of the first permanent teeth continues throughout these years. There are also marked changes in jaw formation, closely related to the development of the teeth. The importance of adequate dental attention and good nutrition cannot be overemphasized. Persistent thumbsucking has been associated with malformation of the jaw. However, its effects appear to be temporary if it is not continued beyond the age of 5 or 6, and in some instances self-correction has been noted as late as 10 years.[4]

Trends in Motor Development

As the child grows older, his motor skills reflect increasingly the kinds of opportunities he has had. We can, however, gain some idea of his increasing power by examining some of the trends in motor development revealed in normative studies.

We have already noted that the 3-year-old walks and runs easily and smoothly. He can jump down 12 inches with his feet together. He can ride a tricycle. By 4 he walks more steadily and with a gait similar to that of the adult. He enjoys a variety of stunts, such as whirling, swinging, somersaulting. He can make a running broad jump of 23 to 33 inches. He can skip with one foot. His starting and stopping facilities are well developed. By 5 grace, ease, and economy of movement characterize his activities. He can skip with both feet.[5]

Similar progress is noted in ball throwing. The 3-year-old hesitates before throwing and throws mostly with his shoulder and

[4] Lewis, Samuel J. "The Effect of Thumb and Finger Sucking on the Primary Teeth and Dental Arches." *Child Development.* 8 (1937), 93–98.
[5] Gesell, Arnold, and others, *The First Five Years of Life.* New York: Harper and Brothers, 1940. P. 73.

elbow. By 4 years he has acquired a more definite stance, throws the ball straight ahead, but does not time its release well and has poor control of its height. By 5 the ball is directed from the side of the shoulder and trunk, and leg movements begin to be incorporated into the whole pattern. Some 5-and-6-year-olds, particularly boys, show considerable maturity in throwing.[6]

For typical progress in small motor co-ordinations, we may consider the way the child holds a pencil or crayon. At 3 the child picks up the pencil by placing the thumb at the left of its shaft and the fingers at the right. Then he adjusts it between the thumb and index finger in imitation of the adult. At 4 the pencil is also picked up in adult fashion. " Writing " is small and cramped, but he can draw a fairly round circle. By 5 he is quite an expert with the pencil. His writing hold is very like that of the adult. He can copy a square or a triangle and trace a path within two parallel lines. By 6, though his movements are slow and laborious, he is really " writing."[7]

Individual variations from these patterns are many. An occasional child (Celeste is an example) becomes fairly adept at small co-ordinations although his large muscle activities remain awkward and poorly co-ordinated. Many children at 6, as is quickly apparent to any observer in first grade, have little skill for writing and manage to print their own names only with great effort.

Eating, Sleeping, and Elimination

Eating. When we consider differences in body type, rate of growth, and customary activity, it is evident that we can expect increasing variation among children of 3, 4, and 5 years in so far as requirements for food, rest, and elimination are concerned. All of them need appropriate amounts of protein and minerals to build skeletal and muscular structure, vitamins to insure the best use of other food elements, sufficient fats, starches, and sugars to supply needed energy, and water and roughage for efficient functioning. With these available, there would seem to be no reason why the child might not as effectively " self-select " his diet in these years as in infancy and toddlerhood. Moreover, since by the age of 3 most

---

[6] *Ibid.* Pp. 86–89.
[7] *Ibid.* Pp. 90–91.

children's digestive systems can handle most of the foods adults eat, adequate nutrition for children of this age should not be difficult to achieve. Unfortunately, a number of factors may complicate the situation.

Perhaps the most important of these is that the child so readily uses the eating situation to serve his own psychological as well as physiological needs. He learns that a sure way of gaining mother's full attention is to pick his way through his dinner. Or, feeling unloved, he comforts himself with more food than his body would ordinarily require. Current emphasis on the wisdom of the child's own appetite and on the fact that a diet may be poorly balanced at a given meal and yet average out over a period of a week to include all the necessary food elements, has helped parents to treat eating more casually. The nursery school teacher, for example, may encounter far fewer " feeding problems " today than was the case in the early thirties when each day's rations were rigorously prescribed. Unfortunately, however, the facts that the basic food elements must be available, and that too great an abundance of highly sweetened rich foods take the edge off the " natural " appetite, may be forgotten. Sometimes parents unwittingly teach children to overvalue candy and desserts by offering them as bribes for finishing the rest of the meal.

Once the child has learned to feel that some kinds of food are very much preferable to others, his appetite becomes a less reliable guide to an adequate diet. It is clear that parental attitudes and feelings have a great deal to do with the child's eating.

Economic factors may also considerably influence nutritional adequacy. Where incomes are insufficient to provide all the needed food elements, the effects on children of this age will be apparent.[8] (Malnutrition was widespread during the depression years in which the youngsters we have been interested in were small.)

Sleep. Adequate rest is essential to good growth in these years. As with food requirements, individual needs vary widely. Some children soon after 3, or even before, begin to concentrate all of their sleep-

[8] Jeans, Philip C. " Feeding of Infants and Children," in *Handbook of Nutrition — A Symposium,* prepared under the auspices of the Council on Foods and Nutrition of the American Medical Association. New York: The Blakiston Company, 1951. P. 291.

ing in the night hours. The nap drops out. Others may nap regularly until 5 and even 6. Most children continue to benefit from a rest period after lunch whether or not they go to sleep. As with eating, emphasis today is on the wisdom of the child's own body, and parents are encouraged to be flexible in their expectations. But here, too, the child's psychological needs or those of the parents may create difficulties. Children in this age period are easily overstimulated. Sometimes they appear to " absorb " tension from the adults around them and become more and more wound up. Under such circumstances they are apt to abhor the idea of rest or a nap, even though they may need it desperately. Rather than wait for the child's behavior to signal his fatigue, parents, who are sensitive to the child's needs, tend to find it wiser to plan a regular time when he rests, even if resting is only a matter of stretching out on his bed quietly with a toy or two. This provision seems particularly necessary for children who live in cities, or in any situation in which there is a great deal of social stimulation. They seem less inclined to rest themselves spontaneously than do children who live in somewhat less complex environments.

Elimination. Eliminative control is usually fairly well established by the age of 3, at least in the daytime. Some children, who are particularly tense, may be slower. Many youngsters, particularly boys, continue to wet at night until after they are 4. Any occurrence which is upsetting or exciting to the child may cause a relapse. The arrival of a new baby brother or sister is frequently the occasion for regression.

Mental Growth

As we indicated in our discussion of intelligence in Chapters 2 and 3, at present there is no way of measuring mental growth in any such direct fashion as physical growth. We discuss mental growth in this section on biological aspects of development, recognizing that children do differ in their inherent capacities for such growth. But we also bear in mind that any measure of mental growth we may have reflects the child's experiences and opportunities as well as his capabilities.

In Chapters 5 and 6, we suggested some of the ways in which an infant's or toddler's responses and also his ways of looking at his world become more and more organized. A number of infant tests have been devised to measure this progress, but there is general agreement that not until after speech is established, do the tests begin to have predictive value.[9] This suggests that it is only as the child gets into the period with which we are presently concerned, that we can begin to measure " the average level of performance which has been built up through previous learning " which is represented in mental tests.[10] It appears that prior to this, the child has in a sense been " learning how to learn." Now it is assumed that we can begin to measure something of what he has learned and from that make a rough approximation of his capacities for learning. Actually, results from one test to another during this period vary so much and the child is so sensitive to a new situation, a different examiner, fatigue, or emotional upset that great reliance cannot be placed upon these measures. As Murphy has suggested, an intelligence test given to the child under 6 may reveal as much or more about his personality than about his intellectual capacity.[11] Nevertheless, research in which the same children have been tested repeatedly during these years has thrown some light on the probable nature of their mental growth.

It is generally agreed that the most rapid mental growth occurs during infancy and early childhood. Some workers have assumed that the child achieves about half of his total mental growth before he is 3. Others place the midpoint at the age of 5.[12]

For our purposes, the pertinent fact is that the child does attain such a major part of his eventual mental stature in these early years. It should not be overlooked, however, that just as children differ from one another in rate of physical growth, so they may vary in rate of mental growth. Longitudinal studies reported by

[9] Goodenough, Florence. " The Measurement of Mental Growth in Children," in *Manual of Child Psychology*, edited by Leonard Carmichael. New York: John Wiley and Sons, 2d ed., 1954. P. 481.

[10] Jones, Harold E. " The Environment and Mental Development," in *Manual of Child Psychology, op. cit.* P. 631.

[11] Murphy, Lois B. " The Appraisal of Child Personality." *Journal of Consulting Psychology.* 12 (1948), 16–19.

[12] Goodenough, Florence, *op. cit.* Pp. 478–479.

Bayley and by Honzik and others [13] indicate some of the fluctuations which may appear.

PROBLEM 5. The research which is referred to above is condensed in *Psychological Studies of Human Development* edited by Kuhlen and Thompson, pages 149–158. An earlier report relating only to the preschool period is reprinted in *Readings in Child Psychology* edited by Dennis, pages 320–323. Read these articles or plan to have them reviewed or discussed in class. In the light of the evidence they present, what cautions will you need to bear in mind in generalizing about the mental abilities of preschool children? About the mental growth of a particular preschool child?

Significance of Biological Aspects of Development

Despite the fact that he is much more socialized than as an infant or a toddler, the personality of the 3-to-6-year-old still reflects to a large extent his uniqueness as a biological organism. His size and his abilities to use his body are important factors in the way he views his world. His impulsiveness, his drive for activity, his sensitivity, the way his tempo and rhythm fit with those of the adults who are patterning his existence, all of these tend to make life go easily or with difficulty for him. They are operative in the impression he makes on other people and in the picture he builds of himself. When the demands of socialization are appropriate to his unique capabilities, it is likely that he will learn vigorously and view himself pleasantly.

The patterns of behavior for which he has potentialities for learning during this period are, it seems, almost limitless. What he actually does learn will, of course, depend upon the particular culture group and family to which he belongs.

SOCIAL FACTORS IN DEVELOPMENT FROM 3 TO 6 YEARS

Visitors to the United States from foreign countries do not remain long before they begin to notice some of the ways in which Ameri-

---

[13] Bayley, Nancy. "Consistency and Variability in the Growth of Intelligence from Birth to Eighteen Years." *Journal of Genetic Psychology.* 75 (1949), 165–196.

Honzik, M. P., and others, "The Stability of Mental Test Performance Between Two and Eighteen Years." *Journal of Experimental Education.* 17 (1948), pp. 309–324.

can 3-to-6-year-olds differ from the same age group in their home lands. They comment, " American children are so active." or " They talk so much. They do not wait for an adult to speak to them." or " They seem so jealous of each other. Our children do not fight as they do." The nature of the likenesses or differences they see are less important for us than is the evidence that by this age children demonstrate so vividly their acquisition of certain typical patterns of behavior. Not only do they speak their native language, but their ways of walking, of gesturing, of responding to each other are also characteristically " American."

Despite the many ways in which their ways of behaving and thinking may resemble each other, there are as many other ways in which they are different. In this section we shall consider first some of the major social factors which in one way or another tend to create differences. Some of these we have mentioned before, while others are introduced for the first time. In any event, we believe that it is in this period of development that children become aware, although dimly, of such influences. Later we shall consider the more specific expectations for the child's socialization which may be held within his family. Finally, we shall concern ourselves with the knowledge of social roles he may be acquiring during this period.

Major Social Factors Influencing Development

We have dealt previously with the effects of socio-economic status on child-rearing practices. Here, however, we shall examine independently some of the factors which affect socio-economic status.

Income level. Many of our foreign visitors, particularly those from the more disadvantaged nations, may well question whether any American children suffer from inadequate income, and perhaps on the contrary, whether some may not suffer from an overabundance of the world's goods. But since a high standard of living is a major American value, the standing of any family is bound to be measured against that which is regarded as typical in the United States. A study of family incomes, made at the time of the Midcentury White House Conference on Children and Youth in 1950, indicated that $2,000 a year could be regarded as an inadequate income for a family with children. At that time somewhat more than a fourth of the children in the country as a whole were in families with an income of less than $2,000, while about half were in families with incomes under $3,000, and a little less than a tenth were in families with incomes of $6,000 or more. Many of the children whose family incomes were inadequate were in broken homes. Where both parents were in the home, the major reason for low income was the father's occupation. Farm laborers and some farm operators and workers with low skills (such as day laborers and domestic servants) made up the bulk of the group. A large proportion of these were Negro.[14]

The relationships between low income, inadequate nutrition, and a high incidence of disease have already been indicated. The effects of low income on mental growth and personality development are less direct, but of no less importance. Studies of the measured intelligence of preschool children have revealed a difference of about twenty points in I.Q. between children of the highest and lowest socio-economic groups.[15] Several hypotheses have been proposed to account for this discrepancy. Some evidence favors each, but none provides a completely satisfactory answer. An early assumption was that the differences were largely hereditary, with the more intelligent individuals tending to move into more advantageous occupations, leaving in the lower-class groups primarily those with few potentialities. However, analysis of the content of the intelligence tests has indicated some tendency for such tests to emphasize problems more readily solved by children who have enjoyed certain material advantages. Studies have also shown increases in average I.Q. when children have better educational opportunities. These findings throw considerable doubt on the idea that low-income groups are necessarily lacking in mental potentiality. On the other hand, the fact that the differences between lower and higher socio-economic groups tend to remain constant rather than increasing as the children grow older, when one might expect the advantages of the more privileged to exercise a cumulative effect on their test

---

[14] Witmer, Helen L., and Kotinsky, Ruth, editors. *Personality in the Making. The Fact-Finding Report of the Midcentury White House Conference on Children and Youth.* New York: Harper and Brothers, 1952. Pp. 123–131.

[15] Jones, *op. cit.* P. 648.

scores, tends to argue against the idea that the discrepancy is entirely environmental.

The significance of the effects of low income on the mental development of the 3-to-6-year-old may be lost if we deal too exclusively with averages. It is possible, for example, that a child with considerable innate ability may be born into a home in which there is little to stimulate the imagination, a dearth of materials for play, and no one much interested in answering his questions. As a toddler, he manipulates and explores the environment as fully as possible, but it does not offer him much challenge toward testing his powers as a 4- or 5-year-old. As Isaacs has put it, " Little children are profoundly at the mercy of grown-ups and of the environment which grown-ups determine, and are always ready to draw in the sensitive feelers which they put out to test the world." [16]

Unfortunately, we lack reliable experimental evidence to indicate what the long-term consequences might be if children from low-income families had some opportunities during this age period to experience less stultifying environments.

The effects of low income on personality development also need further study. Undoubtedly, much depends on how the parents feel about their lot. If they are resigned and see no possibility of improvement, they may even in this early stage discourage the child's budding initiative. When their attitudes are apathetic, it is not likely that the child will add zest and enthusiasm to his copying of their behavior. On the other hand, some parents with low income have considerable ambition and may not only encourage the child's enterprises, but even goad him to greater endeavor.

It would be erroneous to imply that only low income has a disadvantageous effect on development during these years. Although research evidence is lacking, it has often been pointed out that extreme economic privilege also has its hazards. Elaborate toys may be offered the child in lieu of warm parental relationships. The child's playthings may so elaborately reproduce reality that he has no scope for the exercise of imagination.

In only one of the families we have been studying (Jane War-

[16] Isaacs, Susan. *Intellectual Growth in Young Children.* London: Routledge and Kegan Paul, Ltd., 1930. P. 82.

ner's) was the income consistently adequate. On the other hand, none of the families experienced the dire and prolonged poverty which so often characterizes migrant workers or Negroes and others to whom only certain menial jobs may be available. Some of the kinds of strain which were undergone are apparent in the following notes.

Pat Plummer. The financial situation in this family continued about the same as it had been. The relatives shared whatever ups or downs were experienced in employment.

Andrew Drosky. Andy was a little over 3 years old when his father lost his job. Since Mrs. Drosky was pregnant and their savings were sufficient to carry their expenses for only a month or so, their worry was considerable. They considered moving in with relatives, but gave up the idea when Mr. Drosky obtained a clerical job which provided a minimum income for food and rent. Mr. Drosky had sufficient skills so that after about a year he was given a small raise. However, the temporary aspects of the work were continually emphasized and the family never dared plan beyond the next month. These insecurities continued for over two years.

Dan Mallon. Mr. Mallon's income throughout this period was marginal, but it was steady, and he regarded himself as lucky.

Charles Brown. The Browns experienced increasing financial pressure throughout this period. The factory where Mr. Brown worked as a cabinetmaker shut down periodically. He secured occasional jobs to fill in, but the total income was less and less adequate. When Charlie was not quite 6, the factory closed down completely, and the family faced real hardship.

Celeste Collins. Like Mr. Brown, Mr. Collins experienced some layoffs during these years, but his situation gradually improved, and by the time Celeste was 5, he had begun to feel that the chances of his staying on at the small factory where he worked were pretty good. Whenever his work had been slack, Mrs. Collins had managed to get in a few weeks at the garment factory, so that they had not run so far behind as some families did.

PROBLEM 6. Discuss the variety of ways in which the above circumstances might influence the children concerned. Consider such factors as the parents' own feelings of adequacy, the amount of time spent with the children, and their attitudes toward their occupational status.

Occupational status. Above subsistence levels the actual amount of income may be less important in the determination of an individual's socio-economic status than is the prestige attached to the particular job he holds. Thus in most communities professional and managerial positions are regarded as superior to those held by clerks, schoolteachers, small business owners, and skilled workers, and these in turn outrank the unskilled laborers and domestic workers. The exact value attached to a particular job will vary with the community, and the status of any individual may also be influenced by other factors including his family's position, the clubs to which he belongs, and so on. The 3-to-6-year-old is not likely to have much direct awareness of the prestige value of his father's occupation. (According to Stendler's study of children's awareness of the symbols of social class, the first grader is only on the threshold of awareness.) [17] Nevertheless, we need not overlook the possibility that in this period, as the child plays at being the father or the mother, or as he takes on some of the roles of other adults, he is to some extent influenced by the attitudes with which the adults regard these occupations. Mostly the child identifies with the dramatic and active. Thus, with him, gas station attendant, truck driver, fireman, and policeman are popular roles. What does the son of a lawyer whose mother comments, " You may as well get those ideas off your chest now, for your Daddy'll send you to law school " learn about occupations? We may be sure that one such remark will not influence the child's social perceptions much, but the cumulative effect of such parental attitudes is not so certain.

His parent's occupational status unquestionably influences many of the child's specific learnings during this period. Although the differences between groups are by no means rigid, there are, for example, many ways in which the behavior of the 5-year-old son of a physician might be expected to differ from that of the 5-year-old son of a day laborer. The physician's son would likely have learned to discriminate between dress clothes and play clothes; shower and tub baths; salad forks, butter knives, and the more usual knife and fork. He would expect to find a napkin by his place at lunch. He

<hr>

[17] Stendler, Celia Burns. *Children of Brasstown.* Urbana: The University of Illinois, 1949.

would certainly have traveled by car and possibly by train and plane as well. He might have visited a farm, the beach, the zoo. Among the many objects in addition to toys, with which he might be personally familiar, would be tennis rackets, golf clubs, cameras, picture books, magazines, freezers, automatic washers. The day laborer's son, depending in part on whether he was living in a slum area or in a shack or in decent housing, would likely know one kind of clothing (though he might have one very special outfit for Sundays); one way to clean oneself up; and expect nothing more of a meal than to find some kind of food on his plate. His travels would be limited, as would the variety of gadgets with which he was acquainted. To what extent television may alter this state of affairs has not been established. Since the young child learns so much from direct sensory experience, it is questionable whether the child who sees a picture and hears a description has the same knowledge of an object as the child who is able to touch and move about it.

But the most striking difference between the experience of such children as these is probably in the language they relate to it. Professional and managerial groups tend to emphasize words in their work, whereas action is all that is required of the unskilled laborer. Occupational groups in between will vary in the emphasis placed on verbal ability. Thus, it may well happen that children from certain groups are unable to communicate the richness of the experiences they have had because they have never learned language sufficient to describe them.

Parental education. As would be surmised from the discussion thus far, the education of the parents is an extremely influential factor in the development of children in this period. In fact, when the child has reached the age of 2, one can better predict his intelligence at 18 years from a knowledge of the parent's education than from the child's intelligence test score.[18] This finding may mean that as children grow beyond infancy, they tend toward a level of intelligence set by their heredity. Or it may mean that better-educated parents provide environments more stimulating to mental growth. However, there seems to be little question but that the chances of a child's realizing whatever intellectual potentialities he may have

[18] Jones, *op. cit.* P. 645.

are considerably dependent on the amount of education his parents had.

Rural-urban differences. Much more is known about city and suburban children than about rural children, particularly in the period of development with which we are currently concerned. The farm child's experiences, even where standards of living are about equivalent, may be very different from those of his city cousin. Levinger and Murphy suggest that:

The cause and effect of a child's activities are likely to be much clearer in the farm setting. If a city child leaves open a forbidden door, arbitrary punishment may follow. If a farm child leaves open a gate, he sees the young turkeys head for the highway, and this direct experience puts meaning into the punishment that follows. Inhibitions that stem from concrete things doubtless have a different meaning from those that stem from mere words spoken by people; not only are the " do's " and " do not's " much easier for the young child to grasp in the natural-consequence setting but it is likely that there is not the same kind of tension as that which comes from violating the arbitrary orders of older members of the family. The process of gaining clarity about objective dangers may stimulate more self-confidence than the process of constant yielding to adult demands.[19]

One might thus expect to find that farm children would consequently be better equipped for later educative experiences, or that they might appear to be more intelligent. Such has, however, not been the case. Most studies of the intelligence of rural and urban groups have found the average intelligence of the urban children to be higher than that of the rural children. Test items may tend to favor city children, and the effects of a tendency for the more able individuals to move to the city have not been sufficiently evaluated. A further possibility is that the farm child is less likely to be as highly motivated toward accomplishment as is the city child. Casual observation suggests that farm children are accepted somewhat more " as they are " and that there is considerably less tension among them.[20] Although there is need for much more study

[19] Levinger, Leah, and Murphy, Lois B. " Implications of the Social Scene for the Education of Young Children." *National Society for the Study of Education.* Forty-Sixth Yearbook, Part II. Early Childhood Education. Chicago: The National Society for the Study of Education, 1947. P. 20. Quoted by permission of the Society.

[20] Lewis, Claudia. *Children of the Cumberland.* New York: Columbia University Press, 1946.

in this area, we can safely generalize that the power-testing experiences of the 3-to-6-year-old brought up on the farm, and probably their effect upon the development of his sense of initiative, are likely to be quite different from those of the child who spends these years in the city.

Race and religion. The disadvantaged position of Negro children has been implied in the discussion of income level. Moreover, membership in such a minority group also carries with it the threat of prejudice and discrimination. Despite the progress being made toward the provision of equal opportunities for all citizens, there are still many areas in which rigid restrictions are placed on the behavior of individuals who are readily identifiable as members of a minority. Research has begun to reveal how early these restrictions are learned, and the effects which they may have on personality development. The development of the sense of initiative may be seriously hampered when parents, fearing that the child may offend someone, find it necessary to place unusually severe restrictions on his attempts to test his powers. A number of studies of the attitudes of young children reveal that the minority group child learns early that his is a special status and comes thus to tend to devalue himself. Clark and Clark,[21] for example, asked Negro children of 5, 6, and 7 years to fill in an outline of a child with the color closest to their own. Eighty percent of the 5-year-olds selected the appropriate color, but when asked to pick the color they would prefer to be, only 37 percent selected the same color. Goodman [22] in an extended observational study of Negro and white children in mixed nursery schools found a rather high degree of race consciousness among both groups. It is significant to note that the recent Supreme Court decision on segregation in the public schools was based almost entirely on recognition of the psychological influences of segregation on the developing personality.

The Negro child, because his color differences are so readily identifiable and because the restrictions on his group are probably

---

[21] Clark, Kenneth, and Clark, Mamie P. " Emotional Factors in Racial Identification and Preference in Negro Children." *Journal of Negro Education.* 19 (1950), 341–350.

[22] Goodman, Mary E. *Race-Awareness in Young Children.* Cambridge, Massachusetts: Addison-Wesley Press, 1952.

more consistent and more pervasive than those on any other minority, most likely becomes conscious of his status somewhat earlier than do members of other minorities. However, the few studies which are available regarding Jewish children suggest that they, too, are aware of their special status and more conscious of their religious identity than are Catholic or Protestant children.[23] That it may be highly desirable for the child to be " properly introduced to his real situation at the age of three " has been suggested by Lewin in an article on bringing up the Jewish child. " It is of first importance that a stable social ground be laid very early," he adds.[24]

The meaning to the young child of his religious affiliation will, of course, depend upon its meaning to his parents. If religion is a strength and a support to the parents, it is likely to be an important influence to the child. But, as Jersild has indicated,

. . . the younger the child, the more his ideas in matters of religion as in other matters will be built upon his own concrete experiences. These are likely to be elaborated by fantasies.[25]

The child of this age cannot deal very well with abstract ideas. The effects of specific religious convictions and practices on the child's development during this impressionable period need much more study than they have had thus far.

Educational opportunities. In 1953 an estimated 43.5 percent of *all children* of kindergarten age in the United States were currently enrolled in kindergarten.[26] In addition, many children attend nursery school, although specific figures are not available. Since kindergarten programs vary widely, states differ in their requirements for the registration of nursery schools, and some children have group experiences under auspices which are not primarily educational, it is exceedingly difficult to evaluate the actual effects of these on the children's development. One rather comprehensive

[23] Hartley, Eugene, and others. " Children's Use of Ethnic Frames of Reference: an Exploratory Study of Children's Conceptualizations of Multiple Ethnic Group Membership." *Journal of Psychology.* 26 (1948), 367–386.

[24] Lewin, Kurt. " Bringing Up the Jewish Child," in *Resolving Social Conflicts.* New York: Harper and Brothers, 1948. P. 176.

[25] Jersild, Arthur T. *Child Psychology.* New York: Prentice-Hall, 1954. P. 535.

[26] Information furnished by U. S. Office of Education, May 1954, and based on 1953 Bureau of Census report.

study reported in 1938 [27] indicated that children who had kindergarten experience were much less likely to experience retardation or non-promotion in first grade or beyond than were those who did not have such experience. The nineteen-thirties also saw a number of studies, many carried on by the research staff at the University of Iowa,[28] which, although always controversial, have frequently been cited as evidence that nursery school experience tends to stimulate mental growth. This conclusion is no longer considered fully acceptable. However, Olson comments:

> One should not jump hastily to the conclusion that nursery schools and kindergartens because they are unable to erase individual differences among children or to make readily discernible and durable changes do not perform important functions. . . . The immediate values for parents and children are sufficient justification, and many important areas and long-range effects are not readily appraised by existing instruments and methods.[29]

The possible values and effects of educational opportunities for young children should become apparent as we discuss personality development in the years from 3 to 6. We shall, however, mention some of them here since they constitute an important social influence in the lives of perhaps *half of the children* of the United States.

We have stressed that this is a period of power-testing. A well-equipped nursery school or kindergarten offers the child a safe environment in which to practice his running, jumping, climbing, and stunting skills. It provides props for the dramatic play and other creative activities in which he lives through some of his fears and fantasies and anticipates his future roles. At the same time it gives him opportunities to test out on a reality basis some of the ideas he has as to the nature of the world around him — it encourages his scientific inclinations. It is true that all of these *might* be found at home, but as living becomes more complex, as people tend to

---

[27] Morrison, J. Cayce. "Influence of Kindergarten on the Age-Grade Progress of Pupils in New York's Elementary Schools," as quoted in Association for Childhood Education. *Examine the Evidence — Studies in Relation to Kindergarten Experience as a Factor in School Life.* Kindergarten Portfolio, Section 4, 1938.

[28] The Iowa studies together with others stimulated by the research there may be found in National Society for the Study of Education. *Intelligence, Its Nurture and Nature,* 1940, Thirty-Ninth Yearbook, Part II. See Jones, *op. cit.,* for a review of these and later studies and a complete bibliography.

[29] Olson, Willard C. *Child Development.* Boston: D. C. Heath, 1949. P. 105.

live closer to one another, as space is increasingly costly, fewer and fewer homes are able to offer children really suitable places in which to carry on their power-testing activities. Further, much of their meaningfulness to the child is dependent on his having an adult near by who appreciates his imagination and fantasy, but who is also alert to his need to know the world of reality, who understands and accepts his strong feelings and impulses, but also helps him to keep them within safe limits. Some parents can serve this function, but many, because of their own strong (and quite normal) emotional involvements with the child, are not as effective in this respect as the teacher may be. Finally, as the child grows beyond the self-centeredness of toddlerhood, he appears to be " ripe " for the companionship of a small number of his peers, so that the years from 3 to 6 are especially propitious ones for encouraging social understanding and cooperation.[30]

Unfortunately, present overcrowding and understaffing in the public schools has resulted in many kindergartens being operated with perhaps two or three times as many children to a room and to a teacher as are considered desirable. It is extremely doubtful that the child's sense of initiative is greatly furthered when he must be herded together with fifty others and put through a highly regimented two or three hours of looking at books, crayoning, singing, and other quiet activities. Nor is attendance at nursery school necessarily beneficial. In communities where standards for their operation have not been established, they may be operated with inadequate space and equipment and without professional staff. Such nursery-schools-in-name-only offer real hazards to the physical and emotional well-being of young children.

Although experiences outside the home assume increasing importance as the child grows toward the age of 6, the most important influences continue to be those within his own family.

Expectations for Socialization

In previous chapters we discussed the socialization of oral, eliminative, dependent, and aggressive behavior, and made brief refer-

[30] An excellent summary and discussion of the research relating to the effects of nursery school experience on social behavior is found in Jersild, Arthur T., *Child Psychology*, New York: Prentice-Hall, 1954, pp. 273–283.

ence to sexual behavior. By the time the child is 3, particularly in our culture, he has already undergone a considerable amount of training in regard to oral and eliminative behavior. His socialization in these areas is, however, still somewhat tenuous. Under stress, he is likely to regress to baby ways, and his baby impulses are frequently evident in his play. Thus, even a 4- or 5-year-old may suck gleefully from the bottle intended for feeding the doll babies or indulge in much " silly " toilet talk. He has, if all has gone well, some sense of independence, but his socialization in this respect will, in most instances, not be completed until adolescence. So far as aggression is concerned, he is likely to have learned not to respond to *every* major frustration with a temper tantrum, but such explosions may be not uncommon. He has some sense of property rights, but his growing power and strength create new potentialities for destructiveness. Likewise physical aggression, verbal aggression, and disobedience may assume new possibilities. Indeed, from the child's view a central problem in the years from 3 to 6 is " How much self-assertion is safe? " If the relationships he has had and continues to have with adults tend to be too unsatisfactory and frustrating to him, his aggressive impulses may become charged with hostility, thus adding to his uneasiness.

Sex training. Sex training, to which we have so far given little consideration, also becomes an important aspect of socialization in this period. As the child grows in awareness of the world about him, he is likely to notice the ways in which he resembles or is different from those about him. The boy becomes interested in himself as a person with male characteristics, while the girl begins to identify her female attributes. Masturbation may increase. Curiosity may lead to social sexual play. In some cultures these manifestations of sex interest will be encouraged, or at least tolerated, in others it will be discouraged or punished.

Although we may consider sex and aggression training separately, we should note that the child may not yet draw such a distinction between the two. When socialization in either or both areas is usually severe with little provision made for the child to channel his impulses in directions satisfying to him, we may look for restricted initiative and evidence of guilt feelings.

PROBLEM 7. One of the best ways to gain a perspective on the socialization of American children is to study the ways that children are trained in other cultures. Plan a panel discussion on socialization in several primitive societies. Specify the procedures by which oral, eliminative, dependence, and aggression training are accomplished. Discuss the extent to which training in one system of behavior is consistent or inconsistent with that in the other systems. To what extent would a 6-year-old in each of the cultures under consideration have established a sense of trust, of autonomy, and of initiative? In what ways would his view of himself resemble or differ from that of a typical 6-year-old in a comfortable middle-class American family? To what extent would the socialization procedures used in each primitive culture be adaptable or inappropriate for a complex culture such as ours?

Material on which to base reports on child rearing in primitive cultures may be found in *Readings in Psychology*, edited by Dennis, in the following articles: Mead, Margaret, "Child Care in Samoa," pp. 507–577, and Malinowski, Bronislaw, "The Form of the Family and Child Behavior," pp. 491–506.

Of interest also in *Readings in Child Development*, edited by Martin and Stendler, are: Hogbin, J. Ian, "A New-Guinea Childhood: From Weaning till the Eighth Year in Wogeo," pp. 149–159; Beaglehole, Ernest, and Beaglehole, Pearl, "Personality Development in Pukapukan Children," pp. 160–169; Kluckhohn, Clyde, "Some Aspects of Navaho Infancy and Early Childhood," pp. 177–193; and Whiting, John W. M., "The Frustration Complex in Kwoma Society," pp. 194–198.

In the American culture considerable differences in both sex training and aggression control may be expected from group to group. To some extent these may follow social class lines. One finds, for example, fairly consistent evidence that lower-class families are more strict about modesty training and more apt to punish masturbatory activity.[31] On the other hand, since they frequently live so closely together and more often play without adult supervision from an early age, young lower-class children appear to have considerably more sex information and sex experience, of an earthy kind, than do more protected middle-class children.

---

[31] Kinsey, Alfred C., and others. *Sexual Behavior in the Human Male*. Philadelphia: W. B. Saunders Company, 1948.

Aggression training. So far as aggression control is concerned, the findings of different studies are not completely consistent. Maccoby [32] reports that upper-middle-class mothers allow at least as much aggression among neighborhood children as do upper-lower-class mothers. This finding runs counter to the general observation supported in some other studies that middle-class children are less apt to settle their disputes by use of their fists than are lower-class children. Maccoby also found that neither group of parents was very tolerant toward aggression expressed against parents, but the middle-class parents were somewhat more inclined to overlook it.

We must re-emphasize the fact that we do not yet have sufficient information as to how social-class membership affects child-rearing practices or personality development to be able to predict the likely course of a child's socialization from a knowledge of his socio-economic position. Not only is there need for many more studies dealing with this factor, but also for exploration of a variety of related factors. For example, religious convictions of the parents, the amount and the kind of education they have had, their housing arrangements, may make for significant differences in child-rearing attitudes among families whose social position is identical.[33]

The psychological environment. In this connection studies focused on the psychological environment in which socialization takes place are noteworthy. Of particular relevance to this chapter, since personality studies of children of the age period with which we are concerned are included, is research initiated at the Fels Research Institute. The Parent Behavior Rating Scales which have been devised to describe home situations suggest the number of factors needed for consideration in appraising the expectations held for children. Among them are warmth, which includes the child-centeredness of the home, the parents' approval, acceptance, affectionateness, and rapport with the child and the intensity of their contacts with him; democracy, depending on the parents' justification of policies to

[32] Maccoby, Eleanor E., and others. "Methods of Child-Rearing in Two Social Classes." *Readings in Child Development,* edited by Martin and Stendler. New York: Harcourt, Brace and Company, 1954. P. 384.

[33] For a penetrating analysis of the hazards of over-generalization on the basis of social class see Gross, Neal, "A Critique of 'Social Class Structure and American Education.'" *Harvard Educational Review.* 23 (Fall 1953), 298–329.

the child and his participation in family decisions; intellectuality, the parents' striving to hasten the child's rate of development, their readiness to explain to him, their understanding of his abilities and needs; indulgence, their babying, protectiveness, and solicitousness; adjustment, the satisfaction, stability, and achievement of the home, its discord, the effectiveness with which policies are carried out and the overt parent-child conflict.[34]

In a study relating the kinds of socialization experienced in the home to his nursery school behavior, Baldwin noted that democracy tended to raise the child's activity level to produce an aggressive, fearless, planful child who was likely to be a leader, but also overtly more cruel than the average child of his age. When the parental attitudes emphasized control without democracy, the child tended to be quiet, well-behaved, nonresistant and at the same time socially unaggressive and restricted in his curiosity, originality, and forcefulness.[35]

PROBLEM 8. The Baldwin study referred to above is condensed in *Psychological Studies of Human Development,* **by Kuhlen and Thompson, New York, pp. 138–146. A supplementary report is found in** *Readings in Child Development,* **edited by Martin and Stendler, pp. 337–345. Plan to review these articles and discuss the issues raised in them. What practical implications, if any, could parents draw from the studies?**

One reason for the discrepancy in findings regarding the kinds of socialization procedures parents use and their effects on personality is that in some studies (those at Fels Institute, for example) the parent's behavior is observed directly while in others (the Maccoby study) the parent is interviewed regarding her practices. In some instances what parents do and what they say they do may agree rather closely. In other instances, they may differ. Some idea of the complexity of the problems involved in evaluating parental expectations for child behavior may be gained by consideration of the following incidents relating to sex or aggression training taken from the lives of some of the children we have been following.

[34] Baldwin, Alfred L., and others. "Appraisal of Parent Behavior." *Psychological Monographs,* 63 (1949), 1–85.
[35] Baldwin, Alfred L. "Socialization and the Parent-Child Relationship." *Child Development.* 19 (1948), 127–142.

Pat Plummer. Patty, according to her mother, was always asking a great many questions. When she was about 4, there were several new babies in the family, and she was very curious about their origin. Mrs. Plummer felt that such information should not be given children before puberty and was always extremely evasive in her answers to Patty.

She believed that insanity was often traceable to masturbation and was careful to see that Pat was always tucked in bed in a way that would make it difficult for her to attempt it.

Pat had quite a repertoire of cute sayings and " pieces " she had learned from various of her many relatives. Mrs. Plummer liked her to repeat these for any visitors, but, as she put it, Patty had " a mind of her own " and as often as not would refuse to comply. When she did, Mrs. Plummer usually cajoled and promised, ending by the withdrawal of some promised reward.

At 4, Patty was able to dress herself completely, but her mother said, " I just won't let her. After all, she's still only a baby."

Dan Mallon. When Danny was a little more than 4, arrangements were made for him to be taken to nursery school by a member of the staff whom he did not know particularly well. When she called for him, he dashed up the stairs and hung over the banister. His mother called to him in a sharp authoritative tone to come down at once. This he did. She told him to get ready for nursery school. He immediately ran back upstairs, yelling down, " I ain't going! " She said he should be ashamed when there were other children in the neighborhood who would like to go, but didn't have the chance. He only yelled again that he was not going. Then she suggested that she would buy him a lollipop when he came home. He said, " I ain't going! " Finally his mother said, " You can either go or go to bed! " and went to get his pajamas. He was still hidden behind the banister, but when she told him to come down, he did so, still crying. She put his coat on and carried him to the car. He stopped crying and she kissed him before she closed the door. He waved goodbye to her.

When they returned that afternoon, the nursery school staff member asked if he had had a good time. He said, " Yes." She questioned further, " Even after all that crying you did? " He said, " Well, I didn't mind going after my mother kissed me."

. . . . .

Sometime later the teacher who knew Dan best, paid a home visit. Mrs. Mallon held Dan in her lap for a while. Then he got restless and climbed from there to a near-by table. He began to spit at her. She took him into the kitchen and told him to stay there until he could behave. He cried a little, but soon came back.

. . . .

Mrs. Mallon and one of the other mothers were discussing the problem of making children mind. Mrs. Mallon said that she sometimes had to spank Dan, but it worried her to do so lest the punishment would somehow destroy his affection for her.

Charles Brown. Charles' mother's discipline was direct and spontaneous. She often threatened punishments which sounded dire. Sometimes her comments implied favoritism for Charles. Observation of her actual behavior, however, made it clear that she was really a warm mother with the welfare of both boys uppermost in her mind.

PROBLEM 9. Assuming that these descriptions typify the kinds of control exercised by these particular parents, what would you say each child is learning about himself and his relationships to other people? What other factors may influence the child's learning?

PROBLEM 10. It is difficult to compare parental expectations when each parent and child are seen in a different situation. For an example of a study in which parents and their children are observed under similar circumstances read Barbara Merrill's " A Measurement of Mother-Child Interaction " in *Readings in Child Development* by Martin and Stendler, pp. 346–357. Does this study suggest additional factors which you might add to your thinking about Problem 9?

As we consider the variety of comments parents make about their children and the different ways they praise, cajole, threaten, reward, and punish them, it becomes clear that not only do one parent's expectations differ from another's, but also a particular parent's expectations may shift from one time to another. Some of these shifts come with changes in the circumstances of the parent and reflect the pressures he is experiencing and some undoubtedly arise out of his relationships with his child. In any event, so far as the child is concerned, the way he channels his impulses, the way he sees and feels about the expectations which are held for him, and the way he feels about himself will depend on the cumulative effect of all the socializing experiences he has had.

Social Roles

It is in this period that the child begins to show an awareness of the organization of the social world around him. The simple mimicry of the toddler becomes the more elaborate, " You must be the mother and I must be the father," of the 4- or 5-year-old. He is learning the nature of social roles, the customary ways of behaving as husband, wife, policeman, doctor, teacher, and so on. In our discussion of the psychodynamic aspects of development during this period, we shall discuss in more detail the process through which the child comes to identify himself more and more consistently with certain roles. The point which we should like to emphasize here is that this is a period of exploration of possibilities. The roles the child tries out and the behaviors he associates with them are dependent on the " models " which his particular family and associations make available to him. For example, a young teacher working with a group of 3-year-olds in an economically deprived neighborhood was appalled at the paucity of the children's dramatic play. She attempted to stimulate them by proposing that they have a tea party, but received only blank stares. How could they play the role of tea party host or guest when they had never seen either? As she came to know them better, she found there were many roles with which they were familiar and which they could play with real dramatic flourish. Included in these were " bride " and " funeral-director," fruit- and vegetable-peddler, as well as the more usual mother and father. When it comes to learning the appropriate roles usually associated with one sex or the other, working-class youngsters appear to be somewhat advanced over middle-class children.[36] This is evidently because working-class families tend to distinguish masculine and feminine occupations more carefully and also because middle-class mothers seem to spend more time with their children than do lower-class mothers. This provides middle-class children of both sexes more opportunity to copy feminine roles.

PROBLEM 11. As you observe children of these ages, see what evidence you can collect as to the social roles of which they are aware. Do you notice differences among children whose mothers work outside the home and those whose mothers do not? Among those whose fathers do " desk " work in a remote office and those whose work the child observes?

[36] Rabban, Meyer. " Sex-Role Identification in Young Children in Two Diverse Social Groups." *Genetic Psychology Monographs.* 42 (1950), 81–158.

Significance of Social Factors

The major importance of social factors in the period from 3 to 6 years lies in the way in which they structure the child's learning. His parents' income level, their education, occupation, race, and religion, whether his home is in the country or in the city — all of these will influence the patterns of behavior available for him to learn. Further, within these limits, the expectations his parents and other adults significant in his life have for his socialization, the methods they use in training him, and the models they provide for his imitation will have considerable influence on the way he views himself and his world. It is to these inner aspects of development that we shall turn in Chapter 8.

8

༺ɲༀɲༀɲༀɲༀɲༀɲༀɲༀɲༀɲༀɲༀɲༀɲༀɲༀɲༀɲༀɲ༻

Testing Their Powers:

Psychodynamic Aspects of Development from 3 to 6 Years

THIS IS A PERIOD in which children become increasingly competent at controlling and directing their own behavior according to the demands of the society in which they live. The child's feelings and emotions are increasingly differentiated. He learns new wishes and desires. He learns to distinguish " right " from " wrong " according to the precepts of his parents or those adults of significance to him. His perceptions continue to be dominated by his feelings, but increasingly he is moving from fantasy toward reality, from an egocentric view of the world toward greater social awareness.

PROGRESS IN EGO DEVELOPMENT

From time to time we have spoken of an inner control system and have implied that the increasing complexity of the child's perceptions, his thoughts, and his actions parallel the development of that system. We have indicated that the nature of the learning processes through which this is accomplished are not yet fully understood, although a considerable amount of research is currently devoted to them. Eventually we shall expect to be able to explain in terms of a consistent learning theory many phenomena which at

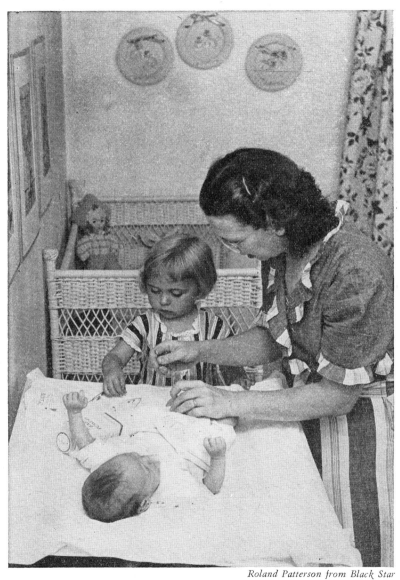

Developing basic attitudes toward oneself and others.

present, at least within the scope of a beginning text, can only be dealt with descriptively.

In infancy and toddlerhood the child has developed some degree of control. He has learned to wait and to anticipate, he can differentiate one experience from another, and has a conscious awareness of some of the prohibitions of his parents. But his mental life is still filled with considerable confusion. There are many mental images which are dominated by emotion. He must learn to differentiate the various aspects of the world around him more clearly. He must learn to distinguish between the real and the fanciful. He must learn more effective ways of coping with his environment. Through such learnings he develops a mental organization which enables him to relate himself to his environment in typically human fashion. It is his capacity for achieving such organization which distinguishes him from other members of the animal world.

The period now under consideration may be thought of as one during which the child's mental organization becomes increasingly more differentiated — that is, more capable of carrying on different functions at the same time, more specialized. At the same time we may say that it also becomes more integrated — that is, its equilibrium is less disturbed by a diversity of functions.

To understand something of this process, we shall have to take into consideration the development of the child's *conscience* and his changing feelings and identifications.

The Development of Conscience

In toddlerhood, as we have seen, the child discovers that he is unable to control the world according to his wishes. He gradually finds it to his advantage to accept for himself the desires of his parents. These become a part of his inner mental life and serve as controls on his behavior. This is the " still small voice " of conscience, in psychoanalytic terms the " super-ego," representing the demands of society. The period of development which we are now considering is in a sense a period in which the child learns to live comfortably with his conscience. As he grows more powerful, there are more and more areas in which he needs the guidance which conscience offers. But at the same time as he matures and is increasingly experienced, he develops increasing ability to make judgments of his own and no longer needs the same prohibitions he did as a toddler.

In the following observation made by a student of child development, he demonstrates very well the way conscience may function in the life of a 3-year-old. There is an awareness of "right and wrong," but such does not necessarily guide behavior.

Observational Notes	*Comments*
Sally is just 3. She is very independent and will not let her mother do anything for her that she thinks she can do for herself.	This is a good description of the development of autonomy.
For her birthday a week ago she received a toy electric stove which can be plugged in. When she received it, she insisted on cooking immediately. Her mother let her make applesauce in one of her toy aluminum pots. She had also made tea in her whistling tea kettle and boiled water for Jell-o. Her mother never let her use the stove unless she was properly supervised. One Sunday morning, I heard the clanking of pots in the kitchen. Curious as to who could be there so early, I slipped out to see. I did not go in, but stayed outside the door watching.	We may surmise that the joy in use of this stems in part at least from identification with the role of her mother. She too can cook. (In some cultures one is not limited to the "play" participation in domesticity, which is typified here.) Parental prohibitions serve the very real function of protection from danger.
Sally had climbed on the kitchen stool and had taken down her stove from its high perch. She had just plugged it in and had put out her little frying pan. She opened the refrigerator door and took out a container of milk and placed it on the floor. Then she reached in for the butter and finally reached for the eggs.	Consider the tremendous amount of previous learning that went into these procedures, and the competence with which they are carried out.

Observational Notes

She accidentally dropped an egg on the floor. She stared at it blankly and then said, " Ooo-Ooo Sally is naughty girl, Mommy will scold you! "

She took a dish towel and wiped up the mess as well as she could.

Then she went back to her tasks. She climbed up on a stool, took down a bowl and proceeded to crack the eggs (with a good amount of shell) into the bowl. She opened the container of milk with difficulty, spilling most of it on the floor in her efforts. She poured the remainder of it into the bowl with the egg and then beat it up with a fork. After the eggs had been beaten until they might have been black and blue, she turned on her little electric stove, put some butter in her play frying pan and heated it up. She poured the mess into the pan stirring so vigorously that she spilled a lot of the eggs all over the stove. When the eggs were " done," she scraped them onto a plate and sat down to eat them with gusto.

At this point I could contain my-self no longer and walked into the kitchen, saying, " Good morning, Sally, what are you doing? " Sally replied, " I made myself some scwombled eggs."

Comments

At 3, one's co-ordinations are not completely reliable!

This is the voice of conscience!

She has some understanding of what the situation demands in the way of correction.

She is not deterred from her goal. Note how much less distract-ible she is than were the toddlers described in the last chapter. The ability to plan and carry through an activity, which is demonstrated here, reflects increasing mental ma-turity and the ability to make use of previous experience.

Again, note the minute detail with which she carries out the pro-cedure she has evidently observed.

In many ways this episode dem-onstrates a degree of organization and planning which is typical of the 3-to-6-year period of develop-ment. Many 3-year-olds would, of course, not be able to carry such a project through to quite such a successful conclusion as does Sally.

PROBLEM 1. We close the above incident just before Sally's mother appears on the scene. If you were the mother, how would you respond to the situation? What might you deduce from the above incident

about the nature of Sally's relationships to her parents? Suppose you had time to think through the possible consequences of your response in terms of Sally's future development (Sally's mother didn't have this opportunity), would your response be different? How important is a single episode such as this in the child's development? Would it be better if parents could have time to deliberate on each such episode?

When we speak of conscience as an inner voice, or even as super-ego, we are, of course, using a figure of speech to symbolize the child's experiences of associating a present situation with a past in which certain behaviors similar to the ones he now contemplates were forbidden.

Conscience, the control which comes from reliance on the prohibitions of the adults significant in his life, often affords the child considerable protection and sometimes saves him from real disaster. The child who has never encountered an effective " no " must test every situation for himself. He is safe only so long as he remains in a protected environment. Examples of the problems he faces can be drawn from the experience of one 4-year-old who had been brought up in a family which always temporized with his demands. When he was entered in a nursery school, his troubles began. Whereas the other children had long since learned to control a variety of impulsive behaviors, he had not. If he built with blocks, and the structure started to topple, he kicked it, even though doing so might bring it crashing on his own head. If the toy truck with which he played suddenly lost a wheel, he threw it with little regard for whether it might land on another child or a teacher or go through the window. If another child or a teacher got in his way, he hit or bit them. As might be expected, he was an exceedingly unhappy little boy when the teacher began gently but very firmly to help him to acquire the " thou-shalt-nots " appropriate to good group living. Over and over he encountered her, " I will not let you hurt other people," " I will not let you destroy things the rest of us enjoy," " I will not let you do something which may hurt you." Gradually it seemed he took these into himself and though life in his vicinity was seldom completely serene, his energies were more and more channeled in constructive directions. Some idea of what it meant to him to know that some kinds of activities were forbidden and not to be indulged, may be gleaned from a comment he made to a child who was having difficulties similar to what his own had been — " Some things grown-ups decide. It's better that way! "

Yet the grown-ups must not decide everything. A conscience evolved from too many prohibitions enforced with too little regard for the child's sensitivity and need for self-expression, may handicap him almost as much as a lack of an adequate conscience. If he feels guilty and deserving of blame in too many areas of his living, his behavior becomes increasingly constricted; and he is less and less able to realize all of his potentialities. Children differ greatly in their feelings about parental rules and regulations. Some are inclined to take them as inexorable commandments applicable for all time and in all circumstances, while others are much less easily influenced. Unfortunately, it is not possible to tell how many and what kinds of prohibitions are " enough " for a particular child and what is " too much."

An example of a child who evidently felt excessive guilt for what her mother regarded as a relatively mild transgression, is seen in an incident involving an intelligent almost-4-year-old. She had become intrigued with the sewing machine. Her mother, fearing that she might be injured, removed the needle and put it out of her reach. Later, when her parents had gone out for the evening, and she was being cared for by her grandmother, it was discovered that a seam in her snowsuit was ripped. The grandmother proposed to repair it and opened the sewing machine. Finding the needle missing, she asked the child if she knew where it was. The youngster replied that her mother had hidden it so she couldn't get it. Her grandmother observed mildly that she would then not be able to fix the snowsuit until later. Whereupon the child burst into uncontrollable sobbing, saying over and over that she wouldn't touch the needle again.

One of the major tasks of the power-testing period (and probably of most of growing up) is to learn to exercise conscience appropriately. The problem the child faces is illustrated in a comparatively simple form in the matter of cleanliness training. As a toddler, the child may learn that his parents are annoyed when he is messy. They may express strong disapproval when, as sometimes happens, he soils himself with a bowel movement, or they may merely see to it that he is always kept shining clean. Even when their prohibitions on getting dirty are relatively mild, he sometimes overlearns them. Do they still apply when he is confronted with an opportunity to play in the sandbox? What about clay or finger paint? In the following records compare the reactions of Celeste and Dan to their first experiences with finger paint, presented at nursery school.

Celeste Collins. She hesitated a little about putting her hand in the paint, then started with the right hand and seemed to enjoy it. She said, " I couldn't go home with hands like this." She made a house in the red paint, then said, " I'll rub it all out," and made another house adding blue paint to the mixture. Then she said, " I don't like doing this, but I have to cause I want to. It'll come off, won't it? "

Dan Mallon. He asked for yellow paint. The teacher put some on the paper and rubbed it about. He said, " Hey, you're painting the picture." The teacher replied that she was just starting it for him and withdrew. He put his hands into the paint with hesitation, looked a little dismayed and said, " How do you get your hands clean? " He worked with both hands a little stiffly and after a few moments said, " It's all done." He asked for another paper and used brown paint on it, working more vigorously and talking about busting and smashing the lumps. Once he said to the teacher, " Hey, look it, there's some on your finger. Hey, will it come off? " When he went in to wash his hands afterward, he said immediately, " Hey, it won't come off." The teacher told him to rub, and he said with obvious relief, " See, it'll come off if you want it to."

PROBLEM 2. From the above incidents which of these two children would you think had stronger feelings about the importance of cleanliness? (It is likely that Celeste's mother had actually emphasized it more.)

Under what circumstances is the nursery school justified in offering the child an activity that may seem to him to go against the dictates of his conscience?

It would be unfortunate if we seemed to imply that conscience is necessarily something acquired once and for all. As the child grows, he encounters new problems for which the " rules " he learned earlier are no longer adequate. Her parents continue, in one way and another, to provide him with the new standards he needs. But he also learns in our culture that other adults have similar or different criteria for right and wrong. Not until he is an adult, and sometimes not even then, will he work out a satisfactory resolution between the demands of society and the demands of his own individuality. It is in the period which we are now considering, however, that he takes his first steps in that direction. He is developing his own control system, learning to deal in an increasingly effective way with the world of reality.

Feelings and Attitudes

In the period with which we are concerned, feelings, it seems, become more intense and more directed. Sometimes, for reasons which will shortly be apparent, the same situation may call forth seemingly at the same moment both love and hatred, or the child may indicate tremendous desire for something which he very shortly rejects.

Take the matter of possession. The " mine " which was so characteristic of the toddler continues. To gather things to one's person seems to enhance the sense of selfhood. Possessiveness at this stage is not ownership in the usual sense. Anything which the child uses may become " his " and, therefore, precious and unique. Taking turns with equipment is arduous apparently because the child finds it so hard to accept the fact that the tricycle that so recently extended his person is now serving the same function for someone else. With his limited sense of time he seems to doubt that he will ever have it again. Offer three 4-year-olds ice cream in what look to the adult to be identical green saucers. Then listen for, " I got more than you did," or failing that, an assertion of pride, " *My* dish has the crack in it! " Yet with all this, there is a growing awareness that giving up brings social approval — a reward which begins to seem as ego enchancing as the things have been. In most groups of young children there comes to be about as much giving and sharing as getting and grabbing.

Then there is power and self-assertiveness. To the child who has so recently discovered a degree of independence, it is a heady thing to dominate another human being, or at least to make a pretense of it. Small wonder that this is a period in which children are prone, as one 4-year-old put it, " to hit, bit, or spit." Nor that, to use another's phrase, there is so much " smashing and crashing." Sometimes the aggression is purely verbal. " I am going to cut you up in little pieces and put you in the garbage can. Then I'll throw you out the window," is not an uncommon threat. But even while in the midst of the expression of such strong feelings, the child may make a loving comment to an adult or pat consolingly the child he has just hit. As his feelings of possessiveness are occasionally balanced with altruism, so his desire for power is mixed with a wish for protection.

Another feeling which comes to the fore in this period is that of rivalry. In a culture which never made comparisons between one person and another this might loom less important than it does in our competitive society. Several circumstances may combine to accentuate the child's feeling of jealousy. One is the obvious fact that he is in many ways less able than the adults and older children around him. Yet in a variety of ways he is encouraged either openly or subtly to emulate them. He is reminded of his actual inferiority, " That's a big boy! " " He's almost as good a mechanic as his Daddy! " " Don't be a baby. *Big* girls don't do that." These are all remarks which indicate to the child that his position is somewhat precarious.

In some societies not as much is made of these   s as we make. Benedict, for example, cites an incident from the Papago Indians.

A grandfather asked his three-year-old granddaughter to close the door. It was heavy and she had a hard time managing it. Nevertheless, no one jumped to the child's assistance. No one took the responsibility from her. . . . It was assumed that the task would not be asked of her unless she could perform it, and having been asked, the responsibility was hers alone just as if she were a grown woman.[1]

But it is not alone the child's inferior status which makes him feel rivalry. His affectional ties are also involved. He comes to a point where he begins, as it were, to take stock of his place in the

[1] Benedict, Ruth. " Continuities and Discontinuities in Cultural Conditioning," in *A Study of Interpersonal Relations,* edited by Patrick Mullahy. New York: Hermitage Press, 1949. P. 300.

family. He is still immature, and he neither thinks nor feels exactly as would the adult in a similar situation. Nevertheless, as he begins to perceive his parents' relationship to each other and to the other children in the family, it may seem to threaten his own position. He realizes that he is not the sole object of parental attention. He must share mother with father, father with brother, and so on. In view of his lack of experience and the extent to which fantasy continues to dominate his thinking, it is not surprising that the boy may become considerably engrossed in the possibility, that his mother's devotion to his father has in it some elements which are not in her affection for him and which he would greatly desire. His preoccupations may come to the surface in comments on his intention to marry his mother, assertions that he is a "big man," and sometimes open expressions of hostility toward the father.

In a family in which the relationships between the mother and father are truly loving and respectful of personality, these jealous feelings are likely lived through without too much disturbance since the mother is able to make it clear to the child that he has his own special place in her affections and that she approves and believes in his manly potentialities. In some cultures there may be relatively little jealousy of this kind experienced because, as Benedict points out ▓▓▓▓▓▓▓ between child and adult sex roles are not emph▓▓▓▓▓▓▓ t they are in our culture.

▓▓▓▓▓▓ analytical theory, on the contrary, sees rivalry as being ▓▓▓ ▓▓ble and as having its roots in the child's concern over his sexual adequacy as compared with that of his parents. The validity of this theory and particularly its application to all human beings has been much questioned. Nevertheless, if we use the theory to symbolize the inner struggles the child goes through as he develops conscious awareness of himself as a person with potentialities and takes his place in a family situation in which much adult behavior and emotional expression cannot help being puzzling to him, it can serve a very useful purpose for us.

Celeste provides us with an example which may be interpreted as revealing attitudes of rivalry. In nursery school, when she was 4, her conversation with the other children tended to be quite boastful. An exchange with Ralph in the doll corner follows:

Celeste: I've got a telephone. You haven't.

Ralph: I have so.

Celeste: Not a really truly one that people talk through and has a wire. Not where you say, " Operator, give me 2791." My mother lets me use the telephone. Once I had to call my grandmother . . . Say you don't know Mr. McDougall, do you?

Ralph: My mother and father got married.

Celeste: So did mine. Mine got married last week. I was a bride and so was my mother. You weren't a groom. Your father was.

Ralph seemed to have lost the drift of this and wandered away.

. . . .

At another time, Celeste, arranging doll furniture, commented, " Sometimes I sit in the middle and sometimes in my mommie's place."

Changing Identifications

During the period from 3 to 6 years we observe many instances in which a child adopts the attitudes of some other person or seems to accept another's behavior as a model for his own. We say that he is " identifying " with the other individual. Such identification is not necessarily limited to parents. The child may identify with other adults, and, as he grows older, with other children. The early identifications, perhaps by sheer virtue of being practiced longest, tend to be most persistent.

Identification may be thought of as having two aspects, emotional and behavioral. The emotional aspects are concerned with the nature of the relationship between the two individuals. This may be one which is basically warm, positive, and integrative — that is, the adult involved is both affectionate and appreciative of the child as a unique human being. Or it may be less healthy as when the adult consciously or unconsciously " uses " the child for his own purposes. An immature, anxious, or hostile adult may see the child as an enhancement to himself, or as a source of gratification of his own need for affection, or as an object for domination.

The behavioral aspects of identification involve the child's attempts to do what his model does. This may be influenced by such factors as the closeness of their association, the clarity of the behavior the child tries to copy, and the extent to which their intellectual and temperamental characteristics facilitate or hamper copying.

Identification appears to take place most readily when there is both a warm relationship and an ease in copying behavior. We may point out, however, that eventually the child, if he is to develop appropriate adult controls, must develop patterns of behavior which are appropriate to *him* as an adult.

Emotional identification, that is, the acceptance of the adult as an ideal, may occur without much behavioral identification. For example, despite the relative anti-sissy emphasis in our culture, early " he-man " behavior may be relatively difficult achievement for a little boy brought up in a home in which father and mother share and share alike in most household activities. Or as one mother remarked of her 4-year-old son, " He's confused. He adores his daddy, the wonderful stories he tells, and the way he helps him answer questions. But the most active thing his daddy does, is to pound the typewriter. *I'm* the one who drives the car, works in the garden, and makes repairs."

On the other hand, behavioral identification may occur without warm emotional identification. It may be a defense against the anxiety the child feels in the relationship with the parent. For example, the hostile, aggressive, threatening father may have a son whose behavior takes on the same qualities. It is as though the child were saying, " Perhaps I can be bigger and worse than you, and then I will not need to fear you." [2]

PROBLEM 3. If possible, read the article by Stuart Stoke, " An Inquiry into the Concept of Identification," which is included in *Readings in Child Development*, edited by Stendler and Martin, pages 227–240. The case study material provides a number of examples of both kinds of identification. If it is possible for you to observe a child and his parent over a period of several weeks or more, see how much evidence you can gather as to the apparent nature and progress of his identifications.

The child's learning is considerably influenced by the nature of his identifications. Depending on them, for example, he may be accepting — readily inclined to take whatever a relatively pleasant

---

[2] The point of view in this statement derives primarily from two sources: Stoke, Stuart. " An Inquiry into the Concept of Identification." *The Journal of Genetic Psychology.* 76 (1950), 163–189; and Ausubel, David. *Ego Development and The Personality Disorders.* New York: Grune and Stratton, 1952.

and reasonable adult offers him — or he may be skeptical — unwilling to accept anything which he cannot test for himself. He may reject learning which seems inappropriate to him in the light of his established identifications, as in the case of the lower-class child who rejects " manners." The possible variations in such orientations to learning are, of course, many. Even in the period under consideration we can see some differences in the way in which children approach new experiences in their play which are to some extent prophetic of later learning.

PLAY AND CREATIVE ACTIVITIES

We can best understand the progress children of this age are making in personality development, the extent to which they are still dominated by feelings and impulses, and the extent to which they are able to deal with reality by studying their play and creative activities.

The following records of children's play were made by a student in the nursery school which Jane Warner attended. In her effort to include all of the interaction between Jane and the two boys, Earl and Ralph, the student was unable to include all of the finer details of the children's behavior. Nevertheless, it reveals very well the typical quality of play among children who are about 4 years old. (Jane was 3 years and 10 months while the boys had already had their fourth birthdays.)

Most of the activity in the records centers around the playhouse which was a sturdy structure large enough to hold three or four children at one time.

Ralph and Earl are playing with some small wooden figures. Jane picks up one, asks how it got broken. The boys look up. Ralph asks where it is broken, and Jane shows him. The boys continue their play.

Jane: " I'm going to wear the beads." Ralph watches her, and Jane chatters about them. Then she goes over to the playhouse, walks in, talking to herself. Ralph follows her and peers into one of the windows.

Jane: " Come on. You're my child." Ralph goes in, peeks his head out the back window.

Ralph: " Hi, everybody."

Earl, from the block area: " Look at him! Humpty Dumpty."

All three play quietly and without comment for a time. Then Earl gets up on his tiptoes, saying, " Sssh! ", goes quietly over to the playhouse. Suddenly he opens the curtain covering one window.

Jane: " This is morning now. Don't come in."

Earl walks around to the back, peers in that window, then goes over to toy telephone, and calls to Ralph, " Hey, Ralph, this is for you. Get up and answer it."

Jane: " Chicago, Chicago! "

Earl, shortly and gruffly: " No! "

Jane: " It's my Chicago, Chicago, or isn't it Chicago? "

Ralph sticks his head out the back window of playhouse: " Hello, everybody."

Earl goes to the back of the house with the telephone, but Ralph retreats inside it. Earl goes around to the front and knocks there.

Jane: " Who is it? " She speaks in a " telephone " voice.

Earl rings the phone again.

Ralph comes out, then quickly goes back in again.

Earl gets a wooden mallet and bangs on the house. They all laugh and peer out at him. He shows them the mallet. They laugh more.

Earl, from the front of the house, calls: " Hey, Ralph, open this door! "

Jane sits by the doorway, looking out at Earl and smiles " No, you can't open the door, 'cause you aren't somebody from our company."

Earl: " I gotta fix the house." He hammers on the front part gently.

The three play separately for a bit. Ralph and Jane come out with dolls. Then they go back in. Earl pretends to paint the house.

Ralph sticks his head out: " Hi, everybody! "

Earl runs up to him, saying: " Let's paint the house." They laugh. Earl knocks on the window.

Jane, from the inside, says: " It's another night and you're still hammering." Then: " What was that noise? Was it a bow and arrow? Was it a bad Indian? "

Earl makes a noise, somewhat resembling an Indian war whoop.

Ralph puts his head out the back window. He and Earl laugh.

Jane to Earl: " You don't have to be a bad Indian any more. You can be a good Indian and watch me fix the babies."

Earl: " No. I am painting the house." Later: " The house isn't fixed yet. Gotta put the nails in yet."

Ralph, from inside the house, evidently to Jane: " Oh, thank you, honey." They continue to play with the dolls.

·   ·   ·   ·

The next two days were fair, and the children spent almost all of the morning outdoors. On the third day, which was Saint Patrick's Day, it rained and the following episode was recorded. The same children were involved.

Ralph is riding the trike. Earl is playing with the small wooden figures, talking to himself.

Ralph: " I am going to fix the house up." He goes over to it. He calls to Jane: " Come on, let's go in the house like we did the other day."

Jane goes to the house, while Ralph mutters: " Gotta get my dollies," and goes to the cupboard evidently trying to decide which to take.

Jane murmurs: " Come on, let's go in the house. It's raining out." After a moment, " Come on, Ralph, where are you? "

Ralph joins Jane. Earl from his play with the wooden figures says: " When I come over, I'll ring the phone, huh! " But he continues to play where he is.

Jane and Ralph are now busily arranging the dolls in the house. Earl tiptoes over, saying: " You mustn't see me coming over. I am the father." He goes close to the house with the phone, ringing it outside. There is no response from inside. Then he knocks on the door: " Hey, let me in! I'm the father! "

Jane: " There mustn't be any father."

Earl: " I must come in from working." He goes on in.

Jane: " Don't let anyone else in."

Earl: " We're all in now. I got the phone in here. The phone has to be on my side. Something has to be on my side." Considerable discussion follows as to what shall be on whose side, where the napkins and the books shall go.

Earl: " Hee, when I go out, I'll take a napkin, and the phone must ring, and it must be for me. . . . I'll fix the house." He goes outside the house. Inside the house, one of the children rings the phone: " Hey, who is it for? "

Jane: " Ralph." She talks into it. " Yesterday. All right. Goodbye."

Earl climbs up on to the roof of the playhouse, then climbs down and looks in the window: " Hey, Ralph, did you know I was up there? "

Ralph comes out, and he and Earl bang on the roof. Jane calls: " Hey, don't do that. It is giving me a headache."

Ralph wanders away.

Earl: " I am going to get up there and break the house." He continues to bang. " I'll get way up there, and she won't see me," he says softly. He climbs on the roof, and continues to pound.

Jane sticks her head out the door and murmurs softly: " Don't! "

Earl, mockingly: " Who's hammering on this house? It gives me a headache."

Jane rings the phone inside the house.

Earl: " Hey, that must be for me." He climbs down from the roof and goes into the house.

Jane: " It's for Jennie."

Earl: " My name is Jennie." . . . " Well, you must ring the phone, and it must be for me." He walks out of the house and starts climbing on the roof again, calling: " If it's for me, tell them, I am up on top of the house."

Earl bangs on the housetop alternately with a rubber mallet and a wooden mallet, getting a nice effect: " Hey, this must be a St. Patrick's Day parade. You come to the door, and you'll see it." He gets down from the roof and goes over to the trike.

Jane comes out: " Oh, I didn't see it. Will you start it up again, so that I can see it? "

Earl pretends to blow a horn and peddles furiously on his trike. Jane smiles.

As he passes the house, Earl calls to Jane: " Oh, that house must be on fire." " I got-a get the hose to put it out."

Jane jumps up and down, saying hurriedly: " Don't let me get on fire. You take the children and the books." They are both very busy dragging things out of the playhouse.

Earl gets back on the trike. " You mustn't know a St. Patrick's Day Parade is coming, but you must see a new car coming, and then you must look all the time, and then see a new car coming, and then see the parade."

Jane: " Don't blow the horn until I get asleep."

She goes in the house. Earl " blows " the horn, and Jane comes running out.

PROBLEM 4. On the basis of the above episodes, what characteristics would you attribute to children's play? At what points do you think this play record reflects the fact that the children are still relatively inexperienced? At which points do you think feelings or motivations of which the children are not consciously aware may be revealed?

Characteristics of Children's Play

The play of young children is *active*. They are not idle bystanders. Even the most peaceful of domestic scenes demands much climbing, walking about, opening and shutting of doors, painting, hammering, manipulation of the phone, and so on. This activity seems to stem from the fact that developing motor skills demand exercise. But the child of this age is an active learner, in all respects. In a sense he "thinks" as much with his muscles as with his mind.

His play is obviously *imitative*. The wearing of the beads, the telephone voices, the "fixing" of the house, the playing of the father and mother roles, all reveal the identifications the child is making. But the imitations are not complete. We can observe that there are places where either the child has not acquired enough information to fill his role completely, or he has become emotionally involved in some one aspect of the role and so is not impelled to copy it in its entirety. In these episodes we note, for example, that Ralph at times seems to be filling the role of the father, but does not imitate very much of the behavior of a father. Earl, on the other hand, although he does not specify (except by implication) the role he is playing, carries on a number of imitative activities.

The play of children of this age has in addition to its purely imitative character a more strongly *imaginative* flavor. The bow and arrow, the good and bad Indian, the fire and the parade are not such everyday occurrences as were depicted in the housekeeping and fixing incidents. Here we see the power of the child to transform and elaborate bits of his experience into quite fantastic occurrences. In some of these, the child is obviously aware that he is "only playing." Jane's comment on the good Indian implies this. On the other hand, at the moment when Jane and Earl are taking the "children and the books" from the playhouse, they are as flurried as though panic were really upon them. This typifies much of the play of this period. The child comes to distinguish the "pretend" from the real, but he still involves himself with as much feeling as though there were no such distinction.

If we consider that children learn through play, its *repetitious* quality is not surprising. In effect, children practice the life they see in the social world about them. The repetition of the telephoning may fall in this category. Some kind of play may also be repeated because of the child's emotional investment in what it represents. Thus fire engine play, which offers a legitimate outlet for strong feelings, is frequently repeated. (For example, the playhouse described in the above record, "burned" innumerable times in the play of these three youngsters and that of other children as well.) Sometimes repetition assumes a somewhat stereotyped and compulsive character, as when a child always builds the identical block buildings. Then we may suspect that it may be providing some kind of protection against anxiety.

There is also a *thematic* quality to children's play. Thus, in the first of the records presented here, the themes or central ideas shift from simple domesticity to the unwelcome visitor, to house repair, to violence, and back to domesticity. In the second record, the same themes are apparent. Themes such as these may appear characteristically when one group play together, while a different group of children may reveal a different variety. For example, Jane's absence and her replacement by a boy might considerably alter the play themes.

Play themes also vary from child to child and reflect their individual concerns and interests. The following notes based on the play of Pat, Dan, and Celeste when they were 4 and 5 years old, suggest some recurrent themes.

Pat Plummer. Clothing and Personal Appearance. A considerable amount of Patty's time was spent dressing and undressing the dolls, calling attention to the details of their clothing. She frequently adorned herself with scarves and hats from the costume box. In addition, she frequently stopped her play to call attention to items of clothing she was wearing or possessed: " These are my new *pants*," " I have new dancing shoes at home," " Did I show you the gloves I wore today? " " Would you like to see my pretty slip? "

Nursing and Feeding. In both doll play and water play, Patty's interest centered around feeding and nursing. She usually held the dolls and bottle-fed them. When playing with water, she poured the water from one container to another, but usually spent a considerable amount of her time filling the nursing bottle and sucking from it.

Windows. Unlike any of the other children in the group, Pat exhibited much interest in the windows in the playroom and in the playhouse. She often incorporated incidents of window opening into the ongoing play. " How I must open that window. I bet I can. Do you want to see me? " Her drawings also often included windows.

Cutting. All of the children used the scissors from time to time, but Patty spent much more time at it than the rest of them. She usually ended by completely destroying whatever she cut out. The paper dolls, which the 5-year-olds were beginning to enjoy, were always in peril of being gradually snipped to bits when Pat joined the game. Several times when she played in the doll corner, she managed to smuggle in the scissors and chop at the hair of a doll or hack at a blanket.

Noise. A recurring comment in Patty's play was, " I make enough noise, don't I? " It mattered little what her activity was — playing with water or in the dollhouse or sitting at the table with crayons or scissors, one could be fairly sure that at least once she would refer to noise.

Dan Mallon. Destruction. Danny was inclined to treat all toys and materials roughly. His destruction was usually accompanied by threats of something worse than he actually accomplished. Typical instances: " If you don't get that table out of my way, I'll snap the scissors." Holding the scissors tightly about the head of a wooden doll, " I'll cut his head off, because I feel like it." Hitting a toy house, " I'll crack the house." Tearing off two tires from a toy truck, " My lord, look at that crazy tire." Putting one toy car on top of another, " Watch I can bust these wheels off. Want to see me? " Grabbing a baby doll and breaking off its leg, " Is it still good? Look at her; she has to hop." Dumping toys from a box on to the floor and kicking them, " Hey, I kicked them."

Death. In Danny's dramatic play, people were always dying or being buried. A typical incident: Danny picks up the phone, and the following conversation ensues, " Eh? Yeah. Could I speak to Richard Wright? What's that? How? All right. Goodbye. Goodbye." He hangs up momentarily and then, " Hello, Richard? Could I speak to Richard? Because I want him to know that the soldier is dead in Detroit. He will be dying tomorrow in Chicago. Yeah. He's an old man. He don't want to be king." Somewhat later, talking to another child, " He was killed today. He was going along, and a car came, and he was going and he tried to put off the brakes, and then he was going in the station, and bang! And he was hit."

Celeste Collins. Hiding. Most children of this age enjoy concealing themselves in some tight place and teasing the other children or adults to find them. Celeste especially delighted in this. Examples are: On the playground, climbing into a large box which happens to have a knothole in it, through which she can peer, she calls, " Can you see me now? You can't see me now! " In the playroom, she often deserts the play to go to the end of draperies which extend to the floor. Enfolding herself in them, she asks, " Can you see me now? "

Curiosity. Celeste played a good bit with the many dolls the nursery school offered, some of the rubber baby type, some " older " ones appropriately dressed as girls or boys, some wooden figures painted to represent policemen, firemen, and so on. Whenever she picked up a doll, her typical response was to examine it closely, removing the pants whenever possible, before she proceeded with whatever other activity her role in the dramatic play demanded.

Destructiveness. This theme appeared much less frequently in Celeste's play than in Danny's or Patty's, but it was observed in such incidents as these: Playing with five small cars, she " crashes " them together. When seated at the table where there are both crayons and scissors, she cuts up some of the crayons. Dumping everything out of a cardboard box, she said, " I'm going to rip up this box, I'm dumping it all out." With the scissors and some cloth she had been given to cut, " You know, what I would like to do — cut, cut, cut, and never pick up."

PROBLEM 5. As you observe the play of children of this age, note whether any persistent themes emerge. Are there some which, you think, are common to most children? Do you observe some which seem unique to a particular child?

The Meaning of Children's Play

How much significance should be attached to such recurrent themes in children's play? What do they tell us about the child? It appears that many recurrent themes represent the child's efforts to clarify for himself experiences that he has had and to which some confusion is attached. On this basis we might expect to find that each theme, if it could be traced to its origin, would be seen to arise out of some incident of the child's personal experience. For example, Pat may have frequently been warned not to make so much noise, and wishes to test out how much is " too much." Dan's concern with death may have arisen from his uncertainties regarding the loss of his grandfather when he was 3; Celeste's curious exploration of the dolls may have been an attempt to establish sex differences, about which she has had insufficient information.

Other themes appear to stem from strong feelings on the part of the child. For example, the destructiveness that appears so frequently in Dan's play and to a somewhat less marked degree in Celeste's and the cutting theme in so much of Patty's play would suggest that all three of them are somewhat hostile. The question then arises as to the underlying causes of their feelings. We have already indicated that to some extent all children have such feelings. Are theirs more marked than those of other children? This question cannot be answered until all of their play patterns have been carefully compared with those of their peers. Even then we may err, since the amount of expressed destructiveness is apparently not necessarily related to the strength of the child's feelings.

For example, Korner in a study of underprivileged children [3] found four patterns so far as the expression of hostility was concerned: some children showed hostility in both play and real life; some showed little hostility in either; others showed strong hostility in play and little in real life; and still others showed mild hostility in play and strong hostility in real life.

A question somewhat related to strength of feelings is that of the relationships of observed themes to the child's treatment in the home. For example, has the child, whose doll play themes always include vigorous spanking of the dolls, been accustomed to spanking at home? A number of recent studies [4] have explored this matter, and appear to be in general agreement that doll play patterns are related to the actual relationships the child has experienced, but they are not necessarily directly reproductive of them.

In any attempt to appraise the significance of the child's play themes, it is a mistake to generalize from too little evidence. The play themes seen in a particular nursery school may emerge as much from the situation, the guidance (or lack of it) given the children, the kinds of play materials available, and so on, as from the child's

---

[3] Korner, Anneliese F. *Some Aspects of Hostility in Young Children.* New York: Grune and Stratton, 1949.

[4] Representative studies are:

Hollenberg, Eleanor, and Sperry, Margaret. " Some Antecedents of Aggression in Doll Play." *Personality.* 1 (1950), 32–43.

Sears, Robert R. " Effects of Frustration and Anxiety on Fantasy Aggression." *American Journal of Orthopsychiatry.* 21 (1951), 498–505.

Sears, Pauline. " Doll Play Aggression in Normal Young Children." *Psychological Monographs,* Vol. 65, No. 6, 1951.

more deep-seated concern. So far as their meaning in terms of the child developing personality, consideration must be given not only to the nature and variety of his play themes, but also to his living in general, his moods, abilities to get along in friendly fashion with his peers and with the adults around him, and to show increasing understanding of the world around him. Nevertheless, if we keep these cautions in mind, observation of the child's play affords an excellent opportunity to learn about typical ways of feeling toward the world and toward himself.

A final characteristic of children's play is its fluidity — one theme merges into another with no apparent rhyme or reason. At least so far as casual observers can tell, there is no plot which demands that, for example, Earl's pounding on the roof should precipitate a St. Patrick's Day parade, or that it in turn should give way to a fire. Whatever logic there is appears to stem more from the emotions than the intellect.

We shall need to keep these characteristics of children's play in mind as we come to a consideration of their changing perceptions. But first we shall note their drawings and paintings, for they, too, reveal something of the nature of their fantasy and thought.

Comments made by Dan when he was asked to draw a picture (he was 4 then) reveal fluidity and the fusion of several different ideas:

He first said he couldn't, but then said he would draw a " lionager." This he did in orange. When he finished, he said he would do another in green. He was asked if this were another " lionager." He replied, " No, the first one ain't finished; this is just another part." Then he drew what appeared to be part three in purple and commented, " It wouldn't be a lionager, it would be a ' clet ' if it didn't have as many as it's got." He did not reveal the identity of a " clet." Later, perhaps fearing too many questions from the adult, he drew on another piece of paper, but said quite firmly, " I ain't making anything now." Then, softly, " It's going to be a big lion king."

Drawing and Painting

The children's drawings shown in Figure 4 likewise reveal qualities similar to those we have noted in children's play.

The top drawing, which is the creation of a girl of 3 years and 10

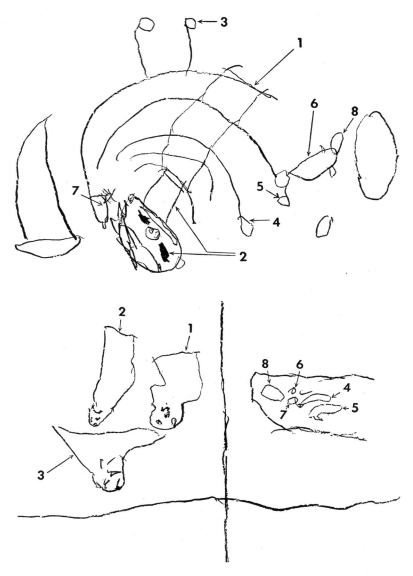

Figure 4

months, shows strong imagination. She chattered as she worked, and these are her comments. (The numbers indicate the area in which she was working as she talked.)

1. "This is a rainbow in the wock. Here's a big round circle, two little round circles, one teensy-weensy one."

2. "Here's a man; his eye . . . he has two eyes."

3. "See what happened to him: He stayed out too long in the air, and he blowed up fat!"

4. "He has a balloon in that hand, and he goes out like that."

5. "Look, there's his glove on a string, and the string is around his waist."

6. "We forgot the suitcase."

7. "He has keys in his hand."

8. "He has a suitcase. That's the handle. That's the little tag. I have a suitcase at home. This one has two tags."

Like some of the play incidents, this drawing is vividly imaginative and filled with symbols through which unconscious fantasy may be expressed. Or perhaps the story is concocted from elements of conscious experience. Except through deep psychological study, it would be impossible to know all that the picture may represent. We can say that it was typical of the child who was an affectionate, highly verbal, and rather sensitive child who seemed to have a capacity for noticing details of her environment which other children often missed. Attention is called to the fact that the drawing is reproduced as she did it — it is not "upside-down."

The bottom drawing was made by a boy of 4 years and 7 months. He began at (1) to make a man, naming eyes, mouth, nose, and stomach. (2) This is a woman with the same parts mentioned and legs as well. (3) Here is a little boy.

Like the picture above, the child has disregarded the customary top and bottom of the page. He apparently does not yet clearly differentiate the sexes.

The figure to the right is a car in which a man is riding. (4) and (5) are the man's legs. (6) and (7) are his nose and mouth. (8) is the steering wheel.

The cross lines extending through the center of the page were referred to as a "train."

All of these drawings reveal a degree of fluidity. The top drawings, although both may be characterized as representation, do not deal with the subject matter nearly as realistically as does the bottom drawing. In both the drawings the child singles out the objects which are of concern to him, but neither reveals a strong conviction of reality. Taken together, they illustrate nicely the principles which Werner Wolff has set forth regarding the difference between art expression in the child and in the adult:

The adult is guided by his impressions — the child by his expressions; the adult by imitation — the child by symbolization; the adult by selection — the child by a search for relationships; the adult by intellectual principles — the child by emotional principles; the adult by objective standards — the child by subjective standards. Hence, as is the case with the other manifestations of the child, there is no bridge between the art of the adult and that of the child, since both have their own criteria and their own values.[5]

From this point of view, every so-called scribble of the child in this period of development has meaning and significance, though it may be quite impossible for any but the therapist or psychologist, who studies the child deeply, to know precisely what it is.

Children's paintings follow a similar trend. At first, the brush seems to be but an extension of the child's hand. He enjoys the manipulation of marks on the paper and the colors he produces, but he does not appear to offer any comments on it.

Sometimes he makes " accidental " designs which adults are prone to label, or in which he may himself see some resemblance to reality. Later, as he gains in manipulative skill, and as he deals more and more with reality and less in fantasy, he may make deliberate designs, and finally come into a stage of representation. The paintings shown in Figure 5 (pages 256–257) include (1) and (2) the experimental, manipulative product of 3-year-olds, and (3) a single selection from a series of ten " designs " made by a 5-year-old which finally culminated in the half-representative, half-fantasy abstraction seen in (4).

In the language of the child, all of these stages are important, for, as Alschuler and Hattwick in reporting a longitudinal study of painting and personality indicate:

[5] Wolff, Werner. *Personality of the Pre-School Child.* New York: Grune and Stratton, 1946. P. 262.

Children can use paints and crayons to express absorbing experiences and preoccupations which they are not yet able to express in words. Sometimes this may be because the experiences are still at a *feeling* level, not sufficiently clarified to express in words, or again it may be that children of this age have not sufficient vocabulary to express their feelings which are, nevertheless, impelling and forceful.[6]

PROBLEM 6. If possible, make a collection of children's paintings or drawings noting the varieties of expression at different ages.

Dance and musical expression. Play, painting, drawing, dancing, chanting, singing, playing an instrument — for the adult these are distinctly different activities, but for the child all of them offer a mode of body expression, and all are characterized by activity, imagination, repetition, and a thematic patterning unique to each individual. Not all children will choose all of these activities with equal zest, but every child appears to have potentialities for creativity in each medium.

Studies[7] of the rhythmic expression of children have indicated that under 5 years of age individual patterns vary widely, and children do not respond to efforts to teach them to keep time. This does not mean, however, that he cannot, in an environment which offers some encouragement, develop his own repertoire of movement.[8] Along with this primitive form of the dance goes chant and even experimentation with musical instruments. Reports from an intensive study of young children closely parallel findings in the area of painting and drawing:

The roots of their earliest music are their rhythmic bodily movements and the sounds which they make or which come from their surroundings. Much of their early activity is instinctive or occurs near the borders of the subconscious, and its conscious control is a matter of slow growth and understanding.[9]

[6] Alschuler, Rose, and Hattwick, La Berta. *Painting and Personality.* Chicago: University of Chicago Press, 1948. P. 5.

[7] See, for example, Jersild, Arthur T., and Bienstock, S. F. *Development of Rhythm in Young Children.* New York: Teachers College, Columbia University, 1935.

[8] For descriptions of the character of children's dance, see Sheehy, Emma Dickson. *There's Music in Children.* New York: Henry Holt and Company, 1946.

[9] Moorhead, Gladys Evelyn, and Pond, Donald. *Music of Young Children. II, General Observations.* Santa Barbara, California: Pillsbury Foundation for Advancement of Music Education, November, 1942. P. 4.

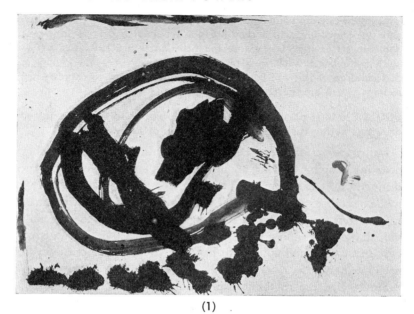

(1)

(2)

Figure 5

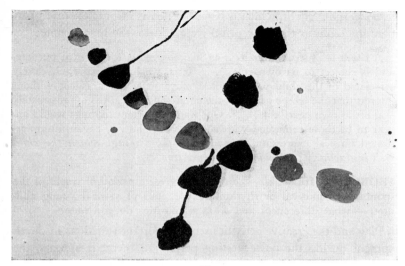

(3)

(4)

Concerning chant, which is regarded not as incomplete or embryonic song, but as the most primitive art form, the reports note:

A chant is ordered after its own manner, exists for its own purpose, and is subject to its own rules. . . . It is, we have discovered, closely associated in the child with physical movement, and it is not without interest that the tempo at which the child sings a chant is approximately that of his own heartbeats. . . . Our most important findings would appear to be those connected with chant as a primitive, pagan, unsophisticated musical expression, *arising from those things which the child feels instinctively to demand such expression.*[10]

PROBLEM 7. If possible, keep a record over a period of weeks of the spontaneous musical or rhythmic expressions of several young children — what differences and what similarities do you note?

Play and the creative activities serve important functions in development during the power-testing period. In them, it appears, the child may work through some of the strong feelings which tend to arise at this time. It is not necessary for him to be explicit as to their nature. Indeed, he may still lack words to describe them, but as he paints at the easel or pounds the drum or scolds a doll, he finds an " out " for impulses that are often better not expressed directly. If the adults are sensitive, they will reinforce his developing understanding that there is nothing basically wrong with having strong feelings — human beings all crave affection, feel aggressive, get angry. They will, however, even while respecting his rights to those feelings, help him to find the best ways for both their control and their expression.

At the same time, play and creative activities offer good possibilities for testing reality.

In his play the child finds not only answers to such questions as " What will happen if . . . ," but also learns increasingly how he himself can control the physical world about him. Again, he is dependent on adults who understand his need for protection against whatever destructive tendencies he may have, and who respect his questions and provide an answer in which he can find answers.

Play with other children, when it is properly supervised so that the child does not run hazards which are too much for his inade-

[10] Moorhead and Pond, *op. cit. I, Chant.* May, 1941.

quately developed control system, offers him an opportunity to learn that the satisfactions that come from giving and sharing are at least on a par with getting and taking.

It may also be that as play and creative activity in this period are better understood, they will be seen as opportunities for the child to find out and even develop conscious awareness of himself as a unique human organism with certain potentialities which differ from those of his peers. Some nursery school teachers already understand the importance of this. They are not so concerned that all children develop " well-rounded " personalities, but rather that each one learn what is most satisfying to him. They want all children to test out all the possibilities — clay, paint, blocks, gardening, dramatic play, dancing, singing, and so on — but they have no stereotype of what each child should be in each activity.

THE CHANGING CHARACTER OF THE CHILD'S PERCEPTIONS OF THE PHYSICAL WORLD

In earlier chapters we indicated some of the difficulties involved in studying children's perceptions before they have developed verbal abilities. Now that we are dealing with an age level which has language, the problems are still many, primarily because only a limited amount of experimental work has been done in this area.

If we may properly infer the character of the child's perception from his play, his drawings, and other creative expressions, we see his view of the world as one in which objects often tend to fuse one with another (lion and tiger become lionager, for example); certain qualities of objects are perceived while others are ignored (a tree is represented by its branches, a car by its general configuration and a steering wheel); movement and action are dominant, emotion and feeling are pervasive.

Such an inference is upheld by research carried on in Europe [11] and especially by the work of Piaget,[12] a Swiss child psychologist.

[11] See studies cited in Werner, Heinz. *Comparative Psychology of Mental Development*. Chicago: Follett Publishing Company, 1948.

[12] See the following books by Jean Piaget:
The Language and Thought of the Child. New York: Harcourt, Brace and Company, 1926.
Judgment and Reasoning in the Child. New York: Harcourt, Brace and Company, 1928.

Dennis, in discussing Piaget's views on the child's perception, says:

Social factors permeate the child's perception of his environment from a very early age. He has interiorized certain aspects of his culture by the time that he can first give a description of his perceptions. . . . He does not distinguish clearly the objective and the subjective. They are fused. Almost from the beginning some acts are inherently naughty, some good; some people are evil, some benevolent; some things are dirty, some clean; some people are cowardly, some are brave; some are ugly, others are pretty; some objects are personal property, some are not. While society supplies these characteristics, the child sees them as natural.[13]

Piaget sees these factors dominating the intellectual life of the child until 7 or 8 years of age. A belief in magic and the tendency to regard all objects in one's world animistically or as living beings and animals anthropomorphically or as people thus tend to considerably distort the child's perception of reality. Consequently, he has difficulty in reasoning and in making generalizations.

Isaacs' observational study [14] of the intellectual development of young children made in England shortly following the initial studies of Piaget failed to support the idea that the perceptions of young children were so fanciful and so egocentric, as he had found. Rather, the children she observed were strongly interested in the things and events of the physical world and capable of reasoning. True, they showed some characteristics attributed to them by Piaget. These could be attributed to the child's ignorance or lack of experience.

The child doesn't *believe* . . . that " everything is alive "; he simply doesn't *know* that everything isn't alive. . . . He does not *know* that locomotives don't want biscuits — how should he? He doesn't know this until he offers a biscuit to a locomotive (or things like it), and the locomotive takes no notice whatever, behaving quite differently from his brother or the dog.[15]

The Child's Conception of the World. New York: Harcourt, Brace and Company, 1929.

The Child's Conception of Physical Causality. New York: Harcourt, Brace and Company, 1930.

[13] Dennis, Wayne. " Cultural and Developmental Factors in Perception," in *Perception, An Approach to Personality,* edited by Blake and Ramsey. New York: Ronald Press, 1951.

[14] Isaacs, Susan. *Intellectual Growth in Young Children.* London: Routledge and Kegan Paul, Ltd., 1930.

[15] *Ibid.* P. 108.

Considerable support can be found for Isaacs' point of view, that at least within the period which we are considering in this chapter children's perceptions of their world are mixed. Some objects with which they lack experience may be distorted, but many are perceived quite accurately. This, however, is also true of adults. Like children, when they deal with phenomena with which they are unfamiliar, they may reveal tendencies toward animistic and magical thinking.

Although the general trend is for children's perceptions to be less accurate than those of adults, current studies of perception indicate that the way the individual sees objects depends in part on the field or context in which he is operating and in part on his own individual psychological organization.[16] The power-testing period, with which we are presently concerned, is undoubtedly important in the development of this kind of individuality. We may expect that the future will see more research devoted to individual differences in perception, particularly as they relate to personality in this period and in later development.

The important influence of experience on the child's perception of his world and on his growing abilities to see relationships in it, that is, to reason, to solve problems, to generalize, and to develop concepts has been supported in several studies,[17] but there is rather a dearth of material to show how the child's perceptions shift with his experience. Because the child's meanings may be so different from those of the adult and because of his difficulty of expressing adequately the meanings he has, one can frequently only infer the processes involved.

Undoubtedly a great deal of the child's observation at this stage is a matter of differentiating among perceptions, noting regularities, the qualities of things which remain constant under varying circumstances. His experience gradually leads him to set up expectations about the properties of things. The fact that these properties may alter brings to his attention the matter of relationships.

[16] Witkin, H. A., and others. *Personality Through Perception*. New York: Harper and Brothers, 1954. P. 467.

[17] See, for example: Deutsche, J. M. *The Development of Children's Concepts of Causal Relations*. Minneapolis: University of Minnesota Press, 1937; Oakes, M. E. *Children's Explanations of Natural Phenomena*. New York: Bureau of Publications, Teachers College, Columbia University; Wolff, Werner. *The Personality of the Pre-School Child*. New York: Grune and Stratton, 1947.

The Process of Concept Formation

Something of the ways in which a child observes and generalizes may be seen in the following incidents taken from the continuous records of the activities of one little boy from the time he was 3 years and 2 months old until he was 6. The parent, who made the observations, was attempting to record all instances which might reveal the child's conceptual development. The incidents in the sequence reported here were selected from some four thousand stenographic records to show the growth in the child's concept of melting. (The comments are those of Navarra, the parent, author of the study of which the records are a part.[18]) The little boy is referred to as "L.B." His mother's name is Celeste. She is not the Celeste we have previously met.

RECORDS	*COMMENT ON PERTINENT FEATURES*

1IM222 — August 9, 1951

L.B.: Please give me a drink of water — my mouth is thirsty.

He was given a glass of fruit juice. L.B. drank some of the juice and then scooped the ice cubes out of the glass. He rubbed the cubes over the table. As he played, little puddles of water began to collect on the table.

The child has had many contacts with ice cubes as they were placed in water and juice drinks. This record is typical of many of the experiences he has had. The water which covered the table provided a definite feeling of melting ice. Although there was no verbalization, the relationship of ice cube to water was well within his experience.

2IM223 — August 9, 1951

L.B.'s mother was replacing an ice tray in the refrigerator. L.B. patted a shelf of the refrigerator.

L.B.: It's cold in here. Is this where the ice lives?

The child has recognized that it is cold inside the refrigerator. He seems to be aware that cold and ice go together since the refrigerator is where "the ice lives." However,

---

[18] Navarra, John G. *The Development of Scientific Concepts in Childhood. A Study of a Young Child's Interaction with the Physical Phenomena of His Environment*, unpublished Doctor of Education Project, Teachers College, Columbia University, 1954.

The author is most appreciative to Mr. Navarra for permission to use this excerpt.

RECORDS

Mother: Yes.

L.B.: Why do you put the ice in here?

Celeste withdrew the tray which had just been placed in the freezing compartment and showed him what she had just placed in the tray.

Mother: We put water in the trays and the water freezes and becomes ice. After the ice cubes are made, they have to be kept cold or they will melt.

3IM736 — November 27, 1951

L.B. wanted to sail a small boat in the sandbox which presently did not have any sand in it. Celeste asked if he wanted her to open the valve while he used the hose to fill the box, but L.B. answered, " We have lots of water." Then as he approached the sandbox, he exclaimed, " Hey, it's like ice. Look it's all ice." Mother asked, " Is it hard? " L.B. responded, " Yes! It's ice." L.B. attempted to pick up pieces of wood which were imbedded in the ice. Shaking his head, he said, " You can't even move the wood — Hey is that cold! " L.B. cracked the ice by chopping it with a toy rake. Much to his surprise he discovered water under the ice. As he broke through, he said, " There's water under there."

4IM737a — November 27, 1951

John came out to play with L.B. As he approached, L.B. called to him, " Look, John, it's all ice."

COMMENT
ON PERTINENT FEATURES

he is not sure why the ice is put in the refrigerator. This would seem to indicate that he is not familiar with water-to-ice relationship. The question would also suggest that his concept of melting ice does not imply any other conditions such as heat.

Change in atmospheric temperature brought about the freezing of the water which was in the child's sandbox. L.B. was surprised when he found that the sandbox contained ice. From his actions, he also seemed surprised when he found water under the ice. Thus, in this record we find the items water, ice, and cold. However, the relationship between the items is not made explicit by the child.

In the previous record, L.B. indicated that he expected to find water in the sandbox. In this rec-

RECORDS

Mother inquired, " I wonder how all this ice got here." L.B. answered by asking a question of his own, " Did the water turn to ice? "

5IM737b — November 27, 1951
L.B. and John cracked the ice.
L.B.: Let's play that we're icemen and we can put the ice on the back of the truck.
John: No, it's too cold.
L.B. proceeded to play as he suggested and John very quickly joined him.

6IM738 — November 27, 1951
L.B. and John were playing with ice which they had gotten from the sandbox. They were transporting it in a small truck. They placed some ice in a small container of water. Mother asked, " Why did you put the ice in the water? " L.B. said, " So it would melt." They continued to play, and then, a full ten minutes later, John asked L.B., " Did it melt yet? " L.B. looked at the ice in the container of water and said, " Some of it." Mother interjected, " How do you know? " L.B. replied, " It's not so big."

7IM739 — November 28, 1951
A stick was protruding from the ice in the sandbox. Part of it was

COMMENT
ON PERTINENT FEATURES

ord his greeting to John seems to imply that he recognizes the change from water to ice, but his answer of a query with a query would seem to indicate that he is not quite sure, and may have some reservations as to what happened.

The item " cold " seems to be fairly well established within their experience as a quality of ice.

L.B.'s initial contact with ice was probably as it was placed in water or some other liquid. From such experiences he probably formulated an expectancy that when ice is placed in water, it gets smaller. This growing smaller has now been associated with melting. His last statement in this record would indicate that " not so big," or growing smaller is his test as to whether the ice has melted. The actions in the record indicate that time is recognized as a factor in melting, i.e., it takes time for the ice to melt; but there is also a suggestion in the record that although the ice becomes smaller as it melts, it remains as ice to the child while it melts.

The significant feature of the record for the present purposes

RECORDS

encased in the ice. L.B. attempted to pull it out without success. He filled a container with water and poured the water over the stick. Then L.B. tried again to pull the stick free from the ice. With all his efforts, he was unable to free the stick. L.B. picked up the toy rake and said, " I can break it with this." He chopped at the ice with the rake and rather reflectively said, " Gee, this is hard! " It took a good deal of concentrated effort to finally free the stick.

COMMENT
ON PERTINENT FEATURES

seems to be the pouring of the water over the stick. Obviously this was done by the child in an effort to loosen the stick. He realized the ice held the stick in place. From the previous record one might say that the child had a developed expectancy that ice melts when placed in water. In this record he has used this expectancy to direct his activity. His unverbalized thoughts may have been: Pour water over the ice, and it will melt, then the stick will be loosened. However, in this case his expectancy did not predict accurately for him, and he had to resort to other means.

8IM759 — November 30, 1951

John and L.B. were playing. L.B. passed the sandbox, looked at it, and said, " It melted, John, it's nearly all water."

Obviously the child is referring to the ice. His statement indicates that the ice melted. The items " melted," " ice," and " water " have assumed a relationship within his conceptual framework.

9IM761 — November 30, 1951

John was breaking up what was left of the ice in the sandbox.

John: I'm gonna make lemon ice.

L.B. began helping John. They smashed the ice and now were placing the small pieces in a basket. Mother asked why the ice was being put in the basket.

L.B.: It has to warm up first.

Mother: Why?

L.B.: So it'll get juicy so we can make lemon ice.

The child has given verbal evidence that he is aware of the role of heat in ice melting. But he has not applied it explicitly in very many of his activities.

RECORDS	*COMMENT* *ON PERTINENT FEATURES*
10IM766 — December 1, 1951 L.B. was playing with the water in the sandbox. He was playing with some boards which he placed in the water. As he played, he rather pensively said, " Sometimes it's ice, and sometimes it's water."	L.B. has recognized the changing conditions in the sandbox. The relationship ice and water is well within his experience. In the previous record he has verbalized on the importance of heat as a factor in ice melting. He has not explicitly stated the role of " coldness " in the water-to-ice formation.
11IM830 — December 6, 1951 L.B. was describing some of the things he did and had planned to do with the water in the sandbox. *L.B.:* I was playing with the water — there wasn't any ice in it. . . . *Dad:* Why wasn't there any ice in the sandbox? *L.B.:* It melted.	The child qualified his description of the water by saying there wasn't any ice in it. His reply to the father's question was that it had melted. The " warming-up " phase of melting has not been integrated into the concept to the point where it is used extensively in replies.

Throughout the child's activities the concept for melting was continuously enlarged and revised. The following excerpts from the records are indicative of the nature of later experiences which contributed information, and aided the growth and refinement of this concept.

CM2148 — June 5, 1952 — 8:45 P.M.
A metal strip on one of L.B.'s small wagons was broken. L.B.'s mother explained that it could be fixed by taking it to the shop where they would " melt some metal " and " pour it on " the broken piece to fix it. L.B. seemed puzzled as he inquired, " Yeah, but *how* can you *pour metal* on the wagon? " Mother replied, " Well, it's melted. . . ." L.B. cut his mother short and asked, " *How* does it get melted? " The mother explained that the metal was heated, and when it became hot enough, it melted. L.B. listened and then said, " Oh! I didn't know that."

CM3816 — December 6, 1952 — 8:10 A.M.
As part of his breakfast, L.B. was given a slice of buttered bread.
L.B.: The butter isn't melted.

Mother: Do you want it melted?
L.B.: Yes.
Mother: Well, how should we melt it?
L.B.: Toast the bread.
Mother: O.K., but why will that melt the butter?
L.B.: Because it's hot.

These records do reveal some apparent animism ("My mouth is thirsty," "Is this where the ice lives?"), but this is considerably outweighed by the child's evident effort to know his world more thoroughly and more accurately. The records suggest several important influences in concept formation. This child has many opportunities for observation and for experimentation. Some children are undoubtedly limited in this respect. On the other hand, it is likely that others have "experience" pushed at them more rapidly than they are able to absorb it. (We are thinking of the youngster whose overzealous parents make frantic efforts to take him to visit the zoo, the farm, the railroad station, and so on.) Fortunately, there seems to be some tendency for the youngster to perceive selectively, to shut out those elements of experience in which he has no inherent interest, and to focus on those which do intrigue him. From the standpoint of many adults, L.B.'s experiences seem amazingly simple and unimportant. Yet it is from thousands of such "simple" learnings that the adult has finally achieved his own ability to cope with the world.

Obviously the child learns much from his own observation and experimentation. But it is doubtful that this alone is sufficient for the development of understanding. The ability to use language facilitates the child's ability to reason; [19] providing him not only with an efficient means of holding on to and organizing his memories (although this can only be inferred, not directly observed), but also a way of checking and verifying his observations.

It may be noted in passing that environments differ widely in the emphasis they give to language, a fact which may considerably

[19] See, for example: Kuenne, M. R. "Experimental Investigation of the Relation of Language to Transposition Behavior in Young Children." *Journal of Experimental Psychology.* 36 (1946), 471–490; Hunter, W. S., and Bartlett, S. C. "Double Alternation Behavior in Young Children." *Journal of Experimental Psychology.* 38 (1948), 558–567; Alberts, E., and Ehrenfreund, D. "Transposition in Children as a Function of Age." *Journal of Experimental Psychology.* 41 (1951), 30–38.

influence the child's ability to express whatever understanding he may have. Perhaps children of this age, given rich opportunities for experimentation, but little encouragement to talk about them, may be able to demonstrate their abilities to reason and to solve problems in a concrete fashion, even though they are not able to express verbally the principle on which they are working. This is a possibility which has been raised in recent years by investigators of social class differences in measured intelligence.[20] Unfortunately, it has not been tested experimentally.

The role of adult influence cannot be overlooked. A child growing up with parents who are sympathetic to his interests in observation and experimentation has a very different experience from the child whose parents are unaware of those interests or who tend to restrict his opportunities. L.B.'s parents made a conscious effort to assume a " nondirective but helpful " role in response to his questions and interests. It should be noted, however, that, although they did not insist on making each of his inquiries an occasion for the dispensation of information, they did structure situations so that he could find out what he wanted to know. They did not give him wrong information. And their occasional throwing of a question back to the child may have helped him to clarify his observations. This is in line with much of what is now known about the nature of learning. The child needs some clues in order to solve problems. To some extent he learns to recognize clues as he tries and rejects various trial and error procedures. However, learning is more efficient when he has some sense of the elements in the situation which are likely to be significant in solving the problem.

The Process of Problem Solving

How past experience and the use of clues may contribute to the solution of a problem may be illustrated by a block building constructed in a nursery school by a vigorous 5-year-old boy. The building started with the construction indicated at (1) in Figure 6. It was a rectangular enclosure within which toy houses and a cart had been placed. The child who had been in a somewhat dis-

---

[20] See, for example: Davis, Alison. *Social Class Influences Upon Learning.* Cambridge: Harvard University Press, 1948; and Eels, Kenneth, and others. *Intelligence and Cultural Differences.* Chicago: University of Chicago Press, 1951.

organized mood all morning seemed about to move on to some other activity. The teacher, feeling that he needed to engage in something constructive and knowing that block building was ordinarily a considerable source of satisfaction to him, said, " Maybe that could have a roof." The child accepted the suggestion and proceeded with what he called a " double decker " (2), a " triple decker " (3), and a fourth (4) which he did not name. In the top he placed several small automobiles, and then roofed over the whole construction. Then he said to the teacher, " How do I get them out ? " The teacher

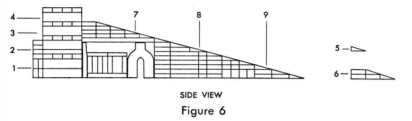

SIDE VIEW

Figure 6

saw this problem in the light of what she knew to have been the previous experience of the child — a downtown garage with a long, long ramp down which cars came at a great rate often with horns blowing and sometimes brakes squealing. The clues she offered were in line with her assumption as to the nature of the problem. Had his experiences been with garage elevators, the clues she gave would have been different. Taking one of the block wedges (5), she said, " Would this help ? " The child looked a little puzzled, so she demonstrated (6) the ramp effect that could be gained with the use of the wedges on top of a step arrangement. The child, without further assistance, built parts (7), (8), and (9). At last he could get the cars out!

This building was left up (and proudly displayed to the child's mother, the nursery school director, and so on). However, at some point it was used by other children, and portions eight and nine were demolished. The blocks which had made them were put away. The following day, another child who had observed the construction came to school early and wanted to " use the garage." He confronted the same problem as the other youngster and was given the same clues by the teacher, but was unable to work out the solution, even when the teacher used additional blocks for demonstration purposes.

Whether the failure of the second child is to be attributed to a difference in chronological age and coincidentally to a lack of sufficient experience, to differences in native intelligence, or to disparities in emotional orientation is not known. Even if it could be established that intellectual capacities were equivalent (which is doubtful), there is little question of a difference in outlook between these two boys. Both, though functioning well within the limits of " normal " behavior, tended to be somewhat tense and anxious. The first child, however, evidently found release in an active, aggressive coping with his environment. The second child apparently lived more within his own private world and more shut off from contact with the outside. Such differences in perspective need to be taken into consideration in any appraisal of learning during this period.

PROBLEM 8. If possible, as you observe children of these ages, keep records of the varieties of ways in which you see evidence of concept formation, problem solving, and reasoning. Discuss your examples in class.

PROBLEM 9. In preparation for the above discussion plan to have the following two articles reviewed:

Maier, Norman F., " Reasoning in Children," pp. 81–87, and

Oakes, Mervin E., " An Analysis of Children's Explanations," pp. 223–226, in *Psychological Studies of Human Development*, edited by Kuhlen and Thompson. What additional light do these studies throw on material presented in this chapter? Do they clarify any situation in which you have observed children's behavior?

LANGUAGE DEVELOPMENT

Children's language in this period not only reveals the child's understanding of his world, but, as we have seen, also facilitates it. At the same time it reflects his unique personality.

Jane chattered constantly. At 3 her babyish enunciation was coupled with intelligent observations — " Fwoors (floors) usually get dirty, don't they? " At 4 her humor was revealed: " Ralph, I'm writing a letter to you: Dear old father, we want some ice cream for the little children."

Pat progressed slowly, both quantitatively and qualitatively, with a gradual upswing at about the age of 4, then a period of incessant questions at home and a retreat into the protection of reticence after 4. Andy increased his volubility from 3 until well beyond 4. He made defensive use of language instead of his fists — " I'm the big, bad man of Ruppert Park! " His " Why's " were incessant at home. Dan's bluster was much more noisy and insistent than Andy's and colored from 4 on with words usually indicated by dashes. Charles' rather slow progress suddenly flowered into nonsense at almost 5 — " Jack the buck, buck the garbage up." Celeste's flair for the vivid expression — " Flowers are like candy — only they aren't candy " — slowly disappeared after she was 4.

The above are some of the ways language flourishes during the years from 3 to 6.

Most striking is the tremendously rapid growth in complexity of structure and in vocabulary, both so far as number of words is concerned and meanings for those words. To some extent, the language of children of this age, according to various studies, is egocentric, but the general trend appears to be toward social give and take. As we have suggested in other connections, there is considerable evidence that children in lower socio-economic groups are less advanced in language than are more privileged groups. In both instances it is likely that individual differences are in part dependent on the amount of stimulation of language interests the environment affords. On the average, girls tend to be more advanced in language development than boys. The reasons for this are not yet established, although some interesting ones have been proposed. Among these is the possibility that the affectional bond with the mother tends to favor the girls' speech development somewhat more than the boys'. In any event, the idea that language development flourishes in a close relationship between mother and child may partially account for the fact that speech difficulties, such as stuttering and a continuation of baby talk, are often associated with the birth of a younger brother or sister.[21]

For many children the rate of language development appears to

[21] Detailed references for these statements may be found in: McCarthy, Dorothea. " Language Development in Children," in *Manual of Child Psychology*, edited by Leonard Carmichael. New York: John Wiley and Sons, 2d ed., 1954. Pp. 492–630.

rise to a peak sometime during this period, but usually around 4 years. Interest in nonsense words and rhyming is marked, and the use of language may be very creative. The testing of limits and the embroidering of skills which is seen in so many other areas of development thus appears in language also. Frequently the child has acquired " power words," ranging all the way from relatively mild expletives like " stinkpot " up to major obscenities and profanities. Wise parents and teachers are concerned with what the child's power language may mean. For some, it may manifest only a healthy self-assertiveness. For others, it may be a cover-up for uncertainty or guilt or anxiety. Unfortunately, despite his tremendous language growth, the child in this period often cannot find words for the feelings which are of most consequence to him.

PROBLEM 10. If possible, keep a record of the language of a child of this age over a period of several weeks. If your classmates keep similar records on other children, you can discuss the trends you observe.

Readiness for the Three R's

In the American culture any consideration of the child's perceptions, his conceptual development, and his language development leads inevitably to the question of reading readiness. A kind of magic seems to attach itself to the age of 6, at which point the child is supposed to enter " regular " school and begin the important business of learning to read, write, and figure. Whether or not a child attends kindergarten, the parents regard the first grade as his major step toward adulthood. He himself thinks of first grade as a major achievement, and, interestingly, many teachers also consider it the real beginning of his school life, when he must begin to " work, not just play." Oddly enough, both parents and teachers are prone to think that because the child has reached the age of 6, he ought to be ready for this new experience. In the next chapter we shall consider more specifically what entrance into first grade does mean in the life of the child. Here, however, we need to examine the idea of " readiness," for it is supposedly in these years before 6 that it is developed.

The meaning of " readiness." " Readiness " is an educational concept concerned with the timeliness of what we wish to teach the child in the light of his ability to make use of it. It would seem, therefore, to put emphasis on understanding of the child's total development. One asks not only " *Can* the child learn this? " but also " What effect will his learning have upon him? " Unfortunately, however, the concept of readiness, particularly in relation to reading, has often been taken in a much narrower sense. As the process of learning to read has been analyzed, it has been noted that the elements involved seem to include the ability to pay attention, to discriminate likeness and differences, to move the eyes from left to right, and so on. Increasingly attention has also been given to the fact that the child's background of experience is an important influence in the process. The question is then raised, " What can be done to help children develop the skills and the experiences necessary to learning to read? " The answer too frequently is a program in which the child is to be given opportunities to practice the various elements involved in the reading process, without sufficient regard for the many other important experiences which he might be having, which in the long run would also contribute to his abilities for reading. In these instances kindergarten becomes a mere " reading-readiness " program. Instead of being a situation in which the child is offered opportunities to channel his energies into constructive and creative activities, to learn to deal more adequately with both his positive and negative feelings, so that he can participate more and more freely in a give-and-take relationship with his peers, it becomes one in which he must put the major part of his energies into fitting himself into the particular patterns for dramatic play, art and music expression, science exploration, and so on, set by the teacher. Above all, he must perform well in whatever reading-readiness exercises are given him. Such a program betrays a curious lack of insight into the true nature of children's growth and learning. It is as though the individuality in rates of growth and in ways of perceiving and understanding as well as individuality in experience could suddenly be erased and all children somehow made ready for first-grade reading. Rather than furthering the child's development of an effective inner control system of his own, it may in some instances retard it. He may indeed be " ready " for first-grade reading, able to cope with the primers and first readers, but true zest for learning and a genuine intellectual curiosity may be stifled. Rather than initiative and spontaneity, he learns only compliance and conformity. On the other hand, should he fail to achieve the desired standards of readiness, he may enter first grade already burdened with a sense of despair and defeat.

Perhaps we paint too gloomy a picture. Obviously the child, who has a rich and satisfying out-of-school life will not be ruined by his kindergarten experiences. On the other hand, one finds so many children for whom reading difficulties constitute a major heartache all through school life, that we think clarification of the processes involved in learning to read are essential. There is no area in which more educational research has been done, and it is likely that there is no area in which confusion is likely more prevalent. Increasingly, however, it appears that the process of learning to read cannot be viewed as something apart from the child's developing personality.

It has its beginnings in his first dim differentiation of his environment, his developing perceptions, and his increasing abilities to attach meanings to words. It is facilitated as he finds reading materials in the world around him and observes the use other people make of them. Depending on the successfulness of his identifications, he also begins to want to become a reader. Further, reading as a process comes to have personal meaning for him. It is something that makes the adults very happy. When he asks, " What does that say? " he does not miss the look of " See, what a bright boy we have " that passes from his father to his mother, and he is equally alert to their approval when he later comments, " That sign says stop." He knows, too, when reading has more than usual meaning for the adults, not merely a useful tool for living, but a means to some important end, like entering medical school before the age of 20. It is something of which his brother is afraid. It is something that his brother does so well that he himself is afraid to tackle it. It is a mysterious process which reveals " secrets " that he would like to know, or of which he is a little fearful. Or perhaps it is something completely foreign to him. Nobody he knows bothers about it. Or he himself is so absorbed in so many other concerns — why don't his parents love him as much as they seem to love his new sister, how can he find his place in the group of children with whom he plays — that he is oblivious to the fact that people do read.

Research [22] has indicated that a considerable amount of home teaching takes place in the area of reading. Sometimes this is a mere answering of the child's questions, sometimes an effort to teach the letters, sometimes a more thoroughgoing effort accompanied by workbooks and regular " drill " and various rewards and punishments. In the light of what is now known about learning to read, there is no reason why the child who asks what a word is should not be told. If he is genuinely interested in learning to read and really " ready," he may seem to teach himself. The major danger lies in parents or other adults, somehow magnifying the importance of this accomplishment, so that the child begins to feel that reading is more valued than anything else. Actually, at this stage a rich play life with its social stimulation and its reality-testing is of much greater consequence. Unpressured by his environment, a very bright child may find time for both.

Readiness for number. The way that children reach out with varying degrees of interest toward the reading possibilities in their environment, is more or less paralleled in their awareness of number, size, and quantities. Increasingly, the child who at first views a collection of objects as a whole in terms of a single characteristic later tends to discriminate among them. The possible number experiences of the young child seem almost limitless — as he handles playthings which are duplicates, dispenses cookies his mother gives him for his playmates, fits small boxes into larger ones, fills a large cup of water with a smaller one, and so on. Yet it takes time for these experiences, like others, to become dependable, assimilated, and meaningful concepts for him. For example, one youngster who can count to thirty at 5 and who can get out the required number of spoons, knives, and forks for the family supper table may not yet be able to comply if mother switches her request to " Please set the table for *four* tonight." Others can deal readily with such an idea as,

"If you have three pennies and I give you two more, how much will you have?"

Readiness then, whether it be in reading, or writing, or arithmetic, is not something which can, as it were, be applied to children so that they reach first grade all primed for the same kind of instruction. It is rather a matter of the extent to which the experiences the child has already had and the growth he has made equip him to meet the expectations which will be held for him. Fortunately, there are many schools which will not wish to make him fit a particular mold, but will rather welcome him and value him as the unique and individual personality he is.

PROBLEM 11. If possible, visit several kindergartens. From your observations, what evidence do you have as to how the teachers and the schools regard readiness. To what extent are the children having meaningful experiences which may help to build a good background for later learning? Are the experiences suitable to the kinds of homes from which the children come? To what extent are they practicing elements of the reading process?

INTERPERSONAL RELATIONSHIPS

Relationships with Adults

In this period, perhaps to a greater extent than in any other, the child's personality reflects his relationships with the adults who are most important to him, usually his mother and his father. Gradually, as he grows in his abilities, they, if all goes well, help him to test out his powers, encourage him toward a realization of his own uniqueness, clarify his confusions. But the very closeness of their emotional attachments for one another often makes for difficulties. For this reason, other adults may assume an important supplementary role in the child's living.

Some of the variety of relationships (the many ways children may view the adults in their world and interact with them) in this period may be seen in a consideration of some of the outstanding characteristics of the relationships between our six youngsters and their mothers and fathers.

Jane Warner. On the whole, Jane was accepting and compliant of her mother's wishes and desires. The standards held for her were high, but she was capable of performing as expected. Her mother enjoyed showing her how to do things properly, setting the table, putting away dishes, and so on. Not until Jane was nearly 6, was there much evidence of any rebellion on Jane's part and even then it was expressed more in stubbornness than in any real outbursts.

The apple of Jane's eye during this period was her father, and it was with him that she shared many delightful moments. She loved to go with him on errands and to have his interest in her imaginative play. Like her, he had a nice sense of humor and was not above " pretending " with her at times.

Pat Plummer. Pat's relationship with her mother was much more a " bedeviling " one, particularly as she got beyond the age of 4. On the other hand, Mrs. Plummer sometimes nagged at Patty when she wanted her to perform or show off in some way or other so that perhaps Patty's tendencies were merely imitative.

So far as her father was concerned, Patty remained the center of his affections as the " little " one of the family. He was the one to whom she turned for information, usually after she had been " after " her mother and had not received any satisfactory answers.

From the time she was 4 or so, Patty had another important male admirer in the person of a cousin who had no children and took special delight in indulging Patty's whims. Patty was very responsive to this.

Dan Mallon. Dan's mother was inclined to be fairly lenient with him, although on occasion she could let him know in no uncertain terms what she expected. She was quite sensitive to the possibility that she might lose his affection if she were too harsh, and this tended to temper her discipline considerably.

It appears to have been Dan's kindergarten teacher who helped him to channel his energies most effectively.

Dan's father was much more inclined to be the disciplinarian in the family, and there is considerable likelihood that Dan not only respected his word, but also feared it.

Andrew Drosky. During the larger part of this period Andy's mother tended to regard him, despite her pride in his abilities, as a very little boy who needed a great deal of protection. Thus, even when he was in kindergarten, she took him back and forth despite the fact that none of the other mothers in the neighborhood felt it necessary to do so.

Andy's relationships with his father were never particularly close, although on occasion his father took him on small excursions which might have been expected to excite a warm comradeship. It is possible of course that Mr. Drosky's uncertainties over his job crept into his relationship with his son, or perhaps he found it impossible to compete with the attentions his wife lavished on the child.

In general, Andy got on well with adults outside his family and was usually considered an appealing youngster by them.

Charles Brown. Charlie continued to be his mother's implied favorite during this period. He was evidently never overawed by her threats nor her highly emotional behavior.

Just how well Charles was able to identify with his father is not very clear. It is evident that Mr. Brown's methods of handling the youngsters was much more definite, direct, and unemotional than his wife's.

Adults outside the family tended to regard both Charlie and Chet as "terrors." It is likely that, because of their closeness to one another, neither was as much influenced by other adults, as some children are.

Celeste Collins. Mrs. Collins seemed to see Celeste during this period as a rather bold, aggressive little girl, although most other adults thought of her as retiring and somewhat forlorn. Since her mother worked a good deal of the time during these years, it is possible that Celeste's relationships with her grandmother or with others who cared for her, ranked nearly equal in importance. In any event, although she did not express it very directly, there is considerable evidence that for some reason Celeste was often inclined toward hostile feelings where women were concerned.

Celeste's relationship with her father was generally a happy one despite the fact that he occasionally disciplined in rather harsh-seeming ways — making her stand in the corner for a considerable time, for example.

It is important to emphasize that in all these instances the important influence on the child's personality was not a matter of the specific techniques used, but rather of the basic relationships between the two individuals. The parent brings to the relationship his own rather well-established ways of looking at the world and himself. The areas in which he has himself had difficulties may be the ones in which he finds it hard to guide the child. For example, Mrs. Mallon's uncertainties may have been tied in with the problem of the extent to which love can be relied upon. Mrs. Drosky evidently needed to have Andy's dependence. We are not implying that any of these parents are "abnormal." But to the extent that they are themselves anxious or hostile or guilt-ridden, parents are less able to sense the child's individuality as a person and more likely to respond to him more in terms of their own needs than of his.

But the children bring something to the relationship as well. Thus a more volatile, high-strung youngster than Andrew might have forced his mother to emancipate him earlier. With a more placid child than Danny Mrs. Mallon might have felt more certain. Further, circumstances may sometimes accentuate problems. For example, several of these children may have had more than usual difficulties in their relationships with their fathers. However, the reasons may have lain not in any basic personality problems, but rather in the fact that the fathers were irritable, anxious, and uncertain of themselves because of their inabilities to find work. We tend to think that children respond to the deeper levels of the parent personality rather than to surface or temporary manifestations. Nevertheless, children differ in their sensitivity and some may be affected where others would not be.

Here again we would point out the salutary effects which other adults may have. A grandmother, without necessarily placing herself in competition, may allow more spontaneity than the mother will permit. The child sees himself in a new way and grows accordingly. A baby-sitter may expect from a dependent little boy a self-reliance which helps him to consider the possibility of being more on his own. The teacher, if she is both sensitive and effective, may help the child to feel more comfortable about himself and to direct his energies into constructive channels. Without the effectiveness of such influences, dependent of course on the individuality of the child, we should be hard put to explain some youngsters' emotional survival.

PROBLEM 12. As you observe children, note how they relate themselves to various adults, as father, mother, teacher, yourself. What constant behavior do you note and what shifts? What do you think may be the basis for the shifts?

Relationships with Children

Although the child's primary concerns in this period may be centered around his parents, his relationships with other children are beginning to assume more and more importance. Let us examine some of the relationships between our children and other chilern.

Jane Warner. Jane remained an only child until she was 6. In nursery school she was well liked by the other youngsters for she had a pleasant adaptability, fell in easily with most play ideas, and offered some interesting ones of her own. She was never aggressive and when the play took such direction usually retreated to adult protection.

Pat Plummer. Pat's relationships with children underwent marked changes during the course of this period. In the beginning she was timid and solitary. At nursery school, when the teachers tried to set up an activity which would include her, she had a nice protection in the comment, " I did that at home last night." However, Pat's relationships underwent a considerable shift at the point where she began to play in the neighborhood around 4 and acquired herself a pal in the person of Frankie, a boy whom she stoutly maintained she intended to marry. Perhaps she found give and take easier to learn in the simpler relationship with one child than in the larger group situation. In any event, she became much more interested in group activities and participated rather actively although usually with little conversation.

Andrew Drosky. Andy's sister, it will be remembered, was born when he was 3 years and 7 months. His nursery school teacher felt that this helped him to grow out of his dependency on his mother. His role with his mother then tended to be one of helping her to care for his sister. With other children he tended to be somewhat more of an imitator than an initiator. He was only occasionally aggressive, usually with children younger than himself.

Dan Mallon. Dan also had a small sister, but she was born while he was still a toddler. Their associations were consistently close, and in general Danny tended to express considerably more positive than negative feelings about her. Occasionally, he liked to tease her, but aside from this, the strong hostile feelings which he evidently had on a deeper level were never openly directed toward her.

Dan's relations with other children have been described in fair detail in earlier portions of this chapter. To the picture of obstreperousness found there may be added an incident when he was a little more than 4. He became involved in a wrestling match with another boy the same age and size. The other boy was inclined to puppyish tussling, but even so Danny twice tried to bring the struggle to a close by saying, " No more! No more! " At the same time, he was unable to keep from using his own fists. However, each time he hit, he was guilty and upset. There is at least a suggestion here that his braggadocio covered up a real anxiety lest genuine give-and-take would lead to the expression of more hostility than he could bear.

Charles Brown. Charles' relationships with other children, when Chet was not around, tended to be friendly and agreeable. With Chet, he was more noisy and it would appear that the two of them were exerting considerable domination and leadership. Closer study would usually reveal that it was merely a matter of more noise and activity on their part without the others becoming actually involved. Interestingly, until about 3½ Charles tended to be the more outgoing and aggressive of the two, but from then on the reverse became increasingly true.

Celeste Collins. Celeste becomes increasingly responsive to children in the first part of the year she is 3, but by the time she is 5, she is still quite tentative. When children made advances to her, she was responsive. With those who were more self-sufficient, she appeared to want to attract attention, but not to know how to do so. (Note her boastfulness in the previous play records.)

The variety of relationships which we find here are not too different from those we might find in any group of children of this age. The general trends in social relationships during the years 3 to 6 are from tentativeness, as seen in the child who plays beside another child and occasionally interchanges a remark, toward cooperation of the sort described in the record of Jane, Ralph, and Earl. Spontaneous groups seldom exceed three or four children even at 6. Some children, by the time they are 5, in such small groups are able to devise fairly elaborate projects which they carry through cooperatively. Such cooperation depends on the personality characteristics of the children, the equipment provided, and the extent to which the adult's role tends to be an integrative one.[23]

The close relationship between the child's personality characteristics and his ability to enjoy friendly social relationships has been implied in the material in this chapter. There are some other factors which must also be taken into account. One of these is the environment in which the relationships occur. Where there are very

[23] For reports of research in these areas see: Jersild, Arthur T. *Child Psychology.* New York: Prentice-Hall, 1954. Pp. 195–235; and Anderson, Harold H. "Social Development," in *Manual of Child Psychology,* edited by Leonard Carmichael. New York: John Wiley and Sons, 2d ed., 1954. Pp. 1163–1215.

few toys, for example, one may expect fighting. On the other hand, if the environment should contain equivalent toys for every child, there would be no need for socialization. Further, some kinds of equipment, such as housekeeping toys, large boxes, and climbing apparatus, tend to encourage socializing, while others, such as puzzles, crayons, and so on, do not.

More important than the equipment is the personality characteristics of the adults. Some tend to dominate the children's activities. One could almost say that they want the children to play *their* way. Such teachers tend to excite similar behavior in the children. They impose their ideas, their desires on their fellows with little regard for their feelings. On the other hand, other teachers are much more alert to possibilities for helping the children to develop cooperation.

Even when the teacher's behavior tends to be such as to encourage the children to be friendly and helpful with each other, she is likely to find that some combinations of children tend to engender fighting and hostility, whereas others will be more likely to cooperate with each other. In nursery schools there has been a general trend toward dividing groups according to age, even within a few months. A deeper understanding of the personality characteristics of children would suggest that it would be wise to consider their influence in establishing groups. For example, some children, like some teachers, seem to have greater capacities than others for resolving conflicts effectively. One child will say to an intruder in the dollhouse, "You can't come in," but another will say, "Oh, that must be the milk man." It may also be wise to explore more thoroughly the effects of group experience on children. For example, left to their own devices in a group of volatile, aggressive youngsters, some children will remain shy little violets. This may well be the kinds of people they are. On the other hand, they might really find themselves capable of considerable good give-and-take if provisions were made for them to get better acquainted with each other or with others more like them. Despite all of the research in social relationships which has been done, there is still much to be done before we know how certain kinds of experiences effect certain kinds of children and to what extent social experiences in these years may influence later development.

PROBLEM 13. As you observe young children, if possible, focus your attention on two or three who play together a good deal. Try to note what each child gets out of and gives to the relationship. Also note how each child reacts with other children. Helpful to an understanding of changing social relationships are the following reports of research:

In Barker, Kounin & Wright, *Child Behavior and Development:*
Barker, Roger, and others, " Frustration and Regression," pp. 441–458;
Anderson, Harold H., " Domination and Socially Integrative Behavior," pp. 459–484;
Parten, Mildred, and Newhall, S. M., " Social Behavior of Preschool Children," pp. 509–526.
In Dennis, *Readings in Child Psychology:*
Jersild, Arthur T., " Children's Social Adjustments in Nursery School."
In Kuhlen and Thompson, *Readings in Human Development:*
Greenberg, Pearl J., " The Growth of Competitiveness During Childhood," pp. 337–344;
Van Alstyne, Dorothy, and Hattwick, La Berta, " Behavior Patterns of Children with Nursery School Experience," pp. 411–415.

CHANGING VIEWS OF THE SELF

It is in the period of toddlerhood that the individual establishes self-awareness. The power-testing period may be thought of as one in which the self acquires many new attributes depending on the kinds of experiences the child has.

Some of these attributes relate to his body and his feelings about it. He may feel good about it, proud of its maleness, pleased with the color of his hair and eyes, and so on. Or he may be uneasy about it. For example, one 6-year-old remarked in a troubled tone, " I don't like my face." The reason was readily apparent to a visitor who had just thoughtlessly assured the boy's mother that the new baby did indeed look like the boy's father. The mother's suggestion that the boy did not and the visitor's apparent assent were more than he could take. One incident of this sort is not likely to alter a child's picture of himself, but an accumulation of them will. He revises his attitudes toward himself in accord with the attitudes others express toward him.

This is nowhere better established than in the previously cited studies which indicated that many young Negro children could pick out the color which they were, but also indicated that it was not the color they preferred. It is obvious that to a large extent the way the child sees himself is a reflection of the way he is appraised by others. In the period under discussion it is the family appraisals which count the most. Goodman [24] illustrates this with the story of the 3-year-old Negro child who asked her father, "What am I?" His fond reply, "You're a tantalizing brown!" and the other positive replies she always received to her questions stood her in good stead. In a nursery school discussion she was able to assert both that she was American and a "tantalizing" brown.

Little girls sometimes suggest their dissatisfaction with certain aspects of their body in their refusals to wear feminine clothing or in cutting off their hair so that, as one 4-year-old put it, "Now I look just like my brother." Dissatisfaction of another sort was suggested by one child who, drawing a picture of herself omitted arms and hands and then commented confidingly to an onlooker, "I'm not going to bite my fingernails."

Some of the creative activities, as we have suggested earlier, particularly dance and movement, seem to have considerable potentialities for helping children to feel that their bodies are attractive, capable of good things. Obviously, if they are made to feel that they are out of step, can't keep time and so on, their self-concept is not likely to be enhanced.

It would seem that by the end of the period under consideration the child ought to have a somewhat realistic concept of himself in terms of what he can and cannot do. One notices this shift toward greater reality in the comment of the 6-year-old who is not quite so bold about his drawings as he was at 4 and may ask how you make "the girl run." If he has come through years in which he has had reasonable opportunities to test his powers, but in which he was not permitted to do things which endangered him, he should, however, have a good sense of positiveness about his abilities.

The Role of Anxiety

From one point of view, anxiety is a continual threat in this period. Primarily this is because the child's power to express his

[24] Goodman, Mary E. *Race-Awareness in Young Children*. Cambridge, Massachusetts: Addison-Wesley Press, 1952. P. 19.

impulses is considerably greater than it was earlier. He is strong enough to hurt those who get in his way. He may be deliberately destructive of something cherished by someone else. Consequently, the chances of his running into danger either actually or in terms of his own conscience are greater. His vivid imagination and lack of experience add to his uneasiness. It is hard for him to draw the line between what he would like to do if he followed his impulses, and what he actually does do. In the case of the child who has an adequate conscience, anxiety can be avoided by following its dictates, but since the dictates of conscience are often strict and the impulses strong, hostility may be engendered along the way. He resents the restrictions he feels against having such strong feelings. If he feels possessive, he can effectively ward off transgressors.

The problem is for the child to find ways of channeling his impulses in directions which will give him sufficient satisfaction so that he has no need to feel hostility. Thus the only way the child can avoid undue anxiety and hostility appears to be through the protection of loving adults who refuse to permit the expression of destructive impulses, but who also help him toward constructive activity. The anxiety he thus experiences is in a sense a goad which pushes him toward greater maturity.

But many children experience anxiety which is far more pervasive than this. Its sources may lie in earlier experiences or in relationships with adults who are anxious or hostile. There are the children who are ceaselessly on the go, who are terrified of what they may do and in a sense ward off anxiety by never doing anything constructive. There are others who withdraw more and more into a world of fantasy, unable to bear the world of reality. Some of these act out their fantasies. Others wall themselves in. Children who present symptoms as marked as these are ill and need skilled psychological help.

Anxiety has many sources in this period. As we have indicated in previous sections, some children are undoubtedly more susceptible to it than others. Aside from this, however, the nature of the child's concerns appear to be such as to provoke a good bit of anxiety on the part of the adults concerned for him. Much of what he has to learn in this period has to do with his fulfillment of his eventual sex role and his expression of aggression. Both of these happen to be areas in which many adults have not fully resolved their conflicts. Small wonder that they find it difficult to offer the child the serene untroubled adult guidance he so much needs.

Contribution of This Period to Personality Development

Erikson defines the central conflict of this period as that between initiative and guilt. He says:

The danger of this stage is a sense of guilt over the goals contemplated and the acts initiated in one's exuberant enjoyment of new locomotor and mental power: acts of aggressive manipulation and coercion which go far beyond the executive capacity of organism and mind and, therefore, call for an energetic halt on one's contemplated initiative.[25]

As this implies and as the previous material in this chapter has indicated, the child gains a healthy awareness of his own potentialities when he has an opportunity to exercise his growing powers under the guidance of adults who keep him within safe limits. Such adults do not hesitate to show disapproval of his mistakes, but they communicate to him at the same time their basic faith in his individuality. They respect his unique personality. He is helped to accept his own potentialities and has diminishing need to be rivalrous of others. They encourage him to show initiative. They help him to channel his possessiveness toward an enjoyment of sharing. Under such circumstances the child is not afraid to exercise his powers and to test out his abilities. He develops what Erikson calls the " sense of initiative."

Let us now consider the extent to which our young people developed this personality component during the years 3 to 6.

PROBLEM 14. Before you read the following material, you may find it interesting to review preceding sections which describe various aspects of these children's living and attempt to list the important factors which may have contributed to their initiative.

Jane Warner. In many respects, Jane has a fine component of initiative. We note especially her ability to use language, her social adapta-

[25] Erikson, Erik. *Childhood and Society.* New York: W. W. Norton & Company, 1950. P. 224.

bility, her humor, and her imagination. There is some evidence that she becomes anxious in situations in which aggression might be expressed. We cannot be sure about whether she will feel free to assert herself in all areas.

Pat Plummer. Patty's sense of initiative is difficult to evaluate. There is considerable evidence of typical little girl interests, including a " boy friend." But there is also evidence of some guilt which may prove hampering.

Andrew Drosky. The precipitating factor in Andy's development of initiative seems to have been the birth of his sister, which freed him from some of his mother's all-enveloping interest. Despite some concern, there is increasing evidence of his good potentialities in this period.

Dan Mallon. Dan's development appears somewhat mixed. He is active and, as his mother puts it, " Gets into everything." But in a number of respects he talks and threatens more than he actually carries out. Fears and insecurities seem to hamper and restrict his exercise of initiative.

Charles Brown. In some areas, Charles seems to have developed the least sense of initiative of any of these youngsters. The significance of his assumption of a less assertive role than his brother is uncertain at this point.

Celeste Collins. Celeste appears to have the least initiative of any of these youngsters. She is, in general, quiet, restricted, and not very assertive.

DESIRABLE GUIDANCE IN THE " POWER–TESTING " PERIOD

Children in the period from 3 to 6 years are both enchanting and disconcerting. As adults we are often charmed by their dramatic interests, their attempts to try out adult roles, their fresh and creative ways of looking at the world; their questions, and their reflections. But we are often appalled at the intensity of their feelings and resentments.

Some of us find it hard to remain adults with children of this age. We are able to feel not merely for the child, but with him. We are not deceived by his behavior. When he is extremely active and never able to be still, we sense the anxiety from which he is fleeing. When he is inactive and restricted, we sense the strength of the inner feelings he is trying to hold in control. To be able thus to feel as the child feels — to experience *empathy* with him — can help us to guide him wisely. But this is only true so long as we are able to maintain with our empathy the clear sense of our own adulthood. When we respond to him as though we, too, were a child, as though we lacked the perspective of all our years of living, we only serve to confuse and disturb him.

The best guidance of children of this age comes from adults who have learned to live with their own childhood. They find it normal and natural to recall that they, too, had in their childhood needs and impulses essentially no different from those of the children who now confront them. Such adults can accept the primitive behavior of children of this age. They can help the child to live with his feelings and to find constructive channels for them. They do not insist that he bottle his feelings inside himself, so that they seethe into more and more hostility. They do not permit him to express his feelings in ways which may be destructive to himself or to other people or to valued property. But they do provide for him all the many kinds of activity, creative and instructive, in which one, whose feelings are mean and resentful, can work off some of his ire. Above all, they do not ask the child to deny his feelings. They do not say, " You must love your little brother. You are a bad boy when you hit him." They may say, in effect, " You were really mad. Everybody gets mad sometimes, but we learn what to do when we feel that way. You'll learn, too."

In the opinion of the author, it is not wise for either the parent or the teacher to attempt to spell out for the child the deeper sources of his feelings — as, for example, the fact that on occasion he does, indeed, hate his parents. This does not mean that his rages are not to be recognized as genuine anger. But the phase where most children need most help, is in learning to recuperate from their emotional outbursts and to perceive reality more clearly. Nothing is more likely to be destructive of good emotional development than leaving a child to chew on his rage for what seems to him an interminably long time. Parents and teachers who understand how the world looks to a 3- or 4-year-old will be quick to " forgive and forget " and to help him to find new satisfactions.

The adult who is comfortable in his own skin is most likely to be able to find the way to help the child to be comfortable in his. Prescribed techniques frequently do not work, simply because they do not respect the sensitivities of a particular child. Momentary isolation may mean extreme deprivation to one child, while for another it offers a welcome opportunity to get a grip on his feelings and impulses. A spanking, administered by a basically loving parent may " clear the air " for one child, and arouse great bitterness in another.

PROBLEM 15. As you observe children of this age, note the variety of ways in which adults attempt to help them to gain control over their behavior. What ways seem to you to be most effective? How do the methods used seem to be related to the personalities of the children and the adults?

PROBLEM 16. Plan a class session on " Discipline for the Young Child." For reference material consult:

Wolf, Katherine, *The Controversial Problem of Discipline.*
Baruch, Dorothy, *New Ways in Discipline.*
Hymes, James L., *Discipline.*
Gruenberg, Sidonie, M. editor. *The Encyclopedia of Child Care and Guidance.*

How do the points-of-view of these authors correspond? At what points are they in disagreement?

If possible, follow the class discussion with a session including several parents of young children. To what extent would they accept the same " formulas " for discipline?

Sex Education

There are a number of specific problems of guidance about which there may be considerable concern which arise during this period. One of them is the matter of sex education. As they become concerned with questions of both origin and potentiality, many children ask what they want to know. Parents do well to answer each question as it comes, in as simple terms as possible. Children of this age are not interested in long expositions. Experiences with pets and their young may help to clarify some of the child's ideas, though it must be remembered that the child of this age is quite literal-minded, and a knowledge of puppy reproduction is not necessarily equated with a knowledge of human reproduction. Parents today probably find it easier to be a little more casual about the child's questions and to give truthful answers (there are innumerable pamphlets and "magazine" articles giving suitable phraseology) than did parents of a generation or so ago. Basically, however, the most important aspect of the child's sex education appears to lie not in what he is told, but in the kinds of family living he himself experiences. If mother and daddy are happy responsive individuals who enjoy mutual respect and admiration, the child's outlook is apt to be good.

A major difficulty with proposing any "formula" for giving sex information is that parents (and other people) seem to convey more to children in what they themselves feel than in what they say. This is why it is probably much more important for all who work with children to come to terms with their own childhood and to work through their own feelings about childish impulses than it is for them to learn what the "authorities" say. Further, what may be right and natural for one set of parents in relation to one child may not be so for the next one. In any event, the child's experience should offer him assurance that his sex interests are basically good and that he has every potentiality for growing up to be a good husband or — in the case of a girl — a good wife.

Fears

Many fears may appear during this period. Sometimes they are specific — the child is afraid of dogs or of the dark, for example. Sometimes they are more vague — the child goes into a panic in a new situation, or he wakes frequently at night from a "bad" dream. To some extent these fears and apprehensions may be a product of the child's rapid mental growth — he is disturbed because situations take on more and more meaning for him, but he has not always had sufficient experience to interpret it. Often, however, the fears go deeper. The child experiences a pervasive anxiety stemming from conflicts over his feelings about his parents, his brothers and sisters, his own impulses. Sometimes he needs to have the standards for his behavior lowered a bit, so that he does not always have to carry the burden of being a "big boy." Sometimes he needs more protection from the adults against his own impulses — more rather than less limits. But often what he needs most is adults who are sympathetic and understanding of his problems, who are able to convey to him faith in his ability to grow. Such adults can help him to come to grips with his fears, to put some of them into words, and in effect to acknowledge that fear is a universal human experience. Again, we must conclude that the important aspect of helping the child is not the technique the adult uses, but rather the relationship which is established between him and the child.

Out-of-Bounds Language

Often it is difficult to know whether to attempt to limit the child's language expression in this period. Some of it, although silly, stays within the limits of good taste, but some becomes exceedingly provocative. Here it seems wise for the adult not to assume that words are equivalent to action. He may tolerate them when he would not tolerate the child's doing of the deeds he describes. The child's words are often clues to his feelings, and it seems unfortunate to close off an important avenue of communication. On the other hand, there is a " time and place " for everything, and gradually the child needs help in understanding this.

Serious Personality Disturbances

Finally we come to the question of the seriousness of problems. How is the parent or the teacher to know when the child's resentments, his interests, or his language reveal problems which are not the ordinary ones of growing up, but rather deep-seated disturbances? It is good to be able to make such a distinction since treatment for a serious problem is often more effective when it is begun in the stage of development than it would be if postponed until later.

One clue to disturbance which may represent a serious problem is the marked *patterning* of behavior. All children have some rituals and resistances and characteristic play patterns. But the child who is disturbed may establish some which are more bizarre than usual. Normally one kind of pattern gives way to another. When they are *persistent* over months, one may begin to question which needs they are serving in the child's life. Some patterns become *pervasive.* The child's living is increasingly organized around them. This, too, signals the possibility that adjustment is costing more than its usual price. When eating, sleeping, and elimination go on as usual, and when the child seems generally happy with his peers and with adults, there is little cause for worry. But when many of his areas of living are affected, then he may need more help than the parent or teacher can give.

A decision to seek professional help for one's child is not an easy decision to make, particularly because parents are so often made to feel that to do so is an indication of their own failure. It should be clear by now that this is not necessarily the case. Children are extremely complex beings, and some of them need more than parents are able to give. Some are unable to meet the parental expectations which would be quite reasonable for another child. On the other hand, it is probably true that in these early years the child's way of relating himself to his world is in most instances primarily a matter of his relationships with his parents.

Sometimes problems are resolved by removing pressure from parents and the child. Thus, a place for parents to talk out their worries may be a great help. One of the reasons why parent discussion groups are so popular seems to be that a degree of relief is obtained when the parent discovers that his child's behavior is not too different from that of his neighbor's child.

Sometimes a problem works itself out as the child has an opportunity to be with other children and to use a variety of play materials. Thus nursery school attendance may have decidedly beneficial effects. But it is wise to remember that when a child is helped by nursery school experience, it is because the nursery school is a good one. The teacher understands what the child needs and how best to provide for him. There are, however, nursery schools and nursery schools. In many communities institutions calling themselves by the name are operated by individuals who have had no training for this important work. Such places are unlikely to be of any benefit to the child, and a wise parent would no more consider patronizing them than he would take his child to a " doctor " who had no license to practice medicine. Even where nursery schools are fully accredited, attendance for a particular child may not be recommended. The youngster in this period of his development is strongly home and family tied. No decision for him to attend nursery school should be made without thoroughgoing consideration of what it may mean to him. For example, to be " sent " when a new baby arrives, or when he has just moved into a new home and is very uncertain about it, or when he is just recuperating from hospitalization can be a very devastating experience to the young child.

The function of most nursery schools is educational, not therapeutic. Teachers, because of their broad experience with a variety of children, can sometimes help parents to evaluate the seriousness of a youngster's difficulties. When these are obviously deep-seated, then the child or his parents, or both, need skilled psychological or psychiatric help.

Whether or not the parent needs such assistance, he is likely to find the power-testing period a challenging one. If he frees himself emotionally to see with the child and to grow along with him, it can also be a tremendously satisfying one. Never again will he be so close to his child, and never again will the child's vision be so fresh.

In some societies, 6- to 12-year-olds master work techniques important to the family living.

9

Mastering the Ways of the World:

Biological and Social Aspects of Development from 6 to 12 Years

SIX TO 12, years usually represented in the first six grades of elementary school, years in which children grow out of their charming interest in pleasing adults into a world set somewhat apart from and sometimes hostile to the grown-ups, these are the years when children learn the skills necessary to effective living.

The " I must be and you must be " of dramatic play gives way to real playwriting and production; the colorful abstractions produced by one child working alone become a cooperative mural depicting an early community settlement. Simple tag games are replaced by elementary kinds of baseball and football; " silly talk " diminishes and in its stead there are riddles and conundrums and code languages; the pockets full of " pretty stones," odd shells, carefully saved string, and other odds and ends are supplemented by more organized collections often carefully labeled and catalogued; crudely nailed airplanes and boats disappear as skill in working with minutely detailed " models " develops; a piece of cloth with a hole in the middle no longer suffices for a doll dress, and the dolls are no longer " babies," but elaborately costumed creatures from all over the world; the girls move into secret clubs and the boys into their gangs; the boys disdain the girls, and the girls profess an equal disinterest, at least for the boys of their own age.

Compared with the growth period which preceded them and with adolescence which follows, these are years of slow physical growth. Because rates of growth differ, however, some children will enter a period of rapid growth — the beginning of the adolescent growth spurt — before they reach the age of 12. Thus, some of the generalizations we make about behavior and interests will be less applicable to children who reach maturity early than to those who grow more slowly. Increasingly, too, we shall have to differentiate between the sexes, for these are the years when the girls' more rapid progress toward maturity becomes increasingly more evident.

At approximately 9 years in most areas of the American culture a number of new behavior patterns appear. The girls and boys move increasingly into their own play groups, and both sexes appear to be less interested in adult standards for their behavior. They often become more difficult for adults to live with, despite the fact that they are in fact considerably more able to look out for themselves than they were in the years from 6 to 9. Because of these shifts in behavior, these older children might well be discussed in a separate chapter.

There are, however, a number of reasons for considering them along with the 6-, 7-, and 8-year-olds. So far as growth is concerned, there are no rapid changes until well toward the end of the 6-to-12-year period. The extent of shifts from 6 to 11 or 12 is no more marked than in the years from 3 to 6. From the standpoint of emotional development, the years 6 and 7 belong as appropriately with the years 3 to 6 as they do with the years 8, 9, 10, and 11. Culturally, the 6-year-period tends to be regarded as an entity — the elementary school years. As we shall see, this may be one of the factors in the apparent resentment of older children for adults.

The basic problem for all children in these years appears to be that of learning how to do well the things which the culture regards as important and necessary. Some children who have not succeeded in developing initiative in an earlier period will be ill-equipped for the challenges of this one. They may continue to struggle with an inadequate or an overpowering conscience. They may lack the kinds of control necessary to the acquisition of academic skills, but there may be other skills which they are ready to learn. Because varying rates of growth and varying backgrounds of experience make for wide diversity among individuals, we shall not expect to find all youngsters learning to master their world in the same fashion or at the same rate of speed. Nevertheless, such mastery is the important basic concern throughout these years.

We turn now to a consideration of the nature of growth and development during these years.

BIOLOGICAL ASPECTS OF DEVELOPMENT

The general trends of physical growth in school-age children are well established and generally agreed upon. At the same time, intensive studies of various aspects of development and longitudinal studies, in which records of the same children are kept over a period of years, are pointing up the wide variation to be found even in " normal " development.

General Trends of Growth in This Period

Generally speaking, growth during this period is relatively uniform and slow. However, there is some tendency for growth to be slightly more accelerated between the ages of 5 and 7 than between the ages of 7 and 10. During this period increases are concentrated in measurements of breadth rather than of height. Trunk, arms, and legs increase in bone thickness. Thus, the general direction of growth during the years from 4 or 5 to 8 can be said to be from slender-to-stocky. This process then gradually slows down.[1] The general effect is to make youngsters of 8 and older seem considerably less fragile in appearance than they did at 4 and 5.

Following this period of growth, there is a period of relative rest preceding the acceleration which initiates the adolescent growth cycle.[2] So great are individual differences, that an occasional 9-year-old girl or 10-year-old boy may already be experiencing an accelera-

---

[1] Meredith, H. V., and Sherbina, P. R. " Body Form in Childhood: Ratios Quantitatively Describing Three Slender-to-Stocky Continua on Girls 4–8 Years of Age." *Child Development.* 22 (1951), 275–285.

[2] Stuart, Harold C. " Physical Growth and Development." *Textbook of Pediatrics.* Philadelphia: W. B. Saunders and Company, 1950. P. 18.

tion in growth. On the average, however, this acceleration occurs after the tenth birthday for girls and not until after the twelfth birthday for boys.[3] This sex difference in rate of growth as well as individual differences in rate of growth are of considerable importance to our understanding of development both in this period and the next. They account for the increasing discrepancies among children of the same age in size, appearance, and motor abilities which appear as they pass their ninth and tenth birthdays. These discrepancies, as we shall see, may be important factors in the way the youngsters view themselves and each other and, indeed, in the expectations which adults set for them.

From the standpoint of the individual child's physical well-being it is also important to know whether a tendency to outrank one's peers in size is a matter of difference in body type or an indication of early maturity. For example, a 10-year-old girl who is taller than other 10-year-olds may be a child who is going to be a tall woman. In this case, she will likely continue to increase in rate of growth for the next two years. If, on the other hand, she is an early maturer, her relative tallness may indicate that she is already in a period of maximum growth. If so, her growth rate during the next two years will likely decrease in rate. When growth is completed, she may be considerably shorter than her peers. As an early maturing youngster, both her appearance and her interests are likely to change rapidly. At 12, she will be, so to speak, a young woman in a group of children.

Some idea of variability in individual patterns of growth may be gained by further study of the growth curves of the six youngsters in whom we have been interested. See Appendix, pages 472–477.

It will be noted that all three of the girls eventually (at age 18) reach approximately the same position so far as height and weight are concerned. Celeste and Jane both had their maximum growth in the period with which we are now concerned. Celeste grew most rapidly in the period from 9½ to 11 years. During this period she gained 4½ inches in height and 15¾ pounds in weight. This early and rapid increase was associated with slightly early maturity, since Celeste menstruated at the age of 11 years and 8 months. Jane's picture is somewhat different. Her body type tended to be somewhat endomorphic, and

3 Stuart, op. cit. P. 44.

from 5 to 8 years she was definitely obese. She did not menstruate until 13 years and 4 months. Pat's period of maximum growth did not come until she was 12.

Andy's growth pattern is particularly noteworthy for the boys because it represents such continuous vigorous growth. When he was 9 years old, he began to put on weight. This acceleration became marked at 10½ and was accompanied by a steady increase in height. By 12 he was, as can be seen from the charts, almost 9 inches taller than either Dan or Charlie. Dan, in contrast, grew relatively slowly throughout this period. Note that he and Charlie followed not greatly dissimilar patterns until they were about 10, when Charlie began to add weight more rapidly than Dan did.

PROBLEM 1. If you can arrange to visit a first grade, make notes on the number of boys and girls who seem outstandingly tall or outstandingly short. If possible, check height and weight records to see how wide the variations in the group are. Be sure to check these against the ages of the children. Repeat the process for a sixth grade. How does the variation compare with that in first grade? Do you see any evidence that discrepancies in size affect the behavior of these older youngsters? If possible, study the height and weight records of these children to see which ones have tended to maintain their positions relative to the other children.

Skeletal development. Although progress in skeletal development is less easy to appraise than progress in height and weight, it is, as we have previously indicated, the best single indicator of the progress the child is making toward physical maturity. In the years now under consideration the process of ossification continues. The bones of the hand, for example, continue to grow in size and to change shape. The spaces between them become smaller. The last wrist bone characteristically forms around 9 years in girls and 10 years in boys. Girls tend on the average to be about two years advanced over boys in skeletal development. However, it should be noted that at any age some boys will be more advanced than some girls. The same child tends to be average, retarded, or advanced in osseous development as compared with others at each succeeding age, although many will shift from one category to another with the passage of time.[4] So far as the children, whose development we have been fol-

---

[4] Stuart, *op. cit.* P. 28.

lowing, are concerned, Celeste is the only one whose skeletal age was consistently advanced. Andy's skeletal development was about average, slightly below before 10 years.

PROBLEM 2. **Explain why Celeste can be said to be advanced in skeletal age and yet develop into a relatively small person, while Andy, whose skeletal age about corresponds to his chronological age, ends up as a large man.**

The bones of the face grow rapidly during the school years, and the features begin to assume more mature characteristics. Another factor in the child's changing appearance is the gradual replacement of the deciduous teeth by the permanent ones. Except for the " wisdom " teeth, this process is completed by approximately 12 years of age. There is considerable individual variation in the time of eruption of the teeth. As would be expected, girls tend to be somewhat in advance of boys.[5]

Other aspects of physical development. As longitudinal studies of development proceed, the relationships between various aspects of growth are better understood. Thus an appraisal of skeletal development becomes meaningful when the development of muscle and fat are also taken into consideration. Type of build is an important factor in appraising the adequacy of the child's muscular development. Lombard comments:

A heavy child may have the same amount of muscle as a light child of similar height, and two children of the same age, height, and weight may have very different amounts of muscle.[6]

Studies such as the one she reports are beginning to show how the distribution of one kind of tissue — in this instance skin and subcutaneous fat — are related to the distribution of other tissues, and how these change with age and sex. Girls have been found to show a consistent pattern of greater fat thickness than boys in all body areas.[7] Girls also tend to show somewhat greater variation than

    [5] Breckenridge, Maria, and Vincent, E. Lee. *Child Development.* Philadelphia: W. B. Saunders and Company, 1949. P. 276.
    [6] Lombard, O. M. " Breadth of Bone and Muscle by Age and Sex in Childhood." *Child Development.* 21 (1950), 229–239.
    [7] Reynolds, Earle L. " The Distribution of Subcutaneous Fat in Childhood and Adolescence." *Monograph of the Society for Research in Child Development,* Vol. 15, No. 1, Serial No. 50, 1951.

boys through age 10, at which time their variation rises markedly above that for boys.[8]

The quantity and distribution of subcutaneous tissue may reflect not only constitutional differences, but many other aspects of growth, physical fitness, and health, including dietary inadequacies.[9] Poor diet, we may add, may sometimes result from inability to procure the proper foods, or a lack of knowledge as to the nature of an inadequate diet, or it may result from the child's unwillingness to eat certain foods or his need from some reason or other to eat foods which tend to go to fat rather than muscle.

In this connection it is interesting to consider the nutritional adequacy during the elementary school years of the diets of the six youngsters whom we have been studying.

In the years from 6 to 8, Jane's appetite was unusually good. She was especially fond of foods with high carbohydrate content. As she tended to put on weight, her mother began to limit her consumption of such food. By the time she was 11, her diet was actually somewhat low in total calories.

Pat's appetite was poor, and her consumption of milk, eggs, cereals, and vegetables was limited. She also tended to eat a considerable number of sweets.

Andy's appetite was consistently good. At the age of 6 he was drinking two quarts of milk a day with no apparent effect from it. His diet tended to be well-balanced and provided good variety.

Dan's appetite was good. The quality of his diet varied, being adequate in calories, but tended to be somewhat low in protein.

Charles' appetite tended to be good, his diet fair.

Celeste's appetite was poor until the age of 7, when it gradually began to improve. Her diet was fair.

PROBLEM 3. In the light of what you know about these children, in which cases would you think emotional factors might be contributing to nutritional problems?

Body mechanics and muscular co-ordinations. We should expect that as children differ in relative size and shape and in skeletal and

---

[8] Lombard, *op. cit.*

[9] Stuart, H. C., and Meredith, B. V. "Use of Body Measurements in the School Health Program." *American Journal of Public Health.* 36 (1946), 1365–1375.

muscular development, they will also vary in their abilities to use their bodies skillfully and well. A recent study of physical growth and motor performance has shown some relationship between some measures of physical maturity and certain gross motor skills.[10]

But the child's skills and his ability to carry his body well are not solely determined by his physical maturity. During this period his vertebral bones and ligaments are relatively malleable. Confinement in positions which are uncomfortable may lead to poor postural habits which can result in permanent changes in the spine.[11] Poor posture may reflect poor nutrition or chronic fatigue, and these in turn may be related to emotional concerns of the child which hamper him from the free use of his body.

Breckenridge and Vincent, in describing activity in this period of development, say:

> Joy in the use of the body is normal for children throughout the elementary school period. Extremely popular are running, chasing, jumping rope, hopscotch, hikes in the woods, roller-skating, bicycle riding, swimming, and all other forms of physical activity which are outlets for energy. Most children from six to twelve are problems to the adults who are responsible for them because of the insistent vigor of their movements, their inability to remain quiet in body or voice, their concentration on physical play and rough-housing.[12]

It is well established that in the years from 9 to 12 most children have increased manual dexterity, increased strength, and increased resistance to fatigue.[13] This fact appears to have important implications both for the understanding and the guidance of these youngsters. Many of their apparent resentments toward adults may stem from the fact that the things in which they do best and are most interested (that is, vigorous physical activities) do not fit very well into the more staid pattern of adult living. At the same time a realization of their own capabilities may make them feel more courageous in resistance toward the adults. Further, their finesse in motor activities

[10] Seils, L. G. "The Relationship Between Measures of Physical Growth and Gross Motor Performance of Primary Grade School Children." *The Research Quarterly of the American Association for Health, Physical Education and Recreation.* 22 (1951), 244–260.

[11] Stuart, *op. cit.* P. 43.

[12] Breckenridge and Vincent, *op cit.* Pp. 311–312.

[13] Blair and Burton, *op. cit.* Pp. 138–145.

tends to set them apart from the younger children very much as their own lack of sex interests separates them from the children older than they who have reached puberty.

Since boys and girls tend to differ considerably even from infancy in various aspects of motor performance, we may expect these differences to be accentuated in the latter part of childhood. Boys tend to exceed girls in muscular strength and in speed and co-ordination of gross body movements. Girls, on the other hand, generally excel in manual dexterity.[14]

It should be recognized, however, that some of these differences are undoubtedly due to differing expectations for boys and girls. Further, motor abilities tend to be rather specific, so that a child may excel in one activity and be quite mediocre in another.[15] This raises the important question of whether sufficient attention is currently given children to help them acquire those skills which would be useful to them in maintaining their place in their group and which might at the same time enhance their own sense of self-worth. It is true that motor ineptness often reflects a child's basic lack of sureness. To attempt to teach an insecure, unhappy child to throw a ball well, may seem to be treating a symptom rather than getting at the basic cause of his difficulty. However, it appears that if such coaching were tactfully and sympathetically offered, it could be a very positive way of conveying to the youngster the idea that someone cared about what happened to him. In this connection it is interesting to note a comment made by Pearson:

. . . Perhaps definite instruction in the specific skills of various games — batting, catching and pitching in baseball; punting, kicking, passing and receiving in football; stance, swing and putt in golf; tennis strokes; technics of basketball, bowling, boxing, wrestling, swimming, dancing, fishing, hockey, whatever game the individual child selected would accomplish more toward the development of coordination and rhythm than the usual physical training of the gymnasium, and it would also enable the child to learn a recreational sport which he could continue in adult life.[16]

[14] Anastasi, Anne, and Foley, John P. *Differential Psychology*. New York: The Macmillan Company, 1949. Pp. 648–649.

[15] Jersild, Arthur T. *Child Psychology*. New York: Prentice-Hall, 1954. P. 165.

[16] Pearson, Gerald H. *Psychoanalysis and the Education of the Child*. New York: W. W. Norton & Company, 1954. P. 239.

None of the youngsters we have been studying appears to have been outstanding in motor skills during this period. The comments on their activity may be studied in relation to what is known about their general physical development, the adequacy of their nutrition, and the emotional concerns they had.

Jane Warner. In the early part of the elementary school years Jane's family moved to a neighborhood where she had more playmates than previously. She became quite active and enjoyed a variety of neighborhood games. Toward the end of these six years, however, her interest in activity slumped, and she tended to take almost no exercise.

Pat Plummer. Pat was outstandingly active throughout these years, sometimes to the point of considerable fatigue. Her muscular development was good and her skills excellent. At times she took dancing lessons.

Andy Drosky. Andy tended to be as active as most children of his age, but particularly in the early part of this period he was inclined toward clumsiness.

Dan Mallon. Dan's posture and use of his body was not too good during these years. He was tremendously interested in boxing and so on, but evidently the coaching he was given was not too effective.

Charles Brown. Charlie was not only very active, but extremely effective in his use of his body. He was always well co-ordinated and carried himself well.

Celeste Collins. By and large, Celeste was less vigorous in her activities than were many of her peers. Her posture tended to be poor, and she did not make a very good showing in any large muscle activities, though she continued to be quite dexterous in fine co-ordinations.

PROBLEM 4. As you observe children in the elementary school years, make an inventory of the variety of motor skills you note. Relate your observations to the ages of the children you observe. If you encounter a suitable opportunity, you may want to try "coaching" a child in some activity. What kind of relationship are you able to establish with the child? How does it influence your techniques?

The effects of illness. In general, this is a relatively healthy period with children having fewer illnesses than during any of the preceding years.[17] Those who have not previously been exposed to such con-

---

[17] Witmer, Helen, and Kotinsky, Ruth. *Personality in the Making.* New York: Harper and Brothers, 1952. P. 334.

tagious diseases as mumps and chicken pox are likely to get them at this time, but modern immunization procedures are such that many diseases at one time hazardous to child life in this period are no longer so menacing.

Longitudinal studies are showing the effects of illness on the child's continuing development. Workers at the Denver Child Research Council report from studies of X-ray photographs of children's chests:

As (the child) grows up, he may have a severe pneumonia or any of a number of other acute infections, but as soon as he has recovered, he will swing back to his own pattern of normality. He will not carry with him the so-called scars of repeated infections, unless . . . chronically ill.[18]

The extent to which illness may affect other aspects of the child's development during this period is one deserving further study. It is likely, for example, that any illness necessitating prolonged absence from his peers or limiting his opportunities to practice his growing skills would be particularly hampering. In one longitudinal study of children's mental development it was noted that children whose scores on the mental tests showed the greatest fluctuations were those whose life experiences had also fluctuated markedly between disturbing and satisfying periods. Frequent illness was regarded as one disturbing influence.[19] However, not all of the children who experienced such disturbance showed variations in the mental test results. Findings of this nature underline the fact of the interrelatedness of various aspects of development, but they also serve to remind us of how much more remains to be known about the nature of the relationships.

Mental Development

It is not until the period of the elementary school years that tests of the child's intellectual abilities begin to have much predictive value.[20] Even then, as we have suggested, the scores of an individual

[18] Gray, G. W. "Human Growth." *Scientific American*. 189 (1953), 65–74.

[19] Honzik, M. P., and others. "The Stability of Mental Test Performance between Two and Eighteen Years." *Journal of Experimental Education*. 17 (1948), 309–24.

[20] Goodenough, Florence. "The Measurement of Mental Growth in Childhood," in *Manual of Child Psychology*, edited by Leonard Carmichael. New York: John Wiley and Sons, 2d ed., 1954. P. 804.

child may vary considerably. Later in the chapter we shall show and discuss the shifts which occur in the child's thinking as he grows. For the present we shall merely emphasize the wide range of individual differences which are to be found.

There is no question that even within a one-year range in a fairly small school one will find a considerable spread in children's abilities to deal with the problems posed by an intelligence test.

In the Stanford-Binet Test, for example, the child would be tested on information with such questions as "What makes a sailboat move?"; on his ability to remember and repeat digits, or to recall the content of a paragraph; on vocabulary; and on reasoning. Included in the reasoning category may be such questions as " A wheel came off Frank's automobile. As he could not get the wheel back on by himself, he drove his automobile to the shop for repairs — what is foolish about that?" and " In what way are wood and coal alike?"[21]

Another individual intelligence test which is increasing in common use is the Wechsler Intelligence Scale for Children.[22] This places somewhat less reliance on purely verbal items since it also includes tests requiring the child to complete and arrange pictures, make block designs, and so on. There are also numerous tests of mental ability which are paper-and-pencil tests and are given to children in groups rather than individually. Results on such tests may be considerably influenced if the child has any difficulties with reading, writing, or with hearing directions, or is easily distracted.

The assumption in all of these is that, depending on his age, the child of ordinary intelligence will have learned answers to the questions posed just in the course of his ordinary experience. There is no doubt that the youngster who can deal with these should also be able to cope with elementary school work. It is good information for the school to have about the child. Unfortunately, however, its significance is sometimes unduly magnified. The child who scores high may be left to his own devices. It is assumed that he is bright and can do well without much special attention. Actually, he may

21 Terman, Lewis M., and Merrill, Maud A. *Measuring Intelligence: A Guide to the Administration of the New Revised Standard-Binet Tests.* Boston: Houghton-Mifflin Company, 1937.

22 Wechsler, David. *Wechsler Intelligence Scale for Children.* New York: Psychological Corporation, 1949.

need considerable challenge to realize his full intellectual potentialities. In terms of his own personal well-being, he may need much help to learn to use his body effectively, to enjoy other people, and to find out fully the kind of person he is. The child who scores low is sometimes thought to be more or less " hopeless," even though he may be a child with a fine warmth of personality, or clever with his fingers, or an excellent ballplayer. Such judgments are, we regret to say, sometimes made on the basis of a single test, not even individually administered. Children are seen only as high, low, or average I.Q.'s rather than as persons, each with many unique traits and characteristics, including certain kinds of intellectual abilities.

Just how mental development is related to other aspects of development, particularly physical development, is not fully understood. In general, brighter children tend to be taller and heavier than children of below average intelligence, but whether this difference is to be attributed to biological differences or to socio-economic differences or to some combination of factors is not known.

Longitudinal studies offer some promise of shedding light on this problem. If we assume that just as there are differences in the rate of physical growth, there may be differences in the rate of intellectual growth, it is relatively easy to conceive a degree of correspondence between the two. Olson, for example, suggests that the child's progress in school is closely dependent on his growth " as a whole." [23] Thus, a child who is growing slowly, as indicated by a composite of such measures as height, weight, bone ossification, and tooth eruption, is also likely to be making relatively slow progress in learning to read. The methods of establishing the rate of " organismic " or true growth are too complex for consideration here. The important point for our purposes is that increasingly interrelationships between intellectual and other aspects of development are being recognized, although their precise nature is not yet understood.

PROBLEM 5. For a fuller description of the concept of organismic age you may find it helpful to review and discuss the article by W. C. Olson and Bryon O. Hughes on " Growth of the Child as a Whole " in *Child Behavior and Development*, edited by Barker, Kounin, and Wright, pages 199–209.

[23] Olson, Willard C. *Child Development*. Boston: D. C. Heath, 1949.

Appraisals of the intellectual abilities of the six youngsters we are following were made from time to time. Note that although they vary in the individual test scores, they tend fairly consistently to retain their positions relative to one another.

PROBLEM 6. Before you read the following statement regarding the mental tests of these youngsters, you may wish to make an estimate of their relative abilities on the basis of what you already know of · them.

Jane Warner. Jane was given the Stanford-Binet Test at 6, 8, and 11 years. At 6 no score was obtained because she grew tired before the test could be completed. At 8 she scored in the " superior " group, and at 11, " very superior."

Pat Plummer. Pat was tested at 6 and at 8. In the first situation, she was inclined to doubt her own ability, asking, " Is that right? " In the second, she chattered so incessantly that it was hard to hold her attention. In both instances her score fell in the " average " group.

Andy Drosky. Andy was tested at 6½, 8, and 12. In the first test he scored well above the average, while in the second he was markedly above, and at 12 "superior." Rather consistently he did better with vocabulary items than with memory items.

Dan Mallon. Only one test was given Dan during this period, and on that, at the age of 7, he scored slightly above average.

Charlie Brown. Charlie was also tested only once in this period, but at 11. His vocabulary was especially good, and he made a very pleasing impression on the examiner. He scored slightly above average.

Celeste Collins. Celeste was tested at 6½. She was very cooperative and interested and made a score slightly above average.

Significance of Biological Factors

In general, this period is one when the physical organism is growing steadily, but relatively slowly. It is a period of comparative equilibrium. The exception to this is most marked for girls, who are likely to begin a period of rapid growth about the 10th year of age. Most boys will not enter this stage until 12.

Just as in physical growth, these years are ones of quiet consolidation, so they tend to be good years for the acquisition of the skills necessary to living in our culture. It appears, however, that in some respects the child learns faster than society is prepared for. In order to understand the personality manifestations of the latter part of these years, we must look to the social expectations which are held for children of this age.

SOCIAL FACTORS IN DEVELOPMENT IN THE YEARS 6 TO 12

We live in a society in which rapid change is characteristic. But the world of 6-to-12-year-olds is not strikingly different from the world they knew as infants and preschool children. Its influences, however, are more direct. The school-age child goes out into the larger community and develops an increasing awareness of life outside his family. He confronts standards and expectations which may either resemble or differ from those his parents have held for him. He meets other children whose values reflect the teachings of their particular segment of society.

In simpler societies, and in our own in earlier times, the transition from dependent childhood to independent adulthood was not so prolonged as with us. Children often began to assume real responsibilities even as early as 6 and 7. In order to understand some of the phenomena which appear around the age of 9 or 10, we need a perspective on the status of children in our society.

The Nature of Adult Society

The changing status of children. Bossard says of colonial children:

Only as they fitted into the pattern of adult life in the community, only as their abilities and interests contributed to the welfare and interests of their elders, were they considered to be of any importance.[24]

In contrast:

Today the child is recognized as a human personality in a peculiarly vital stage of development. He is a coequal personality in the emerging democracy of the family. The guarding of this personality is the child's precious right, and the dangers which threaten it, are recognized social problems: the development of this personality is his most precious opportunity, and the furtherance and guidance of that development are the concern of his elders.[25]

[24] Bossard, James H. S. *The Sociology of Child Development.* New York: Harper and Brothers, rev. ed., 1954. P. 636.
[25] *Ibid.* Pp. 637, 638.

In colonial times the child was expected to be submissive to his parents. He did not have the privilege of sharing in family decisions. But he did have important and worth-while functions to fill. The cows the girls milked, the wood the boys cut, the fruit they harvested, and the cloth they spun, these were all tangible evidence of achievement. They were not merely practicing their growing skills against a day when they *might* need them, but rather putting them to actual immediate use. Today, in many families almost the reverse situation holds. Parents make conscious efforts not to dominate their children. They try to take their wishes into consideration in the making of family decisions. The child's skills are not exploited. Indeed, many families find it difficult to find enough chores to give the children a " sense of responsibility."

The nature of modern economic living is such that it is difficult for children under 12 (or even under 18) to make any very tangible contribution to it. Thus in one sense the " coequality " of personality of which Bossard speaks is impossible of achievement. The turning into small age-sex gangs, which is so typical of the 9-to-12-year-olds, may say in effect, " Since you've nothing worth while for us to turn our efforts toward, we'll see what we can find to occupy our time ourselves."

The pressures of modern living. The uncertainties of present-day living, as we have indicated, affect all children to some degree. But they impinge much more directly on school-age children than they do on the younger ones. The concepts of the child under 12 may be exceedingly hazy, but he is increasingly aware of larger social conflicts and of the fact that they are disturbing to the adults around him and in a sense threatening to him, also. He is becoming sensitive to the ways in which adults cope with social pressures. For example, a bright 6-year-old, after hearing much talk on television regarding the possibility of an amendment to the United States Constitution, was heard to ask his mother why the League of Women Voters did not " do something about it."

Unfortunately, in meeting the hazards of our time, there often must seem to the child very little that the adults can do about many things. Correspondingly, there is not much the child can do, and this in itself may be severely handicapping to the development of the attitudes of industry and accomplishment which are so vital in the child's personality development. When we stress the uncertainties of our time, we do not mean to imply that man has never before known crises. But we do believe that he has seldom had to cope with forces that seemed so impersonal and inexorable as the threat of atomic warfare.

The youngsters whom we have been studying began their elementary school years while the country was still in the grip of an economic depression. We have suggested the effects this had on their parents. As the nation moved into a defense economy prior to World War II, the outlook in the children's homes improved, but along with the increased financial security came the question of the possibility of war service. As it turned out, not one of the fathers was called. But close relatives were so that the children heard much about individuals they knew being sent overseas, wounded in action, and so on. Each of them was to a degree involved in the various drives of their schools — the paper collections, tin-can collections, and work for the Junior Red Cross. Each of these activities served in its own fashion to add something to their sense of accomplishment and of being part of an important effort.

In the postwar years and during and following the Korean war, the issues at stake in world affairs have been so very complex as to confound many grownups. They in turn find themselves unable to clarify the confusions of the children. Further, cold wars and armed truces offer both adults and children little opportunity to feel that they can in their own small ways help to cope with the situation.

The threat of war is but one of the pressures with which youngsters today must learn to live. We have already suggested that a society which is increasingly mechanized and specialized offers children in this age period limited opportunities for worthy accomplishment. Such a society tends also to become impersonal and its members inclined to keep their feelings somewhat walled in. Thus the child, moving from the protection of his family into the larger community, may meet many adults who appear disinterested and unfriendly toward him. Take the matter of entrance into first grade, for example. The youngster who perhaps has never been to kindergarten may find that his teacher is so busy filling in the forms necessary to place him in the school register, that she does not really see him or his mother. If she has forty or fifty other children, as she well may in these crowded days, her lack of perception is excusable. Unfortunately, however, the pattern of impersonality is one which the child may run into again and again, both in school and out.

However, we must not paint too black a picture. Modern society is not completely lacking in adults capable of tenderness and compassion. The dangers to human personality in the trends toward automatization and cold efficiency have been recognized. To bring warmth, spontaneity, and genuineness into human relationships is becoming an important goal in many of the institutions and agencies which deal with children. Individuals, too, are learning to believe that they should be capable of warm expressions of feeling and to seek help when they find themselves lacking in it.

Social influences in the lives of children. Against this picture of the changing status of children and the uncertainties of present-day society let us examine more specifically some of the social influences functioning in the lives of children of elementary school age. Some of these operate informally. The youngsters with whom the child plays and the kinds of neighbors and relatives he has help to shape his experiences in these years, but they are not organized to do so. In contrast, a number of institutions and agencies are set up with deliberate intentions for furthering and protecting the rights of childhood. Some of these are concerned with children from birth, and even prenatally, but many focus on the child of school age and beyond. In any event, it is not until after he is 6 or more that the child begins to develop much awareness of the variety of agencies which are in one way or another concerned about him.

School looms important in the thinking of the child from the age of 6 on, since it is one experience which is almost universally required and anticipated. The church and synagogue, always concerned with children, also begin to look to their instruction at about this time. Many recreational agencies are concerned with protecting the child's right to safe and wholesome places for play and recreation and with providing for his social and cultural needs. Thus, city park and recreation departments, public libraries, community settlement houses, voluntary youth organizations (such as Junior Red

Cross, the Scouts, Police Athletic Leagues, Campfire Girls, Girl Reserves, 4–H), and so on become important in the lives of many children. Health services, including hospitals and associations interested in the study or prevention of certain diseases, operate numerous programs including clinics and camps which may affect children in this age category rather directly. Children of this age may also come in contact with a variety of social services provided through independent agencies, such as Family Welfare Societies, Children's Aid Societies, Community Service organizations, or in connection with schools, health services, courts, recreational organizations, industry, or the military services. Law-enforcement agencies, as represented by the school attendance officer, the neighborhood policeman, and the juvenile court worker, also have their effects.

Many commercial enterprises become influential in the lives of children of elementary school age. We have already mentioned television and the fact young children constitute such a large part of its audience. Older children continue to be viewers. They also are movie fans and comic-book readers. These communication media may, it appears, exert upon youngsters influences at least as potent as those of the deliberately educative agencies, such as the school.

In our more detailed consideration of these socializing influences we shall focus first on the school. We shall concern ourselves not only with the ways it fulfills its basic functions of teaching children the skills of reading, writing, and arithmetic, but also with the additional functions it assumes. In the school the child begins to develop a perspective on himself in relation to the society in which he lives.

The School

Originally the primary function of the elementary school was to teach children to read, write, and figure. Carolyn Pratt, a well-known modern educator, looking back on her childhood in the eighteen seventies, wrote:

> When I grew up . . . school was not very important to children who could roam the real world freely for their learning. We did not merely stand by while the work of our simpler world was done. . . .

No one had to tell us where milk came from, or how butter was made. We helped to harvest wheat, saw it ground into flour in the mill on our own stream; I baked bread for the family at thirteen. There was a paper mill, too, on our stream; we could learn the secrets of half a dozen other industries merely by walking through the open door of a neighbor's shop.

No wonder, school was a relatively unimportant place — a place where we learned only the mechanical tools, the three R's and a smattering about things far away and long ago.

[The modern world is] so far beyond the grasp of children, that only the school can present it to them in terms which they can understand, can prepare them with knowledge of it so that they can take their places in it with confidence when the time comes.[26]

Not everyone would agree that the functions of the school should be as broad as Miss Pratt implies. At the present time when there are more children to be educated than ever before in our history, when we do not have enough classrooms, let alone enough teachers to go around, some people seem to be calling for a return to a school which teaches little else but the three R's. Others believe that many of today's children have little incentive for learning skills, unless the school provides activities which stimulate their interest in learning more about the world around them. Some think that the primary emphasis of the school should be on helping children to acquire knowledge. Others are of the opinion that the development of healthy personalities should be of equal or perhaps greater concern to the school. In some communities representative groups of teachers, parents, and other citizens have studied these matters and reached tentative conclusions as to the kind of education to be provided for the children in the schools. In other communities professional educators have made many of the necessary decisions. In still others school policy is controlled by small groups of citizens, who may or may not represent kinds of thinking going on within the community.

When we add this lack of consensus as to what the school *should* be teaching to the diversity which arises from variations in the amount of financial support given the schools, the difficulties in generalizing about the influence of school experiences are obvious.

Schools differ. Shall we speak of the one-teacher school, no longer

[26] Pratt, Carolyn. *I Learn from Children*. New York: Simon and Schuster, 1948. Pp. xi, xii.

existent in some states but attended by at least 1½ million boys and girls in the United States? [27] Or of the consolidated school to which children are brought by buses from farms often more than an hour's ride from the school? In the city one finds some recently built, spacious schools with gleaming floors, movable tables and desks, and equipment for carpentry, painting, music, and science. A block away is a school built in the eighteen hundreds with the desks squeezed together in tight rows and little room for anything but the children, the teacher, and a few books. Small towns and suburban communities may present equally great discrepancies. And, while the vast majority of children are in public schools, we should not overlook the fact that some are in parochial and private schools and that some, such as those in migrant families, never attend school.

Important as the physical setting is (the possible effects of restriction on the child's physical development have already been mentioned), the primary influence of the school lies in what the child learns there. At first glance it seems relatively easy to appraise that learning. For example, in the schools described above, we may find in all the first-grade classes the same first-grade readers. The same alphabets may serve as models when the children print their names. They may drill on the same number combinations. We could, indeed, travel from Maine to California and from Washington to Florida and find many first grades in which the reading, writing, and arithmetic lessons would be practically identical.

But we cannot assume that each child is learning the same thing. Every one of them brings a different background of experience and different abilities for learning. Some will learn quickly and some slowly. For some the translation of the black marks on the white pages will be important and meaningful. For others it may be a mechanical process, confusing, and not easily understood.

Children differ. Alice, who lives in a white house just like the one in her first reader, enjoys learning to read. Every time she finishes a page, she feels as though the story had really been about her. In another first grade Melinda, looking at the same reader, is

[27] Gaumnitz, Walter H., and Blose, David T. *The One-Teacher School — Its Midcentury Status.* Washington, D.C.: Federal Security Agency, Office of Education, Circular No. 318, 1950.

bored and uninterested. Her skimpy breakfast has long ceased to sustain her. She squirms on the rough bench which is the best equipment this school system affords and longs for the recess period. She does not like reading, and she is not making much progress in it. Sam, a big boy who is almost 7, laboriously copies his name. As always, he reverses the letter S and winces when his teacher calls his attention to it. School, he thinks, is fine, if only it didn't demand that you write. Ruth, his classmate, has trouble with arithmetic. She gathers the eggs at home on the farm every day and reports accurately the number she collects. That the school number combinations she is learning have anything to do with eggs has not yet been made apparent to her.

And so it goes, in classrooms all over the country. Even the simplest kind of reading, writing, and arithmetic has different meanings for each child. The older they grow, the more children differ so that, even though they are taught the same things over the years, some will learn more than others, and each will have somewhat different understandings of what they have learned.

While they are developing abilities to manipulate letters and figures and learning the facts regarded as important for children in our culture, children are also learning attitudes and ways of looking at the world, at other people, and themselves. They learn a great deal which they are not taught.

Subtle learnings differ. The second grade raises ducks. " How do they marry "? they ask their teacher. She changes the subject quickly. " Why can't I divide by zero? " queries a third-grader. " Because you can't," responds the teacher. " My father says the answer to that corn-planting problem in our arithmetic book is wrong," complains a fifth-grader. " Now, let's not have any arguments. I showed you how to do that problem yesterday," is the teacher's reply. These youngsters are learning that the world is an arbitrary place, filled with inconsistencies about which it is better not to be curious.

Mrs. Davidson, president of the P. T. A. and wife of a local businessman, taps on the door to the third-grade classroom. " I'm sorry to trouble you but. . . ." The teacher nods and smiles and carries on an extended conversation while the children continue their work.

Mrs. Zielinski, whose English is barely comprehensible, cowers just outside the door as the class is dismissed, " Teacher, about Sammy . . .", and the teacher says briskly, " Oh, yes. I have just a minute as I am on my way to lunch." Are the third graders learning that their teacher feels some adults are worth while, and others are put up with?

In the fifth grade the teacher moves casually from one table to another as the children work on their arithmetic problems. She pauses to pat Jimmy on the shoulder, saying cordially, " Good work, Jim." She looks at Debby's paper, notes that every problem is correct and the work meticulously arranged. She holds it up for the others to see, commenting on its excellence. Her words are warm, but her manner is cool, restrained. Debby has long since learned, as have her peers, that when you are colored, you are different.

PROBLEM 7. As you observe children in the elementary grades, keep a record of the situations in which you think the child may have learned something the teacher did not intend to teach him.

Fortunately, educators are beginning to devote considerable attention to these subtle kinds of learnings, learnings which are often not intended and certainly not taught deliberately. Students, preparing to be teachers, are looking at their own attitudes and studying their relationships with children in order to become more sensitive to the ways in which their own feelings may be communicated to them. In some cases, attitudes which may stand in the way of the most effective teaching are purely personal ones which stem from the teacher's own experience. For example, a particular child may remind him of someone with whom he has had uncomfortable relationships. Teachers, like parents, often find that certain children, or certain situations, make them uneasy and less able to be helpful than they would wish to be. If the school is to concern itself with personality development as well as with the imparting of information, more attention will need to be focused on the matter of teacher-child relationships. The teacher cannot help the child function more adequately as a person unless he can establish the kind of relationship with him in which such functioning is possible. Thus, the emphasis shifts from the teacher's trying to understand the child and his background to understanding what happens when he with his own background of experience meets the child who has *his* own background of experience.

In addition to individual personal attitudes which may make relationship with certain children difficult, teachers, it appears, often hold values which go counter to those the children are learning from their parents. Research is just beginning to consider the effects of these on teacher-child relationships and on children's learning.

Many studies have focused on the extent to which the values held by the schools differ from those held by various subgroups. A number of these have set forth the idea that the schools reflect the values of a " core class which may be roughly described as the lower middle class. . . ." Emphasis tends to be on the ownership of goods, especially home and land, on cleanliness and tidiness, on avoidance of all forms of overt aggression, and on the avoidance of expression of emotions generally. " Core cultural guides are not readily stated, but appear in terms of what one ought or ought not to do, and what nice people do." [28]

Operating on the basis of such guides, teachers picture the " ideal " pupil as one who is " nice," not hard to handle, easy to work with, clean, well-dressed, moderate in behavior, hard-working. Lower-class children, in contrast, are found to lack the right kind of study habits, to be unable to apply themselves well, to be difficult to control and, because of their physical appearance and lack of tidiness, tend to disgust the teacher. Curiously enough, upper-class children may also fail to meet the teacher's ideal. Although they are alert, have been around so that they know what the teacher is talking about, they are " spoiled," " overindulged," " pampered," and seem to want to run the school for themselves. They, too, may offend the teacher's standards, since their home standards in regard to such matters as picking up after themselves, smoking, and so on may be rather different from those held by the teachers.[29]

A number of authorities consider attempts to account for differences in values solely on the basis of social-class differences an over-

[28] Loeb, Martin B. " Implications of Status Differentiation for Personal and Social Development." *Harvard Educational Review.* 23 (1953), 168–174.

[29] Becker, J. S. " Social-Class Variations in the Teacher-Pupil Relationship." *The Journal of Educational Sociology.* 25 (1952), 451–465.

simplification. Gross, for example, points out that communities are not merely differentiated horizontally into social classes, but vertically along racial, ethnic, and religious lines. He reports on a recent study of a New England community which revealed two social worlds, the Negro and the white. The white world was divided by ethnic origin and religion into Catholic, Protestant, and Jewish contingents. Within each of these, there were additional schisms. The Irish held aloof from the Italians, and the Italians from the Poles. The Jews maintained a religious and social life separate from the Gentiles. Within each of these groups, there was further stratification on the basis of the social values attached to occupation, residence, and education.[30]

Further evidence as to the extent to which elementary school-age children show awareness of such values is needed. Clearly, however, with such diversity in the community, the school needs to consider carefully the values it purports to hold in the light of the values children will bring to it. Questions as to whether it is the function of the school to find the most effective ways to promote middle-class culture, or whether it should more properly concern itself with teaching respect for the goodness inherent in different cultures, have not yet been answered. Meanwhile, schools, whether they are aware of it or not, may convey to children that certain kinds of living and perhaps certain kinds of people are preferable to others. They may reenforce some prejudices and create others.

When our young people were in elementary school, there was considerably less general recognition of the importance of what we have termed " subtle " learnings. In the schools which our young people attended it was recognized that their background of experience and their personalities might make learning easy or difficult, but the effect on his learning of the child's relationships to his teachers and to his peers was likely not as well understood as it might be in those same schools today. At this point let us look at the children's progress in school. Later, in our consideration of their personality development, we shall consider more specifically the contribution of school experience to each one.

[30] Gross, Neal. " A Critique of Social Class Structure and American Education." *Harvard Educational Review.* 23 (1953), 298–329.

Jane. Jane, who, it will be recalled, was a bright youngster, did well in school. However, her record never quite fulfilled the promise which her mental tests seemed to hold. In general, Jane regarded her school experience as "all right," but lacked great enthusiasm for it.

Pat. Pat, in contrast, "loved" school. Her record was not outstanding, but she made steady progress. She was well-liked by her teachers and throughout these years often said that when she grew up she would like to be a teacher.

PROBLEM 8. On the basis of what you already know about these youngsters, can you think of any factors which make for the differences in attitudes of Jane and Pat? Bear this question in mind as you read on through the chapter.

Andy. Andy's elementary school years were characterized by many ups and downs. He was somewhat "slow" in learning to read, but by the age of 7, was doing excellent work. The teacher commented that he did not concentrate well, but was a "quick learner." In third grade his work began to deteriorate. He appeared not to try or to care about learning. He was extremely sociable and had a position of real leadership among his peers, particularly when mischief was afoot. In fourth grade, with another teacher, his work improved. However, increasingly he seemed to be something of a misfit in school and never realized the potentiality which his mental tests wound indicate he had.

PROBLEM 9. On the basis of what you already know about Andy, describe the school situation and the teachers with whom you think Andy would have been most likely to do well.

Charlie. Charlie's school work, though never outstanding, was acceptable. The troubles that he encountered were always on the playground where he and Chet were regarded as both mischievous and aggressive and sometimes something of a menace to the other children.

Dan. Dan brought home good report cards and was extremely "school minded" until the third grade. Until then he hated to be absent and looked forward to going back after weekends and holidays. Sometime toward the middle of third grade he began to lose interest, and his work declined in quality. From then on he put in his time, but never with much zest.

PROBLEM 10. This pattern is not an uncommon one, especially among boys. As you study this chapter, list the factors which may contribute to interest falling-off in school at third or fourth grade.

Celeste. Celeste's enjoyment of school was dramatic. At home, during first grade, she rehearsed over and over again all of the arrangements at school, where she kept her pencil box, who her partner was when they " lined up," and so on. Her work was excellent and won her considerable praise from her teachers. The one exception to this came in third grade when she had a teacher who was " cross." This took most of the joy out of school for that year, but the following year with a new teacher she regained her old enthusiasm.

The Church and Synagogue

Because the religious institution the child attends is customarily one selected by the parent, we might expect that he would find there an extension of home values rather than the conflicting ones he may encounter in the school. In many instances this is indeed the case; in others the child may be confronted with the fact that the standards to which one pays lip service on Sunday are not necessarily the ones to be lived by. Something of this sort may account for the fact that in the relatively small number of studies of the effects of church attendance on resistance to deliquency, honesty, and cooperativeness, the differences between children who attended and those who did not, though tending to favor those attending, have been comparatively small.[31]

In recent years religious institutions have been increasingly concerned about the effectiveness of their work with children. Like the schools, they are beginning to inquire into the subtle learnings which children may acquire without being taught. They are likewise concerned that religious education workers be the kind of people who are capable of positive constructive relationships with children.

A major problem for this period of development is that of treating religious concepts in a way that will not be confusing to the child. Not until the age of 10 or so are most children capable of dealing with abstractions, so that for some time God and His attributes may be taken in an exceedingly literal sense. One child, for example, drew a picture of a bearded gentleman at the wheel of an automobile in which two passengers were seated. This, he explained, was " God driving Adam and Eve out of the Garden of Eden."

[31] Jones, Vernon. " Character Development in Children — An Objective Approach," in *Manual of Child Psychology,* edited by Leonard Carmichael. New York: John Wiley and Sons, 2d ed., 1954. P. 804.

It seems likely, however, that youngsters in this period of development are less adversely affected by inadequate understanding than they are by adults who fail to help them sense religion as a positive and constructive force in their living. Religious tenets may be held over the child's head as threats and may be used to make him fearful or anxious, or they may be used to help him to feel more accepted, wanted, and adequate.

Some children find in their religious participation and education a sense of accomplishment which they may not achieve in their school experience. Hebrew school may offer an intelligent youngster a challenge which is quite lacking in the regular school program which is paced to children of more average abilities. It may, of course, constitute a hazard to the child who is less intellectually inclined. A boy, whose academic record is mediocre, may be an outstanding member of the choir or may serve as altar boy. Some youngsters find friends more easily in their church and Sunday school activities than they do in school. A bright child who is socially less mature than her classmates may remain something of an isolate in school and yet have a very real place in the mixed age groups operating under church sponsorship. This suggests that religious institutions may do well not to pattern their programs too closely on that of the weekday school, but rather provide for greater flexibility and diversity of interests.

In comparison with what is known regarding the effects of parental attitudes and school experience on development, there is remarkably little evidence about the relationships between the child's religious affiliations and his growing personality. Yet the potentiality for important and helpful influence is obvious. Certainly, if we are to understand the development of any youngster, we must not forget to consider the possibility that the church or synagogue may have contributed positively, or negatively, or perhaps not at all.

PROBLEM 11. Plan to observe elementary-school-age children in a Sunday school or other religious education group. If possible, visit several times so that you can observe the experiences of children of different ages, with different teachers, and so on. What are the goals toward which the teachers or leaders are working? How well are these being realized so far as the actual learning of the children is concerned? What similarities and what differences do you note between this situation and weekday school? If several members of the class are able to visit programs in a variety of religious institutions, it might be profitable to plan to compare notes. If you are able to observe and talk with children of this age in their homes, you can be alert to the effects of their religious affiliation on their living and thinking.

Other Institutions and Agencies Interested in Children

Time was when the school and the church were the only social institutions other than his family with which the child from 6 to 12 was likely to have much contact. In some rural communities this continues to be the situation. However, as interests in the rights of childhood have grown and as living, particularly in urban areas, has become more complex, a multiplicity of agencies have developed, concerned with the child's right to good play opportunities, his right to physical and mental health, to an education and to freedom from exploitation.

Leisure-time agencies. Communities vary widely in the provisions which they make for children's out-of-school time. For many children hours after school, on Saturdays and Sundays and during the summer months, may exceed in importance the time spent in school. During this time they work out relationships with their peers, practice many skills, particularly those related to motor development, and develop many interests. In communities where families have spacious backyards and houses come equipped with attic or basement playrooms, children, particularly as they grow toward 9 and beyond, can carry on without too much organization, aside from that provided by themselves and their families. In more crowded areas, or in places where families have little money to purchase play equipment or to supply materials for the hobbies which characteristically develop during this period, children must exercise real ingenuity to find things to do. The dirt thrown up around a sewer-repair job serves as a fortress for gang warfare; the scaffolding surrounding a new building, or the back of a moving bus, becomes a trapeze; the alley is a setting for a game of cards. Small wonder that in an environment which seems to say "No room for you" youngsters so readily wander into delinquent activities.

Numerous organizations and agencies concerned with leisure-time activities attempt to provide youngsters with safe places for play and with activities suitable to their development. Unfortunately, their facilities are not always equitably divided. Thus one may find one town in which, as the parents sometimes put it, "There is too much for the kids to do." Various clubs appear to be vying for the membership of the same children, the churches offer various weekday activities, dancing and music lessons are considered obligatory, and the youngsters want time for baseball, skating, swimming, and so on. In another town, or perhaps even in another section of the same town, organized recreational activities do not exist. Sometimes programs started in city areas in which the need for services appears to be very great are not very successful. Their failure may be attributed to any number of causes, but one of the most frequent is probably a lack of appreciation for the standards and values of the youngsters who might attend. This is particularly true of programs for children of 9, 10, and 11, who are already beginning to regard adult standards with considerable scepticism. For them, programs in which adults "love them, limit them and help them to achieve" have been found most successful.[32] In an atmosphere in which a youngster feels wanted and accepted and in which he is helped to channel his impulses in constructive directions, he feels capable of accomplishment.

Some summer camps provide this type of atmosphere. With a twenty-four hour setting they offer children an excellent opportunity to try out new patterns of response. Often the child behaves at first as he has with his parents, then shifts, as he finds that the counselor's expectations differ from those of the parents. Although a camp session of a few weeks' duration cannot be expected to change personalities, it may help a child to see himself as a person with new potentialities. On the other hand, in some camps the premium put on achievement may be so high that it becomes beneficial only to the few who make the grade and threatening and anxiety-provoking to those who do not. As with other influences in the lives of children, we cannot evaluate the effect of a camp experience without knowing a good bit about the relationships the child has there.

[32] Witmer and Kotinsky, *op. cit.* P. 280.

Andy went to camp when he was 9. He did not like it much the first summer, but returned for two more summers and was increasingly enthusiastic.

PROBLEM 12. After you have finished reading this chapter, summarize what you know about Andy. What kind of camp experience would be most beneficial to him? What would be his liabilities and his assets as a camper?

Dan did not go to camp, but spent several of his summers with relatives in the country. Here he was able to participate in many farm activities.

PROBLEM 13. After you have finished reading this chapter, summarize what you know about Dan. Would there have been any advantages to him in going to camp instead of to the country? Any disadvantages? Discuss these.

The effects on the child's personality development of participation in recreational programs are difficult to evaluate. Undoubtedly some youngsters, finding that some adults genuinely care for them, are given a new tie to society and are saved from possible delinquency and antisocial behavior. Others may be, even at 9 and 10, too hurt, too lacking in basic trust and self-worthiness to be helped in the rather casual atmosphere of the settlement house or the playground.

Social service and health agencies. For children who are emotionally disturbed, neglected, or ill, a variety of social services and health agencies may be brought into the picture. Here again, communities differ widely in the number and kinds of services available and also in the effectiveness with which they are used. Professional workers realize that the mere fact that a community has a large number of services does not necessarily mean better protection of children's rights to fullest realization of their potentialities. Because of a diversity of functions, as many as half a dozen agencies may become involved in a single " case." When this means that the child's parent and perhaps the child as well feel that they are being shunted from one worker to another with no real understanding of the necessity for such shifting about, the services offered are not likely to be very effective. We may suppose, for example, that a child in third grade is having some difficulty in reading. Careful study by the school psychologist indicates that the basic problem is an emotional one, probably centering in his family relationships. The psychologist or the school social worker may talk with the parent, who reveals difficulties between herself and her husband for which psychiatric counseling seems in order. The school worker describes the family service agency and its functions to the mother, who indicates a readiness to go there for such help. In the school worker's conversation with the mother the fact that the child's physical health does not seem very vigorous comes up. It is suggested that the child be taken to the city hospital clinic for a complete physical examination. The mother makes the necessary appointments, but before she is able to keep them, an older child gets into trouble with the police. The mother is then interviewed by a juvenile court worker. If eventually she takes the first child to the clinic and goes herself to the family agency, she will likely have gone over much of the same story at least four different times in less than that many weeks. If the family should require public assistance, another agency will be added to the situation.

The importance of the many social and health services which are available to children and their families must not be minimized, but it is equally important to recognize that their effectiveness is dependent on their actually reaching the child and his parents. When, as is sometimes the case in large communities, periods of six months to two years must elapse between the time the child is referred to a child guidance clinic, for example, and the time he is actually seen, the problem, whatever it may be, has had that much more time to crystallize.

Youngsters in this stage of development tend to be somewhat suspicious of adults. Those needing social services most are apt to be those whose relationships to their families have already given them good reason to distrust grownups. Delays in clinic appointments and shifts in workers simply add to their conviction that it is well to be wary.

Law-enforcement agencies. So far as law-enforcement agencies are concerned, some children will have little contact with them during these years. To many 6- and 7-year-olds the policeman is represented by the kindly .traffic cop who escorts them across the busy street.

As they grow older, their concept expands to include various kinds of policemen, jails, and perhaps courts. But they have few, if any, direct dealings with these. Other children grow up in constant alertness for the approach of the " cops " and have learned to evade them whenever possible.

The effective functioning of police and attendance officers demands that they enforce the authority of the school and the community, but in the light of current understanding of human behavior the ways of accomplishing this may be expected to change. For example, the child who persistently absents himself from school is saying that for some reason his controls are inadequate to the classroom situation. The source of his difficulty may be a teacher with whom he cannot establish a comfortable relationship, or a home situation which fails to give him the support he needs or about which he is upset or worried, or a picture of himself which is inconsistent with the expectations of the school. Only by remedying the cause is the truancy pattern likely to be overcome. When the classroom situation itself is the primary cause of the difficulty, the school can often make adjustments which help. Under some circumstances it can work with the child directly. Often, however, the home must be brought into the situation. It is at this point that the process has often broken down. When the parents were not inclined to want any help, it appeared that little could be done for the child. Basically, people do not change their ways of behaving because someone else thinks they should. Change comes to the individual only as he himself is willing to make it. Recently, however, it is recognized that such wanting to change can come about through the active intervention of someone representing authority, but doing so in an accepting, nonpunishing way. Thus, in effect, the school (and the community) tries to find ways of saying to parents whose relationships with their children are proving detrimental, " We appreciate *your* difficulties, we understand *your* problems, we are sympathetic to *your* needs, but we must insist on the protection of your children."

What is involved here is a knotty problem, to which solutions are by no means simple. It is a question of the wise use of authority, a more complex version of the discipline problems we encounter with children. It involves recognition of the fact that so long as individuals, be they parents or children, feel themselves to be at a disadvantage, discriminated against, unwanted, they will tend to react in hostile and antisocial ways. In order to conform willingly to the standards of society, they must feel themselves an accepted part of it. How to maintain a situation in which at one and the same time the integrity of the individual and the welfare of the group are protected, is, of course, a continuing concern of any democratic society. The many factors which must be taken into consideration of this basic concern are not particularly relevant here. It is important, however, to recognize that whatever solutions are found have definite implications for the personality development of children.

Thus far in our consideration of the school, the church, and various social agencies interested in children we have been dealing with institutions consciously interested in influencing the behavior of youngsters. We shall turn now to consideration of some other important influences.

Media of Communication

Many people believe that TV and the comics and, to a lesser extent, the radio and the movies constitute a more potent influence in the lives of many children than do the institutions which we have just discussed. There is some basis for this thinking in the light of the amount of time which children spend watching TV, reading the comics, and so on.

Unfortunately, it is extremely difficult to appraise the contribution of any one influence to the child's developing personality. Early studies of the movies and of the comics suggested that while they might appear to accentuate a child's difficulties (a youngster who felt left out of the world of adults or his peers might turn increasingly to these media for solace, for example), they seldom precipitated a child's personality problems. This whole question is one which deserves much more study than it has had so far. The trend has been to relate the hours of TV-viewing, for example, to such factors as children's success in school. The results have been somewhat contradictory, but the conclusion reached in one study is significant, " Only after making a thorough case study of each pupil would one be justified in estimating or predicting the effect of TV on the pupil's school achievement." [33] A somewhat similar generalization about the effects of the comics is reached by Jones in a review of the research in that area:

We suspect that different comic books have very different effects on different children. A few may be actually beneficial to some children. Most are probably neutral for most children from the point of view of character. A few are almost certainly marginal if not harmful to all or most of those who read them. The over-all effect is probably small, except possibly in a cumulative way and in combination with other factors.[34]

It is comparatively easy to place the blame for emotional disturbance and delinquency on television or the comics. But to do so is to ignore the fact that both these media, and the others which reinforce them, are products of the adult society. They represent the standards and values to which at least some adults subscribe. If youngsters become confused and assume that these are desirable patterns for them to follow, whose is the responsibility? Have the adults who decry bad influences on children done anything to make them feel comfortable in a real world with other standards and other values? There is good reason to believe that it is not the youngsters who are growing up with parents and teachers who help them to find interesting and challenging things to do, who are the ones spending the major portion of their time at television.

It is true that in all of these media the child is more likely to encounter stereotypes or caricatures than he is real human beings subject to human frailties. The good characters seem likely to be all good. The villains are all bad. Moral issues may be cast in black or white rather than in the shades of gray with which the child himself will have to cope eventually. Yet there is good reason to believe that this has considerably less effect on the children growing up with parents and teachers who are themselves genuine, than it does on youngsters who deal mostly with adults who, like the characters on the screen, go through the motions of living, but never permit themselves to feel or care very deeply about anything.

Given a little help in critical thinking and evaluation, youngsters

[33] Witty, Paul A. " Research about Children and TV " in *Children and TV, Making the Most of It*. Washington, D.C.: Association for Childhood Education International, 1954. Pp. 12, 13.

[34] Jones, *op. cit.* P. 810.

need not be taken in by propaganda. When they are, we may question whether the basic reason may not lie in their own need to believe rather than in the persuasive strength of the medium which brings it to them. In a study of children's reactions to TV advertising, for example, one child wrote, " My hair shines just like the girl in the ad, so I always get —— shampoo now." But a more realistic youngster commented, " They promised me a school-girl complexion, but just look at my pimples. I don't believe *any* of them now." [35]

PROBLEM 14. If possible, plan to interview some children of school age on their television viewing and comic-book reading habits. How much time do they spend? What are their favorites? What do they especially like about them?

A parallel project: a group of students might view the programs and read the comics selected by the children, analyzing the quality of the characters presented, the problems set forth together with solutions offered and the values implied.

Expectations for Socialization

As we have perhaps implied, but not specified, all of the factors which we have mentioned in previous chapters as contributing to differences in children's backgrounds — such as income level, occupation, parental education, residence, race, and religion — continue their operation in the period now under consideration. They determine the kind of social environment in which the child finds himself and they influence the expectations which his parents hold for him. In this period, however, the child's socialization is no longer primarily a matter of adapting to the requirements of the adults. His peers, with whom he has already learned some degree of give-and-take, assume increasing status in his eyes. By the time he has reached the age of 9 or 10, he often seems to value their opinions considerably more than those of his parents or his teachers. He sees himself, his family and their position in the world increasingly through their eyes. They, too, serve as socializing agents for him. When we consider the expectations which are held for the socialization of children, we need to remember the function of the peer group.

[35] Brumbaugh, Florence. " What effect does advertising have on children? " in *Children and TV, Making the Most of It, op. cit.* Pp. 21, 22.

The major requirement for this period is undoubtedly school attendance and at least some demonstration of success there. Depending on the background of the parents the importance attached to
this varies. We shall consider the effects of such expectations on the
child's sense of achievement in more detail later in the chapter.

Going to school by oneself is an important step toward independence. For some children it is but a further loosening of ties that for
some time have been slack. For others it is a real break with home
and mother, perhaps the first occasion for being on one's own. Just
as parents varied in the extent to which they were able to grow
along with the child when he was 3, 4, and 5, so we find differences
in the way in which the growing abilities of the school-age child
are respected. Changes in this period are less obvious than they
were earlier, and some parents appear to shift their expectations
but slightly during this period. The child, however, becomes aware
that he has less freedom than do the other children. Comments
such as " Aw come on, your mother won't care! " " My mother
always lets me go to the park." " Now I am eight, I can stay up a
half hour longer." "Gee, you're a sissy, momma's boy." — all these
have their effect on him, and he uses the group to convince his parent of his right to greater independence. Or, in collaboration with
his group, he may, at the age of 10 or so, simply declare his independence by staying out beyond the appointed hour, maintaining
silence about his plan, his friends, and so on. Yet, as we shall see,
in most families he is by no means completely emancipated even at
12, nor does he really want to be.

Adult expectations regarding aggression also vary widely and
may be the source of considerable difficulty for the child. In many
middle-class families, for example, open expression of aggression,
hitting, and fighting, are discouraged, but competitiveness, getting
ahead of one's neighbor through greater achievement or cleverness
is encouraged. Even here there may be a tacit agreement that boys,
at least, have to do a certain amount of fighting. This is acceptable
so long as the child picks on someone his own size. In contrast, in
some lower-class families, the child, if he is a boy, is expected to be
able to hold his own in a fight, but the expression of aggression
through excelling in school and so on may seem of little importance.

The fact that boys are so frequently dominated by women who may attempt to curb all expressions of physical aggression may also complicate their learning of acceptable patterns. As in the acquisition of independence, the child probably comes eventually to regard as most appropriate the standards held by his peer group.

So far as sexual interests are concerned, the tacit assumption among many adults is that children of this age have none. Some parents expect that the sex information they have given the children earlier should satisfy their curiosity and obviate the necessity for any further consideration of the matter until they approach adolescence. It is likely that even parents who consider themselves an enlightened group will regard with some disapproval any evidence of sex talk or sex play by children of this age.[36] Yet there is fairly consistent evidence in several studies that youngsters in all classes obtain a considerable amount of sex information and experience within the peer group. Most children hesitate to reveal their knowledge to adults, but lower-class children are especially careful. They have learned that they may be scolded for being dirty, filthy, or nasty. Or they may have their mouths washed out with soap, or be severely beaten.[37]

A curious aspect of the relationship between the peer group and the adults is suggested in this and other areas. The adults disapprove or forbid sex talk, or fighting, or too marked manifestations of independence. Yet they are not so old, nor is our culture changing so fast that they should not be able to remember their own sex experiences, their feuds, and their rebellions. It is almost as though they were saying to their children, " This is too much for us — you handle it."

The peer group has become, in many parts of our society, a society in itself. During a period of rapid cultural change, each generation confronts new ways of doing things and new problems. The ways of behaving of the previous generation are no longer appropri-

---

[36] See, for example, Kinsey, Alfred C., and others. *Sexual Behavior in the Human Male.* Philadelphia: W. B. Saunders and Company, 1953. Pp. 101–21. Also Ramsey, G. V. " The Sex Information of Younger Boys." *American Journal of Orthopsychiatry.* 13 (1943), 347–53.

[37] Hollingshead, August. *Elmtown's Youth.* New York: John Wiley and Sons, 1949. P. 415.

ate and so, in a sense, each new generation must learn for itself. It develops its interests, its accepted procedures for accomplishing the enterprises it regards as important, it has its leaders and its followers, in it the members practice various roles. But this apparent separateness and uniqueness is by no means complete. The youngster growing up is at one and the same time a member of a family and generally of several other social institutions, the school, the church, and so on, as well as of the neighborhood play group or gang of these years, or the clique or crowd of adolescence, to which we attach the peer-group label.

The importance of the peer group in the socialization of the child cannot be denied. Yet it is a mistake, in the opinion of the author, to assume that its functions are inexorable. When the peer group comes to regard itself as a group alien to adult society, this has occurred not because of any real desire or need of the children to be so separate, but rather because of the disinterest, the callousness, and the lack of sympathy displayed by the adult world. Even in separateness, the children continue to mirror the world of the grown-ups, suggesting their true dependence on it.

Significance of Social Factors

From 6 to 12 is the period in which the child begins to learn the skills, the customs, the traditions, and the prejudices of the culture in which he lives. As he moves out of his family into the larger social world, he begins to see himself and his family as people with a certain status. The house in which he lives, the job his father holds, the church to which he belongs, and his ethnic origin, all take on new meanings for him. To the extent that the people he encounters in this larger social world are kindly to him, interested in his concerns, encouraging of his abilities, appreciative of him as a worthy human being, he begins to regard himself as a competent person.

To understand the processes through which he arrives at this important point, we shall need to consider the inner feeling aspects of his personality development. In the next chapter we shall discuss the psychodynamic aspects of development in this period.

Elizabeth Hibbs

In our society, 6- to 12-year-olds are expected to master verbal symbols.

10

ᒎᒎᒎ

Mastering the Ways of the World:

Psychodynamic Aspects of
Development in the Years 6 to 12

THE TOOTHLESS, wiggly 6-year-old and the self-critical 7-year-old still slide easily into the world of imagination and fantasy and remain adults' children. The 8-year-old is beginning to be interested in faraway places and prefers his adult ties to be loose. The noisy, grubby 9-, 10-, and 11-year-olds seem by comparison realistic, matter-of-fact, and comparatively uninterested in adults. What is the inner world of childhood like in these years? How much do these children need adults? How well can they control and direct their own behavior? What are the feelings with which they must cope? How do other people matter to them? How do they see their world? How do they see themselves? These are some of the questions we shall need to answer in considering personality development in this period.

What we shall describe as being characteristic must be thought of as typical only of our culture and perhaps only of certain portions of that. For as children grow older, the responses they make and the way they feel about their own developing powers and abilities, depend increasingly upon what the adults expect from them. In our culture, we tend to postpone the child's acceptance as a fullfledged

335

member of society to a point well beyond 12 years. Where there is less differentiation between childhood and adulthood, we shall expect to find that some of our generalizations no longer hold true.

The period is one in which the child develops increasing mastery of the skills and tools of his culture. By and large we expect him to achieve this in school. In a sense, it is an achievement not so much for his present use as his future need. Were his accomplishments matters of immediate necessity in the adult world, as is still the case in some rural communities where children share in the chores, the tilling, and the harvesting, we might find that some of the reserve, aloofness, and even hostility which often characterize his behavior in the years from 18 would be less typical.

PROGRESS IN EGO DEVELOPMENT

In Chapter 8 we suggested that the child's creative activities — his paintings and drawings and his play — provide one kind of evidence as to the progress of his ego development. Figure 7 shows at the top the crayon drawings of an 8-year-old girl, and at the bottom, that of an 8-year-old boy. A comparison of these with those shown in Figures 4 and 5 in Chapter 8 indicates the general trends toward better organization and improved perception of reality which are characteristic of the period with which we are presently concerned.

The increasing complexity and efficiency of the child's inner controls is readily apparent when one compares the behavior at play of a group of 6-year-olds with a group of 11-year-olds. The 6's are very likely to be climbing or stunting on playground equipment, perhaps adding bits of cowboy or space-cadet drama. Just who is participating and who is not, may not be too clear to the observer. But the play will have some obvious structure and direction. The children will be able to take care of minor conflicts without much adult assistance. The 11's, on the other hand, will likely be found in some team game, keenly conscious of its rules and able to abide by them.

The impulses, on which they operated so spontaneously at 3 and to a less degree at 6, have become increasingly organized. Their energy is directed outward to cope with reality, manifested in the

My sister and I are carrying the leaves away. See the squirrels. Judy

Figure 7

rules of the game, rather than absorbed in acting out personal fantasy. Their comradeship with their peers from which they derive so much satisfaction helps to keep them focused on reality and also serves to support them so they no longer depend on the adult.

The difference in intellectual outlook which this implies can be seen in the following incident from a lunch table conversation of 7-year-olds, as compared with a short scene from a play written by a sixth grade. The comments are this author's.

Incident	*Comment*
7–YEAR–OLDS	
Peter said that he wished Hitler and Mussolini had been on the *Hindenburg* which crashed last night. Someone else said that he wished all the Americans had been out of it and only Germans in it. . . .	Even at 7, these youngsters, coming from homes in which current events are discussed and news events broadcasts are heard on the radio, are aware of what goes on in the larger world of adults.
Dick remarked that Hitler was a bastard. Christopher converted this word to " best," referring apparently to both dictators. Dick, with heavy though grinning sarcasm, said, " And *Hitler especially!* He's the best." Christopher added something about the best man, and Dick chimed in, " Hitler and Mussolini are the best men in the world." [1]	Further awareness of adults! Such conversion is typical of the child's efforts to understand at this stage of his development.
	Dick is evidently quite aware that " best " is not an appropriate discription here. Note, however, how the description parallels that used by children in describing things which are close and personal to them. They are dealing with world ideas in the same terms they would use to compare their own possessions.
SIXTH GRADE	
(This is the last half of a scene dictated to the teacher by the children for a play which was to serve as the final activity for a year of social studies devoted to the theme " Living and Growing To-	We assume that the atmosphere of the classroom was such as to provoke a free expression on the part of the children, not overlooking the fact that by this age children have learned to dissemble and

[1] Biber, Barbara, and others. *Child Life in School — A Study of a Seven Year Old Group.* New York: E. P. Dutton and Company, 1942. P. 621.

Incident	*Comment*
gether in the World." It was the year of the first explosion of the atom bomb.)	may respond with what they think the teacher wants.

End of Scene I

First Boy: It sure takes the Americans to do something like this. The Americans have the know-how and the how-to and all the other stuff it takes.	Here is pride and identification. The words that are used, " know-how " and " how-to," appear to have a concrete meaning to the children.
Second Boy: I read that Einstein was in on this, too.	People more than ideas are important at this level of development.
First Boy: Gosh, I think that he was kicked out of Germany by Hitler because he was a Jew.	These children deal not only in the present, but to some extent in the past. This idea was especially meaningful because the children came from a neighborhood with a large group of Jewish refugee families from Germany.
Second Boy: Look at this! A scientist named Fermi worked on this. He's Italian. And he's been working right down here at Columbia University.	The long-ago, the faraway, the world of nations, are important to these youngsters, but so is the here and now.
Third Boy: Hey, look, here's a fellow from Denmark, and his name is Bohr.	The personal emphasis is again evident. Portions of the play not included here indicate how very much these children identify with some of these adult heroic figures.
First Boy: And look! Here's a woman's picture in this article.	
Second Boy: And it says she's German. Her name is Lise Meitner. I'll bet she was kicked out of Germany, too.	
Third Boy: That's just what it says. The S. S. guards came after her, and she was kicked out.[2]	

[2] Mitchell, Lucy S., and others. *Know Your Children in School.* New York: The Macmillan Company, 1954. P. 156.

Perhaps the most striking differences between the groups lie in the considerably greater abilities of the sixth grade to work together and to organize ideas in dramatic fashion, but in accordance with known facts. These abilities reflect the increased complexity of function of their control systems, or egos.

" Knowing " Functions of the Ego

By the age of 10 or 11, if all has gone well, the child has good contact with the outside world. He is able to assess it and to understand it. This applies both to the physical world, as we shall see when we discuss concept formation, and to the social world. He recognizes, for example, that " rules " are essential to fair play, and is not so likely to feel, as he was at an earlier age, that he should be exempt from them. He can appraise rather accurately the relationships between the various members of his group. At the same time he has some awareness of what goes on inside himself. He has some insight into his own motivation, knows what he wants to do, is aware of his urges, strivings, fears. But he can also appraise what is " right " in terms of his own conscience.

An illustration of the development of these " cognitive " or " knowing " functions of the ego may be drawn from Weber's *Country School Diary*. The children had planted a bulb bed and had surrounded it with a sturdy fence. One day the teacher discovered that the bed had been trampled upon, while some of the younger boys had used the fence for high jumping. These boys' knowledge of the effects of trampling on the growth of the bulbs was perhaps not sufficient to keep them from yielding to their desire for activity. Or, perhaps, conscience signaled some protest, but their urges won out. Some slightly older boys, coming on the scene, perceived the possible damage to be done, were not distracted by their own drives for activity, and asked the others to stop. Their additional maturity is revealed in the comment of one of them to the teacher, " They did stop, so I didn't think I had to tell you." [3] He realized that the situation was handled adequately when the destruction ceased. Unlike a younger child, he had no need to tattle.

[3] Weber, Julia. *My Country School Diary*. New York: Harper and Brothers, 1946. P. 51.

Power Functions of the Ego

An adequately functioning ego involves not only "knowing," but "doing." For example, an 11-year-old may see clearly that the reason he is not wanted in the baseball game is because he pitches so badly. Unless he can mobilize himself to practice and polish his skills, his knowledge does him very little good. The attitudes of adults can either help or hinder a child in exerting the power he has. The learning of arithmetic skills affords a good illustration. Many children experience considerable difficulty with long division. Any number of causes may contribute to this, but it sometimes happens that the child has not had sufficient practice in certain fundamentals. The teacher helps him to discover where his weaknesses lie and prepares some drill which should help him. The youngster may understand his difficulty, but do nothing about it. He may sit at his desk and stare at the paper, or he may carry his work home, ostensibly to have someone help him and bring it back next day untouched. But if the teacher really believes in his ultimate ability to achieve and is able to give him genuine approval step by step, his picture of himself as one unable to do long division gradually changes. He is able to use his power because his teacher has helped him to exercise it. It is not the practice alone which counts, but practice which takes place in an atmosphere of understanding and faith.

Selective Functions of the Ego

The child's ego must not only "do" but also be able to choose, to make decisions between one course of action and another. Redl gives us an illustration of this "selective" function in action. A youngster who has been considerably overprotected and is quite lacking in sophistication becomes aware that his gang is indulging in some "dirty talk," which has no meaning for him, although it is pretty obvious that its use gives one considerable status with the other boys. He may deal with the situation in a realistic way, or he may find some way of avoiding dealing directly with the conflict it sets up for him. In the latter event, he may deny any interest in what is going on. He may simply withdraw from the group and avoid further contact with them. Or he may accuse them of crimes of various sorts which have no basis in reality. Or he may push the whole matter out of his conscious awareness, but be troubled by it in his dreams and his fears. If his ego has sufficient strength, however, he will be able to deal with his conflict more openly. Thus he may have a man-to-man talk with his father, or with another boy, and find out what the other kids' talk means. Or he may even submit to the razzing he knows the group will give him and insist on their letting him in on the secrets.[4]

Synthesizing Function of the Ego

Finally, the ego has a "synthetic" function. If development is going well, there is a kind of balance evident in the personality. The child is completely subservient neither to his impulses and feelings, nor to the demands of adults or the peer group. We do not mean to imply that this "balance" will be the same for each youngster. Rather, the synthesis of personality achieved as a unique biological organism grows up in unique social situations should be different for each child.

This kind of integration is, of course, not arrived at all at once, nor indeed once for all. Just as adults will "go to pieces" under certain kinds of stress, children are, if anything, more vulnerable. A youngster may seem pretty much in harmony with himself in the fifth grade with a teacher who is kindly but firm and become considerably disorganized when he encounters a sixth-grade teacher who thinks 11-year-olds ought to be able to make all their own decisions. Or a girl of like age may be "doing fine" until her place of leadership is usurped by a newcomer whose social skills are even better than her own.

However, the general trend through these years is toward a control system capable of the kinds of functions we have described. Important in its development are the child's learning how his conscience best serves him and his learning more and more often to feel positively toward his peers and to expand his identifications.

---

4 Redl, Fritz, and Wineman, David. *Children Who Hate.* Glencoe, Illinois: The Free Press, 1951. Pp. 65–66. Most of the material regarding ego functions which is presented here is drawn from this book, with special reference to pp. 61–73.

The Development of Conscience

As we have indicated, the young child's conscience is primarily determined by the effective prohibitions of the adults who have been most significant in his life, in most cases his parents. At 6, in many instances, this conscience functions almost too effectively. The child may apply his ideas of right and wrong so literally that he sometimes seems quite priggish. In addition, his conscience is often deeply troubling to him. When he yields to impulse, as when he picks a beautiful flower from a neighbor's garden without permission, or swats his baby brother although he has been expressly forbidden to do so, he may carry a burden of guilt quite out of proportion to the actual crime. Some indication of the strength of his feelings about transgressions of the letter-of-the-law are apparent in his readiness to tattle. It is as though he is assuring himself that *he* knows the rules. He tends further to see right and wrong more in black and white than in possible shades of gray.

This tendency has been referred to by Piaget in his studies of the moral judgment of the child as the stage of " moral realism." The child is incapable of judging behavior in terms of its underlying intention or in terms of circumstance. He learns, for example, to distinguish " truth " from " falsehood." He then seems impelled to be truthful even though a declaration of what he perceives as true may carry hurt to another. The " white lie " or the tactful, face-saving comment are beyond his comprehension. Not until the age of 9 or 10 does he become able to appreciate different motives. He begins to conceive that " right and wrong " may be a matter not of imposition from superiors, but of what is necessary and appropriate for the social living of individuals who are equals.[5]

Although there is considerable evidence that many children begin well under the age of 9 to shift from the rigidity which Piaget describes, the child's basis for moral judgment does change during these years. An important factor in that change is his relationships with his peers.[6]

[5] Piaget, Jean. *The Moral Judgment of the Child*. Glencoe, Illinois: The Free Press, no date given.

[6] Isaacs, Susan. *Social Development in Young Children*. London: Routledge & Kegan, Ltd., 1930.

We shall consider the question of peer relationships again later in the chapter, but at this point we should like to emphasize how the kind of conscience the child carries along from early childhood facilitates and hampers the development of personality in this period of development. The child who has taken into himself and accepted a number of " Thou-shalt-nots " is, in one sense, a well-protected child. Rather than struggling with warring impulses, he is free to channel his energies in constructive social directions. For example, when playing with another child, he can concentrate on the progress of their play. He can accept the fact that the toys belong to the other child. He does not try to destroy them, or take them home with him. However, as Redl's studies of " Children Who Hate " have so brilliantly revealed, the conscience, if it is to be effective, must include values which are appropriate to the situation in which the child finds himself. It is conceivable that a youngster might be so very protective of another's property that he could not enjoy its use, fearing its possible destruction. Conscience also must be able to signal danger in advance.[7] It needs, in effect, to say to the child when he begins using a bit of play equipment, " Take it easy." It should not withhold all its prohibitions until after the toy is broken, or has been slyly tucked in a pocket and carried away.

The child whose conscience is too full, for whom too many kinds of behavior have been forbidden, is apt to be restricted in personality. True, he may not be distracted from learning to read, let us say, by his impulses for running around or conversing with his peers. His values are right for the situation. His conscience tells him that reading is a " quiet time." Thus it helps him to realize one of his important potentialities — that of being an individual who can derive meaning from the printed word. Suppose, however, that his conscience functions in the same fashion a half hour later, when he is on the playground. He is unable to realize his potentialities for good social give-and-take.

On the other hand, he may be able to perceive that the playground situation does not call for the same kinds of behavior as the classroom and yield to his impulses there, only to struggle later with a

<hr>

[7] Redl and Wineman, *op. cit.* Pp. 197–208.

conscience which reminds him that he is guilty of nonapproved behavior. An example of this kind can be found in the behavior of one carefully brought-up youngster, who had been taught that it was safe to go barefoot only on the grassy lawn. Yet it was a first-grade custom, whenever the weather became a little warm, to pause on the way home from school to investigate a creek bed, a procedure which always necessitated the removal of shoes and socks. Most of the children then walked home barefoot, but this youngster always had to struggle into socks and shoes. Even though his deception was never found out, it was for some time a source of real guilt and remorse, which undoubtedly colored his responses to his parents in other areas.

As he matures in the ability to see cause and effect relationship in the world about him, as he comes to value the companionship of his peers, and as he comes to be fond of and to make identifications with individuals other than his parents, the child's conscience should begin to function somewhat more flexibly. But the process is not an easy one, for early learnings, particularly those in which the individual has had a deep emotional investment, are not easily unlearned.

The child who has known too few prohibitions, or who has had such uncertain guidance, that he has found the same behavior sometimes condemned and sometimes condoned, is perhaps in a worse position than the child whose " still small voice " is too persistent. Lacking that guide, he is much more the creature of his impulses, much less able to channel, control, and direct them, in a way increasingly satisfactory not only to himself and to his peers, but to the society of which he is a member.

By no means all of a child's problems in relation to conscience come from within. The world of adults he confronts is often a pretty mixed-up sort of place. Many grownups hold and practice values which are inconsistent with one another, or what they do contradicts what they say. If the child is at all intelligent, he is not unaware of some of these, even as early as 6. Indeed, one sometimes feels that one reason some adults tend to shy away from the world of childhood is that they cannot stand the child's ability to see through their subterfuge and self-deception.

Some adults, aiming at democracy in family or school or recreation group living, forget the important role which conscience plays in the child's ability to control his behavior. Rather than maintaining their roles as adults representing the important rules and regulations of a democratic society and in a sense aiding and abetting the child's conscience, they throw too many decisions on him. They may imply to him that *any* kind of activity, *any* way of using materials and equipment is acceptable. They may not help him sufficiently to feel responsible for the consequences of his own behavior. Frequently neither the child's conscience nor his ego or inner control system is strong enough for him to withstand the demands of his own impulses when the environment sets no restrictions on him. Within the family, children suffering from lack of support to their consciences tend all too readily to resemble the little monsters of cartoon fame. In groups, bedlam and destruction are likely outcomes. There is no doubt that children can learn to function democratically and can help to make rules and regulations appropriate for their own behavior, *with adult help*. But to expect them to achieve this alone and unaided, seems to deny the respect for developing personality which is implicit in the concept of democracy.

PROBLEM 1. A classic study having to do with the development of a democratic atmosphere for learning is that by R. Lippit and R. H. White. It is reported in detail in *Child Behavior and Development*, edited by Barker, Kounin, and Wright, pp. 485–508. There is a less technical, but also less graphic account in *Readings in Child Psychology*, edited by Dennis, pp. 531–538. Review one of these accounts. Make a list of impulses with which the children may have struggled in each of the situations. Make a list of the adult controls, both specific and implied which were imposed in each of the three situations — laissez-faire, authoritarian, and democratic. Discuss the effectiveness of each procedure in the light of what you know about the child's development of conscience.

Changing Feelings

When we speak of "changing feelings," we do not mean to imply that the emotions of the young child are transformed as he becomes 6 and 9 and 12. As the individual grows, he develops a capacity for responding with feeling to a greater variety of situations, more ability to exercise voluntary control over his feelings, and a perspective on the role they play in his living. But even the mature adult, unless he has learned to deny completely the reality of his feelings, from time to time must come to terms with emotions, subjectively not unlike those he experienced when he was no more than 2 or 3 years old. The flash of blinding rage, the momentary paralysis of fear, the euphoria found in complete acceptance by another human being, all these are adult experiences which remind us of the basic similarities in human feelings at any age.

Nevertheless, when one is 12, the general run of one's emotional responses and attitudes tends in some respects to vary from what it was at 6, and indeed from what it will be at 16 and at 60. In this section we shall consider what appear to be some attitudes of these years.

During perhaps the first half of this period, the child in many ways resembles emotionally the child of 4 or 5 more than the child of 10 or 11. It appears that around the age of 8 or 9 shifts in differentiation and integration occur, which tend to alter the child's emotional and social outlook. We shall examine the social implications of this shift later.

Listening to a group of 6-year-olds comment on their school experiences, we might well conclude that they are quite mature and emotionally much more stable than they were at 4 and 5. They say: " I'm learning to read. I'm in group I, and we read real hard things." " My teacher says, if we don't make a lot of noise, we get more done." " We're going to the zoo, and we *all* have to take very good care of ourselves and be *very* steady." It is when we watch and listen to them in action, that we sense how dependent they are on the teacher's help in maintaining the maturity of which they boast. Here, for example, are some of the spontaneous comments of 6-year-olds during a first-grade play period:

" I won't be on your side if you do."
" Oh I know that one."
" Look, Rosalie, this is the first page."
" Let's change places in the desks."
" Miss H., do you know what S.F. means? "
" I need an eraser, and I can't find it, and I need one."

" Miss H., I'm going to the bathroom."

" Oh shoot the shoot pifs."

" I'll shoot the mess pot in the middle of the mess."

" You want red. I want blue."

" If he finishes it any more, he'll ruin it."

" Hey, you started it." (snatches book)

" Give that right back." (snatches book)

" You know what I'm doing? "

" Fall. That's when you fall down. That's when the apples fall. That's why we call it fall."

" Hello measles, hello chicken pox."

" Hello whooping cough." [8]

And, moving on a year, listen to the dramatic play of two 7-year-olds:

Amy and Ruth were dramatizing some house play in the wooden shelter. Ruth directs Amy to wash up the dishes, and Amy proceeds to the wall, going through some vague motions. Then Amy, " I'll just wash my hands up, and my face."

They shoo Alex away, run off from the shelter themselves, and then join a large group of children clustered around Miss R.

After a few moments, they return to the shelter, making gestures of entering a house with a key. Once inside, they hunch together in one corner, muttering to themselves and giggling at the recorder. Ruth calls out excitedly, " Get out, you ghost! " as Anne appears with her face covered. Ruth: " I'll pull you and choke you until you are dead." Amy: " Get out of that bathroom door."

Amy goes through the gestures of washing up again and throughout the play seems definitely intent on carrying through the dramatic elements. Ruth suggests going to the park after lunch. Amy brings some mock food, with the command, " Please get off the table." Amy is the wife. The play seems to require unusually frequent washing of hands.

Ruth, on the whole, seems to be taking the more aggressive role. During the driving episode, she drives. Amy attaches herself weakly. The play is dissipated when the assistant calls them to go down off the roof. There is still some giggling and a few last embarrassed glances at the recorder.[9]

Both these records suggest that not too far beneath the surface lie attitudes of possessiveness and rivalry, not too dissimilar from

---

[8] Gesell, Arnold, and Ilg, Frances L. *The Child from Five to Ten.* New York: Harper and Brothers, 1946. P. 125.

[9] Biber and others, *op. cit.* Pp. 198–199.

those we observed in the period we have chosen to label "power-testing." These attitudes, along with the affection which is also there, rather readily find expression in the children's dramatic play. It is well that they should, for one of the hazards of this period of development is that adults may expect the child to grow away from his strong feelings more rapidly than he is really able. He may learn to control his impulses without finding safe ways to direct them. Feelings, both positive and negative, give meaning to life. The child who learns to deny them, may also be learning to live a constricted, futile kind of existence.

Some of the strong feelings of this early part of the child's elementary school years, it appears, stem from much the same sources as they did in the years from 3 to 6. Many of them involve concerns of which the child is not consciously aware. He may still be uncertain about his place in his family, disturbed in his relationships to mother or father, brother or sister. But the world of immediate reality also produces its share of strong feelings.

For many children, if not for most, entrance into school brings with it pride, a new sense of status and considerable positive enjoyment. The child is no longer "a little kid" on the very bottom rung of the prestige scale of his neighborhood group, but has taken one step up and can now look down on those who stay at home or go to kindergarten. Nursery school and kindergarten are now both regarded as "baby stuff." Furthermore parents one way or another imply that being a first grader is something rather special. Even when mother can't bear to "lose" her child to the school and clings to him, as some mothers do, she conveys to him her awareness that "something" extremely important is about to happen to him. If his teacher is sensitive both to his continuing baby needs and his wish to be worthy of his new status, school comes to be a very positive force in his life. But like most other blessings it is not unmixed. In order to reap the rewards of being an approved first grader, the child must increasingly tolerate the needs and wishes of other children as well as the decisions of a new adult. He must adapt himself to some kind of time schedule and a variety of other restrictions in his behavior. He must accept a greater degree of organization and rules and routine in his life than he has likely ever known before.

He finds, if he is fortunate, in the person of his teacher a new adult whom he can love and admire and imitate. Indeed, to a greater extent than we are often aware, many children, in first and even second grade, learn primarily in order to please the teacher. Yet the teacher is not exclusively the child's, but must be shared with his peers.

So the gains that are made through school status are not made without some cost, and the child from time to time very likely feels "put upon" both by adults and by other children. During the period in which they have so much to learn about what is expected from them, many children probably express their resentments in fairly direct ways. For example, a study by Griffiths [10] revealed that both parents and children find aggressive behavior (behavior in which the child is argumentative, talks unnecessarily, resents criticisms, is critical of others, has anger outbursts, is impudent, interrupts, is demanding, was included in this) a matter of somewhat greater concern in the years from 6 to 8 than in the years from 9 to 11. Other children may feel equally pushed, but turn their feelings inward rather than expressing them overtly. Such children, particularly when they feel that they may not meet standards being set for them, may be subject to fears which have no apparent cause, upsetting dreams and such nervous habits as nail biting.

All of the six children we have been interested in got on very well in the first two years of school, with the possible exception of Charles who seems to have been rather more active than his first-grade teacher expected a child should be. Nevertheless, all of them, again not including Charles, showed some evidences of nervous tension.

Jane during first grade showed a considerable tendency to finger sucking. This only appeared when she was excited or bashful, but was fairly persistent.

Pat, during both first and second grades, was inclined to bite her nails or her lips.

Andy's tensions were evidenced in fears. He experienced occasional nightmares.

[10] Griffiths, William. *Behavior Difficulties of Children as Perceived and Judged by Parents, Teachers and Children Themselves.* Minneapolis: University of Minnesota Press, 1952. P. 92.

Dan bit his nails and sucked on a handkerchief, or, failing that, chewed his necktie.

Celeste was also inclined to bite her nails. She did well in school, and it appears that this was a particularly important boost to her. In some ways she became more open and less withdrawn than she had been before she started first grade.

It is doubtful that any child can grow through the years from 6 to 8 without encountering many situations which may make him angry or frightened or jealous. Those who would understand and help him, cannot avoid his exposure to these emotions, but they can see that his life is not dominated by them. When they do not need to meet anger with anger, when they help a resentful youngster to save his face, when they give reassurance to a frightened child, and when they are able to give genuine approval for much of the child's behavior, whatever pain there may be in growing seems small against the satisfaction it brings.

Gradually the child succeeds in getting a firmer command of his impulses and somewhere around 8 or 9 enters into a somewhat different phase of development. We have already suggested that this is a phase about which much more research is needed. We shall indicate here some of the information about the child's feelings which can be drawn from available studies, and we shall also examine some of the creative products of 9-, 10-, and 11-year-old youngsters, to see what they may reveal of their concerns.

The years from 9 to 12 appear to be a period for rejection of adult standards. The parents in the Griffiths study noted an increase through these years in noncompliant behavior (this included untidiness, neglect of school work, dallying, carelessness, silliness, avoidance of assigned chores, poor manners, and so on) and for boys, an increase in withdrawing behavior (shyness, worrying, fearfulness, nervousness, cowardice, discouragement, inattention, suggestibility).[11] Blair and Burton in their comprehensive review of the literature relating to the period say:

There is relatively broad agreement that most of the behavior of these children stems from three basic attitudes toward others. The *first* is the

[11] Blair, Arthur W., and Burton, William H. *Growth and Development of the Preadolescent*. New York: Appleton-Century-Crofts, 1951. Pp. 94–95.

change in authority relations, expressed largely by a seeming rejection of adult standards. . . .

The *second* basic attitude is the apparent antagonism between members of the opposite sex of near the same age. . . .

A *third* underlying attitude is the loyalty to a gang composed of other children similar in age, sex, size and interests.[12]

We have already suggested that these shifts in attitude are to a large extent the product of our culture. How deeply they affect the child's inner life is not fully understood. A study by Sanford, using a number of projective techniques to appraise the nature of children's fantasy as they grow from 5 to 14, revealed that "affective tendencies, tendencies expressive of human warmth, actually reach their lowest point during the middle period, i.e., from nine to thirteen."[13] Primitive impulses continue to be strong, but under the control of conscience are not expressed openly. They continue to be operative in the child's fantasy life. The gregariousness of the 9-to-13-year-olds, according to this study, does not stem from the need for affection. Rather, the child needs to have someone help him carry out some of his practical schemes. Even more important, he needs the support of the other youngsters to help him master his childish fears, anxiety, and guilt.

Not all authorities would agree to this conclusion. Sullivan, for example, describes preadolescence as a period marked by the appearance of a new type of interest in another person.

. . . Nothing remotely like that has ever appeared before. . . . [The] child begins to develop a real sensitivity to what matters to another person. And this is not in the sense of "what should I do to contribute to the happiness or to support the prestige and feeling of worth-whileness of my chum."[14]

He regards these as integrating tendencies basic to love, or "the manifestation of the need for interpersonal intimacy." For our purposes in this volume the important point to remember is that the child's feelings in this period, whether or not they come to the

[12] Blair and Burton, *op. cit.* Pp. 50–51.

[13] Sanford, R. Nevitt, and others. "Physique, Personality and Scholarship." *Monograph of the Society for Research in Child Development,* 8, No. 1, 1943. Pp. 645–647.

[14] Sullivan, Harry Stack. *The Interpersonal Theory of Psychiatry.* New York: W. W. Norton & Company, 1953. P. 246.

surface for full expression, are still influential in his personality development. We must not be deceived into believing that an apparent rejection of adults signifies a lack of any need for warmth and responsiveness. The youngster may look to his chums for these and develops with them a relationship crucially important in his growth toward adulthood, but this does not mean that the basic affection and support of adults is no longer needed.

Let us now look to the children themselves to see what they have to tell us of their wishes and desires, their hopes and their despairs. Following are some stories written by fifth graders. We can note the kinds of people they put in these tales, the problems they face, the solutions they find. We may surmise that the stories reflect the world either as the children see it, or as they would like it to be. (The children's original spelling and punctuation are retained.)

DID TOM SEE HIS UNCLE

One day, a boy named Tom said to his mother, " Will you take me to see Uncle Bill? "

His mother said, " We will see."

All that day his mother said to herself, " Should I take him or not? "

In two days Tom's mother took him to see his uncle.

THE WISH THAT CAME TRUE

Once upon a time there lived a boy and his sister. One day the sister said, " I wish I could go to story land." There was an old fairy who made people's wishes come true if they were honest. She lived by an old well, but nobody knew that it was a wishing well.

One day the girl and the boy were walking by the wishing well. They were wishing. The boy said, " I wish we could go to story land."

All of a sudden the wish came true. They were walking down the path in story land. They were happy to see all their story friends. They read all their favorite books. They read and read until they were getting very sleepy.

Finally the boy said, " I am very tired. I wish we could go back."

Quick as a flash their wish came true.

PROBLEM 2. On the surface neither of these stories seems to reveal any very deep feelings. Do you think they tell you anything about how the children would like adults to respond to them?

In the following, the child's wish for parents to see things " his way " seems fairly clear.

JOHNNY WANTS A DOG

Once there lived a boy named Johnny. He wanted a dog. His father didn't want a dog in the house. Every day his father brought him a new toy. But Johnny would not play with it.

His father said, " John, why don't you play with your toys? "

John said, " I don't want toys. I want a dog."

But his father only said, " I don't want a dog in the house."

Johnny said, " But I want a dog. A dog won't harm anybody."

His father said, " No! Don't ask me again."

" Oh, I'll never get a dog," cried Johnny. " There's no use trying."

It was seventeen days before Christmas. His mother and father went Christmas shopping.

His father said, " Do you think I should get Johnny a dog? "

" Yes! " said mother.

" Here's a pet shop," said father. " I'll tell them to send one over the day before Christmas. I'll put the dog in the attic."

Soon it was Christmas morning. Johnny did not get up early. He stayed in bed late.

His mother called, " Johnny come down to see your presents."

Johnny came down slowly. He opened a box — and there was a dog! He could hardly talk.

" Just what I wanted — a dog — a dog," he cried.

Johnny and his dog lived happily ever after.

These children are healthy, well-adjusted youngsters experiencing no more than the usual problems. But through their stories, as through the play of younger children, run certain themes, suggesting that they have their moments of uncertainty and of loneliness.

The next three stories give a hint as to the nature of the fantasy of their authors. They have not had such experiences.

THE BOY WHO FOUND A HOME

Once there was a little boy, named Jack. He had a little dog named Tippy. Tippy and Jack had no home because Jack's mother died when he was born and his father didn't have enough money to take care of him.

Jack and Tippy were roaming the streets looking for a home. Tippy did not have a collar or license, because all the money Jack earned, was spent on food.

One day Jack and Tippy were out in the country. They passed a farm house. The farmer's wife was feeding the chickens. Tippy wanted to watch her.

Jack asked, " Miss, do you have anything for me to do? "

The farmer's wife asked, " What are you doing way out here? Are you running away? "

" No, Mam," said Jack. " I have no mother or father."

The farmer's wife looked at him sadly for a moment. Then she asked, " Would you like to be my little boy? "

" Oh, yes," said Jack. " Can Tippy stay with me, too? "

" Of course," said the farmer's wife.

And that's how Jack and Tippy got a home.

A BOY WHO WAS LONELY

Once upon a time there lived a boy who was lonely. His mother died, and his father stayed in a tavern. He drank and drank. One day his father died, too. There was no one to take care of this boy. He stayed out late and roamed the streets. When he was 15, he got a job and got married. He lived happy ever after.

THE GIRL AND HER NAME

There once was a little girl who had no father or mother. She had no one. She was alone in the world. She didn't even have a name.

A kind old lady took care of the little girl. The lady gave her a bed to sleep in and food to eat.

One day the little girl said to the lady who took care of her, " I would like to have a name."

The old lady thought and thought. Then she said, " I shall call you Ann. Yes, Ann will be your name."

The little girl was so happy she had a name that she forgot all about everything else. She said to herself, " I have a name! My name is Ann."

Something of the problems faced by the youngster when he is trying to conform to adult ideas of good behavior and his desires to have things come out right are suggested in the following:

MARY AMASON IN THE WOODS

Once there was a little girl just about your size. Her name was Mary Amason. She was 10 years old. She had no mother or father. She lived with her sister and brother. Their names were Carol and James. Carol was 15 years old, and James was 18 years old. Mary told Carol that she wanted to go out into the woods. Carol was washing dishes and told Mary she could go for a walk in the woods, but not to go too far in the woods. It was a nice day, and Mary was enjoying her walk in the woods. She had forgotten what Carol told her. She had forgotten that Carol warned her that it was not safe to go too far into the woods. Suddenly

Mary met up with a wild bear. She turned around and ran as fast as she could. When she got home, she turned to see if the bear was coming. But the bear was not there. Mary never went too far into the woods again, for she never forgot the day the bear chased her.

THE SILLY BUNNY

There was once a silly bunny who was always in trouble, running here and there, making work for the people in town. One day the bunny pulled the lady's dress off the clothes line in the backyard. The people in town were mad at little bunny. The ladies were so angry at little bunny, they decided to catch him and kill him. When they caught him, they could not kill him, for he had some good in him. The ladies let him go, and everybody was happy.

Whatever implications about feelings we may draw from these stories — and we must be careful not to overgeneralize from them — they were not intended by the children to tell us about their innermost selves. What happens when they are asked more directly about their wishes and desires?

Here are compositions from fifth-grade youngsters on "If I Had Three Wishes."

IF I HAD THREE WISHES

If I had three wishes I would wish for a Shopsmith tool which consists of a drill, a saw, a lathe, and a sander. Second I would wish for a new bike with a headlight and a tail light and an extra seat for riders. Last of all I would like one hundred boxes of airplanes. The reason why I would like the Shopsmith tool is that I like woodworking. I would like a bike because my old bike is broke and I get tired of walking to the store on cold days. The reason why I would like one hundred boxes of airplanes is because I like to make wood airplanes and hang them up in my room.

IF I HAD THREE WISHES I WOULD WISH FOR

First I would wish for a puppy because I always wanted a puppy to play with and to take care of.

The second wish would be that my family could go to South America to see the different places and the people who live there and how they are different from us.

The third wish would be that my family will get a car so we can go to New York and other big places.

IF I HAD THREE WISHES

If I had three wishes, I would wish for a farm with all kinds of animals on it and especially a horse. Because I like animals, I want a horse so I can ride it to school and all over my neighborhood. Second I'd wish for about a dozen parrots, so I can teach them to talk and also I like to hear them talk. And third I wish for a baseball mit just like the Yankee's use so I can keep it longer, and also I like them better than the regular mits.

IF I HAD THREE WISHES

If I Had Three Wishes I would wish for a thirty-two foot skiff with a hundred-fifty horse power motor because you know when you go out you are going to come back. You can go almost anywhere you want with a boat that size.

I would wish to have the boat caveked and panted because it takes three to four months to cavek and paint a skiff. If you don't paint of cavek, it you would sink.

I would wish to have someone to pay for the gas and oil because the tank holds eighty-five gallons of gas and ten gallons of oil.

These all seem rather matter-of-fact and not too unrealistic. So in fact do the next three. The first youngster, however, is a girl who is in reality having much difficulty in getting along with other children. Her wish for " friends everywhere " may not have as much relationship to the international situation as it may appear on the surface. The next boy's mother had died recently of an incurable disease, so that his fantasy takes on a special significance. The third boy has also lost his mother through death.

IF I HAD THREE WISHES

If I Had Three Wishes the first one would be to go to South America because I've always wanted to go to South America and I've always wanted to travel. My second wish would be to have a big ranch with lots of animals. So I could see how animals live, and their ways of living. And to train all kinds of animals. And my third, to have the world at peace with other countries and our own, and to have friends everywhere. No war. And no fighting.

IF I HAD THREE WISHES

If I had three wishes the first one would be, to be on the Brooklyn Dodgers as soon as I graduated from high school. You get a lot of money each year and I always wanted to be on that team.

The second wish would be for my father to get the newest and best running cars every year so that he wouldn't have to spend money to repair them.

The third would be for me to become a great scientist so that I could discover a medicine that could cure a disease that was incurable.

IF I HAD THREE WISHES

If I had three wishes first I would wish for a dog because I would play with it and teach it tricks. On rainy days I could have something to do.

Second I would wish for a Airomite so I could go to a big field and fly it. Third I would like some tools so I could fix my plane if it got broken. I could make things like planes, boats, and cars with my tools too.

The following wishes are those of a youngster whose family is continually on the move:

IF I HAD THREE WISHES

I would wish first for my father to come home. We miss him. And because my aunt dosen't like us living with her and we don't have a home to live in.

For my second wish I would wish my mother would become well again.

My third wish I would wish to have Peace On our Earth because men, boys, and lovers are getting killed.

Finally, here are the wishes of a " nervous, jittery boy."

IF I HAD THREE WISHES

My first wishes would be to have a forest full of wild and tame animals.

My second wishes would be for No hunting so the animals could live until they died a natural death.

My third wishes is that ther was a pond in the forest and ther were duck, fish and tultes and no fishing.

Some of these " wishes " give us more insight into the feelings of youngsters of this age than do others. Obviously we should be making a grave error should we assume that the child who records only the most prosaic wishes has no reservoir of strong feeling. On the other hand it is equally erroneous to assume that a fantastic response *necessarily* indicates a troubled child. Techniques such as

these are useful only to the extent that they are used with due regard
for the totality of the child's living.

When it comes to knowing what makes them mad, the youngsters tell us rather specifically. Sometimes their resentments are directed at the adults:

WHAT MAKES ME MAD
When we get our spelling to learn I think that When we learn the
meaning it is to much. Learning spelling is all right. But meaning to
is to much.

WHAT MAKES ME MAD
When I go and ask My father to let the dog out he says No on count
of the next door they do not want the dog to get in their garden. And
they sad the next time they sad they saw it in the garen they would
shot it.

Sometimes the adults and the other children together make them
angry.

WHAT MAKES ME MAD
I get mad when people call me names just to get me mad. And when
people make smart remarks about me. And I get mad when my brother
teases me. I get mad when my Mommy yells at my dog for something
he did not mean to do.

WHAT MAKES ME MAD
I get mad when somebody says hurry yp and then they start talking,
and you get ponished and the other person don't. Like when we have
show and tell and your not finished with your work the teacher says if
your work isn't in in ten minutes we woun't have show and tell. The
somebody nere you says hurry up your holding up show and tell, but if
they don't have anything to show and tell about they take there on
swiet time and don't care about the other people.

WHAT MAKES ME MAD
I told Suesun that the class had a test Friday. I had made a mistake.
Bonnie told Suesun I made a mistake. And Suesun said I was a big fat
lier.

Here is real frustration at the hands of a small brother:

WHAT MAKES ME MAD

The place that makes me mad is at home. My brother breaks thing that I have. Yesterday I was trying to make a bracelet of chestnuts and when I laid them down to go into the house my brother smashed the chestnut all up.

Neither of the following boys is particularly articulate, yet each manages to tell us a good bit about the strength of his feelings in these terse comments:

WHAT MAKES ME MAD

When I build something and I get finished with it, then I don't like it, or it breaks apart.

And if someone doe's something I don't like, and they know I don't like it.

WHAT MAKES ME MAD

What makes me most mad to pick cotten and sucker tobacco.

Changing Identifications

Despite the resentment toward adults which is expressed in this period, the need for someone with whom the child can identify continues. As he grows older, these individuals serve as models for the picture of himself as an adult that he is barely beginning to establish. Through these years the individuals the child admires and would like to be like shift considerably. The first grader may dream of being a teacher, but by third grade it is a ballet dancer whom she would resemble. Gradually her interests shift, and instead of some distant star she begins to play at " dating " and dressing up for the boys, her model the high school girl who lives next door. These varying identifications, though they sometimes frighten parents by their apparent inappropriateness, are in a sense a trying out of roles. As the youngster grows on into adolescence, she will, if all goes well, be ready to select and choose those who are right for her and who can be synthesized into her new image of the person she wishes to be.

The process of identification is similar for both boys and girls. However, the question may well be raised as to whether boys in our society have as good opportunities to make identifications with men as girls do with women. As Blair and Burton have pointed out, there is need for considerable research in this area. For example, do boys who have a close association with men in their home care, in recreation, and in school, react differently from those who lack such contacts? [15]

INTERPERSONAL RELATIONSHIPS

As the child comes into contact with a variety of children and adults outside his family, his contacts with them alter his view of himself, his capabilities, and his potentialities. Nevertheless, his relationships within his family continue to play an important, if not a major, part in his feelings and attitudes.

Relationships Within the Family

The way children of the ages now under consideration view their families has been explored in a study involving psychiatric interviews with some three thousand youngsters and observation of group activities in boys clubs. The children who were happy, friendly, and constructive group-members, revealed a number of significant things about their parents. They saw them as " giving," generous of time, thought, and effort rather than material things. These parents listened to and accepted the child's ideas and ambitions and did not foist theirs upon him. They laughed and joked with their children. When a *good* report card was brought home, they were pleased, but did not attempt to coerce the child into greater effort. If the report card was *poor,* they saw it as an indication of the child's need for help, not for punishment. They assigned children tasks such as lifting, carrying, or fetching, which made the youngsters feel accepted as healthy and strong. In this picture brothers and sisters also had a part. They " fought," wrestled, and played in rough and tumble fashion. They, as well as the parents, were seen as helpful, as doing with the child as well as for him.[16]

These youngsters found within their homes continuing security along with freedom and encouragement to grow. Unfortunately, much as they may consciously desire to do so, not all parents are

[15] Blair and Burton, *op. cit.* P. 216.

[16] Martin, Alexander Reid. " A Study of Parental Attitudes and Their Influence Upon Personality Development." *Education.* 63 (June 1943), 596–608.

able to create this kind of atmosphere. Their own hurts, the lack of appreciation which they felt as children, the ambitions they have for their children's success, all these may get in their way. Many a parent, deeply wounded by his own school experience, vows that what happened to him shall not be repeated. He wants to give the child the help he feels *he* should have had, failing to recognize that his child is different and what was right for him may be wrong for his son. Sometimes the concerns of holding a job, of getting ahead in the world, and of maintaining one's health press too hard, and there is little opportunity for the parent to share with the children in the way these children indicate they like parents to do.

Such sharing is more a matter of spirit and intent than it is of any specific kind of activity on the part of the parent. Here, for example, are some excerpts from a teacher's notes on a happy, energetic 11-year-old Jackie. This youngster has many interests, a good store of knowledge (though he is not much given to book learning) and finds a ready acceptance in his peer group.

We were talking about good manners. Maxine said: " My folks make me say " Thanks for the biscuits," instead of just " I want a biscuit."

Jackie said: " My papa said he was going to slap me if I didn't quit reaching across the table. He make me say ' please ' too." [17]

" Mrs. Adams, I couldn't git my homework. My uncle come last night and we went huntin'."

" What was you huntin'? " asked Bob, the only other child not busy.

" Possums, 'coons, or anything."

" Do you eat 'coons? " asked Bob.

" Naw, shux, they got hands," said Jackie. [18]

Some of the children are bringing samples of handwriting. Bill commented that he " didn't see no use in writin' good."

Jackie said, " My daddy can't read and he can't write nothing but his name, and he can git a job anywhere he wants to." [19]

" We bought us a better house."

" Yea, it used to be a old store," said Tom.

[17] *Fostering Mental Health in Our Schools.* 1950 Yearbook. Association for Supervision and Curriculum Development, National Education Association, Washington, D.C. P. 189.

[18] *Ibid.* Pp. 189–190.

[19] *Ibid.* P. 190.

"Yea, but it sure is a good house. We paid $650 for it."

"Gollee, that old man was high on that ol' place," replied Tom.

"Yea, but it's got four acres around it."

"Who's all them little bitty girls around there?" asked Tom.

"Them's my sisters and they ain't 'all them.' Ain't but three of them. I got one big sister and two little ones and a little brother. . . . If the weather is pretty this weekend we're gonna git our house papered. Our yard is full of old stumps and stuff. I've dug up a whole bunch of them."

"What are you going to do, Jackie, plant grass?" I asked.

"No'm, flowers. Mama's always got to have lots of flowers." [20]

Obviously, Jackie's father's techniques of control are not exemplary. Nevertheless, there is in this family so much warmth, so much appreciation and participation, that Jackie is free to be warm and kindly toward others, including both his sisters and his classmates.

Among the six children, with whom we have been especially concerned, family relationships during this period were quite complex, reflecting in part the strains which all families experienced during the war years, in part the particular strengths and weaknesses of these sets of parents, and of course the individuality of our children and their brothers and sisters.

Jane Warner. More than some mothers, Mrs. Warner seems to have found it difficult to let Jane grow. It was not that she babied her, but rather that she gave her so little leeway to express her own choices. She discovered for example that yellow was an extremely becoming color to her, and that she looked best in dresses made without belts. Jane, it seems, would have preferred pink and yearned for dresses with belts. Another source of irritation to her was her small brother, born when she was nearly 7. Used to having her mother spend considerable time with her, teaching her bits of household lore, it was disconcerting to find herself so often on the periphery of attention. Further, the baby's coming broke into the warmth of the relationship she had had with her father. Bright as she was, she could not have specified all the things which annoyed her, but she did experience an irritation and a disgruntlement which was not openly expressed, but somewhat bottled in, so that she became increasingly less spontaneous in her relationships with her peers and with other adults.

[20] *Ibid.* Pp. 190–191.

Pat Plummer. Pat's relationships within her family during these years were generally warm and satisfying to her. As the youngest she remained the center of attention in much of the visiting and socializing which went on. This approbation plus the fact that she managed to be fairly independent in her neighborhood play, seems to have eased whatever resentment she may have felt toward her parents' reluctance to admit that she was really growing up.

Andrew Drosky. Andy's relationships with his family during this period illustrate nicely the complexity of factors which may influence the way a youngster sees and responds to his parents. It is likely that Andy, having known such encompassing protection from his mother, did experience some resentment as his small sister grew and came into somewhat more direct competition with him. On the other hand, he seemed to find some satisfaction in looking out for her and was generally protective of her. More important, perhaps, was the fact that his father was not particularly well during these years, and his mother was often worried about him. Under these circumstances both of them may have found it less easy to convey to Andy their continuing interests in his activities than might otherwise have been the case. Andy's father was inclined to settle things with him by bribing — " You do this, and I'll give you that," and Andy, it appears, learned to take advantage of the system.

Dan Mallon. Perhaps the most outstanding characteristic of Dan's relationships with his family during this period was the strength of his ties with his sister. She looked up to him, admired him, and appears to have been unusually sympathetic to him. The warm pride in her son's activity, which Dan's mother had appeared to feel when he was small, seems to have been somewhat tempered with concern for his lack of vigorous growth in these years.

Charles Brown. Life in the Brown household was, as always, noisy and spirited. During the early part of these years financial problems took the major part of Mr. Brown's attention. In the latter years his employment involved long hours of overtime, so that Charles and Chet and their older brother continued to be somewhat closer to their mother. Increasingly Charles appears to have found it easier to let Chet take the lead.

Celeste Collins. For the Collins family these were relatively quiet years. From time to time Mrs. Collins worked, and Mr. Collins found his job absorbing. Both of them tended to be somewhat critical of the neighborhood children and to restrict Celeste's contacts with them.

They did appreciate her success in school, and this was perhaps one reason why Celeste accepted their restrictions with relatively little protest. Her relationships with her sister were not particularly close, but neither were there marked disagreements with her.

Satisfactory relationships within the child's family serve as a support to him as he moves out into the world of his peers, where he begins to practice give-and-take among equals. His social skills reflect his learning within his family, but he also has much to learn from the group. Similarly his expectations regarding individuals who are potential group members are largely set by his family's attitudes and expectations. Yet these too may change as he learns.

Relationships Within the Peer Group

When the child begins to go to school and starts to participate in the various recreational and religious activities which his community affords, he comes in contact with a number of youngsters who are about the same age as he. With some of these he may establish close relationships — they become his good friends, the members of his " gang." Such groups are likely to be small, seldom involving more than five or six youngsters. He has more temporary relationships with other children, as he finds himself assigned to this or that work group in his classroom, meets others in Scouts or in Sunday school.

At 6, 7, or 8, the child's group of friends is as likely to have in it both boys and girls. As he grows older, however, he tends to exclude the members of the opposite sex from participation in his group. Since the girls tend to run ahead of the boys developmentally and tend to be interested in the opposite sex earlier, it may be that the boys form their gangs to protect themselves against the girls. Where, for example, one finds a girl member in a gang of boys under the age of twelve, she is characteristically one who apes the boys — a tomboy, rather than one who exploits her femininity. On the other hand, the antagonisms between boys and girls at this stage may be more apparent than real. The teasing the boys do may be an inept expression of their basic interest in the girls. Gallantry, after all, has to be learned. Even while the separate sex groups are maintained, a considerable amount of pairing off may go on.

In occasional small communities a child may work, play, and be good friends with the same group. Most communities, however, are more diverse, and the child has some opportunity to pick and choose his friends. Even where choice is actually limited, youngsters do show preferences. The child society, like the adult society, has its popular members and its unpopular, its leaders and its followers.

The character of the child society depends on the personalities of the children. Youngsters are liked because they have certain approved qualities. The qualities rated as most important tend to reflect the interests of the youngsters at their particular stage of development. For example, popular 11-year-old boys are those who are competent in group games, able to keep a game going, fearless and ready to take a chance, while popular girls of the same age are those who are friendly, pretty, tidy, and gracious.[21]

The older children become, the more difficult it is for the adults to know what goes on in their group life. The parents of a 9-year-old may note that five or six little girls of like age gather in their basement quite regularly, and that the sign on the door reads " Girls' Audubon Club. No boys allowed " but they have to deduce the nature of the activities and character of the social relationships from the relatively few hints dropped by their daughter. They may know that all the members of the club are officers, but they may not know why Mary suddenly stops coming, or why the " meeting " comes to a standstill if for some reason Peggy fails to put in appearance. And the parents of Mary may sense that something is amiss when she begins to come directly home from school every afternoon, but they are likely to find it difficult to appraise why she is no longer accepted in the club group.

Teachers and group leaders are perhaps in a slightly more advantageous position. Not being closely involved with any one child, they may be regarded as more neutral figures by the children. Sensitive adults in this position see, hear, and feel much more than they let on. As they note which children come and go together, who chooses whom in the group games, who sits together at lunch, and so on, they know pretty well what the group structure is, who

---

[21] Tryon, Caroline M. " Evaluations of Adolescent Personality by Adolescents." *Monograph of the Society for Research in Child Development*, No. 4, 1939.

is popular and who is not. It is, however, not always safe to deduce group relationships from what goes on in the classroom. The child who is frequently selected by his classmates to serve as chairman on a committee, for example, is not necessarily the one whose ideas are most accepted in out-of-school activities.

One means of appraising the group relationships is the construction of a sociogram or friendship chart. This is done by asking the children to indicate their choice of companions for some specific activity. For example, one teacher said to her group of 11- and 12-year-olds:

" At various times you have indicated that you would like to make a seating plan for our class. Let's try to work one out together. Here is *one* way to start. On a sheet of paper, please write your name at the top, and then write the name or names of those people that you would like to sit near.

" If it does not matter whom you sit near, then you may not want to write anyone's name. The name closest to your own is the person you would like to sit near *most*. You may write as many or as few names as you wish. Only I will see these slips of paper."

The children's choices were then tallied and ranked and plotted as shown in Figure 8. Note that Nancy with a rank of 1 was chosen more frequently than any other child, while Judy with a rank of 19 was chosen least often. The circles in the diagram represent the girls, while the squares stand for the boys. A solid line indicates a mutual choice. Thus Nancy chooses Harriet, and Harriet chooses Nancy. A dotted line indicates that the child chooses another, but without his choice being reciprocated. Charlotte chooses Anne, but Anne's choices are for Harriet, Sally, and Nancy.

Some subgroups appear, as the triangle of Louise, Barbara, and Marsha, and the cluster of Anne, Nancy, Harriet, Charlotte, and Sally. However, in all instances there are choices outside of each subgroup, so that these are not isolated cliques.

PROBLEM 3. From Figure 8 describe the friendship relationships among the boys in this class.

This method of studying group relationships presents several hazards. If the children do not trust the teacher, they will " fake "

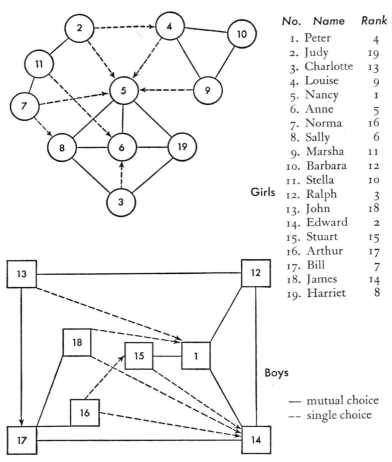

No.	Name	Rank
1.	Peter	4
2.	Judy	19
3.	Charlotte	13
4.	Louise	9
5.	Nancy	1
6.	Anne	5
7.	Norma	16
8.	Sally	6
9.	Marsha	11
10.	Barbara	12
11.	Stella	10
12.	Ralph	3
13.	John	18
14.	Edward	2
15.	Stuart	15
16.	Arthur	17
17.	Bill	7
18.	James	14
19.	Harriet	8

Girls

Boys

— mutual choice
-- single choice

Figure 8. Sociogram for a class of 11- and 12-year-olds, January.

their choices. For example, one second grader confided to her mother that her teacher had asked the group to indicate the children whom they would like to have come to their birthday party. Said the child, " I put down Rachel and Yvonne, because I think the teacher likes them best. But if I *really* had a birthday party, I'd ask Theresa." It is better if the choices made are *actually* used. There are any number of situations in group living in which choices of this kind do need to be made, and the adult can learn much by making note of them. It is also important to bear in mind that group relationships change. Choices for seat mates in school may differ considerably from choices for partners for a ride to a picnic. One realistic youngster, when asked to choose those whom she would like to sit next to, said, " Well, my favorite friend is Ellie, but we whisper too much, so I had better sit next to Grace! "

Individuals also change position as the group gets to know them better, or as group interests shift, or perhaps as the teacher becomes sensitive to those children who can in some subtle ways be helped to contribute in a fashion the other children appreciate. For example, in the class of 11- and 12-year-olds charted in Figure 8 Charlotte attained new status after she had been encouraged to write a play which the class enjoyed presenting.

Figure 9 shows the choices of the group charted in Figure 8 three months later. This time they were choosing individuals whom they would like to have work with them in evaluating a unit of work they were just completing. The diagram suggests the essential stability of the group, but there are some changes. May is a new child in the group. Stuart is no longer attending.

PROBLEM 4. What other differences do you note on this chart as compared with the previous one?

PROBLEM 5. If you are able to observe a class or other group of youngsters over a period of several days or weeks, keep a record of the spontaneous choices you see children make. From this, which children do you believe to be most popular? Also watch for evidence of leadership. Do leadership and popularity coincide? If possible, observe the same group of children with different adults. Do the children's responses to one another differ?

One of the reasons so much importance has been attached to the understanding of the group life of youngsters is the assumption that the ability to get on well with his peers is fundamental to the child's healthy personality development. Basically this is true, but we must not overlook some of its important ramifications.

The mere fact of popularity is not necessarily proof of good personality adjustment. For example, an occasional child in a group may be accepted not so much because he is an active contributor, finding good opportunities in group affairs for the expression of

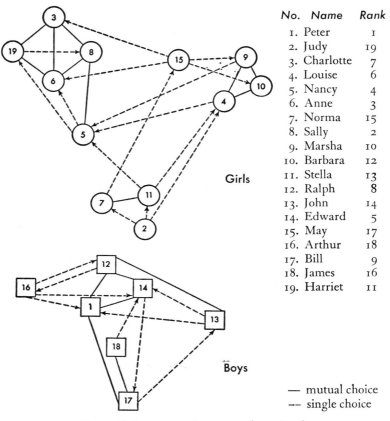

No.	Name	Rank
1.	Peter	1
2.	Judy	19
3.	Charlotte	7
4.	Louise	6
5.	Nancy	4
6.	Anne	3
7.	Norma	15
8.	Sally	2
9.	Marsha	10
10.	Barbara	12
11.	Stella	13
12.	Ralph	8
13.	John	14
14.	Edward	5
15.	May	17
16.	Arthur	18
17.	Bill	9
18.	James	16
19.	Harriet	11

— mutual choice
-- single choice

Figure 9. Sociogram for same class, April.

his own personality, as because he docilely goes along with whatever the rest want. His own self-assertive and aggressive needs may be turned inward, rather than channeled into achievement which would bring him a more genuine kind of satisfaction.[22] It is important to remember that by the time the child reaches school age, he may already have learned to conceal his true feelings, to be alienated from his real self, in a way which is not at all healthy, but

22 See Greenblatt, E. L. "Relationship of Mental Health to Social Status." *Journal of Educational Research.* 44 (1950), 193–204. Also Alexander, Theron, and Alexander, Marie. "Study of Personality and Social Status." *Child Development.* 23 (1952), 207–213 for discussion of this point.

which may deceive the casual onlooker into thinking that he has achieved a serenity which is basically lacking.

PROBLEM 6. Andrew Drosky is an example of a youngster who from time to time achieved a considerable degree of popularity with his peers. Note the comments on his school experience for example. As you review the material in the chapter related to him, consider whether his position in the group was attained as he expressed his true feelings, or as he learned to conceal them.

Teachers and group leaders, though they may be exceedingly astute about the kinds of feelings which may lie hidden well beneath the surface of the child's behavior, cannot know precisely what goes on in the child's inner world. They can, however, be sensitive to the fact that different children will use the same group situation for different purposes, and not assume that what is advantageous, personality-wise, for one youngster, is necessarily so for another.

Also important is the fact that groups differ. A child may find opportunities for healthy self-expression in one group and none at all in another one. For example, an unusually intelligent youngster may be rejected in a group which is not mature enough to appreciate his thinking, while youngsters who see the world pretty much as he does may greatly appreciate him. A quiet gentle child may be "lost" among highly volatile, aggressive peers, and quite a leader among those more like himself.

There is good reason to believe that most individuals learn better in an atmosphere in which they feel wanted and accepted, but if the price of acceptance is conformity to too many group norms, both the individual and the group, in the long run, suffer considerable loss.

Must the small boy, who is more intrigued with butterflies and moths than with baseball be inveigled into the latter? Is the 10-year-old who finds more satisfaction in preparing a family meal than in attending Scout troop meetings necessarily maladjusted? What about the youngster who would rather take the television set apart than watch it? Or the one who would rather read?

Are we, as one author has asserted, bringing up a generation of children who must look always to the approval of the group for their direction?[23] Is it possible to emphasize adjustment to the group to such an extent that the child dares not express the qualities and the ideas which are uniquely his?

The whole matter of how much group life is consonant with the fullest realization of the potentialities of the individual is an important one, and, of course, goes far beyond the scope of the present text. Although we cannot hope to answer the questions which are currently raised, we may, at least, note their relevance to this period of development.

We cannot leave the topic of the relationships within the peer group without noting the extent to which it tends to be structured on the basis of prejudices which the children have learned from their own home and family situation.

According to one study, the social world, as perceived by children even as young as kindergarten age, is differentiated into racial and religious groups. As children grow older, they develop greater awareness of group conflicts, patterns of exclusion and forms of derogation, and greater acceptance of prejudiced attitudes.[24] The effect of this is to deny to certain children the opportunity to participate fully in group life, regardless of how desirable their personality attributes may be. Those who are thus left out have little choice but to band together as best they can, having experienced such humiliation. It is small wonder that they often feel hostile toward their peers who have discriminated against them.

Prejudice often is not merely a matter of information or misinformation acquired from the direct or indirect teaching of the child's family, but may reflect more basic personality characteristics. In one study, for example, children who showed the greatest intolerance toward Jews and Negroes were found to be more constricted, more cynical and fearful, less confident and secure and more suspicious than those who were least prejudiced.[25]

Discrimination is not based entirely on race or religion. Children

[23] Riesman, David. *The Lonely Crowd*. New Haven: Yale University Press, 1950.
[24] Radke, M., and Trager, H. G. " Social Perceptions and Attitudes of Children." *Genetic Psychology Monographs*. 40 (1949), 327–347.
[25] Harris, Dale B., and others. " Children's Ethnic Attitudes: Relationship to Certain Personality Factors." *Child Development*. 21 (1950), 83–91. See also Frenkel-Brunswick, Else, and Havel, J. " Prejudice in the Interviews of Children: Attitudes Toward Minority Groups." *Journal of Genetic Psychology*. 82 (1953), 91–136.

are also aware of socio-economic differences and may select friends in accordance with these. In an old New England community in which adults made rather clear distinctions between upper-middle-class people, the white-collar class, and the working class, the children appeared to choose their friends accordingly. For out-of-school activities, children in grades one and six showed a decided tendency to choose most frequently from their own social class. For in-school activities the same tendency was apparent, although less pronounced. Interestingly, the fourth graders were less inclined to choose according to class position.[26] As the author of the study suggests, this finding may be due to the fact that the working-class youngsters happened to be brighter and hence more likely to take on middle-class behavior. Another explanation of such apparent disregard of social class status is that middle-class youngsters may tend to overlook social class lines at the point when they are forming their own gangs and cliques, that is, at about fourth grade.[27] Some authorities believe the behavior which is typical of the spontaneous group life of the 9-, 10-, and 11-year-olds is patterned on the lower-class child's life in which there is more freedom to explore, and more freeedom to express aggression.[28]

It is quite clear that the prejudices and the discrimination which characterize the adult world do in a variety of ways affect the group life of children. Within such a complex social structure, the problem of how the fullest and best realization of individual personality can be maintained is both troublesome and crucial. Jersild states it thus:

The more fully the members of the majority and the minority, the " ins " and the " outs " and the children of " high " and those of " low " status in the community acquire (in their own self-development) an integrity of their own, the less likely they are to carry further the old prejudices that already exist in the weary and hate-ridden world in which they live and the less need they will have to create a new set of prejudices of their own.[29]

---

[26] Stendler, Celia B. *Children of Brasstown.* Urbana: University of Illinois, 1949.
[27] See Blair and Burton, *op. cit.,* pp. 129–131, for a summary statement of research supporting this possibility.
[28] *Ibid.* Pp. 131–133.
[29] Jersild, Arthur T. *Child Psychology.* New York: Prentice-Hall, 1954. Pp. 297–298.

CHANGING INTELLECTUAL UNDERSTANDING

In Chapter 8 we showed how a young child developed some understanding of the phenomena of ice and melting. We noted that he gradually came to classify certain phenomena as "ice" and to associate with these certain conditions and properties. These processes of classification and association which were described in our illustration continue to operate as the child grows older. However, as the child observes how other people classify objects and as his experiences make possible more and more associations, we expect that he will discriminate more accurately and that the concepts he holds will be increasingly adequate. For example, most children of 6 or older will not mistake crystal or plastic for ice. They have learned to associate a certain degree of coldness with the hardness and transparency which they attribute to "ice." With further experience they may develop understanding of the precise conditions under which ice forms or melts. They note that not until the mercury in the thermometer drops to a certain level does ice appear in the schoolyard puddles. They observe that a bit of ice placed in a pan on a hot stove melts more rapidly than a similar piece left in the sunshine on a winter day. They gradually move from such specific and concrete concepts to those on a more abstract level. For example, the concept of "temperature" becomes meaningful.

As we indicated earlier, there is considerable evidence that the thinking and reasoning processes of children are basically similar to those of adults but more subject to error because of the relative inexperience of the child. On the other hand, there is some evidence which suggests that the child's thinking proceeds through rather clearly defined stages.[30] Certain degrees of abstraction appear to be difficult if not impossible at one age, relatively easy a few years later. Piaget has contended that not until the age of 8 or 9 do the child's ideas concerning a variety of natural phenomena such as plants, animals, the earth, and so on become reasonably correct.[31]

[30] See, for example, Schuessler, Karl, and Strauss, Anselm. "A Study of Concept Formation by Scale Analysis." *American Sociological Review.* 15 (1950), 752–762; Schuessler, Karl, and Strauss, Anselm. "Socialization, Logical Reasoning and Concept Development in the Child." *American Sociological Review.* 16 (1951), 514–523.

[31] Piaget, Jean. *The Child's Conception of the World.* New York: Harcourt, Brace and Company, 1929.

Other studies have not found as rigid dividing lines between the child's way of looking at things at 6 or 7 years and his view at the age of 9 or 11. However, it does appear that beyond the age of 9 the child to a larger extent than previously tends to be realistic and objective in his thinking. Given an opportunity to explain the causes of physical phenomena (for example, what makes the wind blow) he is increasingly likely to offer a logical explanation.[32] His understanding of causal relationships in the area of social affairs appears to develop somewhat more slowly. Children in grades four, five, and six often rather glibly use terms describing various kinds of social relationships without much real understanding of their meaning. A typical example of confusion is that of the 9-year-old whose group leader had been trying to teach her 9-, 10-, and 11-year-old youngsters to apply democratic principles in choosing and organizing their play activities. Irked because he found himself the only member of the group who was disinterested in a particular project, he delivered an ultimatum to the others. " This is a democracy. In a democracy we vote. If you don't vote, then I quit."

When we note that children's social concepts seem to develop somewhat more slowly than some of their concepts concerning the nature of the physical world, we ought not lose sight of the fact that there is much fuzzy thinking in both physical and social areas among adults as well as children. Cronbach points out, " People's meanings are not usually precise. They are not sure just where a concept applies. A *lake* is a body of water — most 6-year-olds have that idea. But how big may it get before we must call it something else? Here is a vast body with no inlet or outlet; can we call it a *lake* even if the map calls it Salton Sea? How about Devil's Lake, which has no stream flowing in or out but is said to be filled by an underground *river?* "[33]

Similar difficulties apply in social areas. Consider, for example, the variety of meanings which a youngster may encounter in using each of the following concepts: Indian, Housing Project, Government, Minority, Communication, President.

[32] Deutsche, Jean M. *The Development of Children's Concepts of Causal Relations*. Minneapolis: University of Minnesota Press, 1937.

[33] Cronbach, Lee J. *Educational Psychology*. New York: Harcourt, Brace and Company, 1954. P. 288.

PROBLEM 7. As you observe children in fourth, fifth, and sixth grades, keep a list of the variety of meanings which you hear children attribute to words such as the above.

Many of the concepts of social relationships which children are expected to acquire appear to be less directly related to their own experiences than are the concepts involving the physical world. Further difficulty may arise from the fact that not until after 11 years of age do most children develop a clear understanding of time in a historical sense.[34] It may be, as Blair and Burton[35] have suggested, that only when the youngster has a clear sense of the relationship between past and present can he comprehend the remote consequences of his own behavior or understand very well the complex patterns by which groups of human beings organize their social living.[36] The general trend of children's intellectual understanding during the years from 6 to 12 is toward increasing objectivity and accuracy. From the age of 9 on, the ability to generalize and to reason logically, particularly in physical and mechanical fields, appears to flourish. Progress in thinking in terms of social concepts is less rapid. However, most children's progress toward understanding of their world is gradual and often uneven. They may be very sophisticated about some of its aspects and quite naïve so far as other aspects are concerned. Children of the same age will differ from one another not only because of their differing intellectual capacities but also because of differing experiences and emotional concerns.

Individual Differences

One of the marks of the highly intelligent child is his ability to generalize — to apply appropriately what he has learned in one experience to a new situation resembling the first. The familiar story of Epaminondas illustrates the problems of the youngster who is unable to differentiate from one situation to another. He may learn

---

[34] Oakden, E. C., and Sturt, Mary. "The Development of the Knowledge of Time in Children." *British Journal of Psychology.* 12 (1922), 309–336. Also Pistor, F. "How Time Concepts Are Acquired by Children." *Educational Method.* 20 (1940), 107–112.

[35] Blair and Burton, *op. cit.* Pp. 160–163.

[36] See Jersild, *op. cit.,* pp. 446–471, for further discussion of children's social concepts.

the "rules," but cannot apply them correctly. Thus, Epaminondas, warned that the proper way to carry his gift of butter was to wrap it in cool green leaves, applied the same technique to a small kitten.

The tale of Epaminondas does not indicate, however, what might have happened had he had repeated experiences carrying each of the several gifts, guided by a teacher who in each instance would help him to analyze which elements in a situation would suggest "wrapping in cool leaves," and which should suggest "tie a string around its neck." Frequently when children appear to be lacking in understanding of some aspect of their world, the basic cause lies not in a lack of sufficient intellectual capacity for understanding but rather in a lack of meaningful experience. For example, a youngster brought up in a remote area of the South in a home without facilities for refrigeration would likely have rather different concepts of "ice" and "melting" than would a northern child. In appraising the intellectual understanding of any child, it is well to consider the extent to which he has had opportunities to develop meanings for the particular concepts he is expected to know.

Recent research also suggests that the emotional concerns of the child may considerably affect his ability to form concepts and to make generalizations. Goldfarb, for example, found that when children whose early infancy had been spent in an institution were compared with children of similar background whose early infancy was spent in foster homes, the institution children showed marked difficulties in thinking "along the lines of abstraction and generalization." [37] Children who have had affectionate care appear to be freer to think in terms of large concepts than those who have lacked such warmth. Clinical experience with emotionally disturbed children also reveals how markedly the child's thinking processes may be distorted under conditions of emotional stress.

The Role of Language Skills

In Chapter 8 we discussed how the child's ability to use language facilitated reasoning and problem solving. In the period now under consideration he develops some important new skills — those of

[37] Goldfarb, William. "Psychological Privation in Infancy and Subsequent Adjustment." *American Journal of Orthopsychiatry.* 15 (1945), 247–255.

reading and writing. The significance of these skills in the development of his intellectual understanding is tremendous. They enable him to expand and to test his concepts in new ways.

The concepts of hardness, coldness, and transparency associated with the spoken word " ice " are also attached to a certain printed configuration — " ice." This same configuration appears in new contexts — a description of the condition of the wings of an airplane under certain kinds of weather conditions or a report of an expedition to the South Pole — and new meanings become associated with it. And so it is with a host of other words, including " melting," " temperature," and " degrees " and eventually, " Fahrenheit " and " Centigrade." When we consider the tremendous number of concepts for which the child must learn a spoken word, a printed word, and a written word, the complexity of the processes of learning reading, writing, and arithmetic become apparent.

Unfortunately the fact that the words the child learns are only symbols for meanings and experiences is sometimes overlooked. The child comes to recognize a word, to say it properly when he comes to it, but he has no idea of its meaning. He " reads " but he does not comprehend. The same state of affairs may occur as the child learns to manipulate number symbols. He may proudly rattle through the multiplication tables but see no relation between them and the problem of whether in four weeks' time he may be able to save sufficient money from his allowance to buy himself a baseball mitt. Undoubtedly, many youngsters fail to learn to use reading and arithmetic skills adequately because they are not helped to bring sufficient meanings to the manipulation of the symbols.

On the other hand, if reading and arithmetic skills are to enhance the child's understanding of his world, he must be able to employ them as efficiently as possible. Adequate provision for his learning will include not only frequent checking and testing of the meanings he associates with the symbols but much practice and drill in using the symbols. His reading teacher will not only want to be sure that he brings several meanings to the word " bear," for example, and chooses the meaning which is appropriate to the context, but he will also want him to have sufficient practice in discrimination so he is sure to see the word as " bear " — not as " hear " or " dear."

Much has been written concerning children who fail in school learning and about those who develop erroneous ideas of the world about them. The fact that some children have such difficulties in learning does not negate the tremendous growth in intellectual understanding which characterizes this period of development. Children in the years 6 to 12 are, in general filled with a zest for knowledge. They revel in acquiring and organizing new facts, in being able to show off new skills. Such understanding is exceedingly important to their self-respect, and basic to their healthy development.

CHANGING VIEWS OF THE SELF

The child carries forward into this period the view of himself which he had begun to formulate during the power-testing period. He appears worthy or unworthy, energetic and enterprising, or constricted and resentful. But this basic picture may be modified as he meets adults and children and has learning experiences outside his family. A child who has been quite uncertain of himself may discover that with a teacher who gives him quiet, gentle approval he dares do many things which once seemed too much for him. A child who has harbored much hostility within him may be relieved as his teacher helps him find constructive channels for his release. On the other hand, a child, whose picture of himself is that of one who explores and experiments, may be made to feel that he is bad when he does so. Thus the adults the child meets can help him to view himself positively and realistically, or they can relate themselves to him in such a way as to make him doubt his own self-worth. The children he meets also contribute to the revision of his self-picture. He compares himself with them, testing his abilities and skills against theirs, and gaining in the process some greater sense of what his own attributes are.

In general, this period of development may be thought of as one in which the child learns to face certain realities about himself. He belongs to a particular sex, family, racial, national, and religious group. He has a certain kind of body and certain facial characteristics. Since growth is relatively slow during this period, he does not have to revise his picture of himself too drastically as he grows older, but some shifts do take place. He has certain kinds of abilities. He can use his fists effectively, construct a model airplane, repair a broken cart, play a game of chess, swim, throw a curve, do long division, and so on.

But all of these are merely personal facts — the various attributes the child has. More important are the attitudes he has toward them. What are his feelings about being left-handed, red-headed, not so good a pitcher as the boy next door, or good in arithmetic and reading, but not so good in swimming or baseball? These feelings will depend on how his attributes are regarded by those around him. If he is constantly belittled for his mediocrity, he will tend to feel more and more unworthy. Unfortunately, in our highly competitive society some youngsters rarely experience the feeling of success and achievement, and the maintenance of a sense of self-worth is difficult if not impossible.

An important shift in the child's view of himself may come from his close friendship with one or more other children of the same sex. With them he may share some of his feelings about himself, and they theirs about themselves. They " understand " one another, and such understanding may bring a healthy perspective on self. One's own fears and apprehensions are not quite so troublesome when one discovers that the other fellows have similar ones. Further, the friend may sometimes help one to acquire new skills and abilities or to accomplish something of which one has been afraid, thus effecting changes in the self-picture.

These changing views of self which we are discussing, can, of course, only be surmised from the child's behavior. The child does not reveal the self he perceives from his inner world, except indirectly. The older he grows, the more important it seems to be for him to keep his view of himself intact. He comes, as it were, to feel comfortable with it, even though it may not be a very flattering view. In such case, he may considerably resist efforts to change. The efforts of well-meaning teachers or other adults to help him may in such instances be distorted in his mind into attempts to destroy his integrity, and he may be quite resistant to them. The child changes his views on himself, it must be remembered, not because someone thinks he should, but because he has lived through experiences in which he has *felt* himself to be different from what he was.

The Role of Anxiety

Provided that the child approaches this stage of development with a considerable inclination to trust other human beings, a good sense of self-worth, and already developed initiative, it would appear that he should be rather well equipped to ward off anxiety. It is well that he should be, for the demands of the period are many and circumstances may be such as to arouse at least temporary anxiety in many youngsters.

A potential source of anxiety lies in learning itself. In order to develop competence, whether in school subjects or in other skills, one must both pay attention and practice. In neither of these activities is there necessarily any immediate reward. The story or the information which the 6- or 7-year-old gets as he struggles with beginning reading is seldom of such intrinsic interest as to outweigh all the other activities in which he could participate. The youngster submits to the requirements for learning at least in the beginning not because he sees himself as being better off because of his accomplishment, but rather because he derives satisfaction from the approval of his teacher or some other adult who is important to him. When approval is lacking, the learning situation becomes threatening in much the same way that the loss of love presents a hazard to the younger child. Most youngsters are sure enough of affection from some source so that they are able to cope with this hazard, but others already uncertain about their acceptance become completely blocked.

Difficulties in certain specific learnings often originate in an experience with undue anxiety. Thus a youngster may always have trouble with arithmetic processes which he should have learned, but didn't because a particular teacher's sarcasm touched off more anxiety than he could bear. We are not implying here that teachers should not be critical of children's errors. On the contrary, a failure to correct them may lead to their perpetuation. We are suggesting that the teacher needs to be sensitive to the ways in which a child who is anxious responds, and to the fact that inattention, apparent lack of interest, and even a " fresh " attitude may bespeak the child who is basically frightened and scared to try.

Anxiety may also be engendered in the child's relationships with his peers. It is easy for adults to assume that in the child's play life, he does whatever he pleases. Actually, the demands on him may be as great or greater than in situations in which he is under close adult supervision. The expectations of the peer group for accomplishment, their I-dare-ya's, their willingness to talk about or even explore matters which the child has been taught are forbidden or dangerous, their defiance of the adult standards, all of these are sources of real anguish for many children. In our culture some such experiences seem to be necessary for the child's eventual emancipation from childish immaturity. But if they are to be helpful and not harmful, they do seem to demand that adults, sensitive to such trials and tribulations, stand by, ready to comfort and support, and once in a while to referee.

Contribution of This Period to Personality Development

Erikson sees the central conflict of this period as that between feelings of industry and accomplishment and those of inferiority. Through its resolution the child learns to be a worker and potential provider. He learns to use tools and skills, to enjoy the pleasure of work. The danger of the period, as Erikson views it, lies in the possibility that the child may learn to feel inadequate in using the tools or skills of the society in which he lives. Or he may despair of his status among his peers. Under these circumstances his ego is constricted, and he is unable to identify with the wider society.[38]

We have implied throughout this chapter that, as society changes so that the work of adults is less tangible to children and rests more and more on the ability to manipulate symbols, the problem of accomplishment for children becomes more difficult. Too narrow a focus on academic skills and learnings means certain failure for some children. To find avenues of expression for all youngsters, while not minimizing the importance of what has been traditionally regarded as " school " learning, constitutes the main challenge of this period.

So far as the youngsters, on whom our interest has been centered, are concerned, all of them were capable of achieving a considerable sense of accomplishment in their school work and in a variety of

[38] Erikson, Erik. *Childhood and Society*. New York: W. W. Norton & Company, 1950. P. 227.

other areas as well. Nevertheless, these years do not seem to have added as much strength in this area as we might have anticipated from our knowledge of them at age 6. There are a number of factors which may account for this. One is the possibility that the involvement of the adults who were close to them in matters related to the war effort precluded their spending as much time teaching them their own interests and hobbies. By and large the six children were not reached by any community programs for children which might have made up for this lack. Another possibility is that the schools which they attended focused pretty much on academic achievement, so that the opportunity for a variety of accomplishments was somewhat limited. Finally, it may be that the personality component with which we are here concerned is difficult to appraise at a stage when youngsters do not too readily reveal basic interests and concerns.

Jane Warner. As Jane approaches 12, she spends more and more of her time " just reading." With her fine mind, it is obvious that during this period she has acquired a considerable amount of knowledge, but she does not seem to be a " do-er." It seems likely that Jane suffered feelings of inferiority and inadequacy at least as often as she felt the joy of accomplishment, or at least that she may have forestalled such feelings by participating as little as she could in the child life around her.

Pat Plummer. In Pat's case, accomplishment so far as school is concerned was not outstanding. In the light of her general abilities it may be considered adequate. However, her skill in dancing, which she continued to practice through these years, seemed a very positive factor in her development.

Andrew Drosky. Andy, like Jane, could have derived a considerable sense of accomplishment from his school, but he did not seem to do so. He had an excellent physique, but did not take a really active interest in athletics until toward the end of this period — although he participated a good bit in various games. That he did not always feel completely adequate, is suggested by his definition of the word " courage " on a mental test at the age of 9 — " Brave, that's not me, I'm a coward."

Dan Mallon. Considering Dan's small size, it is not surprising to find that he did not seem to feel any great sense of accomplishment during these years. Objectively, he did well, maintaining a good school record, and learning all of the games of his peers (swimming gave him considerable difficulty, however).

Charles Brown. Charlie somewhat more than the other youngsters seems to have developed a good sense of accomplishment during this period. His school record was good, he was capable in physical activities, and he seemed increasingly to feel himself adequate in most situations.

Celeste Collins. Celeste, particularly toward the end of this period, always gave the impression of being one who felt somewhat inadequate. Yet there is no question but that she derived an important sense of accomplishment from her good progress in school.

PROBLEM 8. To what extent might the development of feelings of industry or accomplishment during this period have been hampered by earlier experiences the children had had?

DESIRABLE GUIDANCE IN THE YEARS FROM 6 TO 12

What do these busy, active, noisy school-age children, seemingly so self-sufficient, so intent on their own affairs, want and need from their parents, their teachers, their group leaders? Some things are basically no different from what they wanted when they were 3, 4, and 5 — warm acceptance, faith in their potentiality for growth and learning, the protection which comes from reasonable limits, all this plus help in learning and achieving.

Just as the years before 6 demanded adults who could face the strong feelings of the child, this period, too, has its requirements. One of the most rigorous of these is the ability to withstand comparison. The child no longer moves in a world bounded by mother and father. As he finds out what other adults are like and discovers ways of doing things different from those he has learned at home, he questions both the familiar and the new. " I wish you'd wear a *dress* and a *hat,* and *high* heels when you come to our party today — the other mothers do," says Betty. Her mother, contemplating the tweed suit and sturdy oxfords she has so long regarded as appropriate for such affairs, needs a good sense of humor to see her through.

" Syd's father's teaching him how to box. I guess you never boxed, did you, Daddy? " says Mark. No, but Mark's daddy has spent long hours with him tramping through woodland, introducing him to all kinds of nature lore. No wonder he feels some irritation.

And so it goes. The child needs parents who are persons in their own right, who admittedly have certain likes and dislikes, who do some things well, some things badly, and some things not at all. They need not make themselves over to meet the child's demands, but, on the other hand, they do need enough flexibility to let him seek other models for identification without feeling that they have failed because they cannot serve.

To a much greater extent than in the early years, parenthood in this period becomes a matter of standing by, a source of protection when needed. Children have to do their growing on their own. As one youngster put it, when her mother inquired as to what she was doing, " I'm not doing anything, Mother. I'm just being. Can't you let me be? " Yet some recognition of growing up is in order, some loosening of rules and regulations, some increasing of both privileges and responsibilities.

The difficulty is that as children grow toward 9 and 10, they seem so grown-up one day, so careless and childish the next, that parents (and teachers) are often perplexed as to what to expect. In this chapter we have gone into some of the reasons why children's behavior in the latter part of this period may be so unpredictable. But at this point we may sound a note of warning. It is just possible that adult expectations for difficult behavior on the part of the preadolescent child tend to make them see him as more troublesome than he really is. Perhaps the period is a time " when the nicest children often begin to behave in the most awful way," when teachers of the fourth grade do consider marrying men they do not love in order to escape the 10-year-olds,[39] and when " some parents dislike their offspring intensely." [40] The fact remains that *some* teachers infinitely prefer to teach fourth and fifth grade to any other age level, and there are plenty of parents who find these years fascinating. Such adults, it seems, are not unduly disturbed by child rebellion.

Basic to this period is the child's need to feel himself an accom-

[39] Blair and Burton, *op. cit.* P. 1. The first statement is quoted from Fritz Redl.
[40] Reynolds, Martha May. *Children from Seed to Saplings.* New York: McGraw-Hill Company, 1951. P. 169.

plisher. The primary burden for this rests with the school to which is delegated the task of teaching the skills necessary for coping with the physical and social world. Giving the child the sense of achievement he so needs is no mere matter of seeing that all children receive good marks and are promoted from grade to grade. It means appraising the child's abilities, his assets, and his liabilities, seeing that in the light of these he is given a real challenge and that he is helped to meet it adequately. In the light of the variety of backgrounds of youngsters coming to the schools and all that remains to be known about the most effective ways of helping children learn, this places no small demand upon the school and upon teachers.

Finally, we note that it is in this period that signals of later difficulty often appear. The child who is emotionally ill, and the child who is potentially delinquent, can be " spotted " at this time, and the possibilities for treatment and correction are much better during these years than they will be if he is permitted to go on into adolescence unaided.

11

Learning to Be Adults:

Biological and Social Aspects of Development in the Years 12 to 18

TWELVE TO 18, a span of years within which boys and girls — some earlier, some later — take on the physical appearance of men and women and come to think and to feel not as children but as adults. This is the usual period of adolescence.

Drop into a seventh-grade classroom to see 12-year-olds in action. Even in a study period they are in motion — shifting their weight from one side to the other, stretching their legs under their desks, clasping hands behind their heads and yawning exaggeratedly, drumming with their fingers while lost in daydreams. A few of the girls have clearly already reached womanly status, while others are still flat-chested and slim-hipped. Many of the boys retain their little boy look, but some are longer legged than others. In contrast we may think of the 18-year-olds described in the first chapter of this book — no longer children, but young adults.

The intervening years are marked for some youngsters by storm and stress. Others pass through them with relative tranquillity. Typically, however, the behavior of adolescents growing up in the United States seems colorful and conspicuous. They congregate in noisy groups in the school corridors, a popular drugstore or lunch-

In adolescence the peer group assumes major importance.

eonette, or even on the street corners. They form cliques and crowds, gradually pairing off, and perhaps " going steady." Dances, parties, and picnics become popular as the boys gradually learn to accept the girls' ideas as to what constitutes a good time. Increasingly they seek diversion away from home. The movies, the roller-skating rink, the amusement park, and the high school basketball and football games are major attractions with much attendant ritual. " Everybody " wears kerchiefs to the rink, the team's colors in their hair or perhaps on their socks to the game; " nobody " goes to the local hot-dog wagon for refreshments afterwards, but " everybody " drives ten miles to a similar eating place in the next town. But wherever they go, their lack of adult decorum is fairly predictable. Shrieks, swoons, and raucous horseplay are " normal " for most teenagers.

Rebellion against parental wishes may also be regarded as typical. The hour at which one is expected to be in, clothing which the parent insists is inappropriate, the friends one wishes to keep, the course one is to take in school, the plans one makes for a vacation, these and a thousand other matters may set off argument and dissension, and even open defiance.

Yet to emphasize these colorful aspects of adolescence too much may be to overlook other and equally important facts of development during this period. Most youngsters come through adolescence relatively unscathed and emerge from it quite able to take their places in adult society. The years of socializing with their peers, of frolic, and apparent nonsense are also years of learning and often of thoughtful reflection on the world and one's place in it. Some youngsters, in fact, " settle down " in relative sobriety even before the age of 18.

Adolescence may be thought of as a transitional period between childhood and adulthood, and it is to be distinguished from *pubescence,* a term referring more specifically to the period during which certain bodily changes accompanying sexual maturation occur. The age of pubescence usually lasts only two or three years, but it may begin with some girls as early as 10 and with others as late as 14 and with boys at 12 to 16. Hence, youngsters may be undergoing pubescent changes at any age between 10 and 18. For any one individual such changes will, of course, extend through only a portion of these years, but will usually come considerably before the young person's adult status receives social recognition. He must attend school at least until he is 16, and in many instances he continues to be a student well into his 20's. He is not permitted a full-time job before the age of 16. He is subject to the draft at 18, but not until 21 does he acquire the full rights of citizenship. Thus our society tends to prolong the period of adolescence.

Adolescence may also be extended by the individual himself. To come to terms with oneself, to establish a personal identity, to decide for oneself the kind of job that is most appropriate, to face honestly one's potentialities for marriage and parenthood, these are the demands which full-fledged adulthood makes on young people. Some, never having faced their own feelings as children, lacking convictions as to their own self-worth, doubting their own initiative and accomplishment, need many years beyond the teens to establish themselves as adults. Others remain perennial adolescents.

The achievement of adulthood brings no necessary cessation of psychological growth. Indeed, the depth and richness of personality may increase throughout all the years of life. But an important step toward such fulfillment is the individual's recognition and appreciation of himself as an adult. It is during the period of adolescence that the individual learns such self-regard. An essential part of this is learning to live with an adult body. We give our first consideration to biological aspects of development in years from 12 to 18.

BIOLOGICAL ASPECTS OF DEVELOPMENT

The observable body changes associated with pubescence follow pretty much the same sequence in all individuals. For girls this is reported to be: [1] initial enlargement of the breasts; appearance of straight, pigmented pubic hair; age of maximum growth; appearance of kinky pubic hair; first menstruation; and growth of axillary hair. In boys the sequence is: beginning growth of the testes; first pubic hair (straight, pigmented); early voice changes; first ejaculation; kinky pubic hair; age of maximum growth; axillary hair;

[1] Ausubel, David. *Theory and Problems of Adolescent Development.* New York: Grune and Stratton, 1954. P. 95.

marked voice changes; and development of the beard. These changes are but outward evidence of complex shifts which affect practically every system of the body. The extent to which the individual finds such changes disturbing and difficult depends on his particular physiological adaptibility, and, in part, on their timing. For many adolescents, physiological adjustments are rapid and abrupt and the individual's physiological equilibrium is considerably upset until the organism has learned to utilize its available adaptive mechanisms.[2] But even when this "physiological learning" goes on relatively smoothly the fact that the individual experiences it earlier or later than his peers may be psychologically upsetting to him. The late-maturing boy muscularly equipped for track (and not too well at that) at an age when his brawnier peers are football heroes, secretly despairing of his manliness, and in contrast, the early maturing girl harassed by a too obvious femininity, while her erstwhile chums are still collecting dolls, seem most beset by changes which seem to them ill-timed. But the early-maturing boy who tends to be "well-padded" and may be labeled "fat" by his more rangy contemporaries has his problems, just as does the late-maturing girl whose failure to properly fill out an evening dress may be a source of unacknowledged but nonetheless real anguish.

PROBLEM 1. Review the progress of your own physical development in adolescence. Compared to your friends, was it slower, faster, or parallel? Which aspects of the changes it brought, if any, did you find difficult or disagreeable? Which ones pleasant and welcome? PROBLEM 2. If possible plan opportunities to observe young people of known ages together. One observation in a junior high school and one in a senior high school should give good variety. Focus your observations particularly on physical likenesses and differences among those of the same chronological age. Compare girls with boys.

The volume of research related to the changes associated with pubescence is tremendous. Average trends of growth have been established for height and weight and for the various organs and systems of the body. The relationships among the different aspects of growth have been explored. Longitudinal studies in which

[2] Shock, Nathan W. "Some Physiological Aspects of Adolescence." Reprinted in *The Adolescent, A Book of Readings,* edited by Seidman. New York: Dryden Press, 1954. P. 129.

youngsters have been followed throughout the period of adolescence have highlighted the significance of individual variability. Within the limitations of a text such as this we cannot hope to do justice to what is known in this area. Instead we shall focus on a few findings that may help us to understand the nature of the adjustments the young person makes during this period. We shall consider some of the physiological aspects of pubescence before we turn to the matter of physical growth and motor development.

Physiological Aspects of Development

Basic to the growth process, and precipitating the changes of pubescence, are the activities of the endocrine glands, the pituitary, the adrenals, and the gonads (the ovaries and the testes). Each of these secretes hormones, substances which are carried to all parts of the body through the blood stream and which serve to regulate various bodily functions. Pubescence appears to be initiated by the activation of certain growth hormones of the anterior pituitary gland. These hormones stimulate the growth of the testes and ovaries and increase production of male and female sex hormones. Present knowledge of hormone production is based largely on studies of the amounts found to be excreted in the urine. Before the age of 11 both boys and girls excrete both male and female sex hormones. After this age, these hormones increase differentially in the two sexes. Much research has been and continues to be devoted to the relationships between hormone production and other aspects of pubescence. Its significance for our purposes is suggested by Stuart when he says: " With several hormones being produced and interacting on each other, the variations in the timing, character and magnitude of adolescent growth and sexual differentiation are readily understandable. Furthermore, with the production of both male and female by both sexes and in different amounts between individuals, various degrees of femininity in boys and masculinity in girls are to be expected." [3]

Primary sexual characteristics. The organs actually involved in copulation and reproduction are customarily designated as primary

[3] Stuart, Harold C. " Normal Growth and Development During Adolescence." Reprinted in *The Adolescent, A Book of Readings,* edited by Seidman. New York: Dryden Press, 1954. P. 113.

sex characteristics whereas various other physical features which serve to indicate masculinity or femininity are considered secondary.

In boys growth of the testes and of the penis begins to accelerate at about the age of 11 and continues most rapidly through the period of maximum growth in height. The production of mature sperm cells is not established on the average until 15 or 16 years of age, and full sexual maturity probably is not attained until after general growth has slowed down, if not actually ceased. The extent of normal variation is, however, extremely great as is suggested by studies of the growth of the testes. For example, while for 80 percent of the boys in one group studied the age of onset of rapid growth of the testes was between 12 and 16 years, the range of termination of this rapid growth was from 16 to 20 years. Thus, "excluding the extremely advanced and the extremely retarded boys, there was still four years difference in the time of occurrence of these changes."[4]

As Ausubel has noted, the growth of the major sex organs may be of considerable psychological significance to the boy because of "the firmly-rooted belief of our folk-lore that the size of the external genitalia is closely correlated with and symbolic of masculine virility and potency." "Unfortunately," he adds, "adolescent boys are bound by the tyranny of the norm and have little regard for individual differences."[5]

With girls the occurrence of the first menstrual period is evidence that the development of the sex organs has progressed a long way, but the ovaries and uterus are still far from functional maturity and adult size. According to various studies the average age of first menstruation in the United States is about 13 years with a range between 11 and 15. Irregularity of function is rather typical for about two years following this. As with boys, it has been difficult to establish the stage of development at which the individual becomes capable of reproduction, but conception does not usually occur in the first year following the onset of menstruation, and relatively seldom before the age of 16.[6]

Secondary sex characteristics. The secondary sex characteristics, development of the breasts, changes in body contour, in the texture

---

[4] *Ibid.* P. 100.   [5] Ausubel, *op. cit.* P. 82.   [6] Stuart, *op. cit.* Pp. 104–106.

and distribution of hair, in the voice, and in the skin glands psychologically speaking are of almost greater significance than the primary characteristics. They are more directly observable, and it is on them that appraisal of the individual's attractiveness as a male or female person is made. Further, in these traits masculinity and femininity overlap. Thus hairiness, which tends to be associated with masculinity, is also evident in the female. Curves tend to be regarded as appropriate to the female, wiriness and muscularity to the male. Yet individuals with quite adequate male sex organs may be rounded in contour, others not richly endowed as to beard whereas equally adequate females may tend to boyish figures and considerably more hairiness than their sisters. Such deviations may stem from hereditary differences in structure from hormonal malfunctioning or from differences in growth pattern.[7] There is, for example, some tendency for early maturing boys to approximate the broad-hipped, narrow-shoulder pattern regarded as feminine, whereas late-maturing girls tend to be relatively broad-shouldered and narrow-hipped in what is usually regarded as masculine fashion.[8]

Changes in glands of the skin. Changes in the sweat- and oil-producing glands of the skin occur in both boys and girls and are closely related to sexual maturity and functioning. Sweat glands in the armpit and genital regions become markedly active. Many an adolescent urged on both by advertisements which equate attractiveness to the opposite sex with " pleasant " body odors and by the derogatory comments of his peers toward anyone or anything which " smells," wages interminable battle with his own body odors. The tendency for the oil-producing glands in the skin to become increasingly active frequently leads to acne, a skin disturbance which most adolescents fail to escape. (According to one authority 70 percent of boys show some acne during puberty.[9])

Other physiological changes. We have already indicated that a con-

[7] Ausubel, *op. cit.* Pp. 82, 86.
[8] Bayley, Nancy, and Tuddenham, Read D. "Adolescent Changes in Body Build." *The Forty-third Yearbook of the National Society for Education.* Part I, "Adolescence." Chicago: University of Chicago Press, 1944. Pp. 33–35.
[9] Stolz, Herbert R., and Stolz, Lois Meek. "Adolescent Problems Related to Somatic Variations." *The Forty-third Yearbook of the National Society for the Study of Education.* Part I, "Adolescence." Chicago: University of Chicago Press, 1944. P. 94.

siderable amount of what may be called "physiological learning" goes on during this period. Examples of such changing in the functioning of the body can be seen in increasing blood pressure as the heart increases in size and the blood vessels increase in tonus. Sex differences are also evident, with boys showing a greater increase in systolic pressure (the pressure attained on contraction of the heart) than girls. Correspondingly, pulse rate tends to drop. Whether or not the greater cardiac capacity of the adolescent as compared with the younger child involves less physiological strain (as measured by recovery time) for an equivalent amount of exercise is not clear.[10]

Another instance of change is found in apparently increased respiratory capacity as the chest cavity and the lungs are enlarged. However, when body size is taken into consideration, it becomes apparent that respiratory capacity does not increase as rapidly as general body growth. Beyond pubescence the boys are increasingly superior to the girls.[11]

Food intake. Because it is a period of rapid growth the young person's capacity for food shows a marked increase during adolescence. Contrary to popular notion, the food needs of the adolescent are basically similar to those of the adult or of the school-age child except that larger amounts of the foods essential for the building of muscle and bone are required. The fact that young people so often cluster about the soda fountain consuming large quantities of soft drinks, hot dogs, and hamburgers should not be taken to mean that these foods are dictated by any physiological peculiarities of adolescence. Such food tastes are socially dictated, and unless supplemented by a better-balanced diet at other meals will not suffice to maintain the young person in blooming good health.[12] Aside from instances where the food consumption is inadequate because of the poor dietary habits of his family (whether these be attributable to economic or other factors) psychological factors are probably most

[10] Ausubel, *op. cit.* Pp. 97–98.
[11] *Ibid.* P. 99.
[12] Kuhlen, Raymond G. *The Psychology of Adolescent Development.* New York: Harper and Brothers, 1952. P. 69. See also Breckenridge, Marian, and Vincent, E. Lee. *Child Development.* Philadelphia: W. B. Saunders and Company, 1949. Pp. 162–165.

often responsible for poor nutrition in adolescence. A moody youngster, annoyed with his family and wishing to demonstrate his re-
belliousness, may fail to put in appearance at family mealtimes,
or may eat pickily. An unhappy youngster may eat to comfort himself. Or, unduly concerned with her appearance, a girl may diet
unwisely.

Changes in endocrine functioning. Other physiological changes in
adolescence stem from the effects on other glands of the increased
functioning of the endocrine glands specifically related to sexual
maturation. Basal metabolic rates, for example, reflect changes in
the functioning of the thyroid. The general trend is toward a gradual decrease in basal metabolic rate throughout adolescence, with the
rate of fall very small for girls by the age of 16 or 17, but continuing
beyond the age of 18 in boys. However, this pattern, as is typical of
most of the patterns of physiological functioning in adolescence, is
seldom as uniform and even in the individual as it appears to be
when the average is considered. It seems that we cannot overempha-
size the fact that " wide individual differences in patterns and rate
of physiological development occur among so-called ' normal ' children and that children of the same chronological age may be quite
unlike in their degree of physiological maturity." [13]

That the period during which the youngster moves toward physiological maturity is one in which the " internal environment is in a
state of flux " is clear.[14] But whether or not these inner fluctuations
become outwardly disturbing seems also to be a matter of individual
difference.

Physical Growth and Motor Development

Individuality is also apparent in the way young people take on
the stature and acquire the muscular strength and skill of adulthood.

Changes in height and weight. As we indicated in the previous
chapter, acceleration of growth in height and weight, particularly
for girls, may begin before the age of 12. According to one longi-

---

[13] Shock, *op. cit.* P. 125.

[14] Shock, Nathan W. "Physiological Changes in Adolescence." *The Forty-third
Yearbook of the National Society for the Study of Education,* Part I, " Adolescence." Chicago: University of Chicago Press, 1944. P. 57.

tudinal study, average growth in height in girls increases steadily from 9 to 12 years, and in boys from 11 to 14 years. The rate of increase begins to slow down after the age of 13 in girls and 15 in boys. Girls tend to be taller than boys of the same age during the years between 11 and 13. Gains in weight tend to parallel gains in height although the rate of gain is more rapid than for height.[15]

Different parts of the body grow at different rates, a fact to which the various growth studies have given consideration by measurement of sitting as well as standing height, breadth of shoulders, chest, hips, and so on. The period of adolescent acceleration of growth is also entered upon by different individuals at different times. Body proportions thus tend to differ somewhat when children who are early maturers are compared with late maturers. For example, during the preadolescent years the legs tend to grow somewhat more rapidly than the trunk. In the late maturers more rapid growth in the legs continues for a longer period than in the early maturers so that they tend to end up as somewhat longer-legged individuals than the early maturers.[16]

This point is illustrated in Figure 10. The three boys on the left of the illustration are all 15 years old, but the one on the extreme left is postpubescent, while the one in the middle is pubescent, and the one at the right is prepubescent. In contrast, the chronological ages of the three boys on the right are in inverse order to their physical size: The boy on the left is 13 years and 1 month and is postpubescent. The middle one, 13 years and 5 months, is pubescent, and the one at the right is 14 years and 6 months and is prepubescent.

The general trend of differences between those who mature very early and those who mature very late have been summarized by Stuart:

The maximum increment (of growth) is greater in amount; the whole cycle is completed in a shorter time; the children are larger (than their age mates) before maximum growth but are likely to be more alike or even shorter at the end because growth is completed more quickly; and maximal growth occurs early rather typically in broad-hipped persons

---

[15] Simmons, K. " The Brush Foundation Study of Child Growth and Development. II, Physical Growth and Development." *Monographs of the Society for Research in Child Development,* Vol. 9, No. 1, 1944.
[16] Bayley and Tuddenham, *op. cit.* Pp. 38–50.

and those with relatively short legs — that is, in those with a feminine configuration.[17]

Skeletal development. In previous chapters we have indicated the close relationships between progress in skeletal development and progress toward sexual maturity. As we should expect, girls, on the average, at about the age of 12 are advanced in skeletal develop-

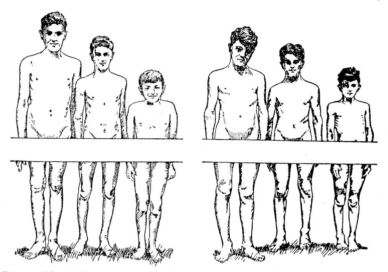

Figure 10. Different stages of pubescent growth. (*From Hedley S. Dimock. Rediscovering the Adolescent. New York: Association Press, 1937.*)

ment about two years over boys of the same age. During the years under consideration the proportion of bony tissue to cartilagenous tissue increases. The breadth of the bones of the arms and legs increases and the characteristic male or female adult structure is achieved.

Muscular and motor development. As the bony structure grows, so does the musculature surrounding it. Sex differences are, however, increasingly apparent. The increase in amount of muscular tissue as in bone tissue is greater for boys than for girls. In addition, the girls who throughout the growth period have shown a

[17] Stuart, *op. cit.* P. 95.

consistent pattern of greater fat thickness than boys continue to show an increase in fat tissue while the boys' fat tissue begins to decline relative to other tissue.[18]

As the individual's musculature increases so does his strength. Thus, youngsters who are pubescent are consistently stronger than those who have not yet reached pubescence. Girls tend to reach their peak of growth in strength somewhat before the boys. The boys' growth in this area continues rapidly for some time.[19] Thus, the already existent superiority of boys over girls is accentuated.

The competence and efficiency in the use of one's body which may be regarded as useful at all stages of development become especially important to the adolescent. Considerable social prestige is attached to athletic accomplishments, and awkwardness becomes a social hazard for both boys and girls. That many youngsters suffer from clumsiness and ineptness during this period seems fairly well established, but the question as to whether the factors responsible for it are primarily biological or primarily social is controversial. Undoubtedly some of it stems from a lack of experience and from self-consciousness. On the other hand, the fact that structural growth may take place rather rapidly, that functional capacity tends to be attained subsequently to such growth, and that there may be rather sudden shifts in body proportions suggest that at least for some youngsters awkwardness may be largely a product of biological factors.[20] Posture commonly improves late in adolescence in association with growth of muscles, increase in tone and strength of ligaments, and improved structural and functional relations with skeletal parts.

Fine muscle co-ordinations do not appear to be much involved in the changes of pubescence. Moreover, they do not seem to be so closely interrelated as are gross motor abilities. There does not, for example, seem to be any general mechanical ability, but rather an individual may be very skillful in one kind of activity and rela-

[18] Reynolds, Earle L. "The Distribution of Subcutaneous Fat in Childhood and Adolescence." *Monographs of the Society for Research in Child Development*, Vol. 15, No. 1, Serial No. 50, 1951.

[19] Jones, Harold E. *Motor Performance and Growth, A Developmental Study of Static Dynamometric Strength*. Berkeley: University of California Press, 1949.

[20] Ausubel, *op. cit.* Pp. 126–127.

tively clumsy in another.[21] Further, there seem to be relatively small differences between the sexes except those which can be attributed to differential opportunities for practice.

We may turn now to the experience of the six young people on whom our attention has been focused to see some of the variations which may characterize " normal " adolescence.

Jane Warner. Breast development began at the age of 11, first menstruation came at 13 years and 4 months.[22] Although periods following exhibited some irregularity, there were no other menstrual difficulties.

Jane, as we have noted, tended to be somewhat obese. From time to time owing to her efforts to control this through diet her total food intake was inadequate. She was relatively inactive until the age of 15 when she began to participate in some sports, and became fairly competent in the use of her body.

Pat Plummer. Pat's period of maximum growth came during the twelfth year. She gained relatively little in height but put on a considerable amount of weight. In skeletal age she tended to be advanced throughout the period from 13 to 18 years. Her first menstruation came at 12 years and 3 months. Regularity was established early, but her periods tended to be painful. At the age of 14 she was subject to acne. She tended toward a somewhat inadequate diet, low in milk, eggs, and vegetables and rather high in carbohydrates. This, however, can most likely be attributed to a continuation of poor dietary habits from childhood rather than to any problems specifically related to adolescence.

Andrew Drosky. Consistently, Andy's physique was such as to warrant favorable comment. He was of average build, but tall and well-proportioned. His period of maximum growth came in the year following his thirteenth birthday. Pubic hair was somewhat evident at 13, and had taken on a characteristic adult pattern of distribution by the age of 14. By 15 his external genitalia were fully developed. He had begun shaving at 14 and had a considerable beard at 15. He suffered from acne from the time he was 15 until about 17. Interestingly, despite his

---

[21] Jones, Harold E., and Seashore, Robert H. " The Development of Fine Motor and Mechanical Abilities." *The Forty-third Yearbook of the National Society for the Study of Education.* Chicago: University of Chicago Press, 1944. Pp. 123–145.

[22] Fels Institute Studies found breast development began on the average two years prior to menarche. See Reynolds, E. L., and Wines, Janet L. " Individual Differences in Physical Changes Associated with Adolescence in Girls." *American Journal of Diseases of Children.* 75 (1948), 329.

fine physique and good motor abilities he was only moderately interested in sports, liking swimming and track about as well as football.

Dan Mallon. Dan, it will be remembered, tended throughout childhood to be a rather slender youngster, active, but not vigorous. Adolescence, however, brought him into the average group for both height and weight. His maximum growth occurred between the ages of 13 and 14½. By the age of 16 genitalia were mature, and by 18 his beard had taken on typical adult characteristics. He had relatively little acne. So far as activity was concerned, Dan was consistently interested in many sports but was not markedly successful in them until the age of 16 when he made the football, basketball, and baseball teams.

Charles Brown. Charles' progress toward maturity appears to have been slightly slower than either Dan's or Andy's. His maximum growth period was in the year from 13 to 14, but he gained almost the same amount in height and more than half as much in weight in the following year. By 16 his pubic hair had taken on adult characteristics and his voice had deepened. His beard grew slowly and was not extensive at 18. He was interested in many sports and generally competent in them. His body mechanics were unusually good so that despite his average size he gave a good impression of bodily strength and vigor.

Celeste Collins. Celeste's first menstruation and year of maximum growth occurred prior to the age of 12. She was troubled with considerable menstrual irregularity throughout the period of adolescence. Aside from the difficulties related to this, these years in many ways appear to have been good ones for Celeste. At 14 she became interested in sports and considerably more active in them than before. Particularly noteworthy is the improvement made in the use of her body. Her posture which had always been fair or poor was, by the age of 16, excellent.

PROBLEM 3. On the basis of what you already know of these young people, what effect would you expect these patterns of physical maturing to have on their social and emotional adjustments during the years 12 to 18?

Mental Development

As we have previously suggested, intellectual development is considerably more difficult to appraise than is physical development. According to present evidence, mental development shows no such accelerated period as we find in physical development.[23] Indeed, there is some thought that the vicissitudes of early adolescence may momentarily slow down intellectual development, but this has not yet been established.[24] The more accepted point of view, based on research that has accumulated during the past twenty-odd years, is that general intelligence continues to gain steadily during the period of early adolescence tapering off at about the age of 23.[25]

During the adolescent period mental test scores tend to be fairly stable, so that the chances of an individual's maintaining his relative position are considerably better than at earlier ages. Nevertheless, illness, extreme emotional disturbance, and so on may considerably influence test results.[26]

A finding of considerable significance in the planning of the educational experiences of young people comes from a longitudinal study which revealed that brighter children tend to grow intellectually at a faster rate than duller individuals during the preadolescent period. However, during the latter years of adolescence, the rate of growth of the duller children tends to continue at a rate equal to or even more rapid than that of the brighter youngsters.[27]

PROBLEM 4. How would this finding apply to the argument that duller children should not be encouraged to finish high school?

So far we have been discussing general intelligence, but as was indicated in Chapter 1 a composite of traits or functions may contribute to this general ability. There is some evidence that these traits become more differentiated, or to put it in another way, that intelligence becomes more specialized as the child grows through adolescence. Garrett, for example, suggests that " with increasing age there appears to be a gradual breakdown of an amorphous gen-

---

[23] Ausubel, *op. cit.* P. 278.

[24] Cornell, Ethel. " Techniques for Evaluating Individual Growth — Some New Ideas." Paper presented at National Council on Measurements Used in Education, February 17, 1953, Atlantic City, New Jersey.

[25] Segel, David. *Intellectual Abilities in the Adolescent Period.* Washington: Federal Security Agency, Office of Education, Bulletin No. 6, 1948. Pp. 6–7.

[26] Bayley, Nancy. " Consistency and Variability in the Growth of Intelligence from Birth to Eighteen Years." *Journal Genetic Psychology.* 76 (1949), 165–196.

[27] Freeman, F. N., and Flory, C. D. " Growth in Intellectual Ability as Measured by Repeated Tests." *Monograph of the Society for Research in Child Development,* Vol. II, No. 2, 1937.

eral ability into a group of fairly distinct aptitudes. It seems highly probable that maturation has much to do with this differentiating process, but increasing experience and diverging interests must also contribute heavily." [28] Efforts to substantiate this point of view through research have been somewhat contradictory [29] and suggest that until closer agreement regarding the nature of general intellectual ability and the conditions of its testing can be reached, we cannot be too sure about its manifestations in the period of adolescence. Such a conclusion in no way hampers us from the observation that in comparison with the younger child the adolescent appears to be more capable of symbolization and abstraction, and better able to reason. We shall concern ourselves with this in somewhat more detail in Chapter 12.

Significance of Biological Factors in Adolescence

Adolescence may be regarded as the period in which the individual comes into his full biological inheritance. The kind of adult body he is to have, its size, shape, and strength, and skills and tempo, all become apparent. In a sense he approaches during this period the limits of his intellectual capacity. This, of course, does not mean that he has by any means learned all that there is for him to learn, whatever his limits may be.

We have noted that there are sufficient changes involved in this period and that the interrelationships between various aspects of development are sufficiently complex as to create at least the possibility of disequilibrium. There is some evidence that some of the storm and stress and the variability and lack of predictability of behavior which seems to go with adolescence may stem from this.

Primarily, however, the significance of the biological changes of adolescence seems to lie in their meaning to the individual. If he likes the adult he sees himself becoming and can prepare himself

[28] Garrett, Henry E. "A Developmental Theory of Intelligence." Reprinted in *The Adolescent, A Book of Readings,* edited by Seidman. New York: Dryden Press, 1953. Pp. 198–199.

[29] See, for example, Doppelt, Jerome Edward. *The Organization of Mental Abilities in the Age Range 13 to 17.* New York: Columbia University Bureau of Publications, 1950. Also McCahan, Gerda Provost. "Mental Organization in the Age Range 9 to 17 Years." *Dissertation Abstracts.* 13 (1953), 123. Abstract of Ph.D. thesis, 1952, Columbia University.

to function according to the limits (and potentialities) which his biology sets for him, adolescence is not likely to be marked off as a time of special difficulty for him. To a large extent the feelings and attitudes of the youngster toward the person he is to be will depend on the kind of self-regard he has already established. But the social world in which he finds himself, the values and opinions of the adults in it, as well as those of his peers will also play an important part. We shall turn now to a consideration of social factors in adolescent development.

SOCIAL FACTORS IN ADOLESCENCE

During the years of adolescence, the period of transition between childhood and adulthood, the young person may be said to be a "marginal man." He stands on the boundary between two worlds — the world of children and the world of adults. He does not belong to either group, or at least he is not certain about his belongingness.[30] True, he has been living in the society of adults, but he has been doing so as a child. As he increases in stature, sees himself take on the appearance of an adult, recognizes that he has strength skills and intellectual understandings not dissimilar to those of the adults, realizes that he too is capable of reproducing himself, he is no longer inclined to regard himself as a child. But the adults are disinclined to recognize him as an adult. Their experience suggests that even though he may have reached his physical prime and the peak of his capacity for learning, he still has much to acquire in the way of knowledge, judgment, insight, and self-reliance.[31]

Whether the young person's acceptance into adult society is made dependent on the acquisition of much or little additional knowledge; whether he need only add to what he already knows or whether he must revise many of his early learnings; whether he receives adult recognition in all areas of his living, or only a few;

[30] Lewin, Kurt. "The Field Theory Approach to Adolescence." Reprinted in *The Adolescent, A Book of Readings,* edited by Seidman. New York: Dryden Press, 1954. P. 33.

[31] Davis, Kingsley. "Adolescence and the Social Structure." Reprinted in *The Adolescent, A Book of Readings,* edited by Seidman. New York: Dryden Press, 1954. Pp. 42–50.

and whether the period of transition is long or short will depend on the particular culture in which he happens to be growing up.

In order to understand the psychological tasks confronting a particular adolescent, we need to know something about the nature of the adult society into which the young person is moving and about the expectations it has for the socialization of youth. Since our concerns are primarily with young people growing up in the United States where the period of adolescent transition is rather long and the world of the adolescent somewhat set apart from that of children and adults, we shall also need to consider the expectations for socialization held by the adolescent's peer group.

PROBLEM 5. As background material for the discussion which follows, it will be helpful to read or to have reviewed and discussed in class Chapter Two of *The Adolescent, A Book of Readings,* edited by Jerome Seidman. This chapter contains articles by Lewin, Davis, and Jones dealing with the adolescent in modern society.

PROBLEM 6. On the basis of the material covered in the problem above and your own knowledge of a particular community (the one in which you grew up, for example) make a list of the specific expectations the adults hold for young people. In what ways are young people guided or helped to meet expectations? To what extent is the responsibility for this left up to the young people themselves? This analysis might also be applied to communities outside the American culture. See, for example, "Adolescence the Hopi Way," by Thompson and Joseph in *The Adolescent, A Book of Readings,* pp. 2–15; and *From the South Seas* by Mead.

The Nature of Adult Society

In earlier chapters we have implied that a considerable amount of similarity underlies the diversity which is so characteristic of the American society. The people of the United States not only share a common territory (large though it is) and a common government, but many ways of doing things, of organizing their living, and of looking at life.

The child maturing in this society takes on these common patterns often without conscious awareness that the demeanor he acquires marks him as American. As he grows toward adulthood, however, the demands of society impinge on him in a somewhat new and different way. As a fullfledged member, it becomes important not only for him to conduct himself in the fashion prescribed by his society but also to have some knowledge of the common ways of life, the traditions, and the values which are held dear. At the same time, these same traditions and values operate to influence many of the choices which he must make as an adult — how he is to make his living, the kind of sex expression he favors, the way he uses his leisure, and so on.

One of the many differences between a complex society such as ours and the societies of earlier times or those of primitive peoples is that in the latter certain values are understood and accepted by everyone. In contrast, the American culture tends to reflect many values.

The rapidity of change. An outstanding characteristic of American society is the rapidity of change within it. Many interrelated factors contribute to this. One is technological invention. A simple illustration of its effects may be seen in the shifting of customary ways of spending leisure time as television became popular, or the changes in techniques of food purchase and preparation in those homes which have acquired freezing units. But perhaps as significant as the inventions themselves are the attitudes of Americans toward them. As this is written, for example, announcement has just been made of a jet transport plane which makes it possible to depart at noon from New York City and arrive at 1:30 P.M. (Pacific time) in Los Angeles. In editorial comment a metropolitan newspaper discusses some of the problems of adjusting mealtimes to such rapid travel, but notes that as air travel becomes speedier these difficulties will be reduced. The problem of clothing appropriate to a take-off in hot weather and a chilly landing may perhaps be solved by the provision of " dressing rooms " where passengers may change en route, says the writer. The column concludes with the comment: " Some of us may not be around to see advertisements reading, ' One Hour to San Francisco! ' but perhaps our offspring will be. Bon voyage, children! And happy landings! " [32]

This seems to reveal an optimism about change, a faith in its benefits which is typical of the values held by most Americans. Faith in, or at least willingness for, change is further reflected in

[32] " Topics of the Times." *New York Times.* (August 28, 1954), 14.

the great mobility which characterizes the American population. Not only do people change residence frequently, they shift from one job to another, start one business, sell it, and "begin all over," and some take on "new" husbands or wives. Vacations are regarded as welcome opportunities for a "change of scenery." Members of some types of social organizations become concerned when they "never see any new faces."

It is customary to assume that the young person will live in a world different from that of his parents and because of this, his rather early break with the traditions of his elders, although often deplored, is at the same time accepted as more or less inevitable. Commenting on this facet of the American value system, an anthropologist and a psychiatrist say:

[The American youngster] is expected to explore new grounds, to seize opportunities, and therefore to abandon the old for the new. In such an atmosphere of constant change, mastery of skill and techniques, the acquisition of information, and the clarification of the self vis-à-vis the world become extremely difficult.[33]

The columnist cited earlier might have demonstrated another aspect of American readiness for change had he made a somewhat different but equally plausible solution to the problem of dressing appropriately for sudden weather changes. We can envision the "One Hour to San Francisco" advertisement paralleled by a spread depicting a "Four-Seasons-Flight-Suit," made from a fabulous synthetic or perhaps equipped with a temperature regulator, but in any event, styled by the Dior of tomorrow and advertised as something without which nobody who is anybody would think of boarding a rocket ship. Thus modern media of communication and the techniques of advertising and propaganda tend both to trade on and to reinforce a tendency to regard the "new" and the "up-to-date" as better.

Some social scientists see the growing importance of the mass communication media as a concomitant of our changing economic situation with profound implications for the American character. A shift from decade to decade from an economy of scarcity toward

[33] Reusch, Jurgen, and Bateson, Gregory. *Communication, The Social Matrix of Psychiatry.* New York: W. W. Norton & Company, 1951. P. 123.

an economy of abundance has put new importance on selling. Advertising is used to create demands for certain products. Increasing numbers of people are involved not in the production of goods but in services related to their distribution and consumption, or in services dealing with ways of spending leisure time. Such individuals, if they are to sell their services must also sell themselves, putting across their personalities in competition with others. Fromm suggests an analogy to handbags on a counter:

> Could they feel and think, each handbag would try to make itself as "attractive" as possible in order to obtain a higher price than its rivals. The handbag sold for the highest price would feel elated, since that would mean it was the most "valuable" one; the one which was not sold would feel sad and convinced of its own worthlessness. This fate might befall a bag which, although excellent in appearance and usefulness, had the bad luck to be out of date because of a change in fashion.[34]

If it is true as Fromm suggests that this "marketing orientation" is increasingly characteristic of American society, it is relatively easy to relate it to the traditions of individual and competitive enterprise and highly valued material success which had their roots in an earlier frontier society. These are traditions which indeed continue to dominate the thinking of great numbers of the American people.

PROBLEM 7. Assuming yourself to be a visitor from a foreign country, read through an American daily newspaper or a weekly news magazine. From this perspective what evidence, if any, do you find that American values change? That personality is regarded as a saleable commodity? That the traditions and material success are of continuing influence?

The tradition of equality. Traditions which grow out of the experiences of a nation at differing times in its history are frequently contradictory to one another. Thus the idea of improving oneself through change wrought by hard work, shrewdness, or even luck runs against an idea which is also basic to American society, that of equality.

The tradition of equality stems in part from the desire of the founding fathers to avoid the kinds of oppressive authority which

---

[34] Fromm, Erich. *Man for Himself.* New York: Rinehart and Company, 1947. Pp. 71–72.

were characteristic of the old countries and to vest whatever authority might be needed in a tribunal of equals. Reflections of their
thinking are to be seen today in opinions that the "least government is the best government," in a tendency to reject authority
whether it be of the family or of government, or at least to take it
rather lightly, and in the continuing wish of most Americans to
be "independent" and "beholden to no one." But equality also
implies a similarity among individuals, and it is in relation to this
that the American society presents some curious contradictions.
What is really regarded as equal, it appears, is opportunity. In line
with this, the American system of free public education has been
developed. Different individuals make different uses of the same
kinds of opportunities, achieve success, and thus become more dissimilar. Evidence of inequality, in the opinion of some observers
of the American scene, makes Americans anxious.[35] So a related
aspect of the high valuation of equality is a strong tendency toward
conformity. So long as people dress very much alike, read the same
magazines, view the same television programs, differences in wealth,
power, or social status are not accentuated. The "average man,"
"the typical American home" are kept in constant view. Idio-
syncrasy, even as the mark of the creative intellect, may be tolerated but is not encouraged. One writer cites a recent illustration of
this from a documentary film put out by a chemical company.
The research team responsible for the company's new products
is depicted as five young men in white coats conferring around a
microscope while the sound track comment is, "No geniuses here.
Just a bunch of good Americans working together."[36]

PROBLEM 8. From your own experience can you cite any evidence
of discomfort in the presence of obvious inequality? To what extent
are you bound by conformity so far as clothes, taste in music, art, or
literature, or the expression of new or different ideas is concerned?
Whose are the standards to which you feel conformity is necessary?

Gregariousness. Those who currently express concern over the
spread of conformity note an increase in another trait typical of

[35] Reusch and Bateson, *op. cit.* P. 104.
[36] Whyte, William J., Jr. "The New Illiteracy." *Saturday Review.* (November 21, 1953), 34.

Americans — gregariousness. According to Reusch and Bateson:

> In America the process of living and interacting with others is sought as a goal in itself. Americans treat others always as people, while Europeans in many situations will treat other people like objects or as if they did not exist. . . . [In America] . . . there exists an awareness that persons have families, want to live, and need a certain environment in order to survive. . . . People are always people; they never become machines or animals.

But they add:

> The treatment of persons as individuals seems to be an expression of the fact that every person is a representative and member of a group, and the group assumes the responsibility for the individual.[37]

Whatever tendency toward greater dependence on the group there may be today can probably be traced in part to the American's mobility. Often separated from his family, or lacking the numerous relatives of earlier families, he seeks substitutes in group memberships. At the same time, the increasing need to sell oneself, to test the value of one's personality by the number of friends and acquaintances one is able to make, becomes another contributing factor.

Riesman, whose thinking somewhat parallels that of Fromm in this respect, suggests that large numbers of people are becoming " other-directed." Rather than having goals which are distinctly personal and unique, the individual learns early to look for his guidance to his contemporaries — " either those known to him or those with whom he is indirectly acquainted through friends and through the mass media." His goals shift with the guidance this group gives him. " It is only the process of striving itself and the process of paying close attention to the signals from others that remain unaltered through life." [38]

Individuals so group-oriented may appear " well-adjusted " in that they are pleasant, and friendly, but they are often lonely and deeply uncertain primarily because they are not able to come to terms with themselves, to recognize, and to express their own unique feelings and talents. They lack the courage to be themselves.

[37] Reusch and Bateson, *op. cit.* P. 109.
[38] Riesman, David. *The Lonely Crowd.* New Haven: Yale University Press, 1950. P. 22.

Each of the characteristics of the American society to which we have thus far given consideration, its commitments to change and progress and to competitive enterprise and material success, its emphasis on equality and conformity, and its gregariousness, are rooted in traditions going back to its frontier beginnings. There is another tradition, that of Puritan morality, which also continues to some extent to affect present-day American society.

Puritan morality. The Puritan code was strict, rigid, intolerant of the desires of the flesh, and placed a heavy degree of responsibility on the individual for its maintenance, with, of course, the help of God. Its influence today appears to lie somewhat less in what people do than in the moral standards to which they give lip service. As some anthropologists have observed, Americans seem more inclined to think habitually in terms of " goodness " or " badness " than individuals in many other cultures.[39] Much as discrepancies between " official pose " and personal living may be deplored, their reality in most of present-day society can hardly be denied.[40]

As we have suggested, any attempt to analyze the common characteristics in a society as complex as that of the United States can at present be based only on evidence from studies of various segments of the population and seems bound to result in disagreement.[41] Not only do different observers draw on differing experience and evidence, but each trend they note tends to have its counter trend, and these shift in importance as time goes on. Thus, for example, the current increase in church membership from some points of

[39] See Mead, Margaret. *And Keep Your Power Dry.* New York: William Morrow and Company, 1942. Also Kluckhohn, Clyde, and Kluckhohn, Florence. " American Culture: Generalized Orientation and Class Patterns," in Conference on Science, Philosophy and Religion, *Conflicts of Power in Modern Culture.* New York: Harper and Brothers, 1947. Pp. 106–129.

[40] Jersild, Arthur T. *Child Psychology.* New York: Prentice-Hall, 4th ed., 1954. P. 543. See his chapter on " Children's Ideals, Morals and Religion," pp. 521–522 for detailed discussion of the effects of society's moral contradictions in the life of the growing individual. Also relevant is Riesman, David. " Values in Context," from *Individualism Reconsidered.* Glencoe, Illinois: The Free Press, 1954. Pp. 17–25. In this he questions some of the current concern about " loss of values " and points out some of the advantages in a society which leaves large areas of living up to the private conscience.

[41] For a discussion of some of the problems inherent in the study of cultural values see Bidney, David. " The Concept of Value," in *Anthropology Today.* Chicago: University of Chicago Press, 1953. Pp. 682–699.

view may represent growing awareness of the threat to self implicit in the " marketing orientation " and in " other-direction." According to such thinking, the question, " What shall it profit a man, if he shall gain the whole world, and lose his own soul? " is as relevant today as two thousand years ago.[42]

The structure of the American society. The fact that all Americans tend to have certain common characteristic ways of behaving and of looking at the world does not deny the reality of the diversity there is among them. We have stressed such diversity throughout preceding chapters, indicating how individuals and groups may be differentiated on the basis of rural or urban residence, social class, occupation, income level, education, race, religion, and so on. We have also indicated that there is considerable evidence that society in the United States is becoming increasingly structured into social classes. Most of the research to which we have referred has defined class in terms of status, emphasizing how people regard themselves and each other. But the concept of class also implies that the group of individuals composing it share relatively fixed patterns of behavior so far as the entire range of human activity is concerned — occupation, consumption habits, education, manner of speaking, mode of dress, philosophy of life, recreational pursuits, social attitudes, family life, and so on.[43] When we examine the extreme ends of the class structure, contrasting, for example, a family which has had money and been in the social register for generations with one in which none of the members has held any other job than that of day laborer, class differences are obvious. But as we move toward the middle, there is considerable interaction and overlapping.

PROBLEM 9. What do you think have been the important values operative in each of the families with which we have been concerned in this book? Are members of a family always agreed on values?

[42] " The numerical increase in church membership was three times greater in the period since 1940 than in the comparable period of 1926 to 1940." *New York Times.* (August 25, 1954), 29. It should be noted that these figures do not appear to take into account population increases during the period. (A foreign observer might well see in this article which gives precise figures for each of the various denominations, typical American characteristics of competition and quantification.)

[43] Bossard, James H. *The Sociology of Child Development.* New York: Harper and Brothers, 1954. Pp. 318–319.

So far as the adolescent is concerned, the structuring of society has two important consequences. One is that to the extent that his family patterns and his associations have been limited to those of a particular class he tends to be better prepared for adulthood in that class than in any other. This is vividly illustrated in Hollingshead's description of the job handicaps of lower-class youth in *Elmtown,* the fictitious name given a highly structured midwestern community. The girls, for example, could do housework or take care of children, but frequently not to the satisfaction of their employers because the ways which they had learned at home differed so from middle-class ways. Even when an individual is able to take on many of the ways of another class, some of his earlier learnings may persist for many years. Thus a college professor describes being tormented by a tendency to revert under stress to the " dem, dese, and dose " for " them, these, and those " which he acquired in his childhood on New York City's Lower East Side.

Another consequence of social class structure is that identification with a certain class position tends either to enhance or to decrease the youngster's opportunities for social participation, and for educational and vocational advancement. This applies particularly in the social area as friendships begin to cross sex lines. An illustration of the process of social exclusion which the youngster may encounter is drawn from the comment of an *Elmtown* girl, a member of class III (the business and professional group):

When I was 15 years old, my parents gave a party for me. They saw to it that only the right boys were invited — children of their friends. Having started out with this group of boys, I have continued in that group. These boys are my Sunday School acquaintances. The friends at my party were my high school bunch, except for one girl and two boys my parents disapprove of. (These youngsters came from class IV: their fathers were mill hands, and this girl's family owned a retail business.) They did not think they rated well enough to come.[44]

Elmtown also affords examples suggesting that the lower-class youngster, even if he is bright and wants to get ahead in school, may struggle against considerable odds. (In fairness it must be noted that the *Elmtown* school appears to have been unusually sensitive

[44] Hollingshead, August B. *Elmtown's Youth.* New York: John Wiley and Sons, 1949. P. 237.

to community cleavages and that the date of this incident is 1937.) According to a working-class mother:

Jean was the brightest girl in high school. When she graduated she was number one in the class. The Hopkins boy was number two, but they recommended the Hopkins boy for a college scholarship. They are some of the big people in town, and we aren't. . . . Last year, about the same thing happened. Joe Brummit and Willa Cross were pretty close together in scholarship. . . . Willa['s] . . . dad's in that Inner Ring. They recommended Willa for the "Special" scholarship. Joe's working down at the Mill for about eighteen or twenty dollars a week — he'll probably be there for a long time. His father's a carpenter, and he can't afford to go away.[45]

How the class position of the young person may affect his job opportunities is revealed in the comments of *Elmtown* employers (these appear to have been made during the period of rapid economic expansion at the beginning of World War II):

[According to the superintendent at the Mill] . . . The relief class is no good. These people have been this way for generations. The kids will be the same way; and if you think you can do anything for them, you are crazy.

He refuses to hire persons who are identified as class V's except as extras and only in unskilled jobs in the yard.[46]

Although the situation presented in *Elmtown* represents what is probably an extreme example of social stratification, it has served the very useful function of pointing out the insidious influences on youth which appear to be inherent in the adult status system.

PROBLEM 10. In your own high school experience of social class differences, how much awareness did you have? To what extent do you think social class influenced the friends students selected? The courses they chose? The success they attained?

Adult Expectations for Adolescents

If one may judge adult expectations for adolescents by newspaper headlines, by popular magazine articles, by the comments of some (but not all) of their parents and teachers, or even by the

---

[45] *Ibid.* Pp. 182–183.   [46] *Ibid.* P. 386.

appraisals of them made by their older brothers and sisters,[47] one may well conclude that mockery of morals and manners, irresponsibility, lawlessness, and delinquency are regarded as more or less inevitable concomitants of the adolescent period. Recently, in a blistering popular article (directed primarily against psychologists), a mother declared that the behavior of teenagers, with which she was fed up, was primarily the result of the adult assumption that adolescents must go through a period of turmoil and general obnoxiousness.[48] In a sense her contention may be correct. Some of the strains of adolescence do arise in part because the adult society ascribes to young people a prolonged period in which their status is that of neither child nor adult. At each stage of his development the child has had to meet certain expectations for socialization. As he learned, he gained in independence and in status. But in adolescence, for many youngsters, the rewards are fewer and the frustrations greater.

Continuously, as we have seen, parents have encouraged the child to be independent, to take increasing responsibility for himself. But as he reaches adult physical status, especially in middle-class families, he is not granted progressively increasing independence. The value and interest systems of the child and the adult are so completely separated that just as he had earlier to go through a period of learning to be an independent child, now he must learn to be a psychologically independent adult.[49] But adult expectations frequently seem confusing and inconsistent. Even within the same social class group some parents abdicate a large part, if not all, of their authority while the child is still in junior high school. Other parents continue to make major decisions for their children even into the years of college.

The economic situation is an important factor in determining

[47] Over a period of years of college teaching, the writer has been struck by the extent to which college students are convinced that their younger brothers and sisters are not only dating earlier than they did, but are also less inhibited and more inclined to do things which they regard as dangerous. One begins to suspect that there is no stage of development more difficult to observe objectively than that of early adolescence!

[48] Heath, Abigail. "I'm Fed Up With Teen-Agers." McCall's Magazine. 80 (January, 1953), 28–31.

[49] See Ausubel, op. cit., pp. 319–327, for an excellent discussion of the cause and effects of prolongation of adolescence in our culture.

when a youngster will be expected to be " on his own." Children from poorer families often enter the work world of adults at the earliest possible moment in order to take the burden of their support from their parents. In time of economic distress, the period of dependence is prolonged. School attendance may be continued, for there is nothing else to do. But it is attendance without zest, for the future seems uncertain. Marriage is postponed, and young people continue to " live at home " with small hopes of a " place of their own." In periods of economic expansion the situation changes, and the young person has a better chance of declaring his independence through part-time, if not full-time employment. In periods of war not only is economic independence quickly acquired, but the enforced breaking of family ties, the pressures on boys to prove their manliness, and on girls to demonstrate their affection and regard for their menfolk, along with a variety of other factors tend to accelerate progress toward maturity.[50]

By the time he arrives at pubescence the youngster has already learned many socially acceptable ways of expressing his aggression and assertiveness. But his increasing strength and power and the tendency to emotional instability which frequently characterizes the period of transition combine with the frustration he experiences in numerous areas to produce a considerable fund of aggression.[51] According to middle-class expectations, this aggression is to be channeled off in the form of social and economic skills to enable them to compete effectively. In contrast, lower-class expectations appear to be more likely to include approval and social reward for physical aggression. Thus, according to one observer, in the low-status group " both girls and boys may curse their father to his face or even attack him. . . . An adolescent who does not try to be a good fighter will not receive the approval of the father." [52]

A somewhat similar situation appears to prevail so far as expec-

[50] The problems attendant upon such acceleration are made evident in an issue of *The Annals* devoted to " Adolescents in Wartime," Vol. 236, November, 1944. For an analysis of these from a psychoanalytic point of view, see Benedek, Therese. *Insight and Personality Adjustment.* New York: Ronald Press, 1946.

[51] Ausubel, *op. cit.* P. 525.

[52] Davis, Allison. " Socialization and Adolescent Personality." *The Forty-third Yearbook of the National Society for the Study of Education.* Chicago: University of Chicago Press, 1944. P. 211.

tations regarding the sexual behavior of adolescents is concerned. But generalizations in this area are difficult, for as Ausubel has put it, "All we can say with definiteness is that in our culture marriage is delayed longer and attitudes toward sex are more heterogenous and more confused than in most other cultures." [53]

In general, it appears that expectations for lower-class youngsters, particularly boys, are much more in the direction of direct and uninhibited sex expression.[54] This does not imply a lack of a sex code but rather standards which differ from that of middle-class persons.[55] Masturbation and petting according to this code are less often regarded as appropriate means of sex expression. A somewhat similar situation applies for lower-class girls, although in many families a considerable effort is made to prevent them from having children before they are married. Lower-class girls, it appears, are given considerably more explicit sex information than are middle-class girls.[56] That middle-class expectations in regard to sexual behavior tend to create major dilemmas for many young people seems an inescapable fact. On the one hand, the naturalness and rightness of the sex urge is maintained. Mass media make frequent appeal to sexual interests, and sexual attractiveness is considerably emphasized. On the other hand, at least according to the expressed code, sex relationships are not to be indulged outside of marriage. Knowledge that the fullest realization of sex as an expression of total personality comes only within the marital relationship does not necessarily relieve the young person from feeling guilty and unworthy about whatever adjustment he makes. In this situation, we may also note, girls find themselves in a somewhat different situation from boys since in general the culture expects them to carry the responsibility for sexual morality. The transgressions of the boys are frequently regarded with a "boys will be boys" kind of tolerance, while girls are likely to be more severely censured.

[53] Ausubel, *op. cit.* P. 396.

[54] Kinsey, Alfred C. *Sexual Behavior in the Human Male.* Philadelphia: W. B. Saunders and Company, 1948. Pp. 327–394.

[55] See, for example, Whyte, William F. *Street Corner Society.* Chicago: University of Chicago Press, 1943.

[56] Davis, Alison. "Child Training and Social Class," in *Child Behavior and Development,* edited by R. G. Barker, and others. New York: McGraw-Hill Book Company, 1942. Pp. 607–621.

To a much larger extent than the younger child, the adolescent is influenced not so much by the expectations his parents hold for him but by the expectations of the rest of the adult community. Basically he recognizes that the test of his own adulthood lies in his acceptance as a peer by adults outside his family. The fact that a widowed mother may turn to her eldest son for counsel does not establish his status so securely as does the fact that the neighbors no longer refer to him as " the Jones kid." To be greeted as an equal by other adults, to share in their activities and decisions, this is what counts. How then, does the community outside the family regard the adolescent? What provisions are made for him in school and in the world of work?

School and the World of Work

By the time the young person has reached physical maturity and has become desirous of social recognition as an adult, he tends to regard school either as a pathway leading to the world of work or as a barrier to be surmounted before entering it. If school becomes too unbearable, or the independence to be gained through becoming a worker seems too alluring, he may contemplate leaving school. In fact, as we indicated in Chapter 1, only about 50 percent of those who enter high school will graduate.

The individual's attitudes toward school and work are determined partly by his abilities and partly by the family from which he comes. But just as there are tremendous differences in elementary schools so there are equally great differences in high schools. Job opportunities for young people and the interests of employers also differ from community to community.

Thus at the beginning of his teens the youngster may leave his elementary school to attend a larger junior high school, or he may continue through the eighth grade and then enter a senior high school. If he attends a junior high school, it may be one with a curriculum carefully planned in the light of present knowledge of the development of the early adolescent, or one only slightly modified from the senior high school pattern. The program may be arranged so that at least one teacher has an opportunity to get to know him well, or it may be one in which he moves from one class to another, each with a different teacher all day long. When he gets to senior high school, it may be one which puts its main emphasis on preparation for college entrance, though offering general and commercial courses as well, or it may include more technical courses. In larger cities, different high schools may have different courses so that one offers vocational training, another general, and so on. In some schools vocational guidance is provided in the junior high school, each student being involved in courses studying career possibilities and in counseling procedures designed to help him assess his interests and aptitudes, his strengths and weaknesses. In other schools the guidance procedure is inclined to be perfunctory and may consist of little more than urging students who have not done well on intelligence or achievement tests to take vocational subjects.

As for work, in many communities jobs go by preference to high school graduates, but there may be little communication between school and employer as to the specific contribution high school experience can make to the job. In other communities employers cooperate closely with the school guidance workers, providing opportunities for young people to visit the stores and factories where they may obtain employment. Some communities have had very successful work experience programs; students receive school credit for work as salespersons, stenographers, nurses' aids, and so on. On the other hand, in the same communities, occasional employers may unwittingly sabotage efforts to keep young people in touch with the school by failing to carry through established procedures regarding working papers.

During the thirties several surveys of youth were made which highlighted their need for a more practical kind of high school education than they were then getting.[57] It became very clear that many young people felt that their high school experience had very little relevance to the life they were to live as adults. Not only were they ill-equipped vocationally, but they faced many problems in their relationships with their families and with each other which schools

[57] See, for example, Bell, H. M. *Youth Tell Their Story.* Washington, D.C.: American Council on Education, 1938. Also Eckert, Ruth, and Marshall, Thomas. *When Youth Leave School.* New York: McGraw-Hill Book Company, 1938.

were inclined to ignore. A study of those who left school in the forties found that rather consistently such young people believed no one in the school cared what happened to them.[58] Not only did they feel that the teachers were uninterested, but often they felt isolated from the other young people as well. As one *Elmtown* youth said about the boys that were " in things ": " They treated me all right. They'd speak to me when they saw me, but I was different from them and they were different from me." Or, according to a girl, " They made me feel like I wasn't wanted." [59]

At the present time high schools all over the United States are beginning to face the indictment of the traditional school program which the " drop-outs " have made. Some schools are focusing on " life adjustment education designed to equip all American youth to live democratically with satisfaction to themselves and profit to society as home members, workers, and citizens." [60] They are as much concerned with those youth who are not preparing for either a skilled occupation or higher education as with those who have these more specific objectives. In other schools, more counseling services and courses in family living, mental health, problems of personal living, and so on attempt to help young people in working through the matters of most vital concern to them. Some schools are making strenuous efforts to involve a wider number of school youth in a greater variety of activities, including not only hobby clubs, and sports, but also the school's own " government " through the establishment of student councils. Such procedures if they are to be successful demand much insight and understanding on the part of the teachers.

At the same time that high schools are blamed for failure to meet the present needs of youth, they are also criticized for failing to give adequate training in the " fundamentals " and for neglecting the important academic areas of history, mathematics, language, and literature. Some disapproval undoubtedly comes from individuals who do not adequately appreciate the breadth of interests and

---

[58] Dillon, H. J. *Early School Leavers.* New York: National Child Labor Committee, 1949.

[59] Hollingshead, *op. cit.* P. 342.

[60] U. S. Office of Education, *Vitalizing Secondary Education,* Report of the First Commission on Life Adjustment Education For Youth, Bulletin No. 3, 1951. P. 1.

abilities which the schools confront when they attempt to educate to the age of 16 or 18 " all American youth." On the other hand, there should be real cause for concern if, as some claim, the level of thinking in high school programs is becoming increasingly mediocre.

Expectations for adolescent learning need not be limited to matters directly related to his immediate adjustment. There are some situations in which the youngsters themselves clearly recognize this. When they do not, they are sometimes not helped to see the relevance of a particular subject, as they are learning it, to their particular life goals. Thus a youngster wishing ultimately to become a dietitian may struggle through an introductory chemistry course with no real inkling of its bearing on nutrition.

In other situations the young person may be expected to acquire knowledge which has no visible relation to either his immediate adjustment or his vocational goals, but which is essential to his understanding and appreciation of the society in which he lives. This perhaps challenges the school as much as providing an atmosphere in which every young person feels accepted.

PROBLEM 11. What kinds of knowledge would you consider essential to understanding and appreciation of the society in which one lives? Consider this question in the light of trends in world politics, the role of science in modern living, the rapid growth of mass media of communication, and the probability of increasing leisure.

As we have suggested before the mere exposure of an individual to " knowledge " is no guarantee of its meaning anything to him, either immediately or later. Educators recognize that every individual perceives the learning situation in his own unique way, and that his feelings toward the subject matter and toward the teacher and the other members of the class may hamper or facilitate his learning. They are not agreed on how (or whether) to attempt to modify teaching procedures in the light of this fact. Jersild suggests:

Social studies might contribute directly or indirectly to a learner's understanding of human problems and motives, including his own. . . . In the teaching of history it would require only a modicum of insight into human behavior to show the psychological content in historical events which often transparently reveal the aspirations and frailties of human beings, their courage or lack of it. . . . In poetry one can hear the echo of one's own feelings, and drama and fiction are filled with conflicts such as occur in daily life.[61]

Truly great teachers it seems have always been able to help students sense that a particular subject had important personal implications for them. But today's high school faces the problem of attempting to provide such teaching for larger numbers of youngsters than ever before and with relatively fewer teachers available.

All of these are important facts to remember when the high schools are blamed for not meeting the present needs of youth nor preparing them adequately for the future. They belong together with the picture of community agencies overlapping in their functions which we presented in Chapter 7. As a people, Americans are committed to the provision of equal educational opportunity to all its citizens, but as Kingsley Davis has pointed out, the purpose of schooling either for the individual or for society is not clear.[62]

PROBLEM 12. To what factors would you attribute a lack of agreement as to the purpose of schooling in our society? How is school support affected?

PROBLEM 13. If possible, find out whether the schools in your community provide any printed statement of aims and objectives for the high schools. Compare these with the courses of study, guidance, and " extracurricular " activities offered. Perhaps you can also arrange to visit some classes or to interview some of the students. School newspapers and yearbooks are useful sources of information as to the extent to which all youngsters are involved in school affairs.

There were no junior high schools in the community in which our young people lived. They remained in neighborhood elementary schools through the eighth grade and entered Franklin High School as freshmen. When they first walked into the front hall and looked up the broad staircases winding up toward the second floor, they had each felt a little awed. It had, however, not taken them long to catch on that the school had been built at " approximately the same time as the Ark " and that most of the teachers were believed to have originated at about the same time. Derogatory as their comments might

---

[61] Jersild, Arthur T. *In Search of Self.* New York: Teachers College, Columbia University, 1952. Pp. 103–104.

[62] Davis, Kingsley, *op. cit.* Pp. 42–50.

be among themselves, each of them would have leapt on any out-
sider who might have dared infer that their building was not equal
to the best. As for the teachers, many of them had seen years of service
at Franklin High. One or two of them did remember the days when
Franklin had had only an academic course; the graduating class was
much smaller than nowadays, and all were " much better students."
Then had come the general course, designed for those students who
might not be entering college, and most recently the commercial
courses. A few of the teachers quite forthrightly indicated their preference for the students who were preparing for college. Some of them
actually appeared to " know the textbook letter for letter " and taught
it exactly that way. But most of them were really concerned about the
young people and wanted them to learn. They would have been the
first to admit that they did not always succeed very well. To a much
greater degree than they were able to convey to the youngsters, they
understood some of the things that baffled them. By no means all of
them could be regarded as old fogies. Perhaps a fifth of them were not
yet 30, and a few, like Mrs. Jordan, were, in a sense, ageless. But the
school organization was such that those teachers with the deepest
concerns for young people seldom succeeded in translating these to
their colleagues who feared the " lowering of academic standards."
The undercurrents of feeling always made the teachers of general and
commercial subjects uncomfortable lest they seem less strict or less
demanding than their colleagues who taught the subjects required for
college entrance.

Although the policy of the school did not encourage the development of a great many social activities, aside from those related to
sports, there were proms given by the junior and senior classes, the
annual Franklin Follies, and several clubs, such as the Debate Club,
and the Literature Club sponsored by English teachers who felt that
youngsters could be interested in " something more serious than the
Follies."

PROBLEM 14. Which of the young people we have been studying
would you expect would derive most satisfaction from the school
described? Which might have some difficulties? How will the influence of the school compare with other influences in the young
person's life?

Jane. Consistently, Jane's academic record was good. But it was never
quite " tops " as her teachers seemed to think it should be. Mrs. Jordan,

going over her school record with her when they were considering what her choice of college might be, was very positive in assuring her that on the basis of the record and the tests she had taken, she should be able to do successful college work. She was, however, struck by Jane's lack of spontaneous enthusiasm for any of her courses and her expressed distaste for even those she had excelled in. Jane took part in sports and in the literary club.

Pat. Pat started out in the general course, managed to hold her own fairly well, but decided at the end of her sophomore year to switch to a secretarial course, so that she would be equipped for a job when she graduated. Her participation in the Franklin Follies took a considerable amount of time, but she did not participate in many other school social activities. She complained to her best friend, Sally, whom she had met through church activities, that since she had transferred to the secretarial program, she never saw any boys, or at least none who were not goons. Aside from that, she was pleased with her decision to change courses and did well in them.

Andy. When Andy was 12, his school standing took such a low dip that he was threatened with failure. He had found school dull and boring and had not exerted himself to nearly his capacity. The following year under a man teacher whom he liked, he pulled out of his slump, and distinguished himself by his fine work. On entering Franklin High, he enrolled in the college entrance course, started off very creditably, then found Latin and math difficult and at the beginning of his sophomore year, transferred to the general course. Here his grades were about average. He was very well liked by all of his teachers. His vocational plans continued uncertain. He worked after school and summers at a drugstore.

PROBLEM 15. Neither Andy nor Jane distinguished themselves academically, yet Andy was regarded considerably more favorably by many of his teachers than was Jane. What factors might contribute to this difference?

Dan. By the time Dan was 12 he was again enjoying school. He elected to take the college entrance course in high school. He found the work hard but managed to maintain average grades throughout. During the summers after he became 15, he worked as a house painter.

Charles. Like Dan, Charlie's school record was just average. He elected college entrance courses but emphasized languages more than

Dan. He had no definite goal in view. Summers and after school, he worked at a neighborhood five-and-ten-cent store.

Celeste. Celeste continued through adolescence as she had earlier to be the kind of pupil teachers prize. She remained on the honor roll throughout high school. She took the commercial course.

For the most part these young people saw very little difference between the way their high school teachers regarded them and the way they had been regarded by their grade-school teachers. Occasionally, they shared in decisions, but for the most part these seemed to them to be made in advance by the faculty. Those who worked after school and during the summers apparently derived a satisfaction which was never quite so well realized in school.

Their experience typifies that of most young people in our society. Neither the school nor the world of work can offer as much status as the adolescent craves. Therefore, he must seek it where it is more readily available — among his peers.

The Peer Group

As we have seen, in preadolescence the society of the peer group becomes an extremely important influence in the life of the child. However, as the children composing it begin to enter the period of pubescence, various shifts in group structure and values take place.

Since the girls tend on the average to reach pubescence before the boys, it is their changing behavior and new interests which seem to precipitate some of the changes which differentiate the adolescent peer group from that of preadolescence. According to one study, girls at the 11- and 12-year level tended to regard with most favor girls who were friendly, pretty, tidy, and quietly gracious. In contrast, the boys of this age valued aggressiveness, boisterousness, and physical skill and leadership in games. By the age of 14 or 15, however, the girls' values had undergone marked changes. They tended to approve buoyant amiability and rather aggressive good sportsmanship with both boys and girls and also sophisticated, glamorous qualities. They admired dominating tendencies which they had previously rejected. Although the boys of 14 and 15 shifted toward some admiration of such characteristics as social ease, personableness, likeableness, and grooming, the greatest emphasis in their value system was still placed on physical skill, daring, and leadership in games.[63] Thus, in the early years of the adolescent period, it is the girls who plan the parties and social affairs which involve dancing and boy-girl pairing. But by the latter half of the period, the heterosexual composition of peer society becomes one of its outstanding characteristics.

As young people become more sophisticated about their relationships to one another, they form definite crowds and cliques. The term "crowd" is used rather loosely to include those individuals who tend to share similar interests and backgrounds and to participate in many of the same social activities. Within the crowd, smaller intimate groups share closer association and intimacy.[64] These groups are referred to as cliques. The crowd sometimes represents a loose amalgamation of cliques, or it may be an expanded clique. The characteristics of the clique are apparent in the following description, dealing with a high school in a midwestern community:

. . . The vast majority of a particular boy's or girl's waking hours are spent in the company of a few pals. When he leaves home in the morning, he generally walks or rides to school with them. In and around the high school he can be seen talking, laughing, walking, playing with them. . . . After school two or three out of a group of five or six may go uptown to the pool hall if boys, or to the drug store or bowling alley if girls. The same two or three boys or girls may be seen early in the evening on their way to a show or a friend's home. . . . Within the clique, personal relations with one another involve the clique mates in emotional and sentimental situations of great moment to the participants. Confidences are exchanged between some or all members; often those very personal, wholly private, experiences that occur in the family which involve only one member may be exchanged with a best friend in the group. Relations with the opposite sex, with adults, and with young people outside the clique are discussed and decisions reached on the action to be taken by the clique, or by a particular member involved in a situation.[65]

Crowds and cliques usually replace gangs in adolescence, except in slum areas. Gangs tend to be more highly organized, to have

[63] Tryon, Caroline. "Evaluation of Adolescent Personality by Adolescents." *Monographs of the Society for Research in Child Development,* Vol. IV, No. 4, 1939.
[64] Hurlock, Elizabeth B. *Adolescent Development.* New York: McGraw-Hill Book Company, 1949.
[65] Hollingshead, *op. cit.* Pp. 204–205.

stronger traditions, and to maintain markedly hostile attitudes toward both adult society and other gangs. Congeniality of interests is obviously the main criterion for membership in a particular clique, but other factors are also operative. Adolescents being, in a sense, in search of status tend to set up prestige hierarchies which greatly resemble those in the adult community. In part this can be attributed to the fact that each young person as a member of a particular family brings with him whatever social standing his family has. In turn, his interests and values reflect those of his family. But adolescent groups may develop a snobbishness and exclusiveness even exceeding that in the adult community.

By derogating other groups of individuals, perceiving them as inferior or undesirable, and treating them with contempt and scorn, it is clearly possible to enhance one's own marginal status relatively without expending the effort or ingenuity required for positive self-enhancement. . . . By making status a scarcer commodity, one makes its achievement a more signal accomplishment; by creating a deprived and to-be-pitied out-group, the advantages and enjoyment of in-group status are considerably enhanced.[66]

In addition to giving him status, the adolescent peer society provides an opportunity for the young person to practice some of the skills and fill some of the roles which are necessary to adulthood. Most of these have to do with getting along with other people, particularly those of the opposite sex, but some relate to other aspects of living which may be more or less taken for granted by many adults.

Youngsters themselves are well aware of this function of the peer group. For example, one of the strong defenses which they make of the high school fraternity or sorority (usually a secret organization which carries cliquishness to its extreme) is that in it they are able to "help the girl who doesn't know how to dress properly," or to "coach the one who is sort of shy." Another of their defenses emphasizes the importance of the various "charity" activities they undertake. Although the adult may often question the inherent value of some of these projects, it is difficult to disregard the fact that the adolescent derives important satisfactions from functioning in the role of benefactor.

[66] Ausubel, *op. cit.* P. 352.

Significance of Social Factors in Adolescence

At one time many students of human behavior believed that the storm and stress so customarily attached to the period of adolescence in our society were primarily, if not entirely, a matter of social imposition. The discontinuities between child and adult life together with the many contradictions which are inherent in the culture do, as we have seen, complicate the transitional period for young people. Were it not for them, many youngsters would likely proceed quite tranquilly through their teens. However, the social factors do not operate in isolation, and we cannot disregard the fact that for many youngsters learning to live with a changing body also accentuates the problems of adolescent adjustment.

We have emphasized the point that in our society the peer group at least during a part of the period under consideration forms what looks to be a society of its own. It appears to have its own standards and values and certainly its own unique patterns for behavior but in most respects it mirrors with some distortions those of the adult society. In some communities it is completely informal while in others it becomes highly structured and exclusive. Its influence on the young persons who are "in" or those who are kept "out" depends both on the characteristics of the peer society and on the psychological needs of the individual youngsters. We shall consider the latter in the next chapter.

12

~~~~~~

Learning to Be Adults:

Psychodynamic Aspects of Development in the Years 12 to 18

DURING AT LEAST a portion of the years from 12 to 18 the individual is perhaps more aware of his feelings and often more troubled by their significance than at any other period of his development. It is not only that a changing body may place new and unfamiliar demands upon him, nor that he may be regarded as neither child nor adult, but also that the ways of dealing with the world which he has previously learned are no longer adequate. The period of adolescence is one in which the ego, or control system, which was quite sufficient to the demands of childhood must develop new strengths. The person needs the abilities and the attitudes necessary to relating himself to other people as an adult and to seeing himself as an adult. It is in the process of such reshaping of the ego that the individual may be beset by puzzling and often contradictory feelings.

PROGRESS OF EGO DEVELOPMENT IN ADOLESCENCE

The suggestion that adolescence brings profound changes in ego is not meant to imply any lack of continuity in its development.

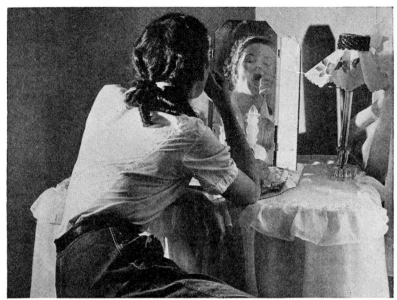

The adolescent learns to live with a changing body and changing feelings.

The ways the young person of 12 or 13 looks at and deals with his world and himself originated while he was still an infant. They have developed as he has lived and learned through the years. The individuality of these ways does not necessarily undergo transformation in adolescence. For example, the youngster who has always been of a stolid, matter-of-fact turn of mind is not likely to emerge from adolescence as a highly imaginative artist.

Despite this essential continuity in development, adolescence demands considerable reorganization in ego structure. The individual must himself assume responsibility for aspects of living previously assumed by various significant adults. We might say that he must learn to take full responsibility for full operation of his own control system. Somewhat as he developed awareness of his physical separateness and independence from those who cared for him, he must now develop an awareness of himself as an adult with a social and emotional identity of his own. Where once he learned to distinguish the real from the fanciful, and to make dependable generalizations in terms of the here-and-now, he must now develop some understanding of the society in which he lives, and to make generalizations in terms of the future and the not-so-close-at-hand. Thus the ego functions of knowing, doing, choosing, and synthesizing to which we referred in the previous chapter become increasingly complex.

In Chapter 7 the knowing, or cognitive, function of the ego was described as including the appraisal of the outer world — physical and social — and the inner world of feelings and emotions, together with an awareness of the dictates of conscience. In this respect the ego of the adolescent often has an exceedingly difficult job. Lacking experience the adolescent often fails to perceive the social world correctly. With new impulses in a changing body and new desires for adult status, the inner world demands are often contradictory. Further, he is at a loss as to whether to apply the dictates of his childish conscience, or the standards and values which he believes may be held by his peers. The following incident is a simple illustration of the complexity of demands which the adolescent ego may have to reconcile.

For weeks, Art and I, both 15, had hitched our way home from our school which was located in a part of the city many miles from where we lived. Each day a series of rides landed us, by a zig-zag route, admittedly within walking distance of home. That winter seemed especially bleak and we thoroughly enjoyed our entrance into each car which stopped to pick us off a corner. But always we were cheerful because each of us kept what we called our " case " dime in our pocket.

One day, we decided to spend our " case " dimes. Art said it would make it more realistic. To the casual observer watching us down a frankfurter with our usual soda, nothing could have seemed out of order. But I still remember the shock of bouncing that " case " dime off the counter. And I remember not enjoying the frankfurter although Art gobbled his down. And how each refusal of a driver led us to curse him when he passed, even if he had a whole family in his car.

We did get home at about the regular time, but I felt that it took us many years. My room looked as good to me as Ulysses' palace must have looked after twenty years of strife. Art didn't seem to care as I did. He had always had more freedom than I. The incident represented, I think, a testing of my self-sufficiency. I had always been, I thought, too sheltered. And it was complicated perhaps by a feeling of guilt expressed as concern over possible censure for being late for dinner.[1]

This suggests how an adolescent may vacillate between wanting to demonstrate independence and wanting the security of the tried and familiar, between wanting to meet the approval of his age-mates, and wanting to hold to the standards his parents have set. It also demonstrates the power and selective functions of the ego. The boy who reports the incident took the action necessary to resolve the conflicts he had.

It is through many similar experiences in which the individual functions independently, appraising his own feelings and making his own choices, that the young person becomes an adult. If all goes well, the ego not only knows inner and outer reality, chooses and carries through action, but brings increasing harmony into the personality. Such harmony or synthesis is not likely to be achieved, at least in our society, until the latter part of the teens and often not then. Important to its realization are shifts in the individual's conscience, his feelings and identifications, his relationships with his family and with his peers, as well as in his intellectual understanding.

[1] From a collection of incidents of adolescence reported by students.

PROBLEM 1. In the light of the information you now have regarding our six young people, which ones would you say have made the most progress in ego development and toward an inner harmony?

The Conscience

The revision in conscience necessary as the child moves into an adulthood in which activities, drives, and impulses once prohibited become permissible, is frequently difficult. As one authority puts it, to the conscience of childhood, " that which was once bad is always bad. It protests against any act that was forbidden in childhood and is deaf to the approval expressed by a more flexible reality world." [2] According to this point of view, the individual confronted by new demands both from within and without begins to sense the inappropriateness of some of the directions of his conscience. In one phase of this recognition he may be very indulgent of his new wishes and desires. Girls, for example, may accentuate and flaunt their feminine charms with make-up, glamorous clothing, and a " come-hither " line. Boys find similarly appropriate ways of expressing their new-found interests. But both girls and boys, particularly in the period of early adolescence, often impose strict limitations on themselves as to how far such expression shall go. Thus by tacit mutual agreement early dates may not involve so much as a chaste kiss. Such prohibitions reflect the alternate phase of development in which the individual displays an almost· slavish devotion to conscience.

During the period in which young people are, in a sense, learning to revise their childish consciences they appear to need, despite their often vociferous protests against the rigidity of their parents, a fairly definite standard of behavior. There is, for example, a kind of protection for them in the fact that parents expect them to be home at a certain time of night, will not permit them to go on unchaperoned week-end parties, and so on. Even when parents no longer assume responsibility for such matters, the youngsters themselves establish codes of behavior which, although they may not confirm precisely to those of the adults, are usually quite rigid. At first these concern matters which seem of relative unimportance

[2] Josselyn, Irene. *The Adolescent and His World*. New York: Family Service Association of America, 1952. P. 69.

in the eyes of adults: the prescribed wearing of jeans, the " correct " words to express approval, and so on. Gradually, however, " As a result of the mutual soul-searching that the individuals in the group experience, standards of the group concerning more basic aspects of social living take shape. Attitudes toward questions of morality, ethics and social custom take form. The standards are rigidly held to by the individuals in the group and gradually become a part of the ' conscience ' of each member." [3] In general, the resulting standards and values appear to be not markedly different from those held by the parents.[4]

Obviously, the extent to which revision of conscience becomes an important factor in the adolescence of a particular young person will depend on the " strength " of his conscience to begin with, and the areas in which it exerts prohibitions, as well as the standards and values emerging in the society of his peers. Even where individuals grow up in a common social environment and behave in pretty much the same way, they may have quite different experiences so far as conscience is concerned.

This is suggested in the findings of the study on adolescent character and personality which was carried on in the same midwest community to which we referred in our discussion of social influences in adolescence (pages 413–428). The young people in the study were classified into several personality types. Included were adaptive persons who fit readily into almost any social situation and are friendly, vivacious, and outgoing in manner; self-directive persons who are ambitious, strong-willed, and self-sufficient, yet inclined to self-criticism and self-doubt; submissive persons who rarely show signs of aggression and appear to live by authority; defiant persons who have experienced so little satisfaction for good behavior that they are ruled by selfishness and aggressive impulses. Of these, the adaptive persons are described as ones who tend to take on the beliefs and principles of their environment readily and without moral struggles. Self-directive persons are described as reflective

---

[3] *Ibid*. P. 75.

[4] For evidence on this point, see Horrocks, John E. *The Psychology of Adolescence*. Boston: Houghton Mifflin Company, 1951. Pp. 540–542; and Ausubel, David, *Theory and Problems of Adolescent Development*. New York: Grune and Stratton, 1954. Pp. 264–265.

and critical. They ask, in effect, " Is this really the *right* thing to do? " They try to work out moral principles for themselves. Submissive persons, though equally concerned, tend to ask the question, " Is this really the right thing to do to keep me out of trouble? "

The authors of the study see these differences in character as dependent on differences in the nature and severity of the conscience together with differences in the development of the sense of self, or ego. They regard the self-directive person as a person having a strong and severe conscience, combined with a well-developed sense of self. They see the adaptive person as one who also has a well-developed sense of self but a more permissive conscience. He is ruled more by social approval and disapproval than by inner feelings of right and wrong.

In contrast, they see submissive and defiant persons as having weaker senses of self. The submissive person, according to their classification has a strong and severe conscience, the defiant person, a weak conscience.[5]

PROBLEM 2. Do any of these personality types correspond to Riesman's other-directed character type?
PROBLEM 3. From what you know about our six young people, which ones would you expect might have most difficulty revising childish consciences? Bear in mind that different individuals may be " strict " in different areas.

Feelings and Attitudes

The evidence is contradictory as to whether adolescence is typically a period of heightened emotionality in comparison to other states of development.[6] However, it is known that the individual may experience a period of physiological disequilibrium, that early or late maturation is often attended with insecurities, and that inability to meet various demands of the society may be attended by frustration. Thus it is not unreasonable to suppose that for many young people feelings may be intense during this period.

As we have suggested earlier, there is a considerable degree of continuity in emotional experience throughout the years of living.

[5] Havighurst, R. J., and Taba, H. *Adolescent Character and Personality*. New York: John Wiley and Sons, 1949. Pp. 183–184.
[6] See, for example, Ausubel, *op. cit.* P. 145. Also Kuhlen, *op. cit.* Pp. 276–282.

Grief and joy, pain and pleasure are as real at 6 and 16 as at 60. But the situations in which these feelings arise do change as we grow older, and emotions in a sense take on new dimensions. Affection affords a good example. The young child loves his parents, his brothers and sisters, an occasional playmate. Romantic attachments to a member of the opposite sex have been reported among children as early as 3 and most of us have known at least one youngster who fell violently in love with a grade-school teacher.[7] But "being in love" takes on a new meaning in adolescence, and new feelings may develop, some of them attributable to hormonal changes, some of them no doubt occasioned by the young person's awareness of his new potentialities.

Feelings of affection. With the steady decrease in the average age of marriage which has been going on since 1890,[8] the chances are increasingly greater that by the age of 18 the individual has already chosen a marriage partner. The shifts of feeling which occur as one moves from the first love to the selection of a mate follow no one pattern. "Each couple makes up a unique plot, weaving together joys and sorrows, disappointments and satisfactions, hopes and cynicisms into a novel as crowded as *Anthony Adverse*."[9] Positive feelings of affection are mixed with other feelings.

One partner may feel uncomfortable unless he can dominate the other; one may regard the other as an enhancement to himself rather than a person in his own right; one may see the other not as he really is but as the dream person he has been seeking; one may offer childish affection more than that of husband or wife.

A good love relationship is one which involves the kind of mutuality in which each partner experiences increasing self-realization. This implies that each brings an already developed sense of his own identity, and suggests that until the adolescent has learned to live serenely with his new-found adulthood, he is not likely to find complete fulfillment in marriage. Young people differ as widely in

[7] Jersild, Arthur T. "Emotional Development," in *Manual of Child Psychology*, edited by Leonard Carmichael. New York: John Wiley and Sons, 2d ed., 1954. P. 908.

[8] Landis, Paul H. *Adolescence and Youth, The Process of Maturing*. New York: McGraw-Hill Book Company, 1952. Pp. 28–29.

[9] Levy, John, and Monroe, Ruth. *The Happy Family*. New York: Alfred A. Knopf, 1943. P. 18.

the rate at which they mature emotionally as in any other aspect of their development. Consequently, the mere attainment of the age of 18 or even 21 is no guarantee of such readiness for marriage. Nor does it necessarily follow that some individuals under special circumstances are not able to find themselves and to grow within the marriage relationship even earlier.

Feelings of aggression. In the process of establishing adulthood, at least in our society, feelings of aggression seem to run high. Sometimes their expression is simply a young person's way of asserting himself, declaring his need for some kind of status. Sometimes it is precipitated by frustration. Families, for example, may find themselves the target of a seemingly unjustified attack in which a youngster " takes out " on them feelings which he did not dare express in the peer group. Sometimes, as the following incident suggests, the adolescent is dimly aware that the individual she has chosen as the target of her aggression has no direct connection with her frustration, but this does not quell the fury of her wrath.

I was 12 when I was asked for my first date. A boy asked me to go to the movies with him. " Oh, no, I couldn't," I demurred. " My father wouldn't let me. But thanks all the same." My response was made with the greatest calmness. It didn't for a moment occur to me that any other answer was possible. A little more discussion of this and that and we walked on down the street toward home together, finally parting at our respective houses with no perceptible overtones of frustration.

I entered the house and started up the stairs without greeting my mother, who, as usual, was waiting to see me safely home. At the top of the stairs I turned around and began shouting at her. All the pent-up fury that I hadn't even suspected I possessed came out in a series of wild imprecations and accusations of the grossest indifference to my desires and feelings. The look on my mother's face was one of complete bewilderment — and well it might have been — for neither she nor my father had ever acted the heavy parent, had ever forbidden me to have a date with a boy. In fact, we had never had any occasion to discuss the matter; I had never made such a request.[10]

PROBLEM 4. What role do you think conscience may have played in this incident?

Sometimes the adolescent's response to his feelings of frustration is to withdraw from close contact with adults or with his peers.

---

[10] From a collection of incidents of adolescent conflict reported by students.

Such withdrawal may be rather pervasive as in the case of the youngster who has no confidants or it may be intermittent as in the case of the one who is sometimes quite uncommunicative to his family or friends, and again willing to share his feelings at some length.

Such withdrawal may be into a world of fantasy, in which the individual who is much too " shy " to ask a girl for a date, is forced to choose between two of the loveliest in his class, or the boy who is belittled for his intellectual pursuits becomes a famous scientist. When the content of the adolescent fantasy world is revealed (as it may be in projective tests), the individual's true feelings about himself can be inferred.

Frequently, it appears the feelings with which the adolescent may struggle the hardest are not new ones, but have their roots in earlier stages of development in which certain conflicts were not fully resolved. The child who at 5 and 6 continued to derive more pleasure and satisfaction from having than from sharing may come uneasily to the intimate relationships of adolescence. The youngster who persistently felt it was his brother that his parents favored, may bring to the sports and competitions of the teens a desire to excel considerably beyond that of one who has learned to appreciate and enjoy his brothers. Or with different life experiences, he may be afraid to tackle any situation in which he might prove himself to be superior.

Some youngsters put on a fine show of indifference. Girls are not interested in boys. They speak in the most derogatory way of the activities of the most popular girls in the school. But often their apparent off-handedness is a little too studied, and a sensitive adult sees behind their cover-up. Other youngsters, aiming at the same concealment of feelings of insecurity and uncertainty, but often quite unaware of their motivation, become ceaselessly busy. Always doing something, though never to any apparent purpose, always chattering, they somehow never quite succeed in escaping the fact that they are not comfortable in their adolescent status.[11]

Ambivalent feelings. The adolescent as much as the toddler or

[11] See Ausubel, *op. cit.,* p. 324, for additional typical adolescent adjustment techniques.

the child in the power-testing period is often caught in situations in which his feelings are markedly ambivalent. He would like to try out for the football team, but is afraid he may not make it. He would like to " go steady," but he is afraid of the very emotional involvements he craves. But most especially as he moves away from the protection of his family into independence, he both chafes to go and longs to stay. A college student's observation of a high school student friend illustrates the behavior which accompanies such feelings:

. . . One Saturday afternoon, Ellie and her mother and I were talking about ironing. Ellie asked me if I did my own ironing. I said I had done it since I was a freshman in high school. About ten minutes later, Ellie went into the kitchen and dampened several articles of her clothing. Her mother didn't refer to it in Ellie's presence but said to me, " She's never done that before without being told." A short while later, Ellie started ironing as though she did it all the time. After she had ironed a few pieces, she said, " I'm going to Ann's for a while and I'll finish this later." It still wasn't done the next day. Her mother finally told her that since she had dampened the clothes she would have to iron them. She did it reluctantly. The desire to be mature and self-sufficient had worn off.[12]

Changing Identifications

This same incident illustrates a rather typical identification of the adolescent. Thus, in many instances it is an individual in the next age group whom the young person chooses to model. This individual may have considerable influence on the thinking and behavior of the adolescent. A simple instance of this is drawn from records of the same student who reported the above instance. This time, Ellie had chosen to wear a blouse belonging to her mother. Her mother had given her permission but indicated that she felt it was too " old " looking. This she would not accept, but when her college student friend indicated that she preferred another, her judgment was immediately accepted. (A certain toughness of skin is requisite for parents of adolescents!)

Sometimes the person who serves as model is a member of the adolescent's own peer group. Thus, a popular girl's choice of cloth-

[12] From a collection of incidents of adolescence reported by students.

ing, or interests, may be quite slavishly imitated by her followers. Or the members of a " pair " may imitate each other.

As the adolescent grows older, the identifications he has made tend to become synthesized and generalized into one. He creates, in effect, a picture of the sort of person he would like to be. This so-called " ego-ideal " may be quite appropriate to his actual interests and abilities or it may be based largely on fantasy.

The process by which the ideal may be arrived at has been described by a 16-year-old in the midwest study of character and personality to which we referred earlier. Asked to write on " The Person I Would Like to Be Like," he wrote, " I have created an imaginary hero and attempted to fit my personality into his. I am not sure who this hero is, but part of him is what I consider myself. I imitate myself and extracts of other people." [13]

According to this study, most 16-year-olds thought of the person they would like to be like in terms of some such composite character. The age of the person was most often indicated as someone between 20 and 29 years.

PROBLEM 5. On the basis of the descriptions of the six young people given in Chapter 1, and the rest of the information you have about them, what individuals would you think might serve as important contributors to the ego ideals of each? Can you trace the process of the formation of such an ideal in your own experience?

INTERPERSONAL RELATIONSHIPS

Relationships within the Family

As the preceding sections of this chapter have implied, adolescence in our society is a period in which some degree of conflict between children and parents seems almost inevitable if the children are to establish themselves as individuals with status apart from that derived from their families. In the periods preceding adolescence most youngsters have already achieved a good deal of independence. Approaching adulthood demands that they extend this into such matters as choosing a mate, a lifework, and developing standards and values, all with appropriate regard both to the society in which they

[13] Havighurst and Taba, *op. cit.* P. 80.

are living and to their own unique qualities as individuals. In order to be sure that their choices are really their own, they must, as it were, rule out whatever ideas they know to be the parents', at least until they are sure that these ideas really fit them too.

One young person, engaged in this process, said to her mother, with considerable irritation in her tone, " Mother, *please don't* be so understanding! " Her comment indicated her need to have something against which to rebel. Standards which parents hold so rigidly that they are unwilling to concede changing times, or the increasing ability of the young person to choose for himself, undoubtedly create undue hardships for young people. But when standards are relaxed completely they lack a much needed home base. As one girl approaching her senior year in college with no very good sense of who she was or who or what she wanted to be said wistfully, " My folks never seemed to care what I did."

Some of the conflict between adolescents and their parents is precipitated by the fact that society changes rapidly, and the parents themselves in many areas do not behave as their parents did when they were adolescents. In addition, each generation is bound to have a somewhat different perspective. Revelations of these differences are sometimes as painful to parents as to the youngsters. For example, one attractive mother of 40 and long accustomed to the apparent adoration of her son was shocked by a comment he made at 14. Dressed for a dinner-party, she appeared in the living-room with two necklaces, inquiring of her husband which he felt was most becoming to her costume. At this point her son interposed, " What difference does it make? Who cares what you wear when you're 40? " In another instance, a mother trying to explain to her daughter, not yet 15, the reasons for a particular rule, observed that she and the girl's father had had more years of experience than she had and were, therefore, able to see situations in a better perspective. To this the daughter's comment was, " I don't think you have had nearly as much experience as I have."

Most studies of conflict between adolescents and their parents indicate that girls tend to have more conflict and that it is more intense than that experienced by boys.

PROBLEM 6. In the light of what you know about differences in the socialization of boys and girls, what factors would you think contribute to this difference?

According to recent research, the conflicts between girls and their parents tended to be focused on broad issues as represented in such problems as parental imposition of goals, parental interference in personal affairs and choice of friends, excessive restriction of freedom of movement, denial of decision, and late hours. Differences about smoking, clothes, and home chores are also sources of irritation. The boys' conflicts tended to be focused on more specific issues including late hours, spending money, smoking, and boy-girl relations. They also experienced some difficulties regarding self-decision and excessive restriction of movement.[14]

Parents, it may be noted, in fairness to them as well as to the adolescent, do not all confront the prospect of watching their children grow into adulthood with equal equanimity. Sometimes it is hard to let a child grow up, particularly a last one, or one who, for some reason such as physical frailty, seems especially precious. Oldest children often complain that parents let the younger ones "get away with murder," and it may well be that the perspective of seeing an older child turn out all right reduces parental anxiety over a younger one. Occasionally parents find their children's adolescence difficult to take, not so much because of any reaction on the part of the child, but because of the particular associations they themselves have with the period. For one it revives heartaches from which they would protect their children. To others it symbolizes the fact that they themselves are no longer young. Unreconciled to their own role as parents, they try to play the role of peer to their child. Rarely are they fully aware of their feelings but they are considerably less well-equipped to deal with teenagers than are those parents whose own adolescent conflicts have been fully resolved.

As some of our earlier illustrations in this chapter have suggested, the issue over which a young person may become most violent often is only a symbol of his more basic concerns. Thus, the conflicts which emerge in adolescence are often not really new but may be traced back to earlier years. Sometimes this fact makes them more

---

[14] Ausubel, *op. cit.* Pp. 225–226.

difficult to resolve. On the other hand, it is at adolescence that both parent and young person are often able to work out difficulties in relationships which have troubled them both.

Jane Warner affords us a good example of this. Throughout her childhood there were times when she felt resentful about some of her mother's decisions for her. Unlike some children who are able to put into words their real feelings, and give parents some clues as to how to help them, Jane tended to keep the things which really annoyed her bottled up inside. However, as she reached later adolescence and began to explore for herself, " What makes me the kind of person I am," she took new stock of some of these early incidents, and even began to discuss them with her parents. Older now, she could appreciate that her mother had always intended the best for her and could even sense, a little uneasily, that she herself might sometimes have changed a situation just by indicating her unhappiness. In somewhat the same fashion Mrs. Warner could sense that there were some situations in which she could have been more perceptive of Jane's feelings. Out of this mutual acknowledgment of misunderstanding, Jane and her mother could begin to build new understandings and eventually the kind of relationship which characterizes two adults who both love and mutually respect one another.

Relationships with the Peer Group

In our discussion of social factors influencing adolescents we described the peer-group society, suggesting that it mirrors the society of adults. It provides young people opportunity to gain status and practice adult roles during the period in which they are not yet accepted into adult groups. In this section we are concerned with the kinds of interpersonal relationships to be found among the members of the peer group.

The importance of peer-group status. Just how much peer-group approval may mean to a young person, and how greatly he may modify his behavior to win it is revealed in the following account. The writer, a young Negro, the son of professional parents of high social status lived in a community with a high delinquency rate. Status among one's playmates in this neighborhood was based on participation in acts of vandalism, street fights, and stealing. He describes his efforts to achieve status without becoming delinquent.

Prestige could be obtained by frequent absence from school. This " achievement " would have to be made known to the others by putting in a swaggering appearance outside the school when classes began or at lunch hour. Again, attending class encumbered by books was taboo for any youth who had achieved neighborhood acceptance. On my way to class, carrying a new book bag given me at Christmas time, I once met several other friends, who, when they espied this " sissy " device, proceeded to shower such ridicule upon the school bag and its possessor, that thereafter the article remained hidden under the bed.

Shortly after entering high school, my attention became occupied with the fact that I had been placed in the role of " doctor's son." Although I had always participated in many of the neighborhood " stickball " and handball games, I had not participated in the regular nocturnal pastimes of street fighting and raids on other nearby blocks. I was never " ganged-up-on," but at best I held only token acceptance by the clique.

The gang's attitude toward my membership was only part of the story. At home my parents were becoming increasingly apprehensive of my getting into trouble, what with there being an almost daily recitation from neighbors of some calamitous occurrence involving one of their own children.

Accordingly, although I had felt that " coming of age " to attend high school would involve a relaxation of parental proscription, I actually was confronted at home with admonitions and anxious expressions. Faced with the choice of receiving more unfavorable mention in the group (and even being ostracized), or incurring parental wrath, I elected the latter. The need to be a " good " part of " the bunch " was too compelling, too important to be ignored.

My attempt to achieve greater or at least a modification of previous status in the group, was abetted by the fact that at the high school level, new standards of " achievement " were now being established. Such skills as dancing, and using slang of a more adult form, were now highly regarded. Also, many members of the group had become aware of their clothing, and how it compared, especially in style, with the attire of other social and ethnic groups.

Straightway, I launched an all out assault designed to overcome the intricacies of the three modal dance steps: the " slow drag " (a one step, which to be properly executed must be accompanied by a bored, disinterested facial expression — along with characteristic " hep " positions of shoulders and arms); the " lindy hop "; and the rhumba. The proving ground at which I developed skills in this vital area was my best friend's living room — he was an excellent instructor, and had a record machine and empty apartment until his parents returned late at night; and later, the neighborhood dance hall, which would be en-

gaged each week by a different club. Continued attendance at these affairs eventually led me to attain proficiency at the necessary steps; as well
as to gain some speaking acquaintanceship with members of the " house-
band," an organization of older youths who were an integral part of
every dance held at this hall; and served as models to be emulated by our
group.

Simultaneously, I also modified my clothing toward conformity
with that of the group. All trousers had to be " pegged " by the neighborhood tailor; and this meant having material removed from the pants-
leg, beginning about a foot above the cuff and proceeding downward.
The desirable form of attire, which would identify one as belonging to
the neighborhood combined these " pegged " pants, a mashed-in felt
hat with ample brim, and an oversized jacket.

The final step in the amalgamation with the peer group comprised
acquisition of its patterns of speech and choice of words. The jargon
acquired was employed with some discretion, since the use of such
words in school, or around the " wrong kind " of adult, might have led
to embarrassing, often painful, consequences.[15]

In contrast to the above subjective account of the importance of
peer-group relationships, we may turn to some of the observations
made by the research team which has carried on the California
Adolescent Growth Study, a longitudinal study of some 200 youngsters who were followed throughout the period of their adolescence.

The structure of adolescent groups. Figure 11 depicts sociograms
for the boys and girls in the ninth grade of a junior high school. It
was prepared during the course of the California Adolescent Growth
Study and shows which children mentioned each other as " best
friends." Each youngster is represented by a circle. A solid line connecting the circles indicates that each person mentioned the other as
a best friend. A dotted line indicates a one-way choice.[16]

The situation represented here is one which appears to be typical
during the period of adolescence. Some youngsters have no friends
(or at least none within the peer group as represented by a particular grade in a particular school). Some have one friend, some more,
but some youngsters rate very high in friends.

In another school, or another community, quite different relationships might emerge, and their significance to young people might

---

[15] From a collection of incidents of adolescent conflict reported by students.

[16] Jones, Harold E. *Development in Adolescence.* New York: Appleton-Century
Company, 1943. P. 43.

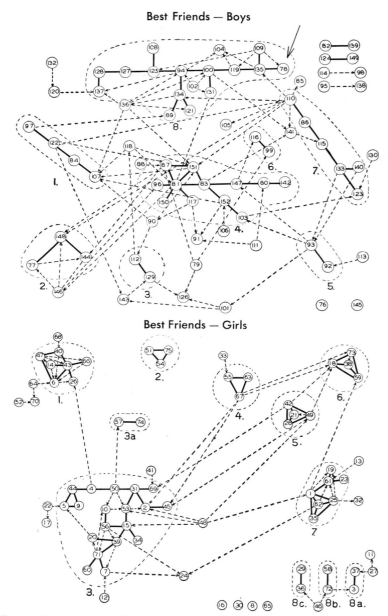

Figure 11. Sociogram for boys and girls based on the California Adolescent Growth Study. (*From Harold E. Jones. Development in Adolescence. New York: Appleton-Century-Crofts, 1943. P. 43.*)

be quite different. Such a diagram depicts only one of the many aspects of the ways in which the members of a group such as this see each other and relate themselves to one another. A picture of leadership choices, for example, would not correspond, although there would be many instances of overlap.

When the sociograms in Figure 11 are examined closely it will be noted that among the girls, there are several cliques.

Group 1, for example, contains seven girls who mentioned no one outside of the group, although three of them were mentioned by others. There are three girls in an evidently self-sufficient triangle at 2. Group 3 is a larger and seemingly less tightly knit group with several outside connections. Note especially that there are four girls who admit to no friends in school, and several chum-pairs, 8a, 8b, 8c. The boys in contrast appear much less likely to limit their best friends to any one group.

PROBLEM 7. How do you account for the differences between the boys' and the girls' sociogram? In which group do you think it would be easier to make friends?

The freedom of movement which comes with the teens and the fact that the high school draws from a larger population than the elementary school tends to give most adolescents a somewhat larger group from which to choose their friends. With differing rates of maturing, interests also shift. Consequently, the adolescents' close friends, as well as the members of his clique or crowd may not be the same individuals he played with in his elementary school years. However, what he looks for in the group and the personal qualities he brings to his relationships with the individuals in it are in part determined by his earlier experiences. If he has customarily been rebuffed by other youngsters his approach to the new group is different than if his place in previous groups has always been assured. Such a youngster may aspire to little more than the finding of one friend, someone in whom he can confide. For another, close friendship is not so important as the mere fact of acceptance in the affairs of the clique, even if not as one who is popular or a leader. Again, a person who has had little acceptance may have a level of aspiration continuously out of line with the acceptance he receives even though he may be fairly realistic about his social position.

Shifts in Status During Adolescence

John Sanders, one of the youngsters whose development was followed in the California Adolescent Growth Study, is an illustration of the social aspirations during adolescence of a youngster who had never achieved marked popularity prior to adolescence. At sixth grade he was rated by his peers as slightly above average in popularity, average in leadership, above average in humor and assurance. "His reputation slipped to a low-water mark in junior high school, recovered slightly at his entrance to senior high, where he was less well-known by those voting; declined again as he became better known and then at the end of his school career showed a promising upward tendency." [17]

John's position in relation to the other members of his group can be seen in the sociogram for his ninth-grade class which is presented in Figure 11. John is represented by the circle marked 78. He mentioned Ralph, 35, as his best friend. Ralph also mentioned him and he was chosen by Will, 109. Six months later, another sociogram indicated that John had been dropped by Ralph and Will. In eleventh and twelfth grades Ralph was again a mutual friend for John, and he had acquired two other close friends.

During most of these years, John's appraisal of his own deficiencies was, for the most part, "alert and candid." This appraisal was based on an inventory which provided the youngster an opportunity to indicate the extent to which he felt he resembled or differed from a number of descriptions of young people such as, "D. is the best ball-player in the school," "J. is the most popular boy in school," "K. has more girl friends than any of the other fellows," and so on. [18]

When it came to what he would have liked for himself, however, John's professed aspirations tended to be extreme. For example, in ninth grade, he wished to be "just like" the best ball-player in the school and to be the biggest and strongest, the brightest, the best dancer, the most popular, and the most outstanding leader. [19]

John's strong desire to be outstanding appears to have been a strong factor in his persistence in staying with the group. Other

---

[17] Jones, *op. cit.* P. 42.   [18] *Ibid.* P. 133.   [19] *Ibid.* P. 135.

boys with similar handicaps — delayed maturity and lack of skill in athletics and other activities popular with boys — might well have retreated. But " John showed a persisting eagerness to 'belong,' to be a member of groups, and to take part in group activities. . . . It sometimes appeared as though any kind of attention, even unfavorable, was more satisfactory to him than no attention at all." [20] The following shows how the peer group expresses disapproval.

Age 14

Clubhouse living room. John chose a chair but was told to get out of it because " it belongs to someone out of the room." There seemed to be a co-ordinated effort to make him uncomfortable, to which he responded in a rather petulant manner.

Clubhouse porch. John came in with his lunch. Asked if someone would play backgammon with him.

Douglas: " I can play but I wouldn't play with you."

Marilyn (to John): " He's beat better people than you." John dropped the backgammon board, and Douglas and Marilyn laughed at him. He was disconcerted, but still remained on the porch and later played a game with Bill. Bill trotted away abruptly as soon as the school bell rang.

John: " I'm always the one that's left to pick things up."

Age 14.5

Evening party at the Clubhouse. Most of those present are playing a game which involves penalties. John is reading magazines in a corner. Louise is given the penalty: " Go up to the best-looking boy in the room and vamp him." When she balked, one girl said, " Oh, you just go up and say 'I love you,' and then give him a kick." Louise looked relieved at the apparent simplicity of this assignment, but still hesitated.

Dorothy: " Say it to sissy-babe John. He doesn't know the difference anyway."

John responded with a sarcastic " Thank you," without looking up from his reading.

In the Clubhouse yard. John rides up on his battered bicycle.

Joe: " Hello, Johnny."

John: " Hi."

Joe: " Aw, don't be so darned stuck up, or I'll knock you off that bike." [21]

That John was not so often exposed to this sort of humiliation as he progressed through senior high school is attributed to several

[20] *Ibid.* P. 55.   [21] *Ibid.* Pp. 54–55.

combinations of factors, illustrative of the changing relationships of the adolescent period. To some extent John's behavior altered as he matured, and to some extent the behavior of his peers changed. Group attitudes and manners no longer permitted such open and contemptuous domination. But apparently more important was the fact that John had the " saving support of a friend. . . . Under the stimulus of [his] fluent expressiveness and with the support of [his] genuine liking and confidence in him, John gradually came to play a more equal role." [22] Of considerable importance to him also were his relationships with some of his teachers and with the research members of the staff.

CHANGING INTELLECTUAL UNDERSTANDING

Within the period of adolescence there seem to be no marked shifts in intellectual outlook such as appear in the elementary school years when the child's ability to generalize, to deal with more abstract ideas, begins to flourish. These are, rather, years in which a young person can apply these abilities in more and more areas.

He can go beyond such a phenomenon as the melting of ice to principles of chemistry and physics, which he can describe algebraically. Using the principles that he has learned he can think through the relationships which will prevail under a particular set of circumstances. As in the previous period, individuals are differently equipped both by native capacity and by their background of experience to deal with abstractions. For many people, however, it appears that not until adolescence does real facility in thinking symbolically develop. The youngster thinks " $a^2 + b^2 = c^2$," instead of " the square on the hypotenuse equal to the sum of the squares of the other two sides," or "πr^2 " for " circumference of the circle." On the other hand, the danger that he may learn to manipulate the symbols without understanding their real meaning is no less than it was earlier.

The adolescent also tends to be better able than the younger child to deal with those concepts and abstractions which relate to the social world. He can move beyond concerns with " rules " and their effects on an individual to consideration of the meaning of such

[22] Jones, *op. cit.* Pp. 56–58.

concepts as democracy. Just as earlier, he may still deal with words rather than with their real meanings so that the importance of having him clarify meanings does not diminish. However, the fact that as an adolescent he appears to be better able to put himself mentally in someone else's place considerably enhances his ability to understand the motivation of others and thus to deal with social issues which at an earlier stage of development he could not have perceived as having any meaning for him.

PROBLEM 8. If possible, plan for several or all members of your class to visit different classes in junior and senior high schools. Keep a record of the generalizations which students make, and the instances in which you believe they are thinking symbolically. Be especially alert to instances of confused thinking as well as to unusually careful thinking. Discuss and analyze these in class.

The kinds of intellectual understandings we are describing here will, of course, be typical of young people who are not handicapped by poor mental capacity, a lack of effective earlier learnings, or too much anxiety related to adolescent instability. Individuals with more limited abilities will not be able to handle ideas on as abstract a level as those with better endowment, but may be expected to improve in the ability to make decisions and to exercise what we usually refer to as "common sense," the ability to put knowledge to practical use.

INTERRELATEDNESS IN DEVELOPMENT

The various shifts we have been discussing are highly interrelated. The ego expands as it revises conscience, deals with new feelings, makes new identifications. The interpersonal relationships which the individual has had in the past continue to exert their influence on the individual's ways of looking at his world, his ways of thinking and acting, but new interpersonal relationships assist in changing these. We may turn to some of the young people we have been studying for illustration of these points.

Pat. Pat's progress through adolescence resembled that of many girls who have been brought up in an atmosphere of warmth and love but with considerable strictness in some areas. As the " little one " of the family her struggle to take over her own direction had to be of a kind to convince her parents that she was no longer a baby. Her campaign on this was waged when she was about 14 and included both appeals to logic (her family had always been able to trust her — now that she was older, could they not trust her further?), and out-and-out defiance and rebellion. That it was fairly successful by the time she was 16 seems to have stemmed in part from the fact that over the years, she had always been fairly free at expressing her feelings and her desires, had already moved away from home somewhat into the neighborhood play group. She was a young person who needed the support of her peers. Fortunately, her development was such that she had no difficulty finding and maintaining a place with young people of her own age. She was then in a position to say to her parents, "All the other mothers let their girls stay out until twelve," and to work out a pattern for herself.

From Pat's earlier training we would expect that she might have had some difficulty dealing with the expression or acceptance of affection if it were clear that sexual feelings were involved. There is a hint of this in the fact that even at 18 she often indicated that she felt more comfortable with the crowd than she did alone with her date.

With the exception of this one area it is evident that Pat, by 18, was functioning on a fairly adult level. She was able throughout high school to balance social life and study and to find time to spend with her family as well as with her peers and to pursue one special interest. At the end of her sophomore year she had appraised herself and the possibilities for the future sufficiently realistically to be sure that the secretarial course was what she wanted.

Celeste. Celeste worked toward the emancipation necessary for adulthood in a quite different way from Pat. Neither she nor her family could quite account for what happened. The early years of adolescence brought no overt rebellion despite the fact of early physical maturity. Rather, more than ever, Celeste seemed to withdraw into herself. She was often obviously unhappy but apparently unable to communicate to anyone the nature of her feelings which were evidently strong. At no time did this withdrawal affect the quality of her school work. At about 15 when her family were beginning to be somewhat concerned about her obvious unhappiness, she began to take more interest in sports, and in social affairs. Together with a friend whom she had known for a long time she began to venture more and more. In the last three years the outside picture of Celeste had changed remarkably. But it appears that the inner world of feeling had not entirely caught up with this outer sophistication.

PROBLEM 9. In what ways does the picture of Celeste in early adolescence correspond to earlier descriptions of her?

Very much as the little Celeste learned to comfort herself with little songs and dances, and later to bring herself approval through her good work in school, she eventually learned in adolescence to gain the good will of the other young people. But some of the feelings of resentment and loneliness which tormented her in earlier years were, it appears, still just below the surface. She might still be likely to select a job or even a mate, more in terms of the possibility of easing these feelings which she had perhaps not yet acknowledged even to herself. Despite this possibility, we must not overlook the extent of progress she had made during the latter part of the years under consideration.

Jane. We have already given sufficient consideration to Jane to suggest that her attempts at emancipating herself, and indeed, the whole pattern of her adolescent development was different from either of the other girls. Her early adolescent " grumpiness " served to irritate her family but did little to help to take over her own controls. When she was finally able to gather her resources together for rebellion, it did not center in the question of appropriate hours for dates as had Pat's but was concerned with issues which often arise earlier — the choice of friends and so on. In the long run, what one rebels about probably makes less difference than the fact that one does eventually decide that he can make choices for himself. This is an essential step in learning to live with new feelings and facing fully one's potentialities as an adult.

PROBLEM 10. What obvious reasons can you find for the fact that Jane and her friend Karen were so much interested in intellectual pursuits? What underlying reasons? Suppose that Jane had gone to a school in which all of the boys and girls had about the same mental ability and intellectual interests. Would you anticipate differences in her behavior and interests? Why or why not?

As we should expect, none of the boys experienced a period of open rebellion as did the girls. Our society makes it somewhat easier for boys to make the transition from childhood to adulthood than it does for girls.

Charles. In many respects Charles appears to have reached more mature insights and functioning than had the others. This does not imply that he had no difficulties, but they were apparently worked through during the early years of adolescence. When he was 13, for example, he was often easily upset and near tears. He seems, however, to have had no very marked problems in emancipation. An important factor in this may have been a close identification with his older brother who somehow seems to have set a pattern the younger boys found not difficult to follow. Or it may have been that his father's directness, and man-to-man approach, gave him status which other young persons have to struggle for. In school Charles approached his teachers realistically, knew the foibles of each, and planned his work accordingly. Until the middle of his adolescence he had been somewhat inclined to let Chet take the lead in making double dates for him, but gradually he prized his own individuality and preferred to operate on his own.

Dan. In contrast to the relative serenity of Charles' adolescence is that of Dan, which demonstrates the important part that physical development may play in changing the individual's outlook on the world and himself. Dan's vigorous adolescent growth was undoubtedly a factor in his improved acceptance among his peers and in his aggressive interest in sports. Although, like Celeste, Dan had probably not really come to terms with his feelings, he had found a way to take care of some of them. Perhaps this freed him somewhat to look ahead and plan a bit, even though he could not yet be too realistic.

Andy. Andy represents the young person who " knows " that his functioning is not quite adequate but cannot yet bring himself to face realistically either the outside world or his own feelings. He first confronted the fact that he was not realizing the potentialities he had when he nearly failed to be promoted in school during his early adolescence. He resolved to do better, but rather than coming to grips with those school subjects in which he expressed interest, he devoted himself to getting on well enough with his teachers to insure his not failing. There are a number of factors which could have been involved in this. One possibility is that he was too preoccupied with his relatively early and vigorous physical growth to devote himself to the demands of school. What seems more likely is that his deeper concerns probably lay in his relationships with his family.

When he was a little boy the same accomplishments could at the same time satisfy him and his mother. As he grew older this was no longer so true, and he needed to find ways of functioning, appropriate for a boy of his age. These perhaps did not correspond with his picture of correct or " rewarding " behavior according to the standards he had incorporated from his mother earlier so that he was uneasy when he attempted them. Or it may be that owing to his father's illnesses he had insufficient opportunity to work through his identifications with him. There is some evidence for this in the marked satisfaction which he found in his relationships to his friends, the recreational worker, and the young college graduate. Or perhaps the school experiences he had were too lacking in stimulation so that he learned to drift along. Whatever the causes, and it is more likely a combination of factors rather than any one, we cannot miss the fact that this fine-looking, intelligent boy has come to his high school graduation without having come to terms with himself, and, as he himself puts it, has " wasted his time."

Changing Views on the Self

The above sketches are suggestive of the shifts in the views on the self which may occur as the individual grows through adolescence. The child begins with an image of self with the body of a child, and the boy ends with an image of himself as a man, and the girl with an image of the body of a woman. Similar shifts occur in the case of his skills, his attitudes, and his feelings. Some youngsters have difficulty revising the picture they have held of themselves because the changes come so rapidly. Others have difficulty because the old pictures, the concepts of themselves as children, were built at considerable emotional cost, and it is hard to part with them. The youngster who has learned to think of himself as worthless and no good does not readily build a new picture just because he is now grown bigger or stronger. Note, for example, how tentatively Celeste who always seems to have had a fair component of self-doubt in her personality begins to act in accordance with her new potentialities. Dan, whose little-boy bravado was undoubtedly a cover-up for self-doubt, presents a similar picture.

Sometimes, too, adolescence brings a new picture of the self which is not attractive. The individual may be for a period awkward or socially inept, or he may experience great guilt over sex or some other aspect of his living. Any of these experiences may be temporarily distressing, but they may assume exaggerated importance and become a part of the self-picture which is carried on into adulthood.

Thus, there is perhaps no period of development when the individual needs more desperately the support of other people who are basically approving of him at the same time as they are realistic. Unfortunately, it may be a time when young people pushed onto their own resources (as in a large and very impersonal high school) establish standards of behavior, dress, and so on, which many cannot hope to meet. It becomes increasingly difficult for many youngsters to regard themselves as worthy, even though they may have many fine qualities which would bring them approval and respect in another setting.

The Role of Anxiety

If we define anxiety as including a dread of the unknown, it is clear that adolescence in its very nature carries with it the threat of anxiety. It is a period when one does not yet " know " the meaning of new biological functions, when one cannot always count on the body to function in its usual predictable fashion, and when physiological instability may in itself be a source of apprehensiveness. Further, the young person, if he has been favored with close family ties, faces some anxiety while he is working through his new status, and assuming new responsibilities for himself. Some young people, unable to bear the anxieties associated with the process of emancipation, temporize in various ways. They become more interested in the intellectual, and do not care for the " freedom " of their peers, or they point to the low moral standards of the group, or they withdraw for a time into the fantasy of what they will do " some day." Only when they feel support from their peers, or from some adult who believes in them, dare they risk the anxiety which seems to them to be inherent in new ways of behaving.

The anxiety of some adolescents may stem from the fact that they confront situations which stir up feelings of apprehensiveness which they had experienced earlier. Coming in at a later hour than the parents approve may revive old fears of losing parental affection if one does not " mind." Sex feelings revive the guilt felt earlier when sex curiosity was reproved, or masturbation forbidden.

Much of the seemingly bizarre behavior of the adolescent may represent attempts to cope with anxiety. Through complying with the self-imposed standards of behavior set up by one's peers, one is able to allay some of the strong feelings which come in a period in which the ways of doing things held in the past no longer seem appropriate and the demands of the future are uncertain and nebulous.

Contribution of Adolescence to Personality Development

Erikson regards the central conflict of this period as that between " identity " and " role diffusion":

. . . The growing and developing youths, faced with this physiological revolution within them are now primarily concerned with what they appear to be in the eyes of others as compared with what they feel they are, and with the question of how to connect the roles and skills culti-vated earlier with the occupational prototypes of the day.[23]

Essentially the task which confronts the individual is that of " knowing " himself, a grown-up self, and of choosing ways of living which will be appropriate to the particular feelings and abilities of that self. Difficulty resides in the fact that over the years the person may have learned to deny feelings in such a way that he no longer really " knows " his self, nor what lies therein. The human being must deal with so many conflicting emotions and must so early learn to take care of those which are at war with one another that it is undoubtedly too much to expect that he should, under most cir-cumstances, have full consciousness of them. However, if, as he grows up, he is able to keep in touch with his emotions, to know that he is angry and at whom, that he is afraid and of what, that he feels warmly and positively, then he is at adolescence in a better position to know his changing self and to make choices which are " right " for it.

Some young people today find it difficult to establish identity not only because their earlier years have encouraged them to deny their feelings but also because the society in which we are living may attach more reward to the presentation of the self, as it were, in a

---

[23] Erikson, Erik. *Childhood and Society.* New York: W. W. Norton & Com-pany, 1950. P. 228.

glossy, well-trimmed package than to its genuineness. Rather than cultivating those of his attributes which are unique and which may offer the expressions of feeling most appropriate to him, the individual is expected to conform to the pattern of " what is being done."

During the process of establishing the sense of identity those individuals who never fully established autonomy or initiative seem to have particular difficulty. In certain ways, the adolescent period has in it struggles not unlike those which the toddler experienced when he began to leave his mother and venture out on his own. Just as the toddler needed to return to his " pivot " of security, so the adolescent is often ambivalent about how much " freedom " to take. Similarly, one sees in some of the behavior of the adolescent a kind of power-testing not unlike that of the preschool years. Much as when he was 4 and 5, the adolescent views himself and his future. Often under the stress of finding identity, earlier unresolved problems of autonomy and initiative are, in a sense, worked through.

This demonstrates an essential point about the nature of personality development. Each stage has in it some elements of each other stage. Growth and experience enhance and enrich. The personality changes, but it remains in a sense the same.

Adolescence provides an opportune time to test the validity of the principle of continuity in development. Neilon's recent comparison of personality sketches of babies under the age of 2 with sketches of the same individuals when they were 17 indicated a considerable degree of " characteristicness." [24]

PROBLEM 11. Pat's enjoyment of pretty clothes and being admired, Dan's concern with death, Andy's ways of pleasing adults — these are a few of the traits which can be noted in our youngsters in early childhood and in adolescence. Reread the material relating to development in the years from 1 to 6 and see what other continuities you can find.

While the central problem of these years is that of identity, the problem of establishing what Erikson has called a sense of intimacy,

[24] Neilon, Patricia. " Shirley's Babies After Fifteen Years." Reprinted in *Readings in Child Psychology,* edited by Wayne Dennis. New York: Prentice-Hall, 1951. Pp. 461–471.

also looms large, and may be worked on almost simultaneously. This demands " self-abandon " or the ability to share oneself fully, not merely in the sex relationship but in close friendship, in work, and in study. Its realization is thus dependent on the establishment of a sense of identity. However, through intimacy one may also come to a more complete and full realization of one's identity.

Although we shall close our discussion of development in this book with the period of adolescence, there should be no thought that resolution of the conflicts of that period bring to an end the development of the personality. Rather the individual has potentialities for growth in richness and depth as long as he lives.

PROBLEM 12. The other components of personality, as Erikson sees them, are generativity, or creativity — the interest in establishing and guiding the next generation — or the " parental sense " and " integrity." The latter implies faith in life and a sense of one's place in the total scheme of things. (See also pages 74–77.) Not knowing what the life experiences of our six young people may be in the future, we cannot with certainty predict the extent to which they will be successful in establishing these additional personality components. On the other hand, we are familiar with the areas in which they may have some difficulty and those in which their strengths lie. In the light of these, what predictions would you make for each?

DESIRABLE GUIDANCE DURING ADOLESCENCE

At all stages of development we have implied that good guidance depends on the nature of the interpersonal relationships between the child and the adult rather than on the particular techniques the adult uses. This principle is equally true in adolescence. But because the young person is himself contemplating adulthood there is perhaps no period when what the adult and the adult society *are* makes greater difference. It is all too easy to view " lawlessness," " valuelessness," and so on as adolescent problems and fail to see that the young person only reflects the confusion of the world in which he lives.

If the adult is to prove helpful to the adolescent it seems essential that he understand the nature of the adolescent's problem — basically that of learning how to manage feelings and impulses and deal with reality in an adult fashion, a process that in our society is often fraught with anxiety. If he is to learn adult ways he must have opportunity to practice them. This suggests that the adults can help by providing opportunities for young people to function in more adult fashion — high school youth, for example, may be expected to participate in the formulation of school policy more than younger children. But while learning is going on, some sense of what is appropriate or " right " is also needed. Otherwise, the young person faces consequences which may be quite frightening and anxiety-producing to him. He may withdraw, as when high school youngsters given more responsibility for student government than they know how to handle, become undependable. Or he may retreat to more childish behavior as when students with too much freedom turn a student council into a farce. Or he may turn his feelings against someone else as when a student group administers punishments which are completely out of line with the nature of the " crimes " committed.

Essentially, we are saying that the adolescent needs adults who remain adults, who do not abdicate their positions and let youth at once " take over." Such adults have respect for their own experience, just as they have appreciation and respect for the enthusiasm and ability of young people. They are not afraid to have youngsters " try their wings." They even encourage them to do so. But they stand by ready to offer support and help if it is asked. And if it is not asked, or if it is asked and then not taken, they are not offended. They do not see the adolescent as being *against* them, but merely *for* himself. The realization of the adolescent self is not regarded as a threat to the adult self.

All of this suggests that the best guidance for adolescents comes from those who have themselves best resolved their own adolescent conflicts, or are at least cognizant of the nature of those conflicts. It also implies that youth may find different kinds of help from different kinds of adults. Parents, for example, would like to feel that *they* could somehow respond to their children's changing needs in a way which would somehow bring them to adulthood with full strength. It is hard for them to face the fact that the very nature of adolescence demands that the child look to other sources for support and for models, for he must find those ways of behaving which are right for him, and he cannot reject the possibility that the parents' ways are not his. Nor, in truth, can any adult really be all things to any adolescent.

Because the adolescent is so much concerned with himself and so often tends to be self-analytical and self-critical, the problem of how he may best be helped to know himself, and to make choices which are truly appropriate to him becomes an important one. Recent years have evidenced increasing provision for this aspect of adolescent development in the form of classes in psychology and mental hygiene in high school, and discussion groups on dating, family living, mate selection, and so on in both schools and in community programs. Much remains to be learned as to the effectiveness of these and the stage of development in which they are most needed. Some youngsters, it appears, can intellectualize fairly well the nature of their problems. But learning to behave in new ways is not so easy. How then to bridge the gap between intellectual understanding and genuine emotional acceptance is a matter with which many adults who care about youth are currently concerned. Surely, if the adult is to live a productive and worth-while life, adolescence would seem to be the appropriate time to insure his readiness to do so. It is because of this belief that we find so much current emphasis on the importance of good guidance for the adolescent.

13

ꙙꙙꙙꙙꙙꙙꙙꙙꙙꙙꙙꙙꙙꙙꙙꙙꙙꙙꙙꙙꙙꙙꙙꙙꙙꙙꙙꙙꙙꙙꙙꙙꙙꙙꙙ

A Look to the Future

IN THE FIRST chapter of this book we were introduced to six 18-year-olds. In numerous ways these young people resembled one another, and in many ways they were different from one another. In an attempt to account for the likenesses and the differences we have considered the interaction of biological and social factors and the psychodynamic processes involved in progress toward adulthood. Incidents from the life histories of our young people have illustrated how development proceeds from conception to 18 years. We have, at least in an elementary fashion, answered the questions which we raised in Chapter 1.

Eighteen-year-olds are alike to the extent that they have completed progress toward physiological maturity. We have noted the ways in which the sequence of this development is similar in all young people. We have seen how at each stage human biology sets certain limits to what the individual can do. Not until he has matured sufficiently can he grasp a cup in his own two hands, stand steadily on his feet, or throw a ball overhand. The younger the child, the more likely it is that it is that his behavior will resemble in many ways that of another individual of the same age. But at any age in the period from birth to 18, youngsters will tend to be more like those of their own or near age than they are like those more remote from them in years. Eighteen-year-olds will also resemble each other to the extent that they have had common learning experiences in their homes, their school, and the larger community.

The expectations set for the child's learning at the various stages of his development differ from one society to another, and also vary within each society depending on the particular subgroups to which the child and his family belong. American 18-year-olds are likely to resemble Australian or French 18-year-olds. However, an 18-year-old brought up in a lower-class New York City neighborhood may differ as much from a middle-class youngster living in a small Ohio town as he would from his peers living in another country.

No matter how much 18-year-olds are alike, there are many ways in which each is also unique. Each has grown according to his own pattern. Each has his own tempo and rhythm, his own sensitivities and vulnerabilities. Each has his particular potentialities, some of which he is already realizing while others remain latent. Most important, each out of his relationships with other people has learned to regard himself in certain unique ways. He has developed his own private world. The ways he functions and the degree to which he fulfills his potentialities are very much dependent on the character of this inner life.

The nature of the individual's inner life as he grows from birth to maturity has been a major concern throughout this book. We have considered the processes by which the infant appears to differentiate himself from the world outside, and how as he grows in experience, things as well as people take on new meanings and significance for him. As a toddler he becomes able to satisfy some of his needs by himself and gradually distinguishes between these means of satisfaction which are acceptable to the adults and those which are disapproved. Continuing to test his own powers, projecting himself into an ever-expanding world both physically and imaginatively, he begins to develop his own inner controls, his own standards of behavior. As he grows, his understanding of his world increases, he appraises it more objectively and becomes more and more its master. With puberty, which brings marked physical changes and opens new social possibilities, he confronts the necessity of dealing with new impulses and desires. He needs to learn to live comfortably with a somewhat new picture of himself.

Much of the behavior of the young person growing up is difficult to understand unless we are able to look at it from the viewpoint of the individual himself. We cannot hope to get inside another's skin to see the world as it looks from there, but we can develop an appreciation and sympathy for the fact that each person (including ourselves) does the best he can in the light of his own unique abilities, experiences, and background. From his own inner perspective his behavior makes sense. This is true even though he may later see situations differently and desire to change.

We have chosen in this book to limit our study to individuals who may be considered rather typical in our society. They have not suffered from any marked physical defects or from any dread diseases. Their intelligence falls within the normal range. They have been brought up in their own homes by kindly intentioned parents who have loved them. Although their families may have experienced financial insecurity, they have never known dire poverty. Had we extended our illustrations to include young people growing up under various handicaps, we should still deal with the same processes of development. The joys and triumphs and the hazards and the heartaches of growing up differ from one individual to another not in kind but only in degree.

Here we may end our study of child development. The growth of our six young people has been followed from birth to young adulthood. They are no longer children. We have set forth some of our present knowledge of the processes of child development. As our reader, you have, we hope, deepened your own understanding and insight into the behavior of children. But if you have thought deeply about the significance of child development, you may wonder what the future holds for these young people, for the growing body of knowledge that we call child development, and perhaps, even for yourself as a student of that subject.

OUR YOUNG PEOPLE'S FUTURES

Our knowledge of the life history of these individuals to the age of 18 is insufficient to predict their futures. With more complete information we might be able to specify some of the circumstances under which they would be most likely to realize their potentialities, but we could not hope to account for all the possibilities. Despite their adult appearance, none of these young people has yet fully come to terms with himself as an adult person. In each, certain aspects of childhood development are still to be worked through. One cannot yet make important decisions for himself because he looks to older people for authority in much the same fashion as he did when he was 2 and 3 years old. Certain frustrations enrage him no less than they did then. Another is from time to time overwhelmed with childish rivalry and jealousy. Still another carries burdens of childish fear and guilt into relationships with members of the opposite sex. At the same time, certain experiences bring special joy and satisfaction because they revive certain pleasant childhood memories.

These young people, like any other 18-year-olds, will vary in the ways in which they integrate their earlier experiences into their adult personalities. However they deal with their earlier years, whether they try to understand or are unable to do so, they are affected by them. The adult one is depends in large part on the child one has been. The child's interpersonal experiences make their own special contribution to his adult personality. We have looked at development as though it proceeded through a series of stages, in each of which the child finds himself involved in certain characteristic conflicts, the resolution of which adds a particular component to his personality. As the persons in his environment respond to him and he to them he adds new attributes to his personality.

In the early months of his life the child, depending in part on his strength and hardiness as a physical organism and in part on the love and protection offered him by the adults who care for him, acquires basic attitudes of trust and security. We have seen that the infant experience of our six young people seemed likely to establish rather well this basic personality component.

In toddlerhood an awareness of the possibilities for independence grows. Through his relationships with others, the child learns to see himself as a person. He feels positively toward himself, or perhaps doubtful. When his attitudes are predominantly positive, the component which Erikson labels a "sense of autonomy," becomes an integral part of his personality. In several instances we noted that the toddlerhood experiences of some of our young people were such as to raise some question about the extent to which they felt fully self-worthy. In the adolescent period some of these early doubts are reflected when the necessity for independent adult status is faced.

Once the child becomes competent in walking and running, he begins to test out his powers both imaginatively and actually and in many spheres. He becomes increasingly aware of his own potentialities. He may confront the social taboos and conventions of his world with a continuing zest for exploration and experimentation for inquiry and creativity. Or he may become fearful and apprehensive about his childish transgressions, real or fancied. Whatever his experiences, they contribute to his later personality development. The varying degrees of initiative, enterprise, and genuine enthusiasm for living we have seen in our 18-year-olds are, in part, a product of their experiences in the power-testing period.

When the child's growth through the formative years before he is 6 is healthy and the interpersonal relationships in which he participates are primarily positive and constructive, he appears to develop a strength of personality, a kind of resilience, which is likely to stand him in good stead throughout his life. But the years beyond 6 are no less important to his later development. In them the child who has lacked trust in himself and others, who has been more inclined to attitudes of shame and doubt and guilt than to self-worthiness and initiative, may find healing in warm relationships with adults who appreciate and understand him.

The years from 6 on are years in which the child becomes an accomplisher, learning the skills and mastering the ways of the society in which he lives. We can see in each of our young people evidence of the contributions of this period. In his own way each of them achieved some success in school, in Sunday school, or in play group, and in taking certain home responsibilities. Each learned many of the social skills essential to living with his peers. We have questioned whether in all instances their accomplishment was in line with their potentialities. Had they been more sure of their own early achievement, their views of their futures at graduation might have been considerably altered.

In the adolescent years the young person comes to terms with all that has gone before and, in a sense, with that which he is to become. Adolescence, we have seen, is often a time of turmoil. But it is also a period of both construction and reconstruction when a person may perhaps for the first time begin to appreciate his own potentialities. In the case of our 18-year-olds it is likely that none of them has yet developed a full realization of his own personal identity, of who he is and where he is going.

Each is still in the process of finding himself as an adult. Not until he has worked through this is he likely to be able to enjoy mature love relationships (involving complete mutuality) or to fill adequately the role of a parent. Beyond this lies the necessity for preserving one's independent adulthood; for deriving continuing significance from work and leisure; and, finally, for taking a retrospective view of one's own life and facing unafraid the inevitability of its close.

Clearly, the eighteenth birthday is not an end point in development. It is merely a convenient time at which to assess how far the individual has come. When we come to know more about development in the later periods of life, we are likely to find that there may be pronounced differences between a " mature " adult of 25 and a " mature " adult of 45 that are just as truly developmental in nature as the difference between a 6-year-old and a 10-year-old.[1] At present, however, we have much less information about these later periods of human development than about childhood and adolescence.

THE FUTURE OF CHILD DEVELOPMENT

To attempt to predict future trends in a field of knowledge such as Child Development is no less difficult than to forecast the future of the young people with whom we have been concerned. It would appear, however, that we may expect rather more emphasis in the future on development in the years beyond childhood and adolescence. With more research in the adult and aging years, child development may be more clearly seen in its proper perspective as one phase of Human Development.

[1] Jersild, Arthur T. " Emotional Development," in *Manual of Child Psychology*, edited by Leonard Carmichael. New York: John Wiley and Sons, 2d ed., 1954. P. 860.

Eventually, life history material, similar to that we have presented here, should be available for complete life spans. Certainly we may anticipate a continuing interest in the life histories of those who may be considered " normal " and healthy. Love, sympathy, integration, and harmony may receive as much attention as has already been given aggression, hostility, domination, and conflict.

The interdisciplinary approach to the understanding of human development appears to have established itself. Specialization in the various fields related to human development will surely continue. But it seems likely that in increasing instances such specialists as the biologist, the psychologist, and the anthropologist will study the same children simultaneously. The eventual understanding of the nature of human learning, for example, seems dependent on both the expansion and the exchange of knowledge in many fields including neurology and physiology as well as psychology.

There is at present no theory of personality adequate to explain all the many facets and intricate relationships in human behavior and development. There is, however, much interest in theory and beginning efforts to bring various points of view into coherence with one another. The prospects for synthesis seem promising.

Currently there is more concern than ever before with the subjective aspects of the child's experience. Child development research is no longer limited to the directly observable behaviors and actions of the child but includes study of his " private world " and his changing views of himself. If the subjective is important in the development of the child, it may be no less important in the development of the research worker or the student in child development. His own early experiences, his understanding of himself, his personal view of the world cannot be ruled out of his study of other human beings. Although the implications of this fact are not yet fully understood or even acknowledged, self-understanding appears likely to receive augmented emphasis in both the study of child development and in research related to it.

FUTURE UNDERSTANDINGS FOR THE READER

Within the covers of this book you have met a few children. You have been given some information about how children grow and learn. You have read how certain experiences have brought young-sters joy or pain, comfort or despair. You have considered how such experiences contribute to the child's developing personality and af-fect his attitudes and behavior as he approaches adulthood. You may stop at this, if you wish. Or you may regard your study of children as only just begun.

If you choose the latter course, you may continue throughout your life to become better acquainted with children wherever you find them as well as with the child that you yourself once were. Your years of living and of watching the children of other people, and perhaps your own as well, may give you new perspective on the significance of childhood, both in yourself and in other people.

Childhood, in point of time, is but a brief interlude in the total life span. Its importance, however, is not measured by its length but rather by its influence which is persistent and pervasive. There seems no better preparation for later life than to live each year of child-hood and adolescence as richly and fully as one's abilities at that stage of development permit. But as satisfying as we may want the child to find his childhood years, we cannot lose sight of the fact that he, like all other human creatures, seems at one and the same time to want to grow and yet to resist change. He would like to be big, but it is comfortable to be a baby. If he is to realize his potentiali-ties, however, he must be encouraged gradually to relinquish child-ish ways. Willingness to grow rapidly and expansively in the years of childhood and adolescence and to grow slowly and in different but no less real ways as an older person is implicit in healthy de-velopment.

We must respect the time values of childhood, remembering that it seems to itself to exist in a huge epic life where good and evil stalk like giants. But if we persist in seeing childhood as a separate and com-plete state of life, an end in itself, the very children will be the first to rebuke us. For they are always pressing forward; the negotiation of every obstacle between them and maturity is a triumph; and each step out of childhood is passionately anticipated, passionately welcomed.[2]

[2] Priestley, J. B. *Midnight on the Desert*. New York: Harper & Brothers, 1937. Pp. 145–146.

Appendix

BOOKS REFERRED TO IN THE PROBLEMS

Barker, Roger G., Kounin, Jacob S., and Wright, Herbert F., eds. *Child Behavior and Development*. New York and London: McGraw-Hill Book Company, 1943.

Baruch, Dorothy. *New Ways in Discipline*. New York: McGraw-Hill Book Company, 1949.

Davis, Allison, and Havighurst, Robert J. *Father of the Man*. Boston: Houghton Mifflin Company, 1947.

Dennis, Wayne, ed. *Readings in Child Psychology*. New York: Prentice-Hall, 1951.

Gesell, Arnold L., and Ilg, Frances L. *Infant and Child in the Culture of Today*. New York and London: Harper and Brothers, 1943.

Hymes, James. *Discipline*. New York: Teachers College, Columbia University, 1949.

Kuhlen, Raymond G., and Thompson, George G., eds. *Psychological Studies of Human Development*. New York: Appleton-Century-Crofts, 1952.

Martin, William E., and Stendler, Celia Burns, eds. *Readings in Child Development*. New York: Harcourt, Brace and Company, 1954.

Mead, Margaret. *From the South Seas*. New York: William Morrow and Company, 1939.

Murphy, Lois B. *Social Behavior and Child Personality*. New York: Columbia University Press, 1937.

Seidman, Jerome, ed. *The Adolescent, A Book of Readings*. New York: Dryden Press, 1953.

Wolf, Katherine M. *The Controversial Problem of Discipline*. New York: Child Study Association of America, 1953.

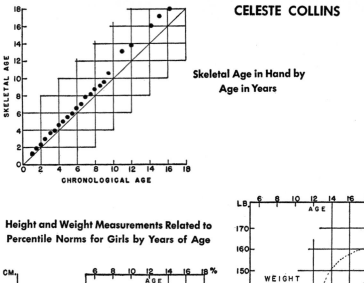

Skeletal Age in Hand by
Age in Years

Height and Weight Measurements Related to
Percentile Norms for Girls by Years of Age

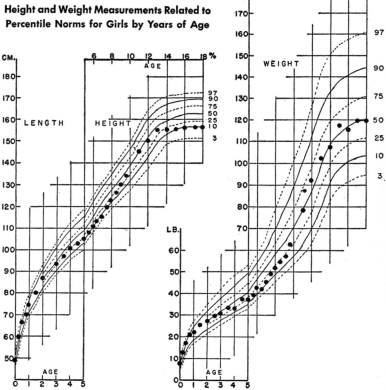

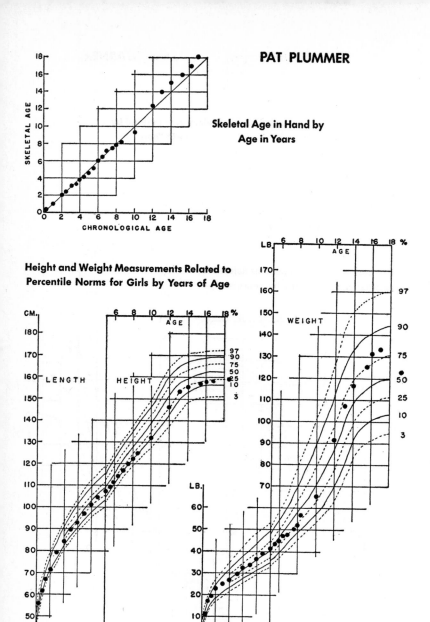

PAT PLUMMER

SKELETAL AGE

CHRONOLOGICAL AGE

Skeletal Age in Hand by
Age in Years

Height and Weight Measurements Related to
Percentile Norms for Girls by Years of Age

LENGTH

HEIGHT

WEIGHT

473

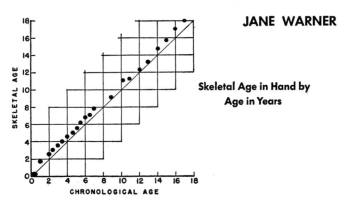

JANE WARNER

Skeletal Age in Hand by
Age in Years

**Height and Weight Measurements Related to
Percentile Norms for Girls by Years of Age**

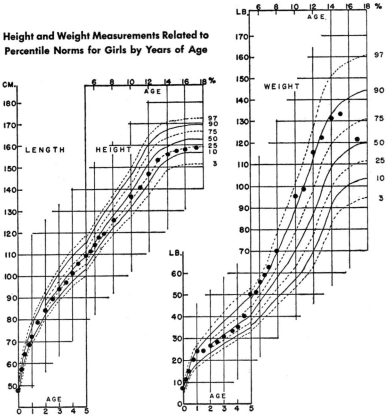

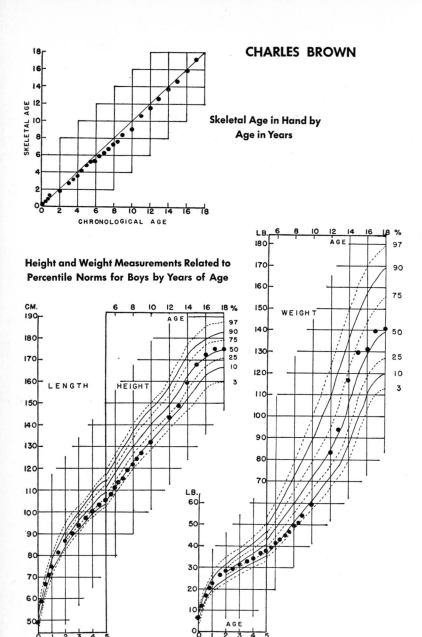

CHARLES BROWN

Skeletal Age in Hand by
Age in Years

Height and Weight Measurements Related to
Percentile Norms for Boys by Years of Age

475

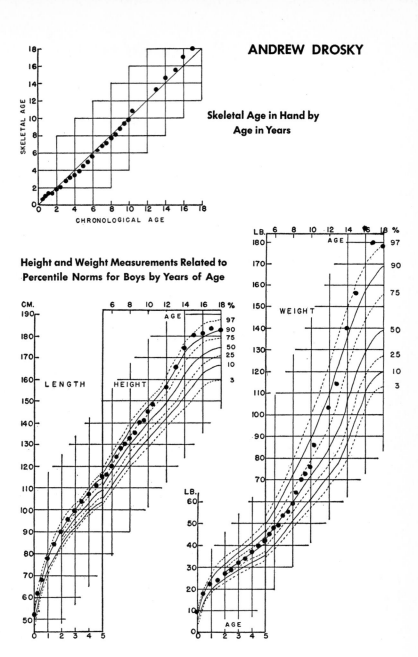

ANDREW DROSKY

Skeletal Age in Hand by
Age in Years

Height and Weight Measurements Related to
Percentile Norms for Boys by Years of Age

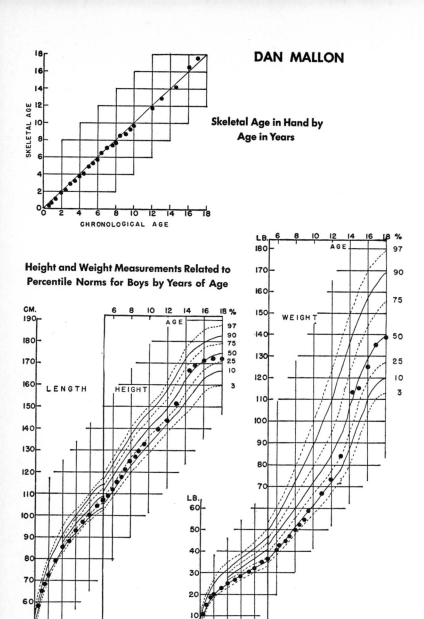

DAN MALLON

Skeletal Age in Hand by Age in Years

Height and Weight Measurements Related to Percentile Norms for Boys by Years of Age

Index

479